Consumer research

The study of consumption is now an important part of many academic disciplines, from sociology and anthropology to history and geography. In business studies, where the customer has always occupied a prominent place, consumer research is growing at an exponential rate. For many commentators, indeed, it comprises the intellectual centre of the marketing discipline.

This growth of interest in consumer research has coincided with a profound shift in how the consumer is conceived and conceptualised. The traditional modernist approach to consumer behaviour, which emphasised rigour, objectivity and quantitative analysis of brand choice, has been challenged by 'postmodern' perspectives, which seek to comprehend the deeply felt beliefs, emotions and meanings that inhere in the rituals, myths and symbols of consumer behaviour.

Consumer research: postcards from the edge is a collection of cutting-edge essays from prominent American and European exponents of 'postmodern' approaches to consumer research. The contributions range from analyses of contemporary consumer lifestyles and the 'consumption' of advertising to studies of the much-publicised 'trolley-rage' phenomenon.

Stephen Brown is Professor of Retailing at the University of Ulster.

Darach Turley is Lecturer in Consumer Behaviour at Dublin City University.

Consumer research

Postcards from the edge

Edited by Stephen Brown and
Darach Turley

London and New York

First published 1997
by Routledge
11 New Fetter Lane, London EC4P 4EE

Simultaneously published in the USA and Canada
by Routledge
29 West 35th Street, New York, NY 10001

Editorial matter and selection © 1997 Stephen Brown and
Darach Turley; individual chapters © the contributors

Typeset in Times by Florencetype, Devon
Printed and bound in Great Britain by Biddles Ltd,
Guildford and Kings Lynn

All rights reserved. No part of this book may be reprinted
or reproduced or utilised in any form or by any electronic,
mechanical or other means, now known or hereafter
invented, including photocopying and recording, or in any
information storage or retrieval system, without permission
in writing from the publishers.

116713386

Learning Resources
Centre

British Library Cataloguing in Publication Data
A catalogue record for this book is available from the
British Library

Library of Congress Cataloguing in Publication Data

Consumer Research: postcards from the edge / edited by
Stephen Brown and Darach Turley.
p.   cm. – (Routledge consumer research series)
Includes biographical references and index.
1. Consumers–Research. I. Brown, Stephen, 1955-.
II. Turley, Darach. III. Series.
HF5415.32.C659 1997
658.8′34–dc21   97–18705
ISBN 0–415–15684–X (hbk)   CIP
ISBN 0–415–17317–5 (pbk)

Contents

Figures

Tables

Contributors

Eric J. Arnould is Associate Professor of Marketing at the University of South Florida, Tampa, Florida, in spite of the fact that the University of Arizona granted him a PhD in social anthropology. He spent ten fruitful/-less years trying to help West African colleagues in more than a dozen nations solve problems of economic development (in agriculture, natural resources, and marketing). Since 1990, he has been a full-time academic trying to pass on his curiosity to university students. His research interests reflect his unwillingness to decide what he wants to be when he grows up and his delight in working with many insightful colleagues. It has ranged from the effects of the development of a regional marketing system on household production strategies in Zinder, the Niger Republic, to channels structure and market organisation in West Africa more generally, to household consumption rituals, to the creation of communitas and magic, and the representation of nature in white water river rafting, to commercial service relationships, and finally, to scientific representation in postmodernity (whew!). Amazingly, his work has appeared in the three major US marketing journals, several anthropological periodicals and a number of books. He has taught at several other universities, including Odense University, Denmark. He is an enthusiastic, if mediocre, guitar player, a slow marathon runner, speaks passable French and Hausa, and adores his children and the American southwest.

Russell W. Belk is N. Eldon Tanner Professor in the David Eccles School of Business at the University of Utah. He has taught there since 1979 and has had previous appointments at the University of Illinois, Temple University, University of British Columbia, University of Craiova, Romania, and Edith Cowan University, Perth, Australia. His PhD is from the University of Minnesota. He is past president of the Association for Consumer Research and is a fellow in the American Psychological Association, Society for Consumer Psychology, and Association for Consumer Research. He is past recipient of the University of Utah Distinguished Research Professorship and a Fulbright Fellowship. He currently edits *Research in Consumer Behavior* and has been an advisory editor for the *Journal of Consumer Research* and associate editor for the *Journal of Economic Psychology* and *Visual Sociology*. He has served on the editorial review boards of twenty-five journals, has written and edited fifteen books or monographs, and has published over two hundred articles and papers. His research primarily involves the meanings of possessions and materialism and his methods have been increasingly qualitative and cross-cultural.

Stephen Brown is The-Professor-Formerly-Known-as-Retailing at the University of Ulster. He has written widely. He has written lots of other words as well, but none so deep as 'widely'.

Richard Elliott is Fellow in Management Studies at St Anne's College, Oxford, and was the first Lecturer in Management Studies (Marketing) to be appointed to Oxford University where he teaches marketing, consumer psychology and advertising on the new Oxford MBA. He has worked in brand management with a number of multinationals, was Marketing Director of an industrial goods company, and Account Director in an international advertising agency. He entered higher education as a mature student, read social psychology at the London School of Economics and has a PhD in marketing from the University of Bradford Management Centre. His research interests include dysfunctional consumer behaviour and socio-cultural aspects of advertising. His work has been published in the *International Journal of Advertising, British Journal of Social Psychology, International Journal of Research in Marketing, Journal of Consumer Policy, Journal of the Market Research Society, British Journal of Management, European Journal of Marketing, Advances in Consumer Research* and *Psychology and Marketing*.

Basil G. Englis is Associate Professor of Marketing in the Campbell School of Business at Berry College, Georgia. He holds a PhD in experimental psychology from Dartmouth College. He was a Culpeper Postdoctoral Fellow in Political Psychology at Dartmouth College (1982–4) and was awarded a Fulbright-Hays grant in 1994/95 in recognition of his research on cross-national media and their effects on consumers. His research interests include mass media and consumer socialisation, political marketing, consumer knowledge acquisition and cognitive representation of lifestyle-related product groupings. He is the co-chair of the 1997 European Conference of the Association for Consumer Research. He has published numerous articles and chapters, and co-edited a volume entitled *Global and Multinational Advertising*.

A. Fuat Firat is Professor of Marketing at Arizona State University West. He received his Licencie en Economie from the Faculty of Economics, Istanbul University, and his PhD in Marketing from Northwestern University. He has held academic positions at Istanbul University, University of Maryland, McGill University and Appalachian State

University. His research interests cover such areas as macro-consumer behaviour and macromarketing, consumption patterns and postmodern culture, marketing and development, interorganisational relations and philosophy of science. His work has been published in *Journal of Consumer Research, International Journal of Research in Marketing, Journal of Macromarketing, Journal of Marketing, Journal of Organizational Change Management, European Journal of Marketing* and *Journal of Economic Psychology*, in several edited books and in proceedings. His article 'Consumption choices at the macro level' with co-author Nikhilesh Dholakia has won the Journal of Macromarketing Charles Slater Award. He has co-edited two books, *Philosophical and Radical Thought in Marketing* and *Marketing and Development: Toward Broader Dimensions*. He was the co-editor of two special issues of the *International Journal of Research in Marketing* on postmodernism, marketing and the consumer. He is currently chief editor of the inter-disciplinary and international journal, *Consumption, Markets and Culture* and president of the Inter-national Society for Marketing and Development.

Gordon R. Foxall is Distinguished Research Professor in Consumer Psychology at Cardiff Business School. He took his first degree at the University of Salford (where he was awarded the Final Year Course Prize for Social Science) and also his master's degree in management economics. He is also a graduate of the University of Birmingham (PhD in indus-trial economics and business studies and DSocSc) and the University of Strathclyde (PhD in psychology). Recently elected a Fellow of the British Psychological Society, he is the author of some fifteen books on consumer behaviour and related themes including the critically acclaimed *Consumer Psychology in Behavioural Perspective* and the best-selling text *Consumer Psychology for Marketing* (co-authored with Ron Goldsmith). He has written over two hundred articles, chapters and papers on consumer behaviour and marketing. His research interests lie in the psychological theory of consumer behaviour, consumer innovativeness, and micro-micro analysis of intra-firm behaviour.

Morris B. Holbrook is William T. Dillard Professor of Marketing, Graduate School of Business, Columbia University, New York, where he teaches courses in communication and in consumer behaviour. Besides his articles in various marketing journals, his research has appeared in publications devoted to research on consumer behaviour, semiotics, cultural economics, the arts, aesthetics, psychology, organisational behaviour, communication, leisure and related topics. Recent books include *Daytime Television Game Shows and the Celebration of Merchandise: The Price is Right, The Semiotics of Consumption, Interpreting Symbolic Consumer Behavior in Popular Culture and Works of Art* (with Elizabeth C. Hirschman), *Postmodern Consumer Research: The Study of Consumption as Text* (with

Elizabeth C. Hirschman) and *Consumer Research: Introspective Essays on the Study of Consumption.*

Laurie Meamber is Visiting Associate Professor of Marketing at Loyola Marymount University. She recently completed her degree at the University of California, Irvine. In 1995/96, she spent the academic year at Odense University, Denmark, as Visiting Scholar. Her research interests include production and consumption of the arts, aesthetics in everyday life, and technology, the arts and popular culture. Her dissertation research focused upon the role of arts/aesthetics in everyday life as cultural production. Her publications have appeared in *Consumption, Markets and Culture* and the *Proceedings of the American Marketing Association.* She won the Best Student Paper award for her paper on product design under postmodernity at the AMA Conference 1995.

David Glen Mick is Associate Professor of Marketing at the University of Wisconsin, Madison. He has also served on the faculties of Indiana University, University of Florida, Copenhagen Business School and Dublin City University. Much of his research has focused on the semiotics of marketing and consumer behaviour, specifically in the areas of advertising, gift-giving and technological products. His articles have appeared in *Journal of Consumer Research, International Journal of Research in Marketing, Journal of Retailing, Semiotica* and *Advances in Consumer Research.* His 'Consumer research and semiotics: exploring the morphology of signs, symbols, and significance' was given the Best Article award in the *Journal of Consumer Research* for 1986–8. He is a member of the *Journal of Consumer Research* editorial board.

Stephanie O'Donohoe is a Lecturer in Marketing at the University of Edinburgh. She is a graduate of the College of Marketing and Design and of Trinity College, Dublin, and completed her PhD at the University of Edinburgh. Her research focuses on consumers' experiences of advertising, and the limitations of traditional advertising theory in accounting for these.

Rhona Reid works as a Marketing Consultant with Capita Management Consultants, Belfast. She previously worked as a Research Assistant at the University of Ulster, Coleraine, where her main research interests were in consumer behaviour and research methods. While at the University of Ulster she lectured in Retail Marketing, Research Methods and Customer Care. She holds an MBA from the University of Ulster and BSocSc from the University of Birmingham.

Mark Ritson was born and educated in the north-west of England. He is currently an Assistant Professor of Marketing at the Carlston School of Management, University of Minnesota. His research focuses on a variety of perspectives within the Interpretive Consumer Research paradigm. In particular, his work explores the role that consumption plays in forming identity and influencing social interactions. He is currently working on ethnographic studies of subcultural consumption, advertising interpretation and consumer behaviour in that notorious behemoth of the post-modern age, the Mall of America.

Michael R. Solomon is Human Sciences Professor of Consumer Behavior in the Department of Consumer Affairs at Auburn University, Alabama. Prior to joining Auburn's School of Human Sciences in 1995, he was Chairman of the Department of Marketing in the School of Business at Rutgers University, New Brunswick, NJ. He began his academic career at the Graduate School of Business Administration at New York University, where he also served as Associate Director of NYU's Institute of Retail Management. He earned BA degrees in Psychology and Sociology at Brandeis University, and an MA and PhD in Social Psychology at the University of North Carolina at Chapel Hill. He was selected as Fulbright Chair to serve as Distinguished Lecturer in Marketing at the Technical University of Lisbon in autumn 1996. His primary research interests include consumer behaviour and lifestyle issues, the symbolic aspects of products, the psychology of fashion, decoration and image, and services marketing. He has published numerous articles on these and related topics in academic journals. He is on the editorial boards of the *Journal of Consumer Research*, *Journal of Retailing* and *Psychology & Marketing.*

Barbara B. Stern is Professor of Marketing at Rutgers, State University of New Jersey, Newark. She has published articles in *Journal of Marketing*, *Journal of Consumer Research*, *Journal of Advertising*, *Journal of Consumer Marketing*, *Journal of Promotion Management*, *Journal of Current Research in Advertising* and other publications. She is on the editorial boards of the *Journal of Consumer Research*, *Journal of Advertising*, *Journal of Consumer Marketing*, *Journal of Promotion Management*, and *Consumption, Markets and Culture: A Journal of Critical Perspectives*. Her research has introduced principles of literary criticism into the study of marketing, consumer behaviour and advertising. Additionally, she has focused on gender issues from the perspective of feminist literary criticism, using feminist deconstruction to analyse values encoded in advertising text.

Craig J. Thompson is Associate Professor of Marketing at the University of Wisconsin, Madison. He joined UW-Madison faculty in 1991 after completing his doctoral work at the University of Tennessee. He has published articles in *Journal of Consumer Research*, *Journal of Public Policy & Marketing*, *Journal of Advertising*, *Psychology & Marketing*, *International Journal of Research in Marketing* and *European Journal of Marketing*. He is on the editorial boards of the *Journal of Consumer Research*, the *Journal of Public Policy and Marketing*, and *Consumption, Markets and Culture: A Journal of Critical Perspectives*. His research in very broad-brush terms has sought to develop and apply hermeneutic approaches to the study of consumption meanings, with a particular focus on gender dynamics.

Darach Turley is Director of the MBA programme and Lecturer in Consumer Behaviour at Dublin City University. His research interests include the senior market, advertising and older viewers and the relationship between bereavement and consumer behaviour.

Caroline Tynan is Professor of Marketing at Nottingham Business School, Nottingham Trent University and a member of the Associate Faculty of Henley Management College. She has published in the areas of market segmentation, qualitative research methodology, consumer behaviour and supply chain management. Her current research focuses on various aspects of relationship marketing in service sectors with particular reference to quality, not-for-profit organisations and small businesses.

Alladi Venkatesh is Professor of Management and Research Associate at CRITO (Center for Research on Information Technology in Organizations) at the University of California, Irvine. His broad research area is technology and social change and his main focus is on the impact of information technologies on families/households. He has an ongoing interest in postmodernism and its relevance to marketing theory and practice. He completed a major study for the National Science Foundation looking at how American families are adapting to the presence of computers at home. He is currently investigating the use of multi-media technologies by families. His theoretical work draws from different streams: household consumption behaviour, economics of time allocation and technology in everyday life. As a Senior Fellow of the American Institute of Indian Studies, University of Chicago, Venkatash recently spent eight months in India examining technology adoption among Indian families, using a cultural model of technology adoption and use. Venkatesh's scholarly publications have appeared in various journals including *Journal of Marketing*, *Communications of the ACM*, *Journal of Product Innovation and Management*, *International Journal of Research in Marketing*, *Telecommunications Policy* and *Irish Marketing Review*. He is co-editor of the journal, *Consumption, Markets and Culture*.

Pre-text: cometh the hour, cometh the man-uscript

People often ask me how I manage to come up with such original titles for my books, articles and conference papers. Well, that's not strictly true. A small number of people have occasionally asked me how I come up with the somewhat idiosyncratic titles of my book chapters, edited volumes and what have you. Hmmm, that's not quite true either. No one has ever asked me how I keep coming up with the weird and wonderful titles for my prodigious academic output, but I live in hope. To be perfectly honest with you, I know only too well that people laugh up their sleeves at the, frankly, lunatic titles of my papers and books. What's more, I have been reliably informed that my prodigious academic output isn't as prodigious as it should be in these RAE-fixated times.

Be that as it may, I have found that, since taking my postmodern 'leap of faith' a couple of years back, the titles of my publications have acquired a whole new significance – for me at least. I don't so much write a paper and then think of a suitable title, as think of a title and then get to work on the accompanying text. Embarrassing though it is to confess, I actually have a stockpile of intriguing (no, make that eccentric – okay, certifiable) titles, which I might get round to developing if you're not careful. Indeed, if I say so myself, I reckon I have become pretty adept at thinking up paper titles. It's the bit that comes after the title that continues to give me problems. But I live in hope and the expectation that inspiration – real inspiration, genuine inspiration, none of your light-bulb-in-the-head nonsense but numinous rays, Road to Damascus, speaking in tongues-type inspiration – will eventually descend. (By the way, I'm considering calling my next book *Brownian Motions*. What do you think?)

The title of the present volume goes back a very long way, I suppose. I have always been fascinated by shops and shopping. One of my earliest childhood memories involves shopping for a pair of shoes. As a special treat, I was allowed to carry the parcel and, to my far from affluent parents' dismay, promptly left it behind in a crowded department store. Infantile trauma aside, the real turning point for me occurred when, as an undergraduate geography student, I was browsing in the library one day, trying to find a researchable topic for my dissertation. I came across Engel, Kollat and Blackwell's immortal textbook on consumer behaviour and suddenly realised the incredible, intoxicating, ineffable fact that some people *actually studied* shops and shoppers. Then and there, I knew that *that* was what I wanted to do with my life. True, I have yet to make a meaningful academic contribution to consumer research, but I live in hope and, as I slide slowly into decrepitude, the increasingly depressing realisation that I'm never actually going to deliver.

If the pre-text of the present text lies in childhood amnesia and teenage ambition, the pretext materialised in October 1995, at the Association for Consumer Research conference in Minneapolis. Inspired by the carnivalesque (sorry, dutiful and earnest endeavour) of the occasion, my colleague and co-editor, Darach Turley, came up with the idea of a grand academic tour. He calculated that he could persuade several distinguished American scholars to visit various collaborating institutions in the United Kingdom and Ireland, thereby spreading the consumer research message to the intellectually unwashed of Business Studies in general and the malodorous of Marketing in particular. Thanks largely to Darach's redoubtable organisational skills, this academic caravan quickly came together and, although the prime mover is much too modest to say so, his Grand Tour of March–April 1996 proved to be a resounding success, both for the American visitors and the host institutions.

As someone who always keeps an eye out for the intellectual main chance – hey, whaddya want from me, integrity? – it occurred to me that Darach's Grand Tour could form the basis of an interesting edited volume. This transcontinental trek, after all, was taking place on the tenth anniversary of the celebrated Consumer Behaviour Odyssey. Most of the participants, what is more, were positioned at the post-positivist, postmodern, post-information processing, post-Howard and Sheth, post-early-for-Christmas – call it what you will – wing of consumer research. Indeed, as a couple of the other US-ual suspects had recently passed through, or were about to visit, my own institution, it seemed that a full-blooded book was in the offing. And, when the title came to me one evening, just prior to the arrival of the first Grand Tourist, I suspected the present text was going to happen in some shape or form.

Now my title, I grant you, was not exactly original, since Carrie Fisher had cornered the market in edgy postcards some time beforehand. (In truth, I had long avoided reading her book – on television chat shows, she comes across as unspeakably smug – though I was very taken by the film, or, to be more specific, by the closing scene where Meryl Streep convincingly demonstrates that she can carry a tune.) However, it struck me that the travel motif, the post-everything positioning of the participants and the cutting-edge qualities of their individual research, made 'postcards from the edge' a singularly appropriate title that somehow succeeded in capturing the spirit of the event. Yet, despite the ostensible appeal of its moniker, the present volume would not have been possible without the unstinting support of Alan Jarvis and Stuart Hay at Routledge, for which I am very grateful. Supplied only with the title, the contributors produced excellent and timely chapters at very short notice and notwithstanding manifold other commitments, both personal and professional. Their efforts are much appreciated. Once again, Dr Pat Ibbotson and Linda, my ever-supportive wife, helped me with the difficult task of assembling the final manuscript. Thank you both. Finally, I would like to express my personal debt of gratitude to Dr Darach Turley for his constant encouragement and infinite patience, even when I was screeching for his overdue chapter. Cometh the hour, cometh the manuscript.

Stephen Brown
Coleraine
February 1997

1 Travelling in trope

Postcards from the edge of consumer research

Stephen Brown and Darach Turley

Directly we arrived at the summit, everybody made a rush for the hotel and fought for the postcards. Five minutes afterwards, everybody was writing for dear life. I believe that the entire party had come up, not for the sake of the experience, or the scenery, but to write postcards and to write them on the summit.

(quoted in Briggs 1988: 366)

PRELUDE

Written in 1900, the above passage suggests that *hyper-reality*, a state where simulacra or reproductions are preferred to the real thing, long predates the postmodern ruminations of hyper-realtor extraordinaire, Jean Baudrillard (1983, 1994a). Such an occurrence, of course, would hardly come as a surprise to the great illusionist of the end. After all, Baudrillard (1994b) has suggested that the final years of the twentieth century will be characterised, not by the fiery fate predicted by countless generations of apocalyptics, soothsayers and Bible-thumpers, but by a systematic process of erasure, where history is thrown into reverse, the past is methodically expunged of its mistakes and misdemeanours, and the terrible temporal slate that is the twentieth century is completely wiped clean in preparation for a fresh start on the other side of the year 2000.[1]

Baudrillard, surprise, surprise, is somewhat imprecise about the precise point at which his hypothesised retroversion will terminate – he posits a 'history barrier', akin to the sound or speed barrier, beyond which the reversal of time cannot pass – but a strong case can surely be made for the late nineteenth century, since the *fin de siècle* appears to be exercising the imagination of innumerable intellectuals at present (e.g. Alexander 1995; Ledger and McCracken 1995; Meštrović 1991). Many latter-day commentators have drawn attention to the intriguing parallels between the dog-days of the nineteenth century and our degraded, some would say decadent, postmodern times. Showalter (1991: 1), for example, states that from 'urban homelessness to imperial decline, from sexual revolution to sexual epidemics, the last decades of the twentieth century seem to be repeating the problems, themes and metaphors of the *fin de siècle*'. Eagleton (1995) notes the 'uncanny' resemblance between the global economic recessions of the late nineteenth and late twentieth centuries, though the latter are accompanied by an all-pervasive air of political lassitude and ennui that was notably absent in the former. 'What we seem left with in the nineties', he concludes, 'is something of the culture of the previous *fin de siècle* shorn of its politics' (Eagleton 1995: 11). For Briggs and Snowman (1996), moreover, the most striking concordance between now and then inheres in both societies' retrospective propensity. Just as we are inclined to reflect on the last *fin de siècle*, so too the late Victorians were prone to ponder on the past and, like ourselves, prone to ponder their ponderings.

One intriguing aspect of La Belle Epoch, which has thus far failed to excite the current crop of *siècle* surfers, is the humble picture postcard. Although blank postcards date from the 1870s, albeit claims for much earlier periods have also been made (Byatt 1982; Coysh 1996; Kandaouroff 1973), the modern picture postcard really only emerged in the middle to late 1890s (Briggs 1988). The passage of enabling legislation (1894 in the UK, 1898 in the USA), coupled with advances in printing technology (collotype, chromo-lithography) and the concomitant growth of the mass tourist industry (see Urry 1990), precipitated an extraordinary picture postcard 'mania', which peaked just prior to the First World War (the so-called 'golden age' of the picture postcard). In Britain alone, the number of postcards passing through the Post Office – a one-to-one ratio of posted-to-unposted cards is assumed by deltiologists – rose from 313 million in 1895 to 926 million in 1914 and it is estimated that by 1910, 2.5 million postcards were sold every day in the United States (Byatt 1982).

This *fin de siècle* fever for postcards is fascinating in several respects, not least with regard to the bizarre believe-it-or-not, Ripley-style achievements it precipitated. One early German enthusiast, for instance, managed to write the first three books of the *Odyssey* on a single postcard and a redoubtable 77 year old, Ms Rita Kettredge of Belfast, Missouri, did likewise for all 15,000 words of President Cleveland's address to Congress (Briggs 1988). From our present perspective, however, one of the most intriguing aspects of this penchant for postcards is the all-important part played by the marketing system. Aside from the mammoth production, distribution and retailing network that emerged in very short order (by 1899, according to Byatt (1982), more than 3,000 different views of Paris were available and a postcard factory in Frankfurt-on-Main, employing 1,200 people, produced 100 new designs each working day), the history of deltiology reveals that the earliest picture postcards were developed by consumer goods manufacturers as advertising vehicles – scenic-type cards came later – and commercial interests lay behind the political campaigning that produced the legislative changes of the 1890s. Indeed, in his compelling chronicle of the postal service, Kandaouroff (1973) reveals that the very first 'letters', found in Cappadocia and dated *c*.3000

BCE, comprised invoices for merchandise, records of diverse traded goods and, no doubt, a tell of prehistoric junk mail.

Another interesting facet of the incredible, late-Victorian postcards fad is the part played by co-mingling, both combative and conciliatory. The growth of the picture postcard is, of course, inseparable from the gradual development of the modern tourist industry – the so-called 'democratisation of travel' (Urry 1990: 16) that accompanied the industrial and communications revolutions of the nineteenth century (paid holidays, railways, steam-ships, travel agencies, etc.) – but it was boosted dramatically by periodic 'comings together' of contrasting cultures, principally in the phonetically contiguous but physically contrasting forms of *warfare* and *world's fairs* (Coysh 1996). Just as the Crimean and American Civil Wars did much to advance the art of photography, so too the Boer War, First World War and, in the pre-*picture* era, the Franco-Prussian War of 1870–1, helped promote La Belle Epoch's passion for postcards. A combination of familial separation, official censorship and the ample fundraising possibilities they afforded, meant that armed conflict was very good for the postcards business (one Aldershot manufacturer, Gale and Polden, specialised in military scenes). Conversely, the commemorative postcards produced by the organisers of world's fairs and analogous exhibitions – Paris Exhibition (1900), St Louis World's Fair (1904), Franco-British Exhibition (1908) – proved enormously popular and did much to engender the 'wish you were here' habit. In fact, the very first official US picture postcards were produced for the celebrated 1893 Colombian Exhibition in Chicago.

A third and, in certain respects, the most captivating component of the *fin de siècle*'s postmastery is the enormous controversy it aroused. Granted, the postcard concept was not short of influential supporters – William Gladstone and the famous Victorian diarist, Francis Kilvert, to name but two – but polite society remained chary of communicating by, if not collecting, these epistolic interlopers. Postcards' inherent lack of privacy, fears of inadvertent libel and concerns about their adverse impact upon the noble art of letter-writing – our moronic inferno of two-minute, soundbite culture is not new, so it seems – meant that many early commentators considered them injudicious, indiscreet, inexpedient and, not to put too fine a point on it, decidedly inadvisable. As late as 1890, a best-selling etiquette manual, engagingly named *Don't*, warned its readers not 'to conduct correspondence on postal cards. It is questionable whether a note on a postal card is entitled to the courtesy of a response' (Briggs 1988: 362). Thus, despite their incredible popularity at the turn of the century, picture postcards were by no means universally beloved. They were frowned upon by philatelists, albeit plain cards were admired by serious collectors. They were largely ignored by professional artists, though some practitioners of Art Nouveau (e.g. Alphonse Mucha, Raphael Kirchner, Hans Christiansen and Paul Berthon) successfully exploited the medium.

And they were treated with ill-disguised contempt in official circles, not least on account of the 'lovely-weather-we're-having' type banalities typically expressed thereon. Some ingenious manufacturers, admittedly, produced picture postcards complete with a sort of proto-sentence completion test – in imitation handwriting! – which was intended to stimulate the writer's creative juices ('It struck me very terribly . . .'). Nevertheless, it is fair to say that the postcard was very quickly relegated to the 'popular' culture sphere, a sphere exemplified by Donald McGill's celebrated carnivalesque cartoon-cards of the inter-war era (Coysh 1996).

INTERLUDE

Although some contemporary commentators consider the picture postcard, with its intimations of imperialism, hints of hegemony and connotations of colonialism, as a sort of *memento mori* for modernity,[2] it is not unreasonable to suggest that the postcard has managed to make a triumphant transition to postmodernity. This survival, however, is not simply a manifestation of post-postcarditis (picture postcards' continuing and heartfelt popularity).[3] We postmodern peripatetics are still required to send some home, albeit with a suitably ironic message – with inverted commas around 'wish you were here?', as it were – and in the foreknowledge that we are likely to get back before our postcards arrive. Nor, for that matter, is it simply due to the imagination, inventiveness and industriousness of postcard manufacturers, whose marketing specialists appear to have succeeded in circumventing the decline stage of the PLC (is it just our imagination, or is the choice of postcards much better these days?). Nor, indeed, is it entirely an instantiation of postmodern de-differentiation, the elision of hitherto sacrosanct boundaries between high art and low. Just as popular culture has been appropriated by the intellectual elite (vernacular architecture, science fiction, street fashions), so too serious treatment is now accorded to 'degraded' cultural forms (rock music, advertising, football, etc.). In such an anti-intellectual intellectual climate, the lowly picture postcard, like comic books, detective fiction, soap operas and so on, cannot be regarded as anything other than a perfectly legitimate area of scholarly inquiry.

There is, in fact, another, somewhat less obvious but nonetheless extremely important, aspect of the relationship between postcards and the postmodern. This connecting element is essentially metaphorical or figurative in character, in so far as it pertains to postmodern theorists' inordinate fondness for a 'postcardite' mode of discourse. In other words, the writings of certain prominent figures in the postmodern pantheon comprise what can only be described as 'postcartography'. Perhaps the most famous example of this propensity is Derrida's (1987) *La Carte postale*, which was inspired, purportedly, by a 1977 visit to Oxford and the author's discovery, in the Bodleian Library, of a picture postcard depicting Socrates writing in the presence of Plato. Inspired by this 'hallucination', this 'acocalyptic revelation' (Derrida 1987: 9), the first 'chapter' of *La Carte postale* – which weighs in at 256 pages and is described as the preface to a book that has not been written! – consists of a long series of anecdotal 'postcards' addressed by the author to all manner of real and/or imaginary correspondents.

Equally epistolary in tone is Baudrillard's so-called, and much-derided, 'metaphysical turn' of the mid-1980s (Best and Kellner 1991). This gave rise to a number of essentially deltiological texts – *America*, *Cool Memories*, *Cool Memories II* and, to some extent, *The Transparency of Evil* (Baudrillard 1988, 1990, 1993, 1996). Described on one back-board blurb as 'wild, often hilarious postcards' and published in a kind of quasi-picture postcard format, the volumes are made up of loosely structured assemblages of aphorisms, asides, comments, reflections and vertiginous, unfailingly brilliant, vignettes. Consider, for example, the following far from atypical observation:

> Modern demolition is truly wonderful. As a spectacle it is the opposite of a rocket launch. The twenty-storey block remains perfectly vertical as it slides towards the centre of the earth. It falls straight, with no loss of its upright bearing, like a tailor's dummy falling through a trap-door, and its own surface area absorbs the rubble. What a marvellous modern art form this is, a match for the firework displays of our childhood.
>
> (Baudrillard, 1988: 17)

Not so much 'wish you were here' as 'wish I were capable of writing a postcard like that'.

Derrida and Baudrillard, of course, are not alone in their postcryptography. Other prominent postcardiologists include the late – that is, late as in late period, not late great – Roland Barthes (*The Pleasure of the Text* and *A Lover's Discourse*, in particular); Walter Benjamin (not only did Benjamin collect picture postcards and dream of writing a book consisting entirely of quotations, but his unpublished masterpiece, the Arcades Project, was also written in a fragmented, hallucinatory, postcardinal point manner); James Clifford (a leading postmodern ethnographer, who has both endorsed and evinced the 'postcards' mode of academic address); and, in many respects, the work of the much-hype(rreale)d media philosophers, Taylor and Saarinen (see Barthes 1990a, 1990b; Brodersen 1996; Buck-Morss 1991; Clifford 1988, 1992; Taylor and Saarinen 1994). True, it can be contended that, with the exception of Clifford, these writings are not 'genuine' postcards, whatever that means (for instance, Taylor and Saarinen's 'book' is a melange of faxes, letters, telephone messages, e-mails and the general ecstasy of postmodern communications technology), but their disjointed, dislocated, disconnected, dissembled and decentred tone is very much in keeping with *l'esprit de carte* of our *fin de siècle*. Indeed, none other than Jean-François Lyotard (1985: 5) aptly describes his work as having been written 'in the spirit of the bottle tossed into the ocean'. What is more, his principal attempt to *do* postmodern philosophy, as opposed to describing what it might be, comprises a discontinuous 'pile of phrases', albeit Lyotard acknowledges that he 'will never know whether or not the phrases happen to arrive at their destination' (Lyotard 1988: xvi).

DELUDE

As the above examples illustrate, the postal metaphor clearly resonates with the postmodern intelligentsia and, by implication, with their copious postcard-carrying academic avatars (what shall we call them? – post-cardigans?, postcard-sharps? or, as in pulling the wool over our eyes, postcarders?). For Baudrillard, it exemplifies the banality, the fragmentation, the phantasmagoria, the proliferation of signs that characterise the late twentieth century, where Gulf Wars do not take place, Disneyland exists in order to demonstrate that the rest of America is fake and the circulation of capital has exceeded escape velocity, only to orbit like a satellite (Baudrillard 1983, 1989, 1995). Lyotard, likewise, envisages the postmodern self as a kind of *poste restante*, through which all manner of messages pass. 'No one, not even the least privileged among us, is ever entirely powerless over the messages that traverse and position him at the post of sender, addressee or referent' (Lyotard 1984: 15). Indeed, in the case of Derrida, the postcard symbolises his entire deconstructive project. It subverts the notion that communication is a closed circuit of exchange, where meanings are clear-cut, completely comprehensible and guaranteed to arrive on time at the appointed place. The act of writing, Derrida argues, exerts a disseminating influence on language, multiplies the possibilities of meaning and serves to undermine the assumption that unadulterated communication can take place. This predicament attains its apogee in the postcard, a 'wandering exile' whose platitudinous message is casually inscribed, open for all to peruse and, paradoxically, makes proper sense only to the ultimate addressee.

Important though the postal/postcards analogy has proved for theorists of postmodernity, it represents only one component – admittedly a key component – of the principal postmodern trope. Notwithstanding the very stiff competition from 'text', 'cyborg' and 'seduction', all of which have been deemed emblematic of our present postmodern times, many prominent commentators consider *travel* and its affiliates (movement, circulation, restlessness, space, etc.) to be today's overarching intellectual conceit. To cite but a few examples: Mike Featherstone (1995: 126) observes that 'In the literature on postmodernism there is ... frequent use of metaphors of movement and marginality. There are references to travel, nomadism, migrancy, border-crossings, living on the borders.' James Clifford (1992) maintains that postmodern ethnographic theorising necessarily involves displacement, going away from home, both physically and epistemologically. Fredric Jameson (1985, 1991) considers 'cognitive mapping' to be one possible means of elucidating the fluidity, the chaos, the disorientating flux that is postmodern culture and society. Megan Morris (1988), by contrast, contends that the motel, which functions as a place of escape yet provides a home from home, comprises a more appropriate analogy for the characteristic diaspora-return processes of postmodernity. For John Urry (1990), postmodernity is typified by 'the tourist gaze', the manifold ways of 'seeing' what we see in today's deliberately manipulated and staged, commerce-soaked cultural milieux. Zygmunt Bauman (1997), similarly, subscribes to the view that 'tourists' and their unfortunate obverse, 'vagabonds', are the key metaphors for late twentieth-century life, since we are all constantly on the move. Elspeth Probyn (1990) posits that postmodernists' predisposition toward the peripheral, marginal and occluded (women, gays, 'deviants', people of colour, etc.)[4] serves ultimately to centre the decentred and decentre the centred, though as Dick Hebdige (1993: 271) makes clear 'the point is not to oversee the collapse of the periphery as exotic relic into the fatal orbit of the centre, but to take the centre to the periphery, to see the idea/ideal of the centre and the institutions of the centre taken to the edge, broken down and taken over *by* the periphery.'

However, perhaps the single most influential contribution to this particular line of tropological thought is the so-called 'nomadology' of Gilles Deleuze and Felix Guattari (see e.g. Braidotti 1994; JanMohamed and Lloyd 1990; Kaplan 1996; Radway 1988). In their pathbreaking book *One Thousand Plateaus* (which also employs avant-garde writing techniques, albeit not of the 'postcards' variety), they distinguish between 'state thought', which is rigorous, disciplined, objective and continually monitored by the apparatus of power, and 'nomadic thought', which is fluid, flexible, disconcerting (to the establishment) and invariably espoused by 'outsiders'. Drawing upon the time-worn military dialectic of barbarian hordes versus civilised society, Deleuze and Guattari (1986, 1988) suggest that, contra the myth of primitivism, nomadic bands are remarkably innovative in many respects (warfare, science, technology, social arrangements, etc.). They represent a vital, Dionysian spur to the uncivilised advance of 'civilisation'. Nomadology, then, is an experiment in creativity and becoming; it is anti-traditional and non-conforming; it is opposed to stultifying orthodoxy; it involves breaking with convention; it seeks emancipation from totalising or accepted modes of thought; it revels in the proliferation of radically different perspectives and philosophies; it postulates a return to pre-cognitive forms of understanding (desire, intuition, spirituality, flow); it stresses the need to challenge disciplinary limits, canonical restrictions, extant ideologies and hegemonic critical practices; and, for Deleuze and Guattari at least, it provides a singularly appropriate blueprint for intellectual life in our present postmodern times.

This travel metaphor, of course, is particularly applicable to post-modernism itself, with its restless, fluid, multiphrenic qualities and its decidedly footloose, not to say circuitous, character. Postmodernism, after all, commenced in the artworld and has gradually spread throughout the entire academic community, though some commentators suggest that its original, genuinely subversive qualities have been systematically shorn in the course of its journey. For Callinicos,

> Postmodernism no longer offers the thrill of scandal and transgression it once had. In some parts of the academy at least, it is now assuming the solemn countenance of orthodoxy. Numerous undergraduate courses introduce students to the ruminations of Lyotard and Baudrillard. Postgraduate theses are written and academic careers launched on the basis of an unquestioning acceptance of the truth of their principal claims . . . The excitement and controversy generated by the first appearance of the philosophical ideas now marketed under the postmodernist label . . . are long gone.
>
> (Callinicos 1995: 134)

Irrespective of its rumoured emasculation or continuing vitality, post-modernism represents a prime example of what Said (1984) terms 'travelling theory', the tendency for ideas, models and concepts to move from person to person, place to place, discipline to discipline and time to time. Such transfers and transplantations are not frictionless, however, nor are they unimpeded, nor are they unproblematical, nor indeed are they easily summarised. According to Said, nevertheless, the nature of the movement of ideas across the intellectual landscape is predicated upon four key factors: first, the point of origin, the specific circumstances which gave rise to the idea; second, the distance travelled and the adaptations that occur as the concept moves further and further from 'home'; third, the set of favourable or unfavourable conditions that confront the trans-planted idea as it diffuses outwards; and, fourth, the extent to which the concept is eventually accommodated within or absorbed into the intel-lectual pantheon of the host domain.

Said's framework – itself a fine example of travelling theory (see Kaplan 1996) – is not simply pertinent to the latter-day postmodern turn, nor a reminder that all academic disciplines engage in intellectual trading relationships, which come complete with metaphorical tariff barriers, customs and excise duties, semi-illicit smuggling operations, bills of lading and the like. The import/export metaphor also draws our attention to the upward mobility of metaphors themselves. Until comparatively recently regarded as 'deviant and parasitic' (Ortony 1993: 2), the disreputable preserve of politicians, poets, advertisers and would-be sophists (Black 1993), metaphors are now considered central to creativity, innovation and outstanding human accomplishment, in both 'scientific' and 'artistic' arenas (Holyoak and Thagard 1995; Morgan 1986). Knowledge claims, furthermore, are held to be inherently metaphorical, tropes deemed to lie at the very heart of our understanding of the world and figurative thinking considered central to discursive formations, regimes of truth and the process of theory articulation (Brown 1997). Metaphors, as Grant and Oswick (1996: 1) make clear, 'are here there and everywhere. They run right through our language. They are used to make sense of the situations we find ourselves in. They shape our perceptions and can influence our attitudes and behaviour.'

For our present purposes, however, perhaps the most important thing to note about metaphor is the rarely acknowledged, yet nonetheless compelling, fact that travel is the metaphorical root of metaphor! Metaphors involve movement, in a manner of speaking, in so far as they bring together two disparate domains (brain as computer, time is money, organisations as organisms, business is war, atom as solar system, etc.) and thereby allow the transfer of information from one (the source domain) to the other (the target domain). By contending, in effect, that source A is like target B, analogies encourage a process of comparison, substitution and interaction between extant images of A and B, which serves to generate new, different and potentially insightful meanings. Indeed, in his detailed analysis of *Travel as Metaphor*, van den Abbeele (1992) observes that the word 'metaphor' comes from the Ancient Greek *metaphorein*, to transfer or transport, and whose modern Greek equivalent, *metafora*, refers to vehicles used for public transportation.[5]

PRECLUDE

The foregoing peregrinations through the prehistory of picture postcards, the poetics of postmodernism and the topography of tropes may strike some readers as self-indulgent at best and unconscionable at worst. What, they may well ask, has it all got to do with consumer research, the fastest growing, most dynamic and intellectually sophisticated sub-field of marketing scholarship? Those familiar with the postmodern penchant for procrastination, postponement and pedantry will, of course, be perfectly at home with our peripatetic prologue. Why, in the promotional words of one tour operator, sail across when you can cruise across? Yet it is arguable that some pertinent parallels can be drawn between latter-day developments in consumer research and our preamble, our preliminaries, our premeditated, not to say meandering, pre-text on postcards.

First and foremost, like picture postcards, academic consumer research dates from the *fin de siècle*. Apart from the celebrated analyses of consumption undertaken by Veblen and Simmel, the first marketing courses were offered in German universities in the 1890s, and the USA and UK followed suit in the early years of the twentieth century (Jones and Monieson 1990). Scholarly interest in consumer behaviour, what is more, has since waxed and waned in intensity – milestones include the classic inter-war work of Lazarsfeld, the mania for motivation research in the 1950s and the multivariate, information-processing revolution of the 1970s – but, as with the picture postcard, the emergence of postmodernism seems to have given consumption a whole new lease of life. So much so, that the burgeoning number of books with 'postmodern' in the title is exceeded only by books with 'consumer' emblazoned on the dustjacket. And just as Coren (1975) suggests that the key to best-sellerdom in Britain is to write a book that combines the nation's infatuation with pets and sport (*Golfing for Cats*), so too the secret of scholarly superstardom seems to be books with both 'postmodern' and 'consumer' in the title. For many academic enthusiasts, indeed, it seems that postmodernity and consumption, if not exactly one and the same, are certainly very closely related (e.g. Featherstone 1991; Gabriel and Lang 1995; Jameson 1985). According to Bocock (1993), for instance,

> Consumption has been seen as epitomising [the] move into post-modernity, for it implies a move away from productive work roles being central to people's lives, to their sense of identity, of who they are. In place of work roles, it is roles in various kinds of family formations, in sexual partnerships of various kinds, in leisure-time pursuits, in consumption in general which have come to be seen as being more and more significant to people. These concerns have become reflected in sociology and social theory as a debate about whether or not western societies are moving towards becoming postmodern.
>
> (Bocock 1993: 4)

Second, the three Cs of commerce, co-mingling and controversy that characterised the history of the picture postcard are no less discernible in the intellectual trajectory of consumer research. A child of marketing, itself a child of economics, consumer research has both broken out of its original home in the business school – as the veritable explosion of non-business orientated consumer research readily attests – and served as a conduit for the reverse flow of non-managerial perspectives. As Belk (1995) makes clear, the emergence of 'new consumer research' in the late 1980s was driven, to a very large extent, by a group of business school-based anthropologists, sociologists, historians and literary critics, who were committed to a much broader, more interdisciplinary approach to consumption behaviour than had previously prevailed. This shift in focus, needless to say, precipitated a deep schism which centred on whether the managerial perspective was beneficial or detrimental to the overall development of consumer research. For some academic authorities, the business school's primary function is to serve business, just as medical schools are designed to meet the needs of medical practitioners, and managerial utility should thus be the *sine qua non* of research conducted therein. For others, any perceived association with a particular interest group in society (marketing managers) inevitably tainted the research undertaken on its behalf and thereby undermined the sub-discipline's aspirations to academic legitimacy (see Belk 1986; Hirschman 1986; Holbrook 1985; Jacoby 1985).

Although it is now widely accepted that the axiological convulsions of the late 1980s did much to invigorate the subject area, it is noteworthy that this confrontation was brought to a head by *travel*, the third parallel between picture postcards and consumer research. Disillusioned by the perceived sterility of the positivistic, hypothetico-deductive, managerially orientated approach to consumer research then prevailing, a group of avant-garde academics abandoned their business schools for a 27-foot recreational vehicle and set off on a three-month voyage into the heart-land of American consumption (Belk 1991). Known as the Consumer Odyssey, this mammoth undertaking, which sought a deeper under-standing of the nature and meaning of US consumer behaviour, generated so much information that not even the most industrious German minia-turist could squeeze it on to the back of a postcard. More significant perhaps than the facts it provided – important though they undoubtedly proved – the Odyssey precipitated a massive shift in the methodology, domain and tropography of consumer research. Methodologically, it opened the door to a host of 'interpretive' research procedures predicated on hermeneutics, semiotics, phenomenology, ethnography and personal introspection, to name but a few. In terms of domain, it focused atten-tion on issues previously considered marginal to the managerial mainstream of brand choice and buying behaviour (collecting, compulsive consumption, flea markets, personal possessions, etc.) and which has encouraged in turn researchers' interest in the tangential, peripheral or hitherto overlooked (homelessness, drug addiction, prostitution, marketising economies, the third world). Above all, however, the Odyssey succeeded in breaking the spell of the sub-discipline's then dominant root metaphor – consumer as computer. Thanks to the endeavours of the Odyssians and Belk's (1987) contemporaneous semi-Swiftian satire, the idea of consumer-as-automaton – acquiring, processing, retrieving and acting upon information inputs – was superseded by a less deterministic, more fluid, open, mutable, socially and culturally embedded notion of consumer as communicator, as hedonist, as explorer, as itinerant (both physically and psychologically).

Ten years on from the Consumer Odyssey, another transcontinental trek inspired the present volume. As noted in the Pre-text, several prominent American scholars accepted invitations to visit a number of academic insti-tutions in Great Britain and Ireland. To coincide with the occasion, each of the participants was presented with our proposed title and asked to prepare a chapter on their specialist subject area. It follows, then, that the overall objective of our postcards from the edge is not to provide an integrated statement on, or outline of, the lineaments of contemporary consumer research. Such an undertaking would be impossible in any event, given the sheer diversity and rapidity of change in the sub-discipline, but it is also contrary to the pluralist, multiphrenic, heteroglossian, discordant, polysemous – call it what you will – character of postmodern marketing scholarship. In keeping with the fragmented tenor of our paradoxical post-modern times, this volume simply offers a vivid tableau of fleeting, disconnected, occasionally disorientating images from the constantly shifting perimeter fence of consumption. While this textual policy may prove disconcerting for some readers, it is arguable that it is much more appropriate to the present, schizophrenic state of consumer research, where 'information processing experiments and experiential consumption ethnographies abut ... one another in the journals' (Belk 1995: 61), than any specious editorial attempt to pour the contributions into a commodious monoglossian mould. If there is any integrating theme, it is the theme of disintegration. The unity of the volume lies in its diversity. It coheres around incoherence, it mixes rather than matches, it offers harmonious discord, peaceable conflict, unanimous disagreement, illogical logic, euphonious cacophony, concentrated dispersal, singular multiplicity, assonant dissonance, homogeneous heterogeneity, particular generalities, sectarian syncretics, sedentary nomadism and civilised barbarity. And that's just the introductory chapter!

INCLUDE

Having set the scene with an attempted postmodern improvisation on our postcards metaphor – postcardiac arrests though it will doubtless induce among our more conservative colleagues – the second chapter deals specif-ically with the truism that travel broadens the mind. In a wide-ranging discussion that takes in Russian folk tales, children's birthday stories, the daily commute, strip-tease, Hallowe'en, and the growth, development and transformation of Las Vegas, Russell W. Belk examines the relationship between travel and creativity, between wandering and wondering, between here and therefore. The process of departure and return, he argues, combined with the public and private rituals that accompany boundary crossings, plays an important part in personal and intellectual develop-ment. The boundaries that exist, admittedly, are more metaphorical than literal, but they are 'real' for all that and have to be traversed success-fully. Indeed, it is the crossing of them, in an open, playful and curious spirit, that ignites the creative spark. Contra the nihilistic nay-sayers, Belk maintains that latter-day advances in telecommunications technology (World Wide Web, virtual reality, etc.) are creating conditions conducive to a new era of boundary crossings and creative discovery.

Creative discovery, albeit of the old-fashioned variety, is equally apparent in the third chapter, where Morris B. Holbrook deploys his celebrated literary and communications skills to extemporise on our over-arching theme. Illustrating his highly allusive argument with a generous selection of stereoscopic 'postcards', the author draws upon his vacation experiences in two very different environmental settings to make a compelling case for 'walking on the edge'. Whether it be in a mountainous or maritime context, the narrow strip between complete safety and mortal peril is where the view is most beautiful and the footing is most firm. The same is also true, says Holbrook, of consumer behaviour and research. As consumers, we seek experiences on the edge of adventure, where we transcend the insipid ordinariness of everyday life. As researchers, we employ methodological procedures on the margin of legitimacy in the belief that epistemological roulette, rather than low-risk, minor twist replication, is the route to academic advance and personal advancement.

Although his publications record is remarkably diverse, the methodology for which Holbrook is perhaps best known is the controversial and much-debated 'subjective personal introspection' technique. As his extraordinary contribution to the present volume exemplifies, this requires the researcher to reflect on his or her own consumption experiences and bring them together in the form of an extended autobiographical essay. A variation on this procedure is employed in the fourth chapter by Stephen Brown and Rhona Reid, which deals with the somewhat neglected yet very timely topic of 'trolley-rage'. Or, to be more specific, it deals with the aversive side of the consumption experience, the sheer irritation, anguish, resentment and despair that shopping can induce, but which has been all but ignored by the consumer research community thus far. Premised upon an interpretive analysis of fifty-five introspective essays, the chapter highlights the manifold frustrations encountered by perfectly innocent shoppers – slow moving queues, surly shop assistants, cramped changing rooms, inadequate car parking facilities, interfering companions, infuriating strangers, ill-fitting or badly made merchandise and many more besides.

Aversiveness is no less apparent in the fifth chapter by Craig J. Thompson, Eric J. Arnould and Barbara B. Stern, although it is aversiveness of an epistemological stripe. Written in an appropriately postmodern mode – riffing, reflexivity and irreverence are much to the fore – the authors employ Derrida's idea of *différance*, meaning both to differ and defer, to argue against the concept of convergent validity and its methodological epigone, 'triangulation'. Contending that the valorisation of consensus and complementarity over dissensus and contradiction is an abrogation of the heterogeneous, pluralistic ethos that characterises (or ought to characterise) postmodernity, they suggest that postmodern consumer research should be centrifugal rather than centripetal, it should emphasise the margins not the median, it should celebrate diversity instead of unity, conflict instead of co-operation and difference instead of similarity. To this end, Thompson, Arnould and Stern offer a radical, postmodern representation of the much-recycled Kuhnian model of paradigm shifts, Gestalt switches, incommensurability *et al.* Divergence, they maintain, must not be regarded as a problem but as an opportunity to understand how different core assumptions, conceptualisations, conventions and research interests give rise to, codify and reproduce the constitution of 'knowledge' and the nature of 'truth'.

In their attempt to challenge the unchallenged assumption that 'post-modern' consumer research comprises a kinder, gentler, 'why-can't-we-all-be-friends?' intellectual nirvana of epistemological, ontological and methodological pluralism, Thompson, Arnould and Stern inevitably traffic in the ideological traffic of Ideology (the very use of the word, after all, speaks volumes about the likely political alignment of the user). This is the theme of the sixth chapter by Richard Elliott and Mark Ritson. Positing that whereas postmodernism provides little of practical worth to consumer research, poststructuralism's critical impulse, its emphasis upon the material as well as the symbolic, offers considerable scope for a politi-cised, 'consciousness raising' programme of empirical investigation. Taking advertising as an example, the authors identify its key ideological mech-anisms – legitimisation, universalisation, unification, fragmentation, naturalisation and enlightened false consciousness – yet also draw atten-tion to the existence of diverse resistance strategies. The recipients of advertising messages are not the unthinking 'cultural dupes' of legend, according to Elliott and Ritson, but individuals and groups of individuals (subcultures) who are highly active, not to say manipulative, in their in-terpretation of textual meaning.

A perfect illustration of this pick 'n' mix propensity is proffered in the seventh chapter by Stephanie O'Donohoe and Caroline Tynan, whose in-depth, para-ethnographic study of young Scottish adults demonstrates that they find advertising highly involving, though the academic construct 'involvement' hardly does justice to the selective, imaginative, sceptical, playful and, not least, socially situated character of the informants' adver-tising-related activities. In particular, O'Donohoe and Tynan postulate that people 'converse' with advertising, they enter into a 'dialogue' with it and are the co-creators of advertising meaning. Consumers, in actual fact, often use advertising for purposes that are quite different from what the makers may have had in mind – structuring time, reinforcing attitudes and values, enhancing egos and facilitating social interactions with friends, family and strangers. However, in order to capture the richness of these forms of advertising involvement, it is necessary to cast off the 'semiotic strait-jacket' of positivistic and experimental research, abandon the formality of the brand choice dress code, and slip into something that is both method-ologically comfortable and theoretically appealing. Our sub-discipline, in short, should sport street-fashion scholarship rather than haute couture conceptualisations.

Commendable though it is, O'Donohoe and Tynan's desire to untie the semiotic strait-jacket almost inevitably raises questions about the design, cut, hang, hemline and bias binding of the garment itself. For David Glen Mick, 'semiotics' is the demi-monde of contemporary marketing discourse and in the eighth chapter he seeks to strip away some of the unnecessary layers of meaning that this highly fashionable term has accumulated. In the popular academic imagination, semiotics is associated with structuralism, post-structuralism, postmodernism, post-positivism, Freudian psychology, qualitative research and 'theory', to name but the most prominent. These are all incorrect, in Mick's forthright opinion, although it remains to be seen whether his curiously Calvinistic, not to say authoritarian, desire to curb the semiosis of Semiotics and impose a singular, agreed meaning upon the S-word will cut much ice among consumer researchers in our polysemous postmodern times. Immolation, presumably, awaits the academic apostates.

Mick's short but provocative dance of the seven semiotic veils, his call for rigour, respect and reverence when using The Word, is met in the ninth chapter by Gordon R. Foxall, albeit within the context of the radical behaviourist paradigm. Widely, if mistakenly, regarded as a pre-modern (i.e. pre-cognitive revolution) mode of marketing understanding, predicated on a crude, contrived and utterly outmoded stimulus-response based conceptualisation of the consumer, radical behaviourism has made rapid strides in recent years thanks to its incorporation of the human capacity for verbal control of behaviour. As Foxall shows, this permits the drawing of a meaningful distinction between contingency-shaped and rule-governed behaviour, and facilitates the development of an interpretive model of the consumer situation, which is applicable to decision taking and choice behaviour in manifold consumption environments.

If the future of consumer research lies in reinventing its past, for Foxall at least, the tenth chapter comprises an entirely different vision of consumption to come. According to Alladi Venkatesh, Laurie Meamber and A. Fuat Firat, cyberspace is the next marketing frontier. A search for alternative forms of life (as opposed to life forms) has begun, new sets of practices and discourses are being articulated and the cybuilders are in the process of creating a whole new world where we can lose ourselves, a place of escape and transformation, a magical milieu that materialises thanks to the technologies of the digital. Acknowledging that it is impossible to observe this all-encompassing, rapidly changing phenomenon, since there is no stable, Archimedian point from which it can be viewed or encapsulated, the authors contend that cyberspace is already part of everyday life, it holds out the inviting prospect of a different consuming 'self', or multiple consuming 'selves', and it is being colonised, some would say invaded, by postmodern marketing organisations. The rhetoric of cyberspace is one of choice, freedom, dispersal, exploration and nomadism, but this is increasingly being redefined and, indeed, commodified by marketers, who now occupy over 80 per cent of the Internet. Like it or not, the postmodern utopia that is cyberspace is having to pay its way and extract a tribute from late twentieth-century IT-inerants.

The penultimate chapter by Michael R. Solomon and Basil G. Englis also deals with the late twentieth-century self, or selves, though it is positioned within the more familiar academic framework of 'lifestyle'. The lifestyle construct, predicated on the premise that people sort themselves into groups organised around things they like to do or ways they spend their money, dates from the late 1960s/early 1970s. Yet despite a vast amount of academic and managerial research, the holy grail of identifiable, definable and generalisable lifestyle categories has proved illusory. Instead of pursuing this chimerical elysium of lifestyle 'types', Solomon and Englis suggest that it is time to reintroduce an all-important but almost forgotten aspect of the phenomenon: living, breathing, thinking consuming, *people*. To this end, the authors offer an alternative conceptualisation of lifestyle based upon two extant models of consumer behaviour – fashion diffusion and communications theory. Summarising an extensive programme of empirical research into college students' self-generated lifestyle categories, they contend that consumer behaviour is frequently motivated, not by the lifestyle group to which the respondent currently belongs, but by the one that he or she aspires to belong to, even though their image of this group is often oversimplified, stereotypical and 'inaccurate'. Distorted though they are, these constructions are more meaningful than the constructs that have dominated lifestyle research to date.

Of course, in the midst of life(style) there is death and the final chapter deals specifically with the after life(style). Aptly portrayed as a postcard from the *very* edge, Darach Turley addresses the relationship between marketing and mortality, arguing that the seemingly taboo subject of death remains unnecessarily neglected by the academy in general and consumer research in particular. However, by drawing upon the hermeneutics of Heidegger and the hyperbolic postmodern cogitations of Baudrillard, the author attempts to challenge the exclusion – the 'social exile' – of death and the associated denial of its central place in contemporary consumer culture. In so doing, Turley brings us full circle to Baudrillard's (1994b) *Illusion of the End*, the principal postmodern prestidigitator's preposterous prediction that the much-prophesied end of time simply cannot take place (since history has run out of puff prior to its proleptic culmination). In the case of the present introductory chapter at least, Baudrillard is sadly but brilliantly mistaken. Time's up. The end. *Fin*.

NOTES

1   Consider the following

> At some point in the 1980s, history took a turn in the opposite direction. Once the apogee of time, the summit of the curve of evolution, the solstice of history had been passed, the downward slope of events began and things began to run in reverse. It seems that, like cosmic space, historical time-space is also curved. By the same chaotic effect in time as in space,

things go quicker and quicker as they approach their term, just as water mysteriously accelerates as it approaches a waterfall. In the Euclidean space of history, the shortest path between two points is the straight line, the line of Progress and Democracy. But this is only true of the linear space of the Enlightenment. In our non-Euclidean *fin de siècle* space, a baleful curvature unfailingly deflects all trajectories ... Each apparent movement of history brings us imperceptibly closer to its antipodal point, if not indeed to its starting point. ... By this retroversion of history to infinity, this hyperbolic curvature, the century itself is escaping its end. By this retroaction of events, we are eluding our own deaths. Metaphorically, then, we shall not even reach the symbolic term of the end, the symbolic term of the year 2000.

(Baudrillard 1994b: 10–11)

2 A word of explanation is probably in order. According to McCannell (1989), the contemporary tourist is a symbol of *modernity*, in so far as the travel industry, and the 'experience' of tourism, involves an ambivalent relationship to the past, technologies of simultaneity, massive population displacement, global economic interconnectedness and, above all, the creation-cum-perpetuation of boundaries, both tangible and intangible (developed/underdeveloped, urban/rural, First World/Third World, etc.). All tourists, he argues, search for verifiable markers of 'authenticity' – of evidence that they were 'really there' – and these are provided by photographs, souvenirs and the ubiquitous picture postcard. In a similar vein, Horne (1984) contends that valid expressions of modernity, of cosmopolitanism, of broad-mindedness, are acquired primarily through travel. Travel, however, requires corroboration, which is achieved through documentation of the experience in the shape of travel diaries, ticket stubs, video recordings, photography and the writing of postcards. Unfortunately, the very act of taking a photograph or writing a postcard comprises a form of possession, a means of 'capturing' the moment, the place, the people, the Other and, as such, inevitably involves the imposition of power relations, of hegemony, of subordination, of domination through representation. As Kaplan (1996: 61) makes clear,

Representational practices of all kinds, from ethnographies, to popular films to postcards, produce views of the world that participate in discourses of displacement in powerful ways. Whether we see representation as 'gaining possession of an experience', 'getting a grip on reality', or expressing a partial viewpoint, the process is never free of power relations. The questions become: what kind of power? exercised in what ways? to whose benefit? and to whose loss?'

Urry (1990: 138), analogously, notes the insatiability of the 'photographing eye', an insatiability that offers new ways of looking at the world and provides new forms of authority for doing so. Photography, nevertheless, is a socially constructed mode of representation. It appropriates the subject being photographed and thereby 'tames' the object of the gaze. It seems to afford unmediated access to reality ('the camera never lies'), but actually necessitates the preselection, composition and, to some extent, aestheticisation of the chosen artefacts. What is more, it gives shape to travel, in that photo-opportunities provide the hub around which holiday experiences revolve. Much contemporary tourism, he suggests, 'becomes in effect a search for the photogenic; travel is a strategy for the accumulation of photographs' (Urry 1990: 139). Urry's thesis, of course, pertains primarily to the humble holiday snap, yet it is equally true of picture postcards, if not more so. Postcards, along with films, television programmes and travel brochures, help create our pre-formed mental images of localities – the Eiffel Tower, New York skyline, Sydney Opera House, etc. – and thus determine what we consider worth photographing when we eventually get there. In theme parks, it is not unusual to see signposts identifying prime photographic vantage points, albeit the resultant snap is almost identical to, if less professional than, the postcards on sale in the souvenir shop! In this respect, Urry asserts that tourism in the late twentieth century is largely hermeneutic, since holidays involve tracking down pre-formed photographic images, capturing those self-same images for oneself and comparing the captured images with the images examined prior to departure.

3   As this neologism may be a bit too subtle (read, contrived) for most readers, I should perhaps point out that 'carditis' means inflammation of the heart. What I'm (SB) trying to say here is that, unlike our Victorian forebears, we postmoderns are no longer inflamed by, or infatuated with, the picture postcard (hence postcarditis) but we continue to write them in an ironic, knowing, tongue-in-cheek manner (post-postcarditis). Pretentious, or what?

4   In this regard, Wolff (1993) makes the important point that the postmodern proliferation of travel-related vocabularies and metaphors serves only to reproduce androcentric tendencies in critical thought, since travel is a deeply, perniciously, almost irredeemably, gendered activity (man ventures forth, woman stays at home).

5   Van den Abbeele also expatiates on the etymology of the word 'voyage', which according to the *Encyclopédie* of 1765, has its roots (like the postal service) in commercial life. It originally referred to the comings and goings of a mercenary (meaning someone working for monetary gain) who transports furnishings, wheat and other things.

REFERENCES

Alexander, J.C. (1995) *Fin de Siècle Social Theory: Relativism, Reduction and the Problem of Reason*, London: Verso.

Barthes, R. (1990a [1973]) *The Pleasure of the Text*, trans. R. Miller, Oxford: Blackwell.

—— (1990b [1977]) *A Lover's Discourse: Fragments*, trans. R. Howard, Harmondsworth: Penguin.

Baudrillard, J. (1983 [1981]) *Simulations*, trans. P. Foss, P. Patton and P. Beitchman, New York: Semiotext(e).

—— (1988 [1986]) *America*, trans. C. Turner, London: Verso.

—— (1989) 'The anexoric ruins', in D. Kamper and C. Wulf (eds) *Looking Back on the End of the World*, trans. D. Antal, New York: Semiotext(e), 29–45.

—— (1990 [1987]) *Cool Memories*, trans. C. Turner, London: Verso.

—— (1993 [1990]) *The Transparency of Evil: Essays on Extreme Phenomena*, trans. J. Benedict, London: Verso.

—— (1994a [1981]) *Simulacra and Simulation*, trans. S.F. Glaser, Ann Arbor, MI: University of Michigan Press.

—— (1994b [1992]) *The Illusion of the End*, trans. C. Turner, Cambridge: Polity.

—— (1995 [1991]) *The Gulf War Did Not Take Place*, trans. P. Patton, Bloomington, IN: Indiana University Press.

—— (1996 [1990]) *Cool Memories II*, trans. C. Turner, Cambridge: Polity.

Bauman, Z. (1997) *Postmodernity and its Discontents*, Cambridge: Polity.

Belk, R.W. (1986) 'What should ACR want to be when it grows up?', in R.J. Lutz (ed.) *Advances in Consumer Research*, 13, Provo, UT: Association for Consumer Research, 423–424.

—— (1987) 'A modest proposal for creating verisimilitude in consumer-information-processing models and some suggestions for establishing a discipline to study consumer behaviour', in A.F. Firat, N. Dholakia and R.P. Bagozzi (eds) *Philosophical and Radical Thought in Marketing*, Lexington, MA: Lexington Books, 361–372.

—— (ed.) (1991) *Highways and Buyways: Naturalistic Research from the Consumer Behaviour Odyssey*, Provo, UT: Association for Consumer Research.

—— (1995) 'Studies in the new consumer behaviour', in D. Miller (ed.) *Acknowledging Consumption: A Review of New Studies*, London: Routledge, 58–95.

Best, S. and Kellner, D. (1991) *Postmodern Theory: Critical Interrogations*, London: Macmillan.

Black, M. (1993) 'More about metaphors', in A. Ortony (ed.) *Metaphor and Thought*, 2nd edn, Chicago: University of Chicago Press, 19–41.

Bocock, R. (1993) *Consumption*, London: Routledge.

Braidotti, R. (1994) *Nomadic Subjects: Embodiment and Sexual Difference in Contemporary Feminist Theory*, New York: Columbia University Press.

Briggs, A. (1988) *Victorian Things*, London: Batsford.

—— and Snowman, D. (1996) 'Introduction', in A. Briggs and D. Snowman (eds) *Fins de Siècle: How Centuries End 1400–2000*, New Haven, CT: Yale University Press, 1–5.

Brodersen, M. (1996 [1990]) *Walter Benjamin: A Biography*, trans. M.R. Green and I. Ligers, London: Verso.

Brown, S. (1997) *Postmodern Marketing Two: Telling Tales*, London: International Thompson Business Press.

Buck-Morss, S. (1991) *The Dialectics of Seeing: Walter Benjamin and the Arcades Project*, Cambridge, MA: MIT Press.

Byatt, A. (1982) *Collecting Picture Postcards: An Introduction*, Malvern: Golden Age Postcard Books.

Callinicos, A. (1995) 'Postmodernism as normal science', *British Journal of Sociology*, 46, December: 134–139.

Clifford, J. (1988) *The Predicament of Culture: Twentieth-century Ethnography, Literature and Art*, Cambridge, MA: Harvard University Press.

—— (1992) 'Traveling cultures', in L. Grossberg, C. Nelson and P. Treichler (eds) *Cultural Studies*, New York: Routledge, 96–116.

Coren, A. (1975) *Golfing for Cats*, London: Coronet.

Coysh, A.W. (1996) *The Dictionary of Picture Postcards in Britain 1894–1939*, Woodbridge: Antique Collectors' Club.

Deleuze, G. and Guattari, F. (1986 [1980]) *Nomadology*, trans. B. Massumi, New York: Semiotext(e).

—— (1988 [1980]) *A Thousand Plateaus: Capitalism and Schizophrenia*, trans. B. Massumi, London: Athlone.

Derrida, J. (1987 [1980]) *The Post Card: From Socrates to Freud and Beyond*, trans. A. Bass, Chicago: University of Chicago Press.

Eagleton, T. (1995) 'The flight to the real', in S. Ledger and S. McCracken (eds) *Cultural Politics at the Fin de Siècle*, Cambridge: Cambridge University Press, 11–21.

Featherstone, M. (1991) *Consumer Culture and Postmodernism*, London: Sage.

—— (1995) *Undoing Culture: Globalisation, Postmodernism and Identity*, London: Sage.

Gabriel, Y. and Lang, T. (1995) *The Unmanageable Consumer: Contemporary Consumption and its Fragmentations*, London: Sage.

Grant, D. and Oswick, C. (1996) 'Introduction: getting the measure of metaphors', in D. Grant and C. Oswick (eds) *Metaphor and Organisations*, London: Sage, 1–20.

Hebdige, D. (1993) 'Training some thoughts on the future', in J. Bird, B. Curtis, T. Putnam, G. Robertson and L. Tickner (eds) *Mapping the Futures: Local Cultures, Global Change*, London: Routledge, 270–279.

Hirschman, E.C. (1986) 'Marketing, intellectual creativity and consumer research', in R.J. Lutz (ed.) *Advances in Consumer Research*, 13, Provo, UT: Association for Consumer Research, 433–435.

Holbrook, M.B. (1985) 'Why business is bad for consumer research: The Three Bears revisited', in E.C. Hirschman and M.B. Holbrook (eds) *Advances in Consumer Research*, 12, Provo, UT: Association for Consumer Research, 145–156.

Holyoak, K.J. and Thagard, P. (1995) *Mental Leaps: Analogy in Creative Thought*, Cambridge, MA: MIT Press.

Horne, D. (1984) *The Great Museum: The Re-presentation of History*, London: Pluto.

Jacoby, J. (1985) 'The vices and virtues of consulting: responding to a fairy tale', in E.C. Hirschman and M.B. Holbrook (eds) *Advances in Consumer Research*, 12, Provo, UT: Association for Consumer Research, 157–163.

Jameson, F. (1985) 'Postmodernism and consumer society', in H. Foster (ed.) *Postmodern Culture*, London: Pluto, 111–125.

—— (1991) *Postmodernism, or, The Cultural Logic of Late Capitalism*, London: Verso.

JanMohamed, A. and Lloyd, D. (1990) *The Nature and Context of Minority Discourse*, Oxford: Oxford University Press.

Jones, D.G.B. and Monieson, D.D. (1990) 'Early development of the philosophy of marketing thought', *Journal of Marketing*, 54, January: 102–113.

Kandaouroff, D. (1973) *Collecting Postal History: Postmarks, Cards and Covers*, London: Peter Lowe/Eurospan.

Kaplan, C. (1996) *Questions of Travel: Postmodern Discourses of Displacement*, Durham, NC: Duke University Press.

Ledger, S. and McCracken, S. (1995) 'Introduction', in S. Ledger and S. McCracken (eds) *Cultural Politics at the Fin de Siècle*, Cambridge: Cambridge University Press, 1–10.

Lyotard, J-F. (1984 [1979]) *The Postmodern Condition: A Report on Knowledge*, trans. G. Bennington and A. Massumi, Manchester: Manchester University Press.

—— (1985 [1979]) *Just Gaming*, trans. W. Godzich, Manchester: Manchester University Press.

—— (1988 [1983]) *The Differend: Phrases in Dispute*, trans. G. van den Abbeele, Manchester: Manchester University Press.

McCannell, D. (1989) *The Tourist: A New Theory of the Leisure Class*, 2nd edn, New York: Schocken.

Meštrovič, S.G. (1991) *The Coming Fin de Siècle*, London: Routledge.

Morgan, G. (1986) *Images of Organisation*, Beverly Hills, CA: Sage.

Morris, M. (1988) 'At Henry Parkes Motel', *Cultural Studies*, 2, 1: 1–47.

Ortony, A. (1993) 'Metaphor, language and thought', in A. Ortony (ed.) *Metaphor and Thought*, 2nd edn, Cambridge: Cambridge University Press, 1–16.

Probyn, E. (1990) 'Travels in the postmodern: making sense of the local', in L. Nicholson (ed.) *Feminism/Postmodernism*, New York: Routledge, 176–189.

Radway, J. (1988) 'Reception study: ethnography and the problems of dispersed audiences and nomadic subjects', *Cultural Studies*, 2, 3: 359–376.

Said, E.W. (1984) 'Traveling theory', in E.W. Said, *The World, The Text and The Critic*, London: Vintage, 226–247.

Showalter, E. (1991) *Sexual Anarchy: Gender and Culture at the Fin de Siècle*, London: Bloomsbury.

Taylor, M.C. and Saarinen, E. (1994) *Imagologies: Media Philosophy*, London: Routledge.

Urry, J. (1990) *The Tourist Gaze: Leisure and Travel in Contemporary Societies*, London: Sage.

van den Abbeele, G. (1992) *Travel as Metaphor: From Montaigne to Rousseau*, Minneapolis, MN: University of Minnesota Press.

Wolff, J. (1993) 'On the road again: metaphors of travel in cultural criticism', *Cultural Studies*, 7, 2: 224–239.

2 Been there, done that, bought the souvenirs
Of journeys and boundary crossing

Russell W. Belk

In the Russian tale, 'The Winter Oak' (Nagibin 1979), a young school teacher Anna Vasilyevna walks to her elementary school classroom along a well-worn path in the snow. As a second-year teacher, she confidently begins her morning lesson on nouns by explaining that a noun is a person, thing or quality and then calls on the class for examples. 'Cat', 'house', 'table' – the examples come flying – until they are interrupted by the entrance of Savushkin, a small boy in battered felt boots and patched clothing, who is late once again. Anna scolds Savushkin and tells him that after class they must go to see his mother before she starts her shift as a scrub nurse at the sanatorium of their peat farm village. She repeats her definition of nouns and asks Savushkin for an example. The child eagerly shouts out 'winter oak', and the class bursts into laughter. Anna explains that 'oak' is a noun, but 'winter' is another part of speech that they haven't studied yet; she further admonishes that this is what comes of being late.

After class, Anna and Savushkin begin their journey to see his mother. Rather than follow the more direct route along the highway, Savushkin leads Anna through the forest – the route he follows between home and school, but unfamiliar territory to his teacher. Anna chides him once more and explains it would be faster to walk along the highway. She tells a saddened Savushkin that he must in the future abandon the circuitous forest trail so he will be certain to get to school on time. As they go deeper into the forest, Anna sees animal tracks and asks what they are. Savuskin explains that they are elk tracks, but that the elk is elusive and most likely they will not see one; he has seen only droppings ('Dung' he self-consciously clarifies when Anna asks). Following a stream, Savushkin shows Anna a place where warm springs keep the water open. Anna soon finds a place where she believes she sees the stream's movement beneath the ice. But Savushkin corrects her that it is simply shadows from the movement of the tree branches above. They soon come to a large snow-frosted tree that Anna realises is the winter oak, 'tall and majestic like a cathedral', – the one that Savuskin had offered so enthusiastically in class as his noun. Carefully prodding among the roots of the tree, Savushkin shows his teacher a hibernating hedgehog, a well-hidden frog, lizards, insects and other curiosities of nature.

Anna's curiosity leads her on to discoveries of her own, until Savushkin realises they have tarried too long and his mother will be at work. But by now Anna has had a change of heart and tells Savushkin that she was foolish to forbid him to take the forest trail. Savushkin thanks Anna and offers to escort her back. When she assures him she will be all right, he gives her a stick and says that she should protect herself by hitting the elk if she should see one. On second thought, he suggests that she merely wave the stick lest the elk become too frightened and leave the forest entirely. Anna returns realising that despite her pride and confidence earlier that day, she still has much to learn about teaching. Turning to see Savushkin watching her, she now knows that the most wonderful being in the forest is not the magnificent winter oak, but a small boy in battered felt boots and patched clothing.

In the short journey of this tale much has happened. In crossing over from the edge of her civilisation into the unfamiliar forest, the tables have turned and Anna becomes the student of her diminutive pupil. She comes to realise that the nouns and examples she had elicited from the class were merely dry abstractions and that the winter oak is both a wondrous part of their world and a source of much knowledge – a tree of knowledge, with all its beauties, enticements, uncertainties and dangers. Like the lesson that beginning ethnographers soon learn with their informants, Anna has learned that others are very happy to act as our kind and patient teachers if we believe that they may have something valuable to teach us and if we are willing to listen to them with sincere interest. Perhaps the elusive elk is wisdom; Savushkin has seen only tracks and droppings, but he has seen enough to fear that Anna might scare it away. Anna has learned that while the well-worn straight and narrow path may be the most expedient one, it is not the best one for learning. To learn, we must leave our comfort zones and pursue knowledge in its wild and natural settings. There is no one correct path, but we are best served if we follow where our childlike curiosity leads us.

In this chapter I would like to consider several types of journeys and explore where they may lead us. Both physical journeys through time and space and metaphoric journeys are of interest. Physical journeys include exploration, tourism, migration, commuting and pilgrimage. Metaphoric journeys include those involved in rites of passage, ecstatic shamanism, vision quests, fantasies, daydreams, 'voyages' of self-discovery and the journeys of behavioural – and especially ethnographic – research. Some common elements in each of these journeys include boundary crossing rituals, hospitality rituals, encounters with 'the Other', the collection of artefacts and souvenirs, and an interwoven fabric of curiosity, fear, learning, and play (see Belk and Costa 1995). By asking what is common to these various types of journeys we may learn why the journey is such a compelling phenomenon as well as such a compelling metaphor both for research and for personal development. We may learn why, in the words of an old Cunard Lines slogan, getting there is half the fun.

These days, however, few of us are likely to take an ocean liner in order to travel between continents. Most of us are in far too much of a hurry. It is also widely recognised that thanks to more instantaneous communication, speedier transportation, proliferating multinational commerce, and rapidly expanding international tourism, the world is becoming a much smaller place than it once was. Thus it is also worth contemplating the impact of these changes on both travel and the places we travel to and from. Accordingly, I shall conclude the brief journey of this chapter by considering the fate of the journey in an age of virtual realities, the Internet, international cuisine, world music, world-wide hotel, fast food, and retail franchises, and the simulated otherness of places ranging from mega-malls to Las Vegas.

THE JOURNEY

From Gilgamesh, Homer's Odysseus, and medieval pilgrimages to Keroac, Casteneda's Don Juan, and contemporary tourism, the journey has long fascinated us. Gulliver travelled, as did Thelma and Louise, Hansel and Gretel, John Steinbeck and Charlie, the Israelites, the Wilburys, Bilbo, Paul Theroux, Herodotus, Lassie, Captain Kirk, Captain Nemo, Jesus, Buddha, Darwin, Peter Pan, Little Red Riding Hood, the Love Boat, Jason and the Argonauts, the Apollo astronauts, Pirsig's Phaedrus, Dorothy and Toto, and countless others. Tourism is the world's largest industry and more people travel greater distances at faster speeds than ever before. There is something about travel that continues to captivate us. I suggest that the essence of this something, whether it is sought over the rainbow, at Lourdes, in Disneyland, in the movies, or among the natives of Papua New Guinea, lies chiefly in the difference that these places promise from what we regard as ordinary. It is not necessarily that they are entirely new, novel or unfamiliar. What matters is that they are regarded as markedly different from the ordinary and in that sense promise to be extraordinary places offering the potential for extraordinary experiences. In Cohen and Taylor's (1992) terms, they represent 'escape attempts', and what we are attempting to escape or even subvert is the potential monotony of our everyday lives and their lack of surprises.

When our destinations are different enough and when they are approached with fitting rituals, they may be not only extraordinary, but sacred (Graburn 1989). Appropriate contemporary travel rituals include ceremonies of departure and return, threshold and boundary crossing rites, hospitality and welcoming rituals, celebrations of communitas and liminality, acts of sacrifice and reverence at significant sites and sights, and the acquisition of relics, gifts and souvenirs. There may be various 'priests' who aid in these rituals, including customs officials, tour guides, sales clerks and museum personnel, or we may perform the rituals ourselves with the aid of sacred texts including those published by Michelin, Rough Guide, Frommer's, Fodor's and Lonely Planet.

Just as the traditional rite of passage (which commonly involves a journey as well) is intended to momentously transform a person from one state or life stage to another (van Gennep 1960; Turner 1969), so in one view is tourism a self-transforming ritual process:

> Tourism can be a ritual in which by moving our bodies from here to there we summon up regenerative forces. It can provide the annual reward for a year's striving; some tourist journeys can be the event of a lifetime. We can gain prestige from tourism. We can 'find ourselves'. Whether physically, intellectually, morally, or spiritually, we can feel better after we have done some tourism.
>
> (Horne 1992: 5–6)

As international touristic travel becomes more widespread it has been suggested that it has become a part of the 'standard package' desired by virtually all of the world's consumers (Keyfitz 1982). One issue as travel becomes more routine is whether it can continue to offer life-transforming ritual, magic and surprise. But while the challenges of most contemporary tourism may be small, transformations of self may still be facilitated by the feelings of having mastered the challenges of today's travel, including lost luggage, breakdowns in transportation, crime, new foods, foreign languages, and general uncertainty. For others, 'adventure travel' and 'eco-tourism' promise something closer to a rite of passage or religious pilgrimage.

Perhaps contemporary urban societies come closest to traditional rites of passage in annual birthday celebrations. It is telling that of a set of ninety-nine stories of children's birthdays that Kim Dodson and I have been investigating (Belk and Dodson 1997; Dodson and Belk 1996), nearly one-quarter involve the focal birthday character in travel. In a typical story the birthday child, often aided by some form of magic, is transported to another place or time where he or she faces dangers, has adventures, meets challenges, and returns a wiser, stronger, more confident person. For example, in a story called 'Knights of the Kitchen Table' (Scieszka 1991), Joe receives for his birthday a magical book from his uncle and on opening it he and two friends are transported to King Arthur's court. There they cleverly defeat the black knight, dispatch a fire-breathing dragon and a giant, impress Guinivere with card tricks, and are knighted by Arthur before returning to the kitchen table where their adventure began. Like the traditional rite of passage and the heroic quest, there has been a journey, a challenge, a triumph, and a rebirth as another person (Campbell 1968). All of this is made more dramatic because in these stories it is a child succeeding against great odds in a world of adults. Such play stories also help the child cross the boundary between fantasy and reality and in so doing may prove both symbolically self-transforma-tive and self-expanding as the child explores and enjoys adventures in imagined worlds (Stott 1994).

There is also an educational aspect of travel that has a long heritage and potentially extends to tourism as well. Jager (1975) notes that in ancient Greece the journey was a part of the tradition of acquiring schol-arly knowledge. In fact, *theoroi*, from which our word 'theory' derives, meant a voyage of inquiry, whether by land or sea. Curiosity drives many types of contemporary travellers, including both tourists and scholars (Helms 1988; Hodgen 1964; Stagl 1995). Curiosity may be seen as a 'world-openness' (Stagl 1995). The traveller or scholar who is motivated by curiosity is open to new experience. New knowledge as well as new insights about self are most likely to come from the external stimulation, obser-vation and comparison of ourselves and our behaviours with the selves and behaviours of other people, places and times. As Zerubavel (1991: 117) suggests, 'Transgressing boundaries is a hallmark of creativity.' Not only as returned travellers made strange by the new knowledge acquired in travel, but also as strangers in foreign lands, we traditionally expect the traveller to possess superior or supernatural knowledge. Without trav-elling to other lands, it is difficult to be a prophet in your own land.

Elsewhere (Belk 1987) I have observed that unlike the linear travel of the immigrant, scholars and tourist travellers follow a circular route that begins and ends in the community (the scholarly community in the former case). In another sense however, such a traveller generally abandons the cyclical time of the home community and its regular rituals and adopts the linear time of a journey filled with singular occurrences and unique and unrepeatable events. The patient ethnographer tries to overcome the limitations of the tourist's one-time chance encounters by more sustained immersion in another culture or subculture.

In addition to the literal journeys of tourists and ethnographers into strange new places, the quest for knowledge generally is filled with metaphors of the journey. Jager (1975) and Wolff (1993) observe that scientific and artistic discourses are full of terms and phrases like progress, advances, discoveries, making breakthroughs, keeping up, falling behind, reaching conclusions, scaling new heights, penetrating the unknown, reach-ing a plateau, following research streams, stumbling on new ideas, pursu-ing grounded theory, running down leads, and advancing the leading edge or being in the avant-garde of research. Similar phrases might be used by someone on a 'voyage' of self 'discovery'. Indeed, as noted above, pur-suing knowledge of others is necessarily bound up with learning about ourselves. It is thus no accident that the 1986 Consumer Behaviour Odyssey and the 1993 Odyssey Down Under were so titled, since they were both literal journeys (through the United States and Aboriginal Australia) and metaphoric journeys exploring new methods, topics, people and places (Belk 1987, 1991; Groves and Belk 1995).

There is one essential ingredient of travel that has not yet been identified. Whether the journey is touristic, religious or scholarly, when it is
approached with curiosity (rather than primarily for economic, militaristic
or evangelical purposes), it has a ludic or playful quality. Curiosity involves
'superfluous' activity with no immediate utilitarian goal (Stagl 1995: 2).
The spectacular rise of mass tourism (Belk and Costa 1995) cannot be
accounted for by a search for either education or economic gain. Rather
it is necessary that such tourism promises to be fun (Urry 1990). Part of
the pleasure is found in freedom from daily routines, inhibitions and
constraints, and the tourist's activity has a certain luxurious novelty, as
Mehrabian (1976) suggests:

> Travelers have special attitudes and prerogatives, amounting to an
> ability to rape the land – see the best that it has to offer, eat at the
> most interesting restaurants, attend the best concerts, and see the best
> plays or shows.
>
> (Mehrabian 1976: 273)

This is especially true of the First World Tourist in the Third World,
where the huge imbalance in spending power allows tourists to be kings
and queens for the duration of their visits. There are individual and
cultural differences, but the tourist typically dresses, spends, eats, drinks
and has sex in a more open and playful way that would generally seem
out of place (literally) at home. But in order to get to this ludic state, the
traveller must first cross some boundaries.

BOUNDARY CROSSING

Terminus was a powerful Roman god who guarded boundaries between
fields and houses and to whom sacrifices were made each New Year –
itself a boundary between the old and the new (Stilgoe 1976). The
threshold continues to mark the physical boundary between inside and
outside, family and stranger, home and world (Altman and Chemers 1980).
Other significant boundaries include those between male and female, child
and adult, insider and outsider, private and public, native and alien, nature
and culture, home and work, life and death, real and imaginary, mainstream and counter-culture, rich and poor, and human and non-human
(Peñaloza 1991, 1994, 1996; Zerubavel 1991). We normally keep firm and
absolute barriers between these categories, and the transgression of these
boundaries is likely to provoke fear. For instance, for some the transgression of the boundary between male and female by gays and lesbians
is regarded as repugnant. However, for many homosexuals the relevant
boundary is between gay and straight and bisexuals are the offending
boundary straddlers. As Douglas (1966) points out, we have feelings of
disgust and horror when categorically different things 'leak' and threaten
to merge with one another. Fiedler (1978: 65) places in this ambiguous

position freaks, monsters and children wondering 'whether they are beasts or men: little animals more like their pets than their parents'. Burglary victims often recoil at the horror that their boundaries of privacy have been violated by uninvited strangers in a manner these victims often compare to rape (e.g. Maguire 1980; Papp 1981). One reaction to the fear of boundary transgression is boundary maintenance rituals. Even the token marking of property boundaries with flower beds and other such symbolic barriers appears to be an effective deterrent to burglary and other property crimes (Brown 1985).

For similar reasons, the itinerant preacher in colonial America threatened the bounded community and was perceived as transgressive threat bringing disorder to the community (Hall 1994). In Hall's view the itinerant helped dissolve the boundaries of isolated communities, replace local festivals with non-local festivals, and link local communities with the broader world. These trends were not always well-received and 'Critics warned, the rule of reason would give way to the tyranny of unchecked passion' (Hall 1994: 44). Similar fears were aroused by the peddler travelling from community to community and using his liminal status as a trickster figure to beguile locals with promises of magical transformations through consumption (Lears 1989: 78). As Spinks (1991: 176) argues, the trickster, like the shaman, 'walks the edges of the Sacred and Profane to practise behaviours which to most "normal" folk are insane, sacred, or blasphemous'. As creatures of the margins, they cross the boundaries that lead to revelation and knowledge. The trickster does this through humour and it is both the ludic event and the resulting laughter that Spinks (1991) insightfully identifies as ways of knowing. As with the 'playful promiscuity' of the circus (Bouissac 1976; Zerubavel 1991: 90), the liminality of the fair and the merchant have at least since the middle ages been associated with transgression, inversion and the marketplace (Bakhtin 1968). Travel is the common denominator in each case bringing transgressive chaos to disrupt local order. But in the process, the itinerant preacher, the roving merchant, the clown, the shaman and the trickster also bring us to knowledge.

For the pilgrim or the initiate undergoing a rite of passage there is a period betwixt and between statuses that is similarly freeing and which Turner (1969) terms 'liminal'. The tourist in a contemporary industrial society may not experience as total a liminal experience as the pilgrim or initiate, and the less intense liminality of the tourist may be more properly denoted 'liminoid' rather than truly liminal (Belk *et al.* 1989). Nevertheless, a similar uninhibited, levelling, statusless quality attends the travel of modern tourists who are more apt to behave like children than like the well-disciplined adults that they are at home. This need not mean that the tourist doesn't learn from the travel experience, but that is not the primary purpose. Paradoxically, the playful open attitude of tourists may actually make them more apt to learn than a more work-like orientation might. It is similarly essential that the creative scholar engage a playful liminal spirit rather than a deadly serious quest for knowledge. As Mary Douglas (1966) recognised, liminal statuses free us of the conventional and rational thought and behavioural patterns that we otherwise routinely follow. Like Anna in the forest, we must stop proceeding with our logical cognitive agendas long enough to follow our emotions and play with other alternatives. While what Freud (1958) labelled secondary process thinking is appropriate for refining and explaining our ideas and insights to others, actually getting these ideas is far more likely to occur if we are in the more playful state of primary process thinking (Belk 1984; Suler 1980). Ultimately to communicate our ideas to others we may need secondary process 'analytical' thought again, but to generate these ideas the 'fuzzy synthetic' thought of primary thought processes are superior (Zerubavel 1991: 121).

Zerubavel (1991) suggests that young children, believing as they do in Santa Claus and the tooth fairy, are less likely than adults to make sharp distinctions between fantasy and reality. While they develop increasingly clear notions of such a boundary as they get older, the barrier remains more permeable than is the case for adults and children have an easy time jumping into the story and acting it out (Scarlett and Wolf 1979). Adults have a more difficult time acting out fantasies, or at least acknowledging that they do so; both Davis (1983) and Cohen and Taylor (1992) find that sustaining sexual fantasies about someone else while having sex with our partners is prevalent among adults. Nevertheless, boundaries generally are noticed more clearly by adults and are crossed with greater difficulty than during childhood. The fact that these boundaries are perceived more clearly by adults is a result of socialisation and conceptual abilities rather than sharper sensory acuity. For boundaries, whether they are between fantasy and reality, childhood and adulthood, or one nation and another, are social constructions. As Zerubavel (1991) points out,

> The proverbial Martian cannot see the mental partitions separating Catholics from Protestants, classical from popular music, or the funny from the crude. Like the contours of constellations, we 'see' such fine lines only when we learn that we should expect them there.
>
> (Zerubavel 1991: 80)

Cultures not only construct such boundaries but also often aid in transcending them through publicly enacted rituals like birthday celebrations as well as more private rituals like sexual intercourse (which helps transcend the boundaries between the participants – Eisler 1995).

In travel there are also a series of public and private rituals commonly employed to reinforce boundaries and help the traveller to transcend them. In ancient Greece there was an elaborate series of hospitality rituals that welcomed travellers (Reece 1993), although in our contemporary age such rituals have been commercialised by the 'hospitality industry'. But non-commercial travel rituals also persist. Together with the separation and reincorporation of metaphorical travel in rites of passage such as birthday celebrations, transitions are often marked by 'threshold gifts' (Hyde 1983). Considering such thresholds and status changes as gradua-tions, weddings, anniversaries, goings away, welcomes home, housewarm-ings, births, birthdays, funerals, and even loss of baby teeth (Clark 1995), threshold gift-giving pervades the entire life cycle and is usually the most common type of occasion we have for giving gifts. In order to cross a geographic threshold for the first time (and thereby potentially to begin to change statuses from stranger to friend), gifts are among the rituals that help the transition by demonstrating good intentions and inviting or repaying the counter-gift of hospitality (Reece 1993).

Thus when Hindu pilgrims make their way to the sacred banks of the Ganges they give the holy men there gifts or *dana* for helping them perform rites to expiate sins, gain merit or honour the dead (Crawford 1994). The gifts of flowers and food at funerals mimic the threshold gifts of coins for the dead to pay passage to be ferried by Charon over the River Styx and into Hades. As with the Hindu pilgrims to Benares, the gift in this case helps to connect the worlds of the living and the dead, the material and the spiritual, the profane and the sacred. It is significant in Greek mythology that Hermes is not only the protector of travellers, but also the guide to the underworld (where he rescued Persephone), and the god of merchants and traders. Early merchants and traders were necessarily travellers, carrying merchandise from one place to another and crossing boundaries of cities, nations and cultures (Crawford 1994). In each case, Hermes helps guide us from the known to the unknown. And for early merchants and traders, operating in other countries generally necessitated rituals of lavish gift-giving (Jardine 1996), which gained them the acceptance to do business in these countries. Just as pilgrims make sacrifices to purify themselves and gain entrance to sacred spaces, these merchant gifts can be seen as a form of sacrifice to facilitate boundary crossings.

Boundary crossing rituals also help to mentally mark our transition into otherness and attaining a state of grace or at least a state of having been with the Other. Two contemporary touristic rituals that do this involve the two institutions that have done so much to supplant religion: art and shopping. Art as well as historic relics are enshrined in the great temple of the museum (Horne 1984), while consumer goods are enshrined in the local equivalent of the shopping mall and department store. Every travel guide these days is replete with listings of museum-going and shopping opportunities. For like sightseeing and eating what passes as local cuisine, no recreational trip by an educated middle-class consumer is complete without museum-going and shopping to help authenticate the experience. In fact, as Kelley (1987) finds, the museum experience for many tourists goes no further than the gift shop. For these tourists, the prestigious sense of having 'been there' and 'done that' is truncated into having 'bought the souvenirs'. Saatchi and Saatchi managed to capture some of this spirit in an advertisement for the Victoria and Albert Museum a few years ago by highlighting the museum's restaurant using the headline 'An ace caf with a rather nice museum attached'. Museum visitation is an important part of the 'cultured' learning experience. While status claiming and affirming is important in this museum-going context (Bourdieu and Darbel 1990), it is also a touristic ritual designed to help mark and highlight having experienced the most significant aspects of another culture: those that have entered the sacred space of the museum.

As with traditional rites of passage, touristic boundary crossing is also often aided by rituals of personal status change. Rituals of separation and reincorporation upon return from touristic travel may range from ceremonial goodbyes and hellos to friends and loved ones to bon voyage parties, welcome home parties or banners, and the elaborate receipt of *senbetsu* travel money and return *omiyage* gifts by Japanese travellers (Graburn 1987; Rucker, *et al.* 1986; Witkowski and Yamamoto 1991). With greater elaboration than in most societies, these paired gift-giving rituals help assure both successful separation from the original community and subsequent reintegration into the community. On a smaller and more frequent scale, Nippert-Eng (1996) found that the daily commute between home and work is a ritualistic transformation from one self to another. Various ritualistic elements such as grooming, hellos and goodbyes, changes of clothing, consumption of caffeine or alcohol, eating certain foods, turning computers on and off, and reading newspapers, help at the boundary thresholds of home and work. The intervening commute is a sacred liminal time for separating from one world and preparing to enter the next. It might be seen as a miniature version of bequeathing possessions and otherwise preparing to leave this life and presumably enter another.

Stagl (1995) suggests that both homecomers and visitors from abroad are also put in virtual social quarantine and are interrogated about their journeys before being (re)admitted into the group. Similarly, customary questions upon returning to work on Monday morning include an enquiry about the weekend and family, just as on returning from work a family member is likely to be asked how the day went and what is new at work (Nippert-Eng 1996). These rituals help reintegrate the person into the workplace and family. Reincorporation into the group following a brief touristic sojourn is also a matter to be dealt with ritually. The gifts brought back to those left behind are often mere sops or tokens, given both to lessen the guilt of the privileged journey and to symbolically assure that others were not forgotten during the journey. At the same time there is tension to be dissolved on such occasions, as such gifts can also be used (under the guise of a thinking-of-you gift) where the real intent is status-claiming. The 'wish you were here' postcard is perhaps emblematic of this perversion of the threshold gift (the present *Postcards* volume excepted of course!). When the gift that eases this tension is something appropriate to the area visited (or *meibutsu* in the case of the *omiyage* gift – Graburn 1987), it shares some features of the souvenir that is purchased and retained by the traveller.

The souvenir, while it too might be used for acquisitive status-claiming, is perhaps more often an attempt to transport some of the sacred quality of the journey across boundaries and back to the home of traveller. Like holy relics (Geary 1986) and authenticating *locta sancta* souvenirs of pilgrimage (Hahn 1990), travel souvenirs are generally meant to serve as 'traces of authentic experience' (Stewart 1984) for the tourist. Of the various types of souvenirs detailed by Gordon (1986), the 'piece of the rock' variety is perhaps most unequivocally authenticating and the closest to holy relics like pieces of the True Cross, participating as they do in the power of contagion. However we are a visual people and the ritual of photography or videography now has a nearly equal claim to act as a trace of authentic experience, especially when framed from the same photo-opportunistic perspective as the travel brochure (MacCannell 1989).

The scholar or researcher also attempts to cross boundaries and to bring back some of the sacred truths discovered, negotiated or shaped there. These boundaries are primarily those between the researcher and the phenomenon being studied: another culture, time period, or a group or activity that is initially unfamiliar. It is more difficult to find truths in our own backyards because we are generally overly familiar with these environments and have difficulty seeing them anew and afresh; with the eyes of a child like Savushkin. By instead going across boundaries and into strange new 'forests', we encounter unfamiliar things that we cannot rely on our habitual perceptions to understand. While the ethnographic formula is to make the strange familiar and the familiar strange, George Steiner (1989) argues that great art goes further and makes the strange even stranger. Or in the words of Hunter Thompson (1971) on encountering Las Vegas, 'When the going gets weird, the weird turn pro.'

A similarly refreshing academic boundary crossing occurs when we seek out other disciplines and other scholars with very different training from our own. As with other boundary crossings into unfamiliar terrain we must learn the language in order to make sense of these new worlds. Besides the rituals of our research methods, we may also aid academic boundary crossings by bringing gifts. As Emerson (1983) suggested, 'The only gift is a portion of thyself.' For academics, the gifts that are most a portion of ourselves are our ideas and insights. While the cynic is apt to see more self-aggrandising motives, Hyde (1983) has suggested that the scholar's freely offered ideas are a form of Potlatch, or ritualistic give-away. And as for souvenirs, our books, our field notes, our data and our artefacts, all serve to fetishistically memorialise our scholarly journeys.

BOUNDARY MAINTENANCE

Because crossing boundaries is a frightening experience that threatens to dismantle our familiar sense of who we are, we also engage in practices that help maintain boundaries. For example, for more permanent immigrants, travel has a different character than is the case with tourists. For immigrants there is still a separation, but the reincorporation is in a new place with new people. In order to provide some sense of continuity, bringing or acquiring possessions that symbolise the homeland is a common occurrence and it is these possessions that take on a sacred quality (Belk 1993b; Mehta and Belk 1991). They also act as transitional objects in the same way that a child's stuffed animal or blanket may act to smooth the transition away from home and mother. Eventually however, for full incorporation into the new culture it seems important that the new home reflect less of the immigrants' former locale and more of their current locale. Thus Hansen and Altman (1976) found college student graduation success was positively related to decorating with artefacts from the college and negatively related to decorating with artefacts from the students' previous home towns and schools. We might similarly predict that the amount of baggage that tourists carry reflects their need for familiar transitional objects during their travels and is negatively related to their degree of integration into the locales visited.

There are very likely individual differences (e.g. Hartmann 1991) and cultural differences (e.g. Mehrabian 1976) in the thickness and permeability of the boundaries that we maintain about our selves. In the context of mixing or keeping separate the realms of home and work (through artefacts, people, language, clothing, communication and activities), Nippert-Eng (1996) terms the extremes 'integraters' and 'segmenters' respectively. Both Nippert-Eng (1996) and Tuan (1982) suggest we live in a largely segmented society. We all have symbolic boundaries that separate 'me' from 'not me' and 'us' from 'not us'. No doubt our most private and well-maintained boundary is that of our own bodies, which we consider tantamount to our selves. We have traditionally held to the belief that the skin, as the 'edge' of the body and the self, forms an impermeable boundary to the outer world, even though this is biologically untrue (Lappé 1996). Violation of this boundary via wounds as well as products from the body, such as urine, faeces, saliva, vomit, semen and blood, produce feelings of disgust and revulsion in most contexts (Belk 1988; Douglas 1966). While it has not always been the case, the revulsion we feel towards dead bodies also reflects the strength of boundaries we have established between the living and the dead. Ingesting materials into the body in eating relies on a series of culture-specific food preparation and eating rituals in order to make the food seem palatable. Because of the ritual significance of eating and because of its nurturing and civilising character (Elias 1978; Visser 1991), the meal or feast is also an important hospitality ritual in boundary crossing (Farb and Armelogos 1980; Reece 1993).

Even, or perhaps especially, strip-teasers, who seemingly visually offer their bodies publicly, employ boundary maintenance rituals that safeguard their inner selves from this gaze (e.g. Silber 1971). Zerubavel (1991: 87–88) notes that in initiating contact with another, we shake hands by literally as well as symbolically interlocking our hands. In order for a would-be sexual partner to gain access to our bodies and our selves, threshold gifts are common and are a significant part of courtship rituals (Belk and Coon 1993). As Collins and Gregor (1995) put it, to love someone is to take loyalty away from the family, community or polis and devote this loyalty instead to a single individual and a dyadic relationship with this person. The tension at the boundary demands a highly ritualised and deeply symbolic series of actions in order to mark and make acceptable this sharp shift in loyalties. At a more aggregate level, despite their artificiality, national boundaries have spawned wars, immigration laws, and trade laws to prevent unwanted contamination of the national 'self'.

BETWIXT AND BETWEEN

While boundaries are places of danger and secular boundary gods must still be appeased, the boundary is also a liminal zone or 'interstitial crack' (Zerubavel 1991: 90) where traditional rules do not apply. Thus on quarter days that form the seam or boundary between seasons, there is an opportunity for both carnivalesque liberation and for the dangerous spirits of the nether regions to escape and roam the earth. During the Celtic celebration of Samhain (which after modification efforts by the Christian Church became All-Hallows Eve or Hallowe'en), bonfires were lit to keep these spirits at bay (Belk 1990, 1994). If our fears of evil spirits are lesser today, we nevertheless have many vestigial remnants in Hallowe'en ghost stories and movies, and roaming witches, monsters, skeletons and goblins of every sort imaginable. In the United States children dressed as such ghosts and goblins still take neighbourhood journeys and 'beg' for treats at the threshold doorway where they are given gifts of candy treats, ostensibly to appease these spirits and nullify their threat of evil tricks, but also in a boundary ritual that solidifies feelings of community. Nevertheless, urban legends continue to raise annual fears of the Hallowe'en sadist who puts razor blades, pins and poisons in treats given to children (Best 1985; Wenhaner and Dodder 1984), thus tapping the traditional element of fear at the same threshold boundary around which we use carnivalesque merriment in an attempt to counter and overcome these fears.

The liminal spirit at Hallowe'en (and at other seasonal junctures such as New Year's Eve, Mardi Gras and the Summer Solstice) is also a time of inversion when status boundaries dissolve: children hold power over adults, the sexes may symbolically exchange roles, and gays and lesbians in drag take to the streets in parades and festivals in many large cities. Besides Hallowe'en, when New York's Greenwich Village, Washington

DC's Georgetown and San Francisco's Castro Street (see O'Drain 1986), all have huge gay parades, Sydney televises its gay Mardi Gras parade and North American cities have their Lesbian and Gay Pride Day parades and street carnivals on or near the Summer Solstice. While, like Hallowe'en trick-or-treating, these are times of joyous celebration for the participants, they may only be 'rites of rebellion' (Gluckman 1963) that solidify the status quo. This is because they allow the dominant community to focus all its fears (of Hallowe'en sadists, sexual inversions, and other 'demons') into a single liminal moment that keeps these fears at bay for the rest of the year. At a psychological level, mastering fears is what boundary crossing rituals are all about. They serve these functions for their more direct participants as well, such that gays and lesbians learn that coming out of the closet with their sexual identities is something of which they can be proud and children learn that they can go to strange houses in the dark of All-Hallows Eve and be welcomed and given treats. The academic crossing cultural, topical and disciplinary boundaries generally learns a similar lesson and is welcomed by congenial informants and colleagues. As has been argued, it is this boundary crossing and the ludic spirit of liminality that is essential to creativity and the production of new insights and knowledge.

THE JOURNEY AND THE BOUNDARY IN AN AGE OF VIRTUAL REALITY

What of the future? What becomes of travelling and boundary crossing in a global, mobile, electronic age? Do natural and cultural wonders continue to amaze us in such an information- and image-rich environment? Are potential travel destinations becoming homogenised and globalised, such that they will lose their interest and powers of stimulation? Will increased and increasingly far-flung travel also make us so accustomed to travelling, as well as to different people and places, that travelling itself becomes a familiar routine? Do multinational corporations threaten to erase national borders as Zerbuval (1991: 113) suggests? As our multimedia environment becomes more spectacular, more interconnected and better able to provide fantasy experiences, will physical travel and metaphoric travel both lose their appeal in favour of virtual travel?

It may seem paradoxical that tourism, which already accounts for more than 10 per cent of the world's economy (Belk and Costa 1995), continues to grow and expand at the same time that we can receive an exponentially growing amount of stimulation electronically through the merging nexus of computers, televisions, sound systems and virtual reality devices. We are coming closer to the experience machine that Robert Nozick (1974) hypothesised. Assuming that we could have any sort of experience we wished from such a machine and that we could not distinguish this experience from the real thing, Nozick asked whether we would ever unhook ourselves from this device in order to deal instead in the non-simulated world.

At the same time that such virtual experiences are coming closer to (and sometimes going beyond) non-simulated life, travel experiences are becoming safer and tamer as more people travel and even the most remote locales begin to cater to tourists (Belk 1993a). While travel tours continue to provide an insulated 'bubble' that shields some tourists from the unexpected (in language, food, transportation, accommodation and personal encounters), independent travel has had to become more 'adventure' oriented in order to escape the growing web of world-wide car rental, hotel, restaurant, credit card, airline and travel chains. Ritzer (1993) bemoans the 'McDonaldisation' of society, which he defines as incorporating efficiency, quantified and calculated products and experiences, predictability, and the substitution of non-human for human technology. Augé (1995) protests against the loss of myth and magic as the places we travel offer little beyond their names to distinguish them from each other any longer. He calls the airports, aircraft, motorways, cars, hotels, shopping malls and other leisure locales frequented by tourists 'non-places' and sees them as increasingly linked by the same televisions, computers, software and cash machines. Relph (1976) calls this 'placelessness' and suggests that it leads only to commonplace and mediocre experiences. MacCannell (1989) objects to the 'staged authenticity' of locales and events presented for their touristic appeal rather than as local cultural events. Kodak's hula shows in Honolulu are one example, but there are many more. In order to compete with such touristic spectacles, museums and other cultural institutions are beginning to 'Disneyfy' and offer similar spectacular productions. Thus, much of the agenda of mass tourism appears to be dissolving into something like the sort of simulated reality experienced at Disney theme parks (King 1991) and mega-malls (Kowinski 1986).

While Disney parks are frequently cited as prototypes of these trends, Las Vegas may be a more revealing exemplar (Belk 1997). Early in its fifty-year history as a gambling mecca, going to Las Vegas was a journey to a vice-dripping dystopia full of associations with organised crime, prostitution and all-you-can-eat cut-rate buffets – a triple threat temptation to greed, lust and gluttony. As Bataille (1985) and Falk (1994) suggest, much of the appeal of such temptations is the titillating feeling of transgression that they provide. The sacrifice for crossing such transgressive boundaries is the ostentatious loss of money. This monetary sacrifice acts as a potlatch of sorts and is accompanied by a liminal journey across stark deserts to the improbable oasis of Las Vegas.

But Las Vegas has gone through many incarnations. The success of these adaptations is evident in the facts that the city offers more hotel rooms than any other city in the world and that tourist visits continue to swell, despite the proliferation of legalised gambling elsewhere. In its most recent incarnation, Las Vegas has become more family-orientated, with casinos incorporating virtual video game arcades, amusement park rides (indoors as well as outdoors) and theme park adventures – all activities aimed at a non-gambling audience. These changes are perhaps indicative of the decline of evil in this former sin city, and the concomitant decline of transgressive thrills as a basis for desire. In place of transgression, the new ethic is that of play. No one takes Las Vegas seriously, with its larger than life faux New York and New Orleans streetscapes, pyramid, pirate ships, volcano, medieval castle and yellow brick road; each spectacle more grandiose than the last. That is the point. Rugoff (1995) insightfully sums up the impact of this presentation:

> Las Vegas is a comic spectacle. The Mirage's ejaculating volcano, so punctual you can set your watch by its eruptions, provides a type of extravagant farce absent from the architecture of our major cities. Rather than beguile visitors with escapist promises, theme resorts like Treasure Island and Luxor appeal to our sense that in today's shrunken world, the exotic getaway is a notion that can be spoofed. Las Vegas has become a place you visit in order to go somewhere else, but your destination is a joke.
>
> (Rugoff 1995: 4)

As Rugoff notes, the referents for a number of Las Vegas resorts are not so much places as they are fantasies: Treasure Island is from Spielberg's *Hook*, the MGM Grand's emerald city is from Flemming's *The Wizard of Oz* and the Caesar's Palace centurions are right out of Kubrick's *Spartacus*. Unlike Disney's sanitisation of Mainstreet USA, these are not meant to evoke nostalgia or feelings of 'being there'. They are instead burlesques of illusions. They are playful fantasies presented with an unapologetic spirit of fun. All this resonates with playful tourism's self-conscious mockery that Urry (1990) calls 'post-tourism', normally accompanied by 'post-shopping'. As with various calendric **times** like coffee breaks, commutes, weekends and vacations (Nippert-Eng 1996), and **occasions** like Hallowe'en, Mardi Gras and New Year's Eve, Las Vegas is among our liminal **places** where normal rules do not apply.

If Las Vegas were an isolated anomaly it would be more difficult to accept as a prototype of future cities and future tourism. But we can see similar transitions from seriousness and fearful transgression to unmitigated fun in other realms including food, fashions, sports and other discretionary consumption arenas. Because it is tied to travel and tourism, let us briefly consider food as an example. Following the medieval period in Europe, table manners became a mark of civility and social class (Elias 1978; Tuan 1982; Visser 1991). In some views, eating at a fancy restaurant is still a nerve-racking test of the patron's gentility and manners (e.g. Finkelstein 1989). For many restaurants and many people, however, I contend that eating has become a playful, pleasure-seeking game. The restaurant need not serve 'happy meals' and have servers in funny costumes for this ethos to be dominant. Consider the playful, even camp, manner in which we have come to regard many world cuisines. Where once regional and world cuisine restaurants, like tourism to these same regional and world locales, involved exoticism and even mild transgression, we now playfully embrace an 'aesthetics of the diverse' (Cook and Crang 1996). We have made eating an indulgent game and restaurants are happy to accommodate.

Tourism and restaurants thus provide a context for examining the supposed globalisation of consumption offerings. McDonald's is often suggested as the global corporate prototype, with a similar menu around the world, now including India. Just as Christmas has been suggested as the first global consumption holiday (with Santa showing up in such unlikely venues as the Ginza in Tokyo – Miller 1993), McDonald's is touted as offering the first global food. But not only does McDonald's décor adapt to local cultures so do its foods, beverages, and promotions. This is seen most clearly in McDonald's adaptations to local holidays. In Singapore during the 1992 Chinese New Year celebration (the year of the monkey), with the purchase of a burger plus 80-cents Singapore, the patron could buy any of four plastic monkeys for the new year – Lucky Lucy, Longevity Larry, Rich Richie and Happy Harry. The western names and the caricatured Chinese clothing on these monkeys offer a nice example of hybridisation rather than globalisation. On the other hand, McDonald's Singapore version of the red *hongbao* (gift) packets that the Chinese use to convey money to children on this holiday provides an example less of syncreticism than co-optation. The corporation gave out red *hongbao* envelopes that show Ronald McDonald distributing such gifts to other McDonald's characters – the Hamburgler and the Fry Babies. Similarly, in Ankara in 1996 during Ramadan, McDonald's modified their menu to meet local traditions. For the period of Ramadan the sunrise to sunset fast is broken at sunset with the *iftar* meal. The McDonald's of Ankara offered free hot 'iftar soup' to those who buy 'menu' meals during iftar hours. Such ploys caused me to wonder whether McDonald's didn't miss an opportunity at their former location just off Tiananmen Square in Beijing. After visiting Mao's crystal tomb there in 1995, I fully expected the McDonald's adjacent to Mao's Mausoleum to have mimicked the mausoleum with a similar glass entombment of Ronald McDonald.

The other quintessential multinational food company is Coca-Cola. One of the ways in which it has begun to promote and aggrandise itself is through corporate museums. The largest is in downtown Atlanta at what became Olympic Park during the 1996 summer games. In the United States and at the Atlanta museum, Coca-Cola enthusiastically promoted itself as a 'proud sponsor of the US Olympic team'. Meanwhile at a second Coca-Cola corporate museum at Circular Quay in Sydney, Australian visitors were invited to enter a booth and 'send a [videotaped] message to **our** athletes in Atlanta' (emphasis added). Here too, rather than a universal globalised appeal, the message is clearly adapted for local audiences, just as amoral politicians are apt to do.

In international tourism, cities and nations have also begun to adapt to their audiences – in this case the liminal free-spending, free-spirited, First World tourist. Rather than providing tourists with unwelcome didactic educations, world travel destinations are increasingly learning to give consumers what they expect and want. What this involves in the majority of instances is an almost caricatured stereotype of the locale. Thus, Peru becomes Inca-land and the Andes, Brazil becomes samba and year-round Carnival, and Mexico becomes a huge theme park for Anglo amigos that might well be dubbed 'Gringolandia' (Belk 1996; Shacochis 1989). As might be expected from such attempts to follow the so-called Marketing Concept, rather than adversely affect tourism, these stylised adaptations significantly enhance it. They may increasingly be taken a bit tongue-in-cheek, like the spectacular spoofs in Las Vegas, but they are nevertheless taken. It may be this almost camp reflexivity that keeps fun-loving travellers from becoming bored with the whole thing.

As for over-familiarity, routinisation of travel and incursions by virtual reality and virtual travel, all of these remain future possibilities. But I think they are unlikely. As the number of tourists continues to grow, so do the number of places offering themselves as tourist destinations and so do the number of diversions offered in these places. Given our apparent predilection for hyperreal fantasies, there is no reason why any place cannot follow the Las Vegas model, and indeed many have begun to do so. In answer to Nozick's experience machine question, Las Vegas and other tourist locales have quickly learned that while it might not suffice to spend an entire vacation holiday in virtual reality, VR offers a paying diversion for tourists once they have been brought to an only slightly more real tourist destination. Besides numerous VR games and VR amusements of various descriptions, a currently popular Las Vegas offering at all of the resort theme parks is to have yourself morphed onto the cover of a magazine. You can quickly become a muscle man, billionaire, starlet, Olympic skier or cheerleader, and have any blemishes electronically erased in the process. These are the authenticating fantasy souvenirs that mark the visit to a fantasy land. From these examples it appears that the future of recreational travel is more likely to benefit than be harmed by VR applications. And if we fear that the virtual communities of fellow consumers of the Internet and world-wide brands threaten real communities, it is worth noting that similar charges were made when itinerant preachers and merchants began to link distant communities with each other (Hall 1994). Our boundaries continue to be maintained and strengthened through sports, ethnic and religious cleavages, paradigm clashes, age gaps, subcultural confrontations, brand and place promotional competitions, and numerous other symbolic conflicts and ritual affirmations of identity.

CONCLUSION

If the journey continues to fascinate us even as its character changes, what then of the need for boundary crossing rituals? In brief, only when there are no longer boundaries will there no longer be a human need for boundary crossing rituals. Our boundaries may now be more between daily life and fantasy, but they are no less significant. We are simultaneously fascinated and frightened by boundaries because on the other side lies the unknown and otherness. The appeal of this unknown otherness is due to our own curiosities (likely to be expanded during times of relative comfort) and the remaining hope for and possibility of the sacred. This continues to be true at all types of boundaries: between cultures, people, sexes, time periods, life stages and research communities. None of these boundaries is immutable and fixed; we construct them so that we can bring order and meaning to our lives. But it is crossing these boundaries that provides the otherness of which creative synthesis is born. If we become overly familiar with some sources of otherness, we will invent new sources. We need the Other because we need to invent our own identities through the imagined contrast. There is a need for the Other because there is a human need for new possibilities, new knowledge, new enjoyments, and new experiences. And if, like Anna, we cajole ourselves into believing that we have no need for new possibilities, we will have done ourselves a great disservice in precluding the possibility and joy of childlike wonder and magic.

The original Star Trek television series began with an opening voice-over announcing that space was the final frontier. Others have suggested that the ocean remains the last frontier (Kyokai 1981), that night will forever remain a frontier (Melbin 1987) or that cyberspace represents the ultimate frontier (Rheingold 1993). Just as we have long been fascinated by the journey, we have long been fascinated by the frontier because it promises new and unique travel destinations. During times of rapidly emerging new frontiers like the European exploration of the New World and contact with the Far East, and United States exploration of its own frontiers, knowledge and ideas of self and possibilities expanded tremendously. The expansionism stimulated by European contact with the New World precipitated the Renaissance (Jardine 1996), collections and museums (Belk 1995) and consumer culture (Mukerji 1983). If we are at the threshold not only of a new millennium but also of a new, more global, electronic age, rather than millenarian doubt and doom-saying, perhaps we should be joyful that we are at the edge of another age of creative discovery. While some might venture that this an optimism born of the uniquely American frontier experience, I think it is a warranted expectation. If we are willing to make the metaphoric journey, aided by whatever boundary crossing rituals we can create, if we are willing to engage in some creative marginality, and if we are willing to take the path of Savushkin through the mysterious forest, then we will, I believe, be well rewarded.

ACKNOWLEDGEMENT

I am very thankful to Stephen Brown for providing such an ideal forum for these ideas, for inviting this chapter, for suggesting my focus on the journey, and for his insightful comments on an earlier draft of the chapter.

REFERENCES

Altman, I. and Chemers, M. (1980) *Culture and Environment*, Monterey, CA: Brooks/Cole.

Augé, M. (1995) *Non-Places: Introduction to an Anthropology of Supermodernity*, trans. J. Howe, London: Verso (original 1992 edn, *Non-Lieux, Introduction à une Anthropologie de la sur Modernité*, Paris: Editions du Seuil).

Bakhtin, M. (1968) *Rabelais and his World*, trans. H. Iswolsky, Cambridge, MA: MIT Press.

Bataille, G. (1985) *Visions of Excess: Selected Writings, 1927–1939*, trans. A. Stoekl, Minneapolis, MN: University of Minnesota Press.

Belk, R.W. (1984) 'Against thinking', in P.F. Anderson and M.J. Ryan (eds) *1984 AMA Winter Educators' Conference: Scientific Method in Marketing*, Chicago: American Marketing Association, 57–20.

—— (1987) 'The role of the Odyssey in consumer research and in consumer behavior', in M. Wallendorf and P. Anderson (eds) *Advances in Consumer Research*, 14, Provo, UT: Association for Consumer Research, 357–361.

—— (1988) 'Possessions and the extended self', *Journal of Consumer Research*, 15, September: 139–168.

—— (1990) 'Hallowe'en: an evolving American consumption ritual', in M. Goldberg, G. Gorn and R. Pollay (eds) *Advances in Consumer Research*, 17, Provo, UT: Association for Consumer Research, 508–517.

—— (ed.) (1991) *Highways and Buyways: Naturalistic Research from the Consumer Behavior Odyssey*, Provo, UT: Association for Consumer Research.

—— (1993a) 'Moving possessions: an analysis based on personal documents from the 1847–1869 Mormon migration', *Journal of Consumer Research*, 19, December: 393–417.

—— (1993b) 'Third World tourism: panacea or poison? The case of Nepal', *Journal of International Consumer Marketing*, 5, 1: 27–68.

—— (1994) 'Carnival, control, and corporate culture in contemporary Halloween celebrations', in J. Santino (ed.) *Halloween and Other Festivals of Death and Life*, Knoxville, TN: University of Tennessee Press, 105–132.

—— (1995) *Collecting in a Consumer Society*, London: Routledge.

—— (1996) 'Hyperreality and globalization: culture in the age of Ronald McDonald', *Journal of International Consumer Marketing*, 8, 3/4: 23–37.

—— (1997) 'On aura, illusion, escape, and hope in apocalyptic consumption: the apotheosis of Las Vegas', in S. Brown, J. Bell and D. Carson (eds) *Marketing Apocalypse: Eschatology, Escapology and the Illusion of the End*, London: Routledge, 87–107.

—— and Coon, G.S. (1993) 'Gift-giving as agapic love: an alternative to the exchange paradigm based on dating experiences', *Journal of Consumer Research*, 20, December: 393–417.

—— and Costa, J.A. (1995) 'International tourism: an assessment and overview', *Journal of Macromarketing*, 15, Fall: 33–49.

—— and Dodson, K. (1997) 'Lessons of altruism and egoism in children's birthday stories', in M. Brucks and D. MacInnis (eds) *Advances in Consumer Research*, 24, Provo, UT: Association for Consumer Research.

——, Wallendorf, M. and Sherry, J.F. Jr (1989) 'The sacred and the profane in consumer behavior: theodicy on the Odyssey', *Journal of Consumer Research*, 16, June: 1–38.

Best, J. (1985) 'The myth of the Halloween sadist', *Psychology Today*, 19, November: 14–16.

Bouissac, P. (1976) *Circus and Culture: A Semiotic Approach*, Bloomington, IN: Indiana University Press.

Bourdieu, P. and Darbel, A. (1990) *The Love of Art: European Art Museums and their Public*, trans. C. Beattie and N. Merriman, Stanford, CA: Stanford University Press.

Brown, B.B. (1985) 'Residential territories: cues to burglary vulnerability', *Architectural Planning and Research*, 2: 231–243.

Campbell, J. (1968) *The Hero with a Thousand Faces*, 2nd edn, Princeton, NJ: Princeton University Press.

Clark, C.D. (1995) *Flights of Fancy, Leaps of Faith: Children's Myths in Contemporary America*, Chicago: University of Chicago Press.

Cohen, S. and Taylor, L. (1992) *Escape Attempts: The Theory and Practice of Resistance to Everyday Life*, London: Routledge.

Collins, J.C. and Gregor, T. (1995) 'Boundaries of love', in W. Jankowiak (ed.) *Romantic Passion: A Universal Experience?*, New York: Columbia University Press, 72–92.

Cook, I. and Crang, P. (1996) 'The world on a plate: culinary culture, displacement and geographical knowledges', *Journal of Material Culture*, 1, July: 131–153.

Crawford, T. (1994) *The Secret Life of Money: Teaching Tales of Spending, Receiving, Saving, and Owing*, New York: G.P. Putnam's Sons.

Davis, M.S. (1983) *Smut*, Chicago: University of Chicago Press.

Dodson, K. and Belk, R.W. (1996) 'Gender in children's birthday stories', in J.A. Costa (ed.) *Gender, Marketing and Consumer Behavior: Third Conference Proceedings*, Salt Lake City, UT: University of Utah Printing Service, 96–108.

Douglas, M. (1966) *Purity and Danger: An Analysis of Pollution and Taboo*, London: Routledge & Kegan Paul.

Eisler, R.T. (1995) *Sacred Pleasure: Sex, Myth, and the Politics of the Body*, San Francisco, CA: Harper.

Elias, N. (1978) *The Civilizing Process: The History of Manners*, New York: Urizen.

Emerson, R.W. (1983) 'Gifts', *The Collected Works of Ralph Waldo Emerson*, A.R. Fergusson (ed.), Cambridge, MA: Belknap, 91–96.

Falk, P. (1994) *The Consuming Body*, London: Sage.

Farb, P. and Armelogos, G. (1980) *Consuming Passions: The Anthropology of Eating*, Boston, MA: Houghton Mifflin.

Fiedler, L. (1978) *Freaks: Myths and Images of the Secret Self*, New York: Simon & Schuster.

Finkelstein, J. (1989) *Dining Out: A Sociology of Modern Manners*, New York: New York University Press.

Freud, S. (1958 [1911]) 'Formulations on the two principles of mental functioning', *The Standard Edition of the Complete Psychological Works of Sigmund Freud*, 12, J. Strachey (ed.), London: Hogarth.

Geary, P. (1986) 'Sacred commodities: the circulation of Medieval relics', in A. Appadurai (ed.) *The Social Life of Things: Commodities in Cultural Perspective*, Cambridge: Cambridge University Press, 169–191.

van Gennep, A. (1960) *The Rites of Passage*, trans. M.B. Vizedom and G.L. Caffee, London: Routledge & Kegan Paul.

Gluckman, M. (1963) *Order and Rebellion in Tribal Africa: Collected Essays*, London: Cohen & West.

Gordon, B. (1986) 'The souvenir: messenger of the extraordinary', *Journal of Popular Culture*, 20, 3: 135–146.

Graburn, N.H.H. (1987) 'Material symbols in Japanese domestic tourism', in D.W. Ingersol, Jr and G. Bronitsky (eds) *Mirror and Metaphor: Material and Social Constructions of Reality*, Lanham, MD: University Press of America, 17–28.

—— (1989) 'Tourism: the sacred journey', in V.L. Smith (ed.) *Hosts and Guests: The Anthropology of Tourism*, 2nd edn, Philadelphia, PA: University of Pennsylvania Press, 21–36.

Groves, R. and Belk, R.W. (1995) 'The Odyssey Downunder: a qualitative study of aboriginal consumers', in F.R. Kardes and M. Sujan (eds) *Advances in Consumer Research*, 22, Provo, UT: Association for Consumer Research, 303–305.

Hahn, C. (1990) 'Locta Sancta souvenirs: sealing the pilgrim's experience', in R. Ousterhout (ed.) *The Blessings of Pilgrimage*, Urbana, IL: University of Illinois Press, 85–96.

Hall, T.D. (1994) *Contested Boundaries: Itinerancy and the Reshaping of the Colonial American Religious World*, Durham, NC: Duke University Press.

Hansen, W.B. and Altman, I. (1976) 'Decorating personal places: a descriptive analysis', *Environment and Behavior*, 8, December: 491–504.

Hartmann, E. (1991) 'Thin and thick boundaries: personality, dreams, and imagination', in R.G. Kunzendorf (ed.) *Mental Imagery*, New York: Plenum, 71–78.

Helms, M.W. (1988) *Ulysses' Sail: An Ethnographic Odyssey of Power, Knowledge, and Geographical Distance*, Princeton, NJ: Princeton University Press.

Hodgen, M.T. (1964) *Early Anthropology in the Sixteenth and Seventeenth Centuries*, Philadelphia, PA: University of Pennsylvania Press.

Horne, D. (1984) *The Great Museum: The Re-presentation of History*, London: Pluto.

—— (1992) *The Intelligent Tourist*, McMahons Point, New South Wales: Margaret Gee.

Hyde, L. (1983) *The Gift: Imagination and the Erotic Life of Property*, New York: Vintage.

Jager, B. (1975) 'Theorizing, journeying, dwelling', in A. Giorgi, C.T. Fischer and E.L. Murray (eds) *Dusquene Studies in Phenomenological Psychology: Volume II*, Pittsburgh, PA: Dusquene University Press, 235–260.

Jardine, L. (1996) *Worldly Goods: A New History of the Renaissance*, London: Macmillan.

Kelley, R.F. (1987) 'Museums as status symbols: attaining a state of having been', in R. W. Belk (ed.) *Advances in Nonprofit Marketing*, 2, Greenwich, CT: JAI Press, 1–38.

Keyfitz, N. (1982) 'Development and the elimination of poverty', *Economic Development and Cultural Change*, 30, April: 650–670.

King, M.J. (1991) 'The theme park experience: what museums can learn from Mickey Mouse', *The Futurist*, 25, November–December: 24–32.

Kowinski, W.S. (1986) 'Endless summer at the world's biggest shopping wonderland', *Smithsonian*, 17, December: 35–43.

Kyokai, N.K. (ed.) (1981) *The Frontier of the Seas: Problems of Delimitation*, Tokyo: Ocean Association of Japan.

Lappé, M. (1996) *The Body's Edge: Our Cultural Obsession with Skin*, New York: Henry Holt.

Lears, J. (1989) 'Beyond Veblen: rethinking consumer culture in America', in S.J. Bronner (ed.) *Consuming Visions: Accumulation and Display of Goods in America, 1880–1920*, New York: W.W. Norton, 73–97.

MacCannell, D. (1989) *The Tourist: A New Theory of the Leisure Class*, New York: Schocken.

Maguire, M. (1980) 'The impact of burglary upon victims', *British Journal of Criminology*, 20, July: 261–275.

Mehrabian, A. (1976) *Public Places and Private Spaces: The Psychology of Work, Play, and Living Environments*, New York: Basic Books, 237–239, 277–278.

Mehta, R. and Belk, R. W. (1991) 'Artifacts, identity, and transition: favorite possessions of Indians and Indian immigrants to the United States', *Journal of Consumer Research*, 17, March: 398–411.

Melbin, M. (1987) *Night as Frontier: Colonizing the World After Dark*, New York: Free Press.

Miller, D. (ed.) (1993) *Unwrapping Christmas*, Oxford: Oxford University Press.

Mukerji, C. (1983) *From Graven Images: Patterns of Modern Materialism*, New York: Columbia University Press.

Nagibin, Y. (1979) 'Winter oak', *Atlantic Monthly*, September.

Nippert-Eng, C. (1996) *Home and Work*, Chicago: University of Chicago Press.

Nozick, R. (1974) *Anarchy, State, and Utopia*, New York: Basic Books.

O'Drain, M. (1986) 'San Francisco's Gay Halloween', *International Folklore Review*, 4: 90–95.

Papp, W.R. (1981) 'Being burglarized: an account of victimization', *Victimology: An International Journal*, 6, 1–4: 297–305.

Peñaloza, L.N. (1991) 'Crossing boundaries/drawing lines: gender trouble in consumer research', in J.A. Costa (ed.) *Gender and Consumer Behavior Conference Proceedings*, Salt Lake City, UT: University of Utah Printing Service, 89.

—— (1994) 'Atravesando fronteras/border crossings: a critical ethnographic exploration of the consumer acculturation of Mexican immigrants', *Journal of Consumer Research*, 21, June: 32–54.

—— (1996) 'We're here, we're queer, and we're going shopping! A critical perspective on the accommodation of gays and lesbians in the U.S. Marketplace', in L.W. Daniel (ed.) *Gays, Lesbians, and Consumer Behavior: Theory, Practice, and Research Issues in Marketing*, New York: Haworth, 9–41.

Reece, S. (1993) *The Stranger's Welcome: Oral Theory and the Aesthetics of the Homeric Hospitality Scene*, Ann Arbor, MI: University of Michigan Press.

Relph, E. (1976) *Place and Placelessness*, London: Pion.

Rheingold, H. (1993) *The Virtual Community: Homesteading on the Electronic Frontier*, Reading, MA: Addison Wesley.

Ritzer, G. (1993) *The McDonaldization of Society*, Thousand Oaks, CA: Pine Forge Press.

Rucker, M.S., Kaiser, S., Barry, M., Brumett, D., Freeman, C. and Peters, A. (1986) 'The imported export market: an investigation of foreign visitors' gift and personal purchases', in N.K. Malhotra (ed.) *Developments in Marketing Science*, 9, Atlanta, GA: Academy of Marketing Science, 120–124.

Rugoff, R. (1995) *Circus Americanus*, London: Verso.

Scarlett, W.G. and Wolf, D. (1979) 'When it's only make-believe: the construction of a boundary between fantasy and reality in storytelling', *New Directions for Child Development*, 6: 29–40.

Scieszka, J. (1991) *Knights of the Kitchen Table*, New York: Viking.

Shacochis, B. (1989) 'In deepest Gringolandia; Mexico: the Third World as tourist theme park', *Harper's*, July: 42–50.

Silber, J. R. (1971) 'Masks and fig leaves', in J.R. Pennock and J.W. Chapman (eds) *Privacy*, New York: Atherton, 226–235.

Spinks, C.W. Jr (1991) *Semiosis, Marginal Signs and Trickster: A Dagger of the Mind*, London: Macmillan.

Stagl, J. (1995) *A History of Curiosity: The Theory of Travel 1550–1800*, Chur, Switzerland: Harwood.

Steiner, G. (1989) *Real Presences*, Chicago: University of Chicago Press.

Stewart, S. (1984) *On Longing: Narratives of the Miniature, the Gigantic, the Souvenir, the Collection*, Baltimore, MD: Johns Hopkins University Press.

Stilgoe, J.R. (1976) 'Jack-o'-lanterns to surveyors: the secularization of landscape boundaries', *Environmental Review*, 1, 1: 14–30.

Stott, J.C. (1994) 'Making stories mean: making meaning from stories: the value of literature for children', *Children's Literature in Education*, 25, December: 243–253.

Suler, J.R. (1980) 'Primary process thinking and creativity', *Psychological Bulletin*, 88: 144–165.

Thompson, H.S. (1971) *Fear and Loathing in Las Vegas: A Savage Journey to the Heart of the American Dream*, New York: Random House.

Tuan, Y. (1982) *Segmented Worlds and Self: Group Life and Individual Consciousness*, Minneapolis, MN: University of Minnesota Press.

Turner, V. (1969) *The Ritual Process: Structure and Anti-Structure*, Chicago: Aldine.

Urry, J. (1990) *The Tourist Gaze: Leisure and Travel in Contemporary Societies*, London: Sage.

Visser, M. (1991) *The Rituals of Dinner: The Origin, Evolution, Eccentricities, and Meaning of Table Manners*, New York: Grove Weidenfeld.

Wemhaner, J.D. and Dodder, R. (1984) 'A new Halloween goblin: the product tamperings', *Journal of Popular Culture*, 18, Winter: 21–24.

Witkowski, T. and Yamamoto, Y. (1991) '*Omiyage* gift purchasing by Japanese travelers in the U.S.' , in R.H. Holman and M.R. Solomon (eds) *Advances in Consumer Research*, 18, Provo, UT: Association for Consumer Research, 123–128.

Wolff, J. (1993) 'On the road again: metaphors of travel in cultural criticism', *Cultural Studies*, 7, 2: 224–239.

Zerubavel, E. (1991) *The Fine Line: Making Distinctions in Everyday Life*, New York: Free Press.

3   Walking on the edge
A stereographic photo essay on the verge of consumer research

Morris B. Holbrook

DIVIDED TIME: WEST AND EAST

During the summer of 1994, quite unexpectedly, my wife Sally and I became bi-directional vacationers.

It all started when the fierce winter of 1993/4 dumped massive piles of ice and snow on top of our weekend house in the Pocono Mountains of Pennsylvania, at a development called Hemlock Farms, about 100 miles west of New York City, where we live and work during the career-orientated part of the week. The ill-conceived hot-tar flat roof of our little Pennsylvania retreat creaked, groaned and then notched downward a couple of feet as the carpenter-ant-infested beams in the south-west wall collapsed, allowing the huge plate-glass windows that they had formerly supported to descend and to leave a broad swathe of clear daylight beneath the tops of the window frames up near the ceiling. Through this window of opportunity passed huge gulps of frigid Pocono air plus an occasional drenching of frozen sleet, frosty hail or blizzard flakes.

When we returned to Hemlock Farms that spring, we immediately realised that our vacation home in the mountains badly needed recon-struction. Soon, workmen had boarded up the big windows with gigantic slabs of ugly plywood. They had erected massive scaffoldings in what would otherwise have been our living room. Our precious forest hideaway had become a certifiable disaster area. Further, once they had started their rebuilding project, the workmen showed no particular inclination to finish the job. It quickly became clear that we should not plan to spend the weekends of summer 1994 in Pennsylvania.

Casting about for somewhere else to invest our leisure time, Sally and I tried the New Jersey and Delaware shores – as far down as Cape May and Lewes – and various parts of Long Island. Eventually, we found ourselves gravitating towards Montauk – a small resort community, formerly a fishing village and seaport, past the fashionable Hamptons, in an area of natural wildness at the furthest eastern tip of Long Island's South Fork, about 120 miles from Manhattan and about 220 miles from the Poconos of Pennsylvania. In Montauk, we spent time taking long walks on the beaches and wandering down the small deserted dirt roads, appreciating nature in a way we had not done in many years.

One day, our hike led us to a place called Rough Riders Landing (so named because it is built on the spot where Teddy Roosevelt and his men had their military camp during the First World War). Rough Riders is a condominium community perched on the side of Fort Pond Bay – looking into Block Island Sound, which separates the North and South Forks – in a reclaimed spot where the US Navy used to test torpedoes by firing them out to sea and chasing them in small planes. The condos sit within easy walking distance of the train station, at the end-of-the-line for the Long Island Railroad, which stops and parks its trains only a few feet from the Landing's gate. The Rough Riders apartments resemble what we have come to think of as hotel suites – a large living room with kitchenette looking out onto a deck, a bathroom and a small bedroom in the back. Being curious, we asked about the availability of these units, and, being a born saleswoman, the property agent began showing us around and quoting us prices. We soon discovered that – after purchasing a unit – the *monthly* maintenance was about the same as what we had been paying *per night* for our much smaller, much less attractive, much less comfortable hotel room on the Atlantic Ocean side. Further, the real-estate agent was responsible for renting out these condos when they were not in use by their owners (helping them, she assured us, more or less pay for themselves).

Pretty soon, the selling-and-renting agent showed us a unit with a spectacular view across Fort Pond Bay into Block Island Sound and, on a clear day, all the way to New London, Connecticut. To the right, the rickety pier of Duryea's Lobster House projected into the water, presenting a classic picture of quaintness. (The owner, Mr Chip Duryea, has since publicly toyed with the idea of selling his formidable dock to the Pequot Indians for the purpose of running a car ferry to their gambling casino in Connecticut; but, at the time, we had no way of anticipating the remotest possibility of such a disaster.) To the left, one saw nothing but blue water stretching toward New England. (As far as we know, no one has yet contemplated violating this majestic vista.)

Not for nothing did I get my MBA and Sally her degrees in clinical social work. Given the financial incentives and aesthetic attractions of this place, we immediately did what any self-respecting experientially orientated proponents of consumer debt would do. We made an impulse investment in real estate on the east end of Long Island.

Thus did it happen that we – Morris and Sally, who did not even own our first new car until after we had celebrated our fifteenth wedding anniversary – began to divide our vacation time between a house in the Pocono Mountains of Pennsylvania to the west and a condo at Montauk on the farthest tip of Long Island to the east.

DIFFERENCES

One might wonder why people ostensibly in their right minds would need or want two weekend-vacation homes within a 120-mile radius of New York City. The answers are (1) that these two places are both very special; (2) that both offer a welcome retreat from the rigours encountered during a week of workdays in Manhattan; and – perhaps most importantly – (3) that the consumption experiences associated with these two locations are *as different as it is possible to imagine*. Table 3.1 lists some of the relevant binary oppositions in a series of structural comparisons that appear to deserve our attention, as follows.

Dwelling

Space

The Pennsylvania home is a small house that nonetheless has a spacious feeling by virtue of its two-storey living room surrounded by balconies that give views through gigantic areas of window glass. The presence of

Table 3.1   Binary oppositions based on life in the Poconos and at Montauk

Basis for comparison	Pennsylvania: Hemlock Farms	Long Island: Rough Riders Landing
Dwelling		
Space	Small house, spacious feeling, indoor focus	Large condo, cramped feeling, outdoor focus
Sense of privacy	Private place, surrounded by woods	Communal living, shared beach
Furnishings	Lovingly furnished to personal tastes	Furnished in homogeneous, standardised Montauk modern
Inhabitants	Solely occupied by owners	Rented to strangers in absence of owners
Transportation	Car, 2–5 hours	Train, 4–28 hours
People	New Yorkers, Bronx/Queens accents	Irish, Celtic accents
Scenery		
Flora	Mountain terrain, green vistas	Ocean setting, seaside views
Seasonality	Four seasons	Two seasons
Fauna	Deer, skunks, (bear)	Sea gulls, (fish)
Activities		
Walking	Hikes on woody hillsides	Strolls on the beach by the sea
Entertainment	Movies at Stroudsburg	TV at home
Eating out	Italian restaurants	Lobster rolls
Broken promises	More tennis	More swimming
Cat play	Spiral stairs (mice)	Wooden deck (birds)

two bathrooms affords the luxury of not having to compete for use of the basin, toilet or shower. There is a stone terrace, but the Pocono insects make its usage almost unthinkable. Hence, the focus is on the indoors. By contrast, the Montauk condo resembles a large hotel accommodation that nonetheless has a somewhat cramped feeling by virtue of its excess of overstuffed furniture, its crowded kitchenette and its lack of cupboard space. Limitation to one bathroom means a constant contest for who gets to wash, pee or bathe first. Thanks to the almost miraculously low numbers of insects, one can comfortably sit on the large wooden deck. Hence, the orientation is toward the outdoors.

Sense of privacy

The Pocono house sits on four-fifths of an acre surrounded by woods, giving it a fairly private feeling (at least by New York City standards). Neighbours live nearby, but – because of the trees and the tendency of people not to come more than one or two weekends per month – one barely notices them. By contrast, the Montauk condo provides an exercise in close communal living. Neighbours gather on their own decks within easy earshot. Sometimes they play ugly music (not jazz or classical) on their tinny portable radios or leave their big rottweilers out on the deck to play (and bark) while they go to a movie or yell in loud voices to their noisy children who frolic obstreperously on the shared beach only fifty yards away.

Furnishings and inhabitants

The Pocono house conveys a sense of personal proprietorship. It has been lovingly furnished – piece by piece – with inexpensive but meaningful objects that we find attractive, amusing or otherwise worthwhile and with built-in furniture that we have largely designed ourselves and constructed with our own hands. Partly because few people really want to spend too much time in the Poconos (what with the declassé image of honeymooners in heart-shaped bathtubs and all), the house does not offer a marketable rental opportunity, is solely inhabited by its owners, and therefore conveys a feeling of privacy. By contrast, the Montauk apartment shares its furnishings with every other unit in the condominium community – oak tables, chairs and cabinets; brown industrial-style carpet; blue-green U-shaped couch; aqua-coloured arm chair; matching lamps; and assorted wall decorations that one would hesitate to call artworks. As one tours the community, one discovers that all one's neighbours have exactly the same furniture and nothing but copy-cat hangings on their walls. Further, because strangers occupy the space when it is rented for income, one constantly feels like a visitor, guest or tenant in one's own home.

Transportation

The only way to get to the house in the Poconos is by car. You drive from 87th Street and Riverside, up the Henry Hudson Parkway, across the George Washington Bridge, west on Route 80 across New Jersey, over the Delaware River Water Gap, up Highway 402 just past the Pickerel Inn on the right to the entrance for Hemlock Farms, and down a few increasingly smaller and more winding roads until you reach Horseshoe Lane, where you find our place at the end of a long, unmarked, dirt driveway. Barring unforeseen events, total time from door to door is anywhere from two to five hours, depending on traffic at the bridges. By comparison, a major reason for the Montauk experiment was the motivating consideration that you can reach our condo by train – offering an opportunity to read the paper, review a journal submission or two, and take a nap – instead of struggling to remain vigilant behind the wheel while following in the tractor-tread wakes of uncountable semi-trailer trucks. To reach Montauk, you walk from 87th and Riverside to the downtown Interborough Rapid Transit (IRT) local on Broadway, change subways at 42nd Street, go to Hunter's Point in Queens, hike a block to the Long Island Railroad (LIRR) station, take the LIRR east to the last stop at the end of the tracks, and stroll a short distance to the gate for Rough Riders Landing. Total time from the Upper West Side to Fort Pond Bay is from four to twenty-eight hours, depending on whether the LIRR engineers are ready to renegotiate their labour contract and unexpectedly decide to conduct a wildcat work stoppage (as they did, for example, on the Friday before Memorial Day, 1995).

People

Most of the people in Montauk seem to be Irish. Apparently, the settlers got as far as the tip of Long Island, thought it looked a lot like the coast of Donegal Bay, and decided to quit while they were ahead. As a result, the women in Montauk all have beautiful red hair atop pretty faces covered with cute freckles and, even after three or four generations, speak with a lilting Celtic accent (which appears to be genetic). By contrast, the Poconos attract hordes of displaced New Yorkers – mostly overweight, middle-aged accountants who drive up for a weekend of relaxation among the pine trees and who fill the air with their Bronx or Queens accents. On the community tennis courts, the nearby player is likely to congratulate his opponent on a particularly skilful return of service with words such as, 'Noice shawt; yer bowl wuz jist awn da loin' (translation – 'Nice shot; your ball was just on the line').

Scenery

Flora and seasonality

The Poconos feature the sorts of heart-stopping scenic views that one associates with mountainous terrain. Driving or walking along roadways, one encounters green vistas – lush valleys heavily wooded with pine, oak and maple trees. During the summer months, the ragweed and pollen count soar into the stratosphere and bring a sniffle or two to allergy sufferers trying to enjoy the cool shade of the green forest. In the autumn a panoply of reds, browns, yellows and oranges bursts forth on the tree-covered hills and attracts hordes of tourists who drive down the major highways gaping in astonishment at the wonderful autumn colours. Winter covers everything with gleaming white accented by sparkling ice crystals. And, with spring, new buds begin to sprout as soon as the last snows have melted. By comparison, befitting what one expects of the ocean-moderated climate on the eastern seaboard, the weather in Montauk has achieved a remarkably streamlined simplicity by reducing everything to just two seasons. The seasons at Montauk are binary or digital – zero or one, yes or no – in short, summer or winter. Whatever the temperature (often rather chilly), summer begins on the Memorial Day Weekend when hordes of pale Manhattanites decide that it is time for their first beach experience of the year. As the summer wears on, the days grow hotter and hotter, fuelled by the burning intensity of a fierce sun that seems to set reluctantly in a blaze of glory, bathing the sky over Fort Pond Bay in wonderful diffuse shades of pink and red, after which the air sweetens into a balmy breeze that wafts across the water for the rest of the evening. After Labor Day, summer becomes Indian summer, which continues until Thanksgiving (usually pretty cool) when the aforementioned Manhattanites discover that they must start staying home to prepare for their holiday responsibilities at the end of December. All the local merchants immediately close their shops and flee to Florida. The ensuing winter season brings temperatures so cold, winds so fierce, and shopping so sparse that Montauk becomes virtually uninhabitable (except by a handful of brave ex-Celts) until Memorial Day rolls around once again.

Fauna

Besides an amazing insect population that never quits, the Poconos feature a burgeoning number of deer that, however beautiful, have become almost pestlike in their plenitude, roaming the woods in large herds of white-tailed scavengers, eating the flowers, and literally begging for food at kitchen windows. During the hunting season, these deer are so tame and friendly that they walk right up to the cars parked by the side of the road and peer curiously through the windows at the men with rifles, who obligingly blow their heads off, referring to this sporting practice as 'harvesting' the 'deer crop' as if these graceful, trusting animals were a patch of rhubarb that needed to be mowed down. Amazingly, we saw a pure white skunk on our terrace last summer. Rumours tell of bear who live in the woods, but they seldom come out to play. By contrast, whatever deer inhabit Montauk keep to themselves, leaving the job of running the wildlife show pretty much up to the sea gulls who strut across the beaches, paddle around in the water, and fill the skies with their flapping wings and hawking sounds, often demonstrating how they can stay in one place effortlessly by gliding on the wind and not moving a muscle. Rumours tell of fish who live in the waters. And men do come to the Rough Riders pier with rods and reels to cast for these mythical sea creatures. But I have never seen any of these men catch anything.

Activities

Walking

In Pennsylvania, we take long hikes in the wooded hills, remarking on the beauties of the forest and commenting on the foibles of our neighbours. At Montauk, we take long strolls on the beach by the sea, remarking on the beauties of the ocean and commenting on the foibles of the other beachcombers.

Entertainment and eating out

In Pennsylvania, with no television, we sometimes drive thirty miles to see one of the mindless movies playing at the multiplex cinema in the Stroudsburg Mall, after which we generally stop off at one of the Poconos' fine Italian restaurants on the way home. (Yankee broadcaster Phil Rizzuto has often touted the merits of these restaurants during what might otherwise have been construed as his accounts of the ballgames.) At Montauk, where the nearest multiplex is on the prohibitively crowded main street of East Hampton – the major motoring bottleneck of the western hemisphere – we are forced to stay at home, where we can watch equally mindless entertainment on the TV that came as standard equipment with our condo. But, more often, we just gaze at the water and munch lobster rolls carried in from Duryea's just up the beach. (We now enjoy such lobster feasts with some misgivings for fear of subsidising the man who threatens to sell us out to the invasive interests of the gambling casino run by the Pequot Indians in Connecticut; but we still do enjoy them.)

Broken promises

In Pennsylvania, we keep promising ourselves to play more tennis. Usually, it is too cool for swimming. In Montauk, the wind usually rules out tennis. We keep promising ourselves to do more swimming.

Cat play

In Pennsylvania, our cat Rocky likes to climb half-way up the spiral stair-case on one side of our living room and then to jump off, gradually increasing the speed of this cycle, running with frenzy and leaping for joy, until he creates a wondrous spectacle of fur flying all around the stairs. At Montauk, Rocky likes to lie languorously on the deck, watching the sea gulls whirling overhead and pouncing on the occasional insect that is foolish enough to wander within the range of his quick paws. Someday, Rocky hopes to catch a mouse in the Poconos or a bird at Montauk. His chances for the former and latter appear excellent and remote, respectively.

Summary and preview

In sum, the two vacation sites between which we now divide our time, whether from the human or feline perspective, could not be more different. Indeed, they serve admirably as the basis for binary oppositions in the series of polar contrasts shown in the table. One could not hope to find two more divergent vacation spots giving rise to two more diverse consumption experiences.

Yet I wish to suggest that both locations do converge in one respect. In one way, they offer experiences that teach us the same lesson about life in general and about consumer research in particular. Specifically – west or east, in the Poconos or at Montauk – the same principle applies: *it pays to walk on the edge*.

THE EDGE

Definitions

In the English language, the term *edge* carries powerful connotations – both positive and negative. Literally, according to Webster, the noun *edge* means 'the cutting side of a blade'. Hence, on the positive side, it is asso-ciated with 'sharpness', 'penetrating power', 'keenness', and 'competitive advantage'. As a verb, *to edge* means 'to defeat' one's opponent (albeit by a small margin) or 'to advance' (by small steps). When 'edge' joins with the word 'cutting', the term *cutting edge* refers to the 'forefront' – presumably, a good place to be – or to a 'sharp effect or quality'. Clearly, as consumers and researchers, we want our experiences and insights to have these cutting-edge qualities of sharpness, penetration, advantage, success and advancement.

But *edge* also carries some negative connotations. It can mean 'a notice-ably harsh or sharp quality' (as in an unpleasant tone of voice) or can refer to a state of being 'tense' or 'irritable' (as in a 'fidgety' disposition). Clearly, except when helping out journal editors by serving in our capacities as ruthless reviewers of other people's cherished contributions, we wish to banish such aspects of edginess from our lives and work.

Moving past these familiar meanings, it is another sense of the term *edge*, neither positive nor negative in connotation without further elaboration, that I wish to emphasise here – namely, 'the narrow part adjacent to the border', the 'brink', the 'verge', the 'margin', the 'line where an object or area begins or ends'. *This* is the sense of the concept *edge* that I wish to recommend to consumers and to researchers when I suggest that in both pursuits, figuratively speaking, *it pays to walk on the edge*.

Mathematical Proof

We can, of course, prove this proposition mathematically. Let us define the *edge* (E) as half-way between the two polar extremes (E_1 and E_2) – in other words, the golden mean or happy compromise: $E = (E_1+E_2)/2$. Assume that, at one extreme (E_1), the probability of success (P_1) is virtually certain ($P_1 = 1.0$) but that the reward for such a success (R_1) is essentially zero ($R_1 = 0.0$). In other words, E_1 represents the tried-and-true approach where we are sure of proceeding correctly but where there is little to gain by such a conservative route. (For example, think of someone submitting a paper to the leading consumer-research journal that reports an experimental test of some hypotheses drawn from established psychological theory as represented by a convincing nomological network.) By contrast, the other polar extreme (E_2) carries the largest possible potential reward ($R_2 = 1.0$) but is so risky that failure is virtually guaranteed ($P_2 = 0.0$). In other words, E_2 represents a departure from conventions so daring that it cannot possibly succeed in its lofty ambitions. (For example, consider the likely fate of someone submitting work to the same journal mentioned previously in the form of an animated cartoon or a poem.)

Further assume that P_L and R_L are linear decreasing and increasing functions of one's location (L) over the range between the two extremes just described: $P_L = (E_2 - L)/(E_2 - E_1)$; $R_L = (L - E_1)/(E_2 - E_1)$. Our job is to maximise the Expected Payoff (EP_L) where $EP_L = P_L R_L$. Toward that end, substituting for P_L and R_L gives: $EP_L = (E_2 - L)(L - E_1)/(E_2 - E_1)^2 = (E_2 E_1 - L^2 + E_1 L + E_2 L)/(E_2 - E_1)^2$. Taking the derivative with respect to location (L): $d(EP_L)/dL = (-2L + E_1 + E_2)/(E_2 - E_1)^2$. Setting this derivative equal to zero and solving for the optimal location (L^*) gives: $L^* = (E_1 + E_2)/2 = E$.

From this, it follows that one's optimal location in consumption and research is at *the edge* [$E = (E_1 + E_2)/2$, as defined previously] between the extremes of safety and risk – at a sort of Golden Mean betwixt the self-deluding safety of 'nothing ventured, nothing gained' and the lunatic riskiness of 'double or nothing'. Thus, it appears straightforward to demonstrate the optimality of walking on the edge via this simple mathematical proof. Indeed, our editor informs me that this proof bears some resemblance to Hotelling's classic prescription for the location of ice-cream vendors on a beach (though I hasten to add that *his* proof referred to the *length* of the beach whereas *mine* deals with its *width*). Nevertheless, we might have more confidence in our conclusion if it were also supported by means of some telling anecdotal evidence. Toward this end, the illustrative cases of recreation in the Poconos and at Montauk prove illuminating.

The edge in Pennsylvania

Imagine that you are walking along a mountain trail, enjoying those scenic Pocono vistas described earlier. As you hike, you ponder the questions of where the view is most exciting or, figuratively, most insightful. It occurs to you that there is some danger in walking too close to the precipice on your right; you might fall off; the momentary view would be spectacular as you plummeted head over heels to your death on the craggy rocks below; but it would all be over very quickly. Alternatively, you could shrink to the left; but if you went too far in that direction, you would enter the forest; you would be completely safe from falling, but all you would see is a few trees, branches, and leaves obstructing your view of the scenic wonders ahead. Wisely, you opt for *walking on the edge* – at the margin between bland safety and perilous danger – at the boundary where you need to proceed with care but where the payoff in terms of a vivid, visually rich imaginative experience is thrilling. In the Poconos, *the edge is where the view is most beautiful.*

The edge on Long Island

Now imagine that you are whisked, from Pennsylvania in the west to 220 miles eastward on the tip of Long Island, where you find yourself strolling along the beach as you admire the oceanic splendour discussed previously. As you stroll, you notice that the tide is going out, and you ponder the question of where the footing is firmest or, figuratively, most true. It occurs to you that, literally and littorally, the receding waves form a line between the very dry sand on the left and the very wet sand on the right. If you walk too far to the left, the sand is too loose; your tennis shoes sink into it; the steps require great effort; you stay dry, but your progress is slow, faltering and awkward. But if you walk too far to the right, the sand is too soggy from the last wave that has washed over it; your feet sink deeply into the muck; your steps again require great effort; and, worse, your Reeboks are likely to be soaked by the next wave that pushes in a little farther than the others. Wisely, you opt for *walking on the edge* – on that margin of damp and firmly packed sand between slow progress on one side and constant threat of a dousing on the other – at the littoral boundary where you need to watch for waves that come in too far but where the sand moistened by the retreating tide still feels solid and secure under foot. At Montauk, *the edge is where the footing is most firm.*

CONSUMPTION AND CONSUMER RESEARCH

Clearly, the stories I have just told represent metaphors for how I believe we should think about our activities as consumers and researchers.

As consumers, we seek consumption experiences on the edge of adventure (flow, the peak moment or ecstasy) where we transcend the bland ordinariness of everyday life without doing physical or mental damage to ourselves. Profound aesthetic experiences, absorbing games or spiritual rapture come to mind as examples well worth striving for.

As researchers, we pursue approaches on the edge of legitimacy (profound insights, stunning breakthroughs or definitive answers to apparently unfathomable questions) where we escape the bounds of conventional aims, concepts and methods to discover new intellectual terrain that deserves exploration. Some of the emerging approaches represented by the present volume – those that draw innovatively on literary, post-structuralist, interpretive, semiotic, ethnographic, social-constructionist, phenomenological-existential, symbolic-interactionist, postmodern or introspective viewpoints – come to mind as illustrative perspectives well worth pursuing.

I have a friend who will be coming up for promotion to tenure in a year or so and who recently discussed his career strategy with me over lunch. Some senior professors have advised him to aim his work at business-orientated problems where he can find quick solutions of interest to marketing managers. Others have urged him to strive for attention-getting leaps of creativity that are less useful than singular in their imaginative sweep. Wisely, he opts for the middle ground, steering a course between the safe sterility of paid consulting and the dangerous idiosyncrasy of wild fancy. Thus, we again find the proposition unfolding before us. Between classic and romantic – between yin and yang, between dust and water, between darkness and light, between earth and heaven, between profane and sacred – we must seek a balance: again, *it pays to walk on the edge.*

In such cases – as consumers or researchers or people pursuing our careers – we gain by heeding the lesson in the analogies drawn from the Poconos and Montauk. We might think of our consumption experiences as analogous to skirting a dangerous precipice while enjoying the magnificent view. We might regard our research activities as directed towards finding the solid ground between the intellectually arid blandness of dry sand on one side and the wet blanket of encroaching surf on the other.

In both cases, we *start* by leaving home. We depart from our familiar turf (Manhattan) and head for new terrain (the Poconos) or uncharted waters (Montauk). Once we have embarked in this new direction (west or east), we *walk on the edge* – skirting the scenic vistas along a mountain trail or stepping down the beach along the fringes of the receding waves. And, almost paradoxically, it is at this brink or on this margin or along this border that we may hope to see most clearly or to tread most firmly. Hence, we have reason to celebrate the virtues of walking on the edge, perhaps by sending a postcard to describe our travels.

POSTCARDS FROM THE EDGE

The preceding reflections have suggested that the creative centre of consumption and the most penetrating insights from research often lie at the boundary – the brink, the verge, the liminal region, the littoral zone – where one realm of experience meets another. As an inspiration for the title and viewpoint of the present book, this theme surfaces in the film *Postcards from the Edge* starring Meryl Streep and Shirley MacLaine, based on a novel of the same name by Carrie Fisher. In building on the comments presented thus far, it strikes me that postcards in general and those from the edge in particular offer an excellent metaphor to motivate concrete illustrations of several points previously made more abstractly.

Postcards

In what follows, I shall present a series of postcards that mimic the epistolary style adopted by Carrie Fisher for part of her book – the part that represents the heroine's visit to a mental institution for drug-rehabilitation treatment. Here, she finds herself living past the boundary of any reality she has ever known, in a strange exile from which she must struggle to fight her way back to the other side of the precipitous brink from which she has fallen. Unlike Fisher's prose, my epistles will consist partly of photographs – picture postcards – that depict relevant aspects of consumption experiences at Montauk, in the Poconos, and from various points of view in between. All have something to say, I believe, about the special nature and profound power of moments spent at the margin between one world and another.

Edge

The particular pictures presented here appear in the form of three-dimensional stereographic photo pairs. As I have described elsewhere at greater length, such stereographs are captured by two camera lenses placed about two and a half inches apart and fired simultaneously to produce images from the vantage points of the left and right eyes. When viewed in a manner that causes the two pictures to fuse into one three-dimensional image, such stereo pairs convey 3-D experiences of greatly enhanced vividness, clarity, detail, and – most importantly – depth.

Most saliently in the present context, the 3-D stereo pairs parallel the concept of an edge – in the sense that two somewhat disparate areas of experience (the left and right views) adjoin one another (side-by-side) while standing apart (as neighbours) but ultimately come together (fuse) to form a moment of heightened awareness (the three-dimensional experience). In this, as a metaphor for liminal awareness, 3-D stereography reflects an ethos reminiscent of that which characterised our earlier descriptions of walking on the edge.

Those wishing to view my postcards in their full three-dimensional depth can pursue one or both of two available options: *free viewing* or *aided viewing*. In *free viewing*, one looks between and past the two photographic images in the stereo pair, moving the display toward and away from the face, while waiting for the two pictures to float together and to fuse into one coherent three-dimensional representation. In *aided viewing*, one makes use of an optical device such as those based on prismatic lenses that shift the images toward the centre of the visual space, thereby helping them to fuse into the desired 3-D experience. Because the stereo pairs presented here are small enough to permit easy fusion by the naked eyes, virtually all readers should be able to achieve fusion via free viewing without the aid of special optics. However, those seeking assistance via aided viewing should contact such suppliers of appropriate optical devices as The Added Dimension (Clearwater, FL), Reel 3-D Enterprises (Culver City, CA), Cygnus Graphic (Phoenix, AZ), The Stereoscopic Society (c/o Eric Silk, Cambridge, UK) or Bode Verlag (Halten, Germany). These vendors sell suitable stereo-pair viewers for under four dollars, three pounds or six marks apiece. More information about stereography can be found on my home page: http://www.columbia.edu/~mbh3/

Postmodern postcards from the edge of the edge: post-post card from the edge(edge) (Figure 3.1)

Dear Meryl: This photo expresses my empathy with the theme of your postcards-related movie in general and with your persona as the marginal edge-dwelling character in particular. Specifically, my affinity for your borderline role places me not only at the edge of the photograph but also at the brink of a bluff overlooking the beach along the Atlantic Ocean at Montauk. Thus, this particular postmodern postcard comments on itself by calling attention to the edge of the edge. In other words, reflexively, this post-post card finds me at the edge(edge) – giving a somewhat pomo twist to my experience of the scene. You'll also notice that I am wearing my snap-on dark glasses of the type you featured throughout the *Postcards* film. This is about as close as I come to the boundary-spanning aspects of cross-dressing. I suppose this sartorial gesture in your direction helps to place me in touch with the more feminine side of my personality. Meanwhile, notice how the three-dimensional effect clarifies

Figure 3.1 **Postmodern postcards from the edge of the edge: post-post card from the edge(edge).** In the postmodern spirit, this postcard comments reflexively on itself by showing the author on the edge of the edge, atop a bluff overlooking the beach at Montauk; also, in this post-post card from the edge(edge), the author wears Streep glasses as a subdued example of sartorial gender bending.

the relationships among the ridges of the bluff and gives a sense of the depth in the plunge down to the waves crashing on the beach below.

Lost cards from the ledge / lost c(h)ords from the stage (Figure 3.2)

Dear Meryl: It's me again, just to say that I have also admired you in many other films – the celebrated *Out of Africa*, of course, plus *Sophie's Choice, Kramer vs. Kramer* and *The Bridges of Madison County* – but also even the less well received movies like *A Cry in the Dark*, where you played the Australian housewife whose baby was stolen by a dingo when she visited Ayers Rock – surely a massive ledge if ever there was one. In your honour, we made a trip to Australia last March, but we stayed away from the central portions of the country and thereby lost the chance to shoot pictures of the outback near Alice Springs where your film was made. Rather, true to form, we stuck to the perimeters along the coast

Figure 3.2   **Lost cards from the ledge / lost c(h)ords from the stage.** The author lost the opportunity to visit the massive stone ledge at Ayers Rock because, true to form, his trip to Australia focused on the coastlines. Here, the Sydney Opera House provides a stage for human vocalists (cords) to perform songs (chords) – a role that can push an actress (Streep) to the edge (country music), but somehow beyond the expressive range of a more 'legitimate' singer (MacLaine).

lines – both east and west. Here we are on the east side of Australia visiting the Sydney Opera House at the gateway to the harbour where the tourist boats constantly circulate. In this photo, stereography contributes greatly to our rounded in-depth perception of the glass-globed lamps that lead to the Opera House. Speaking of operas and singing, what a thrill you must have had playing the heroine in that wonderful film (Carrie Fisher's semi-autobiographical *Postcards*) and working with Shirley MacLaine as your mother (based loosely on Debbie Reynolds). Shirley was right to show such visible pride in her stage daughter on screen. But, we are sorry to say, her almost operatic stage voice did not serve her well in her key moment as a brave but fading cabaret singer. Those with 'big' voices suitable for the stage almost always suffer when they try to execute pop or jazz material – as indelibly conveyed by a recording that we recently heard of the otherwise estimable Elly Ameling (noted coloratura) singing songs associated with Duke Ellington (such as, heaven help us, 'It Don't Mean a Thing If It Ain't Got That Swing' – which, in her case, it certainly don't 'cause it definitely ain't). Far more impressive to us was your own singing performance as Shirley's daughter, who pushes herself to the brink of her talents and triumphs on this dangerous terrain. Pretending to pretend not to be a singer, you begin

'You Don't Know Me' in a halting manner that gradually, almost imperceptibly, verges on a performance of commanding strength. And at the end of the film, as Shirley watches with motherly pride shining in her eyes, you give definitive interpretations of a country tune by Carly Simon – first, as a soulful torch song; then, as a joyous spiritual. I watched this in awe – forcing myself to remember that, after all, you are really *not* a singer. Rather you are an actress supreme who has somehow willed herself into a state of being able to sing – indeed, to sing beautifully. Your stage presence has carried you across the borders of one art form (acting) and into another (singing). Earlier in the film, much was made of your character's skill in looping some of her own dialogue (that is, speaking the words at a later date to synchronise with the movements of your lips on film). The looping scene naturally reminds us of lip-synching music. In this age of Milli Vanilli, reflexively, we naturally expect something similar from this movie about making movies. But when the screen credits roll, when we look to see who dubbed your vocal performance so expertly, and when we find that you sang those songs yourself, we have an on-the-edge experience of our own: thrilling.

Passed cars from the ledge (Figure 3.3)

Dear Carrie: Nowhere does the film of your story better convey your precarious balance at the boundary between frightening fantasy and grim reality than in the scene where Meryl Streep appears to hang by her fingers from a window ledge high above passing cars in the city streets below, but is in fact sprawled on her stomach in a stage set that has been rotated ninety degrees from the orientation of its counterpart in real life. This fascination with precipice-like views from high window ledges – real, fantasy, or somewhere in between – is something that movie audiences share with our cat Rocky. In this photo, Rocky sprawls on the window sill and watches the motor cars passing by the snowy scene in the park below. The radiator warms his tummy while his nose nearly touches the cold glass. After the Blizzard of 1996, as shown here, he would lie this way for hours, contemplating the uncharacteristically white fantasy world below from his vantage point on the window ledge at the edge between in and out, up and down, warm and cold, comfortable and hostile, safe and dangerous. The 3-D effect emphasises the distance between Rocky's real everyday existence as a prisoner in our apartment and the hyperreal world of his imagination.

Most cars as a hedge (Figure 3.4)

Dear Ford Motor Company: Because our trips to the Poconos require the use of an automobile and because our Oldsmobile station wagon had reached the advanced age of sixteen years old, we decided to buy a new

Figure 3.3   **Passed cars from the ledge.** Sprawled on his window ledge (reminiscent of Streep in her visually ambiguous stage set), Rocky the Cat watches cars passing in the street below amidst the snow deposited by the Blizzard of 1996.

motor vehicle for the purposes of making our weekend trips to the country. This purchase decision pushed us past the boundaries of our competence as consumers. So we elected to rely on the simplest of all shopping heuristics (the one I dutifully teach my students *not* to use) – namely, to hedge our bets by assuming that there is safety in numbers and choosing the most popular, biggest selling car, which turned out to be the Ford Taurus. In the photo, our shiny new silver Taurus LX sedan – named Nickel for obvious reasons – sits in the driveway near our house in Pennsylvania next to the leafy and mysterious woods beyond. Notice how the stereographic view allows us to look *into* rather than merely *at* the car.

Rusted car by the ridge (Figure 3.5)

Dear Nickel: Some day (we hope not soon), you may resemble this old rusty shell of a car that lies near a ridge overlooking Fort Pond Bay and that serves mostly as a sort of oversized flower pot for growing weeds. This picture illustrates how those who stay on safe terrain run the risk of growing rusty and ultimately vacuous. By contrast, the 3-D effect draws our attention toward the row of buildings in the distance on the other side of the Bay. These include the condo where we spend our time when visiting the east end of Long Island. It takes about forty minutes on foot to skirt the edge of the Bay and to reach the spot shown here.

Figure 3.4 **Most cars as a hedge.** As a hedge against error in buying a new car, the author and his wife chose the one with the most sales in the United States – namely, the Ford Taurus – pictured here at the edge of the woods that encircle the house in the Poconos.

Figure 3.5 **Rusted car by the ridge.** Across the Bay from the condo in Montauk, this rusted car sits near a ridge overlooking the water.

Doe's heart is for Chet (Figure 3.6)

Dear Chet: On a recent warm summer's day, with all the windows of our house in the Poconos flung open to let in the breeze, I listened to your final beautifully gentle and pensive recording with the vibraphonist Wolfgang Lackerschmid (*Welcome Back*, West Wind 2083). Before long a doe came, lay down beside the terrace just outside our screen door, and listened attentively to the lyrical Chet Baker sound for over an hour. Finally, I could stand it no longer and snuck outside to try to snap her picture. When she heard me, she stood up but remained rooted to the spot, staring at my stereo camera rig inquisitively and continuing to listen to your marvellously melodic trumpet. This photo shows the edge of the stone terrace and the musically fulfilled deer just beyond the ledge with the sun streaming deeply through the trees behind her.

Post and bird with wings spread (Figure 3.7)

Dear Charlie: Speaking of Chet Baker and therefore speaking of jazz, we recall that your nickname (Bird) originated in a mundane way (a fondness for chicken) but has come to symbolise the very force of creativity in the music itself (an ability to fly beyond the conventional boundaries and to soar into the realm of pure artistry). To capture this edge-defying magic of the Charlie Parker mystique visually, I offer this stereograph of a sea gull taking off from its perch on the pier at Gosman's Dock in Montauk. Such a stereo image of a fast-moving object is mechanically difficult to capture because both cameras must be triggered in perfect synchronisation. Here, though the rapid beating of the gull's wings makes them slightly blurred, the 3-D effect remains quite striking.

Past cares on the beach (Figure 3.8)

Dear Mr Duryea: This photo finds us at the eastern end of our trajectory between the Poconos of Pennsylvania and the beach at Montauk on the tip of Long Island's South Fork – where, again, we abandon the cares of the City to seek a littoral state of liminality at the edge of America. In this picture, Sally walks at the edge of the waves along the shoreline where the sand is damp but solid and the footing is most firm. Other beach-combers follow in her footsteps along the margin of the sand. Notice how the stereographic view emphasises the contours of the waves and the length of the shoreline that stretches into the background. The day is warm, the spot beautiful, the moment memorable. Please don't violate the integrity of our borders by selling your dock to a ferry service for purposes of transporting gamblers to a casino in Connecticut.

Figure 3.6 **Doe's heart is for Chet.** By the edge of the terrace at the Pocono house, this doe paused for over an hour to listen appreciatively to the lyrical trumpet of Chet Baker.

Positivistic code for research (Figure 3.9)

Dear Bobby and Alice: Please forgive me for my little interpretivistic 'paroxysm of self-expression'. Of course, I could have stated my appreciation of the beach at Montauk as a falsifiable hypothesis – namely, *H1*: people tend to walk where the sand is damp, not completely dry nor submerged under water. You will be happy to hear that, after setting up my camera to photograph Sally (as just shown), I tested this hypothesis systematically by continuing to photograph the next four people who passed. This empirical study shows a consistent pattern of walking in the manner predicted, thereby supporting my hypothesis and tending to corroborate the mathematically derived theory presented earlier. Further, the 3-D view draws our attention into the backgrounds of these pictures and shows that other people farther down the beach also pursue this intersubjectively verifiable walking behaviour.

Figure 3.7 **Post and bird with wings spread.** Metaphorically representing the musical flights of Charlie 'Bird' Parker, this sea gull takes off from its post on the pier at Gosman's Dock in Montauk.

Pose, carts, front, edges (Figure 3.10)

Dear Reader: In this photo, the author poses for you and shoots a picture of a window display from in front of his neighbourhood frame shop at the corner of 85th Street and Broadway. Figuratively speaking, carts of all sorts appear as reflections in the glass – two taxis, a van, the Boar's Head truck. But literally – and, again, littorally – the theme here concerns edges, boundaries of every description, the whole essence of a frame shop. Thus, each item in the window is framed, boxed, bordered, set off from its neighbours. But, reflexively, the central mirror frames a view of another mirror and, indeed, of that mirror reflecting itself. In the midst of all this, seen in true three-dimensional depth, the author stands with his camera and poses among the carts in front of the store with all its edges – indeed, a festival of edges framed by frames that are reciprocally framed by other frames – reflected in a mirror behind a boundary of plate glass that in turn mirrors aspects of the scene behind him (including buildings, the sidewalk, pedestrians, a garbage can, and the aforementioned motor vehicles).

Figure 3.8 **Past cares on the beach.** Having left the City behind, past caring about the world of everyday responsibilities, the author's wife walks along the edge of the waves on the beach at Montauk in the place where the sand is damp but solid and where the footing is most firm.

Could one find any more hyperreal pastiche-like juxtaposition of jostling images with which to encapsulate our concern for edges?

EDGES AND BRIDGES

The edges/bridges of Monroe County (Figure 3.11)

Dear Clint: Like you, I love to take pictures of bridges, covered or not. Often, bridges span the boundaries demarcated by rivers or streams between counties or states. Whereas you and Meryl enjoyed the beauties of Madison County (presumably named after the fourth president of the United States), our place in the Poconos is in Pike County which borders on Monroe County to the South (recalling the name of our fifth president). Small world, huh? But such verbal associations parallel the ways in which edges force us to build bridges to form connections. For example, when we return to New York from Pennsylvania, we must use one of the three bridges that cross the Delaware River into New Jersey (by contrast with our first president George Washington, who used a boat to cross the

Figure 3.9 **Positivistic code for research.** Pursuing the (neo)positivistic goal of hypothesis testing, the author shot four random photographs that tend to corroborate his theory concerning the merits of walking on the edge.

Figure 3.9 Continued

Figure 3.10 **Pose, carts, front, edges.** The author strikes a pose – between the carts behind and the window glass in front – to photograph himself among the festival of edges found in a frame-shop display.

Delaware but who nonetheless did succeed in having a famous bridge named after himself). This photo shows the smallest of the bridges crossing the Delaware – one so small that only a single vehicle can proceed across it at a given time. However precarious, edges and bridges work together to create possibilities.

Towed barge on the sludge (Figure 3.12)

Dear Clint: Hi, again. I'm back to point out the paradox that, even though edges and bridges work together to create possibilities, these boundary-spanning constructions may also run the risk of misleading us by distracting our attention from the meaningful events that transpire in the space below – that is, the rich phenomena that occur at the borders between one area and another and that thereby fall in the cracks between

Figure 3.11 **The edges/bridges of Monroe County.** The Pocono retreat is in Pike County, Pennsylvania, which borders on Monroe County to the South and on the Delaware River to the East; this bridge (only partially covered) crosses the Delaware to New Jersey, indicating how edges and bridges work together to create possibilities.

the edges. Very often, important insights manifest themselves at the edge so that bridges across boundaries may encourage us to gloss over the key distinctions and crucial differences that really matter. Such conceptual mishaps arise conspicuously in the cases of thinkers who ask, 'Isn't X really just nothing but Y?' where 'X' refers to whatever you are arguing from what you take to be a fresh perspective and 'Y' represents what they already happen to believe from their own entrenched position. As an example, consider the role of Subjective Personal Introspection (SPI) in Consumer Research. Clearly, SPI lies at the fringes of conventional social science (e.g. as a near neighbour to psychoanalysis). Equally clearly, it skirts the borders of postpositivistic social studies (e.g. as a close kin to conventional ethnography). Hence, those consumer researchers who try to build bridges between the more neopositivistic and more interpre-

Figure 3.12 **Towed barge on the sludge.** The commanding presence of this bridge spanning the Ohio River illustrates the danger of ignoring the important phenomena at the gaps between borders – in this case the activities of a coal barge on the polluted sludge-filled river below.

tivistic approaches often continue to disregard the potential contributions of SPI at the edge between the divergent viewpoints (e.g. as a form of autoethnography or participant observation performed on one's own life). Figuratively, this issue appears in this photo of the bridge that crosses the Ohio River between Wheeling, West Virginia and Bellaire, Ohio on the other side. Visually, we tend to notice the majestic expanse of the Wheeling Bridge. But the plunging depth of the stereographic image impresses us with the importance of events that occur *under* the bridge in the space *between* the two river banks – in this case, life on the river in general and the passing of a barge that carries coal (an industry on which Wheeling precariously depends for its increasingly shaky financial survival) and that proceeds down the sludge-filled stream (polluted by the onslaughts of human and industrial waste since time immemorial). Nice photo, huh? And I didn't even get to store my film in Meryl Streep's refrigerator.

Posts and ark under bridge: a bridge too far? (Figure 3.13)

Dear Mr Attenborough: The lesson learned at the Wheeling Bridge reminds us that, too often, a well-intentioned but misguided attempt to span boundaries by homogenising differences may cause us to ignore important distinctions – in which case, a 'Bridge Too Far' may become a 'Bridge to Nowhere'. Here, to illustrate figuratively, we find a footbridge

Figure 3.13 **Posts and ark under bridge: a bridge too far?** While the main visual interest appears in the interplay between three posts, three fishing vessels, and a small rowboat, this footbridge for pedestrians provides a path that leads nowhere.

for pedestrians across the marina at Ogunquit, Maine. Those with metaphorical feet of clay can focus on the small footbridge – pedestrian indeed – but all the visual interest lies in a parallelism between the three posts and the three fishing vessels plus the way that imaginary lines drawn from the leftmost (rightmost) post to the rightmost (leftmost) vessel intersect at the position of the small rowboat in between. A pedestrian preoccupation with the footbridge would encourage us to ignore all that.

Dolts carp at the text / foes harp on defects: a view from the bridge (Figure 3.14)

Dear RichElli: Since you refer to me as MoHo throughout your critique of my book on *Consumer Research* (in the 1996 *Irish Marketing Review*), I trust you will not mind if I reciprocate by calling you RichElli. By attacking Subjective Personal Introspection as falling beneath or beyond your neopositivistic standards for science, I fear that you have missed my

Figure 3.14 **Dolts carp at the text / foes harp on defects: a view from the bridge.** This reflexive stereoscopic image of a stereoscopic apparatus shows the view from a bridge-like observation deck that overlooks Niagara Falls.

central point – namely, that SPI is just one of many potentially helpful perspectives that we might bring to bear on the study of consumers, especially in light of my premises that sometimes things are worth saying merely because they are funny or otherwise entertaining and that always one should be gentle with the text. Unfortunately, as vividly illustrated by your review, when one abandons one's gentle sense of humour and resorts to critical harping or literal-minded carping, one loses the ability to listen accurately (the ACR luncheon) or to read intelligently (the role of cats as illustrative metaphors). Perhaps this photo makes the point more clearly in pictorial form by offering a stereoscopic view *of* a stereoscopic view of Niagara Falls – certainly one of the most dramatic edges one is likely to find. Here, the lesson is that a truly in-depth 3-D experience of the turbulent activity at this boundary between the USA and Canada depends on a fusion of at least two different perspectives into one integrated stereographic image. By insisting on your scientistically unidimensional picture of the world, I fear that you relinquish any hope for such three-dimensional insights. Figuratively, as indicated by the Mighty Niagara seen from the bridge of a nearby observation deck, when one steps over the brink of good sense, succumbs to the strong current of conventional thought, and plunges past one's intellectual depth, one may find oneself in a dangerous epistemological predicament comparable to the fate of a hapless swimmer about to plummet over the edge of a waterfall onto the treacherous rocks below. By contrast, the view is fine from the bridge this time of year. Wish you were here.

Posted bar to the beach (Figure 3.15)

Dear Melanie and Merrie: At the opposite extreme from the sort of pedestrian plodding represented by the Ogunquit footbridge – another name for which is 'triangulation', by the way – we find those exciting but dangerous voyages past the brink of the familiar, beyond the boundaries of the already known, and into the uncharted waters of imaginative experience. Those who wish to remain safe – like the small blonde girl standing at the edge of the beach – will heed the advice of the warning sign that bars access to swimmers. Others may long to escape such restrictions by sailing away on the small boat moored near the shore. Meanwhile, we suggest with some misgivings, the little girl – who obeys all the rules but thereby limits her horizons – will be safe but sorry.

Post, yardage and three bridges (Figure 3.16)

Dear Captain: Lost at sea, we must rely on another kind of bridge – namely, the type from which a captain steers the ship and from where he or she enjoys a commanding view of the greatest possible clarity, depth and breadth. Here, among the tangled yardage of three tugboats (representing

Figure 3.15   **Posted bar to the beach.** As a representation of conventional limitations to innovative approaches, this warning sign recommends the safety of sticking to familiar terrain on this side of the boundary to a world beyond.

the confused chaos of the world), we find a post (representing postmodernism) and three captain's bridges (representing clarity, depth and breadth of vision more than the spanning of boundaries). The latter difference resembles the distinction between a footbridge connecting the two banks of a narrow stream and a self-powered boat set loose upon the open seas. Translated into the terms of Consumer Research, the contrast parallels that between a qualitative study that struggles to maintain the conventional scientific trappings of neopositivism (written records, word counting, member checks, independent audits) and a more free-spirited approach that constitutes a real paradigm shift (say, a form of expression drawn without apology from the humanities). The latter possibilities involve greater dangers, but perhaps one must sometimes brave such risks – must sometimes venture beyond the edge – for the sake of progress.

Boat chartered for a watch (Figure 3.17)

Dear Odysseans: The contrast just noted highlights the major contribution of the project whose commemoration serves as an occasion for the present volume. As initially envisioned, like a whale watch, the Consumer

Figure 3.16 **Post, yardage and three bridges.** A post stands amidst the yardage for three tug boats, each of whose safety depends on the clarity, depth and breadth of a captain's view from its bridge.

Behaviour Odyssey intended to break from the moorings of conventional Consumer Research and to embark upon a liberated journey into the remote corners of Consumption in America. The original aims and aspirations for this adventure embraced an eager openness to new insights from unique visions. True, as the voyage proceeded from west to east – from Los Angeles to Connecticut, from left to right – the original pluralistic acceptance of alternative approaches, the intended flexibility concerning methods, the initial spirit of adventure, and the early imaginative thrust toward the arcane may have tended to fade somewhat as a new set of concepts, methods and aims gradually emerged and acquired some measure of prescriptive authority. Nevertheless, the basic thrust of the Odyssey illustrated one of those famous self-contradictions for which the Ethos of Postmodernism is justly celebrated – namely, the occasional need to depart from the optimality of 'Walking on the Edge' by pushing across borders, past boundaries, or beyond restraints and, yes, by flinging oneself recklessly into the Great Unknown in search of new, dangerous,

Figure 3.17 **Boat chartered for a watch.** As a parallel to the promise of the Consumer Behaviour Odyssey, this chartered cruise boat ventures into unfamiliar waters to watch for something potentially striking – the surfacing of a whale.

or even forbidden experiences. The demonstrable fact that, despite the ultimate conservatism voiced by some of its members, the Consumer Behaviour Odyssey has had such an important broadening influence on subsequent work in Consumer Research makes this a fittingly ironic and paradoxical place to end my series of Postcards from the Edge.

ACKNOWLEDGEMENT

The author gratefully acknowledges the support of the Columbia Business School's Faculty Research Fund.

4 Shoppers on the verge of a nervous breakdown

Chronicle, composition and confabulation in consumer research

Stephen Brown and Rhona Reid

ONCE UPON A TIME

On 13 October 1996, the following one-paragraph story appeared in the News Digest column of the *Sunday Times*:

> A shopper died yesterday in what police are treating as Britain's first trolley rage fatality. Gordon Edwards, 71, a retired businessman, clashed with another customer in the car park of a supermarket in Darlington, Co. Durham. A man was helping police last night.

Compared to the stories of national pith and moment that dominated the front page on that particular day – 'Irish farms buy BSE cows in cash scam', 'Government to ban handguns at home', 'Richard Branson joins exclusive club of Britain's billionaires' – the trolley rage episode doubtless merited its sketchy treatment. For most of us, the tragic events in Darlington necessitate no more than a rueful shake of the head or a spousal comment of the imagine-getting-that-angry-about-shopping variety. Indeed, like all back-page, single paragraph, human interest stories, the newspaper's portrayal of the Co. Durham contretemps raises more questions than it answers. What precipitated the altercation? Were trolleys actually involved? Why the car park? What does 'clashed with another customer' mean, exactly? The pedants among us, what is more, may pause to ponder on the 'helping police' euphemism. (Helping them with what? Their shopping? The trolley patrol? Traffic duty? Drug busts? Unarmed combat? Fabricating evidence? Incarcerating innocent people?) However, it is our contention that this slice of late twentieth-century life also raises a number of empirical and methodological questions for consumer research, around which the present chapter will attempt to construct an instructive tale.

In certain respects, the Darlington shopping tragedy should not come as a surprise to us. Since the mid-1950s we have been cognisant of the fact that many shoppers are shopping averse. Stone's (1954) pioneering study of 124 department store patrons famously identified four 'types' of shoppers: *economic*, those who are motivated by low prices or the prospect of picking up a bargain; *personalising*, individuals who place great reliance on their relationship with store personnel; *ethical*, people who feel a moral obligation to certain retail establishments, such as small, family-run businesses; and, most importantly for our present purposes, *apathetic shoppers*, those who have no real interest in, or actively dislike, shopping and appear to endure rather than enjoy the whole experience. The apathetic shopper, admittedly, was the smallest of Stone's four categories, but it still comprised 17 per cent of the total sample, a not insignificant proportion.

Like most pathbreaking publications, Stone's paper stimulated – and continues to stimulate – a plethora of imitations, modifications and extensions. A rich and varied literature on shopper 'typologies' or 'orientations' now exists. Researchers have identified a veritable host of weird and wonderful shopper types, ranging from 'sensualists' and 'quartermasters' to 'out-shoppers' and 'post-shoppers' (Table 4.1). Indeed, it is no exaggeration (well, okay, a little bit of an exaggeration) to state that there are almost as many types of shoppers as there are researchers in the field. Yet these exercises also highlight – almost without exception – the existence of the apathetic shopper. In many studies, such as those by Darden and Ashton (1975), Westbrook and Black (1985) and Audits of Great Britain (AGB) (1987), the apathetic shopper, or its terminological equivalent, comprises the single largest category in the classification. Clearly, the precise balance of shopper types is partly an artefact of each individual study – sample composition, categories of merchandise, analytical techniques employed, etc. – but the celebrated investigation by Lesser and Hughes (1986), which was based on a balanced, nationally representative sample of approximately 7,000 householders, also concluded that apathetic ('inactive') was the single most common shopping orientation.

Of course, the 'existence' of the apathetic shopper – our familiarity with this 'type', as it were – does not help us comprehend the shocking incident in Darlington, Co. Durham. If anything, it makes the appalling events *less* comprehensible, since anyone approaching the altercation from an academically informed perspective cannot fail to have had their preconceptions utterly confounded. After all, the term 'apathetic', with its connotations of indifference, passivity, neutrality and inertia, simply *does not equate* with the anger, the apoplexy, the emotional eruption, the incandescent 'trolley rage' that presumably precipitated the confrontation in the car park, with all its tragic consequences. Some post-structuralists may seek to explain our unpreparedness, our inability to anticipate such occurrences, in terms of the always uneasy relationship between word and world (i.e. the word we employ – apathetic – helps shape what we see, hence our surprise at the sheer depths of the emotions unleashed). But, like Baudrillard's (1995) notorious announcement that the Gulf War did not take place, such linguistic circumlocutions seem singularly inappropriate, not to say morally reprehensible, when someone is lying dead or mortally injured in a supermarket car park.

Table 4.1 Summary of principal shopper typologies

Author/date	Population	Gender	Sample size	Research format	Shopper types (%)
Stone 1954	Department store shoppers	Female – 100%	124	Questionnaire; cluster analysis	Economic (33) Personalising (28) Ethical (18) Apathetic (17) Indeterminate (4)
Darden and Ashton 1975	Middle-class suburban housewives	Female – 100%	116	Self-administered questionnaire; MANOVA	Apathetic (22) Demanding (9) Quality (19) Fastidious (15) Stamp preferer (12) Convenience (15) Stamp haters (8)
Moschis 1976	Cosmetic buyers	Female – 100%	206	Questionnaire; factor analysis	Specials (n/a) Brand loyal (n/a) Store loyal (n/a) Problem solving (n/a) Psycho-socialising (n/a) Name-conscious (n/a)
Williams, Painter and Nicholas 1978	Grocery shoppers	No reference to gender make-up: assume 100% female	298	Questionnaire; cluster analysis	Apathetic (20) Convenience (27) Price (27) Involved (11) Unclassifiable (15)
Bellenger and Korgaonkar, 1980	Adult shopper	Female – 69% Male – 31%	324	Self-administered questionnaire; discriminant analysis	Economic (69) Recreational (31)
Westbrook and Black 1985	Adult shopper	Female – 100%	203	Structured questionnaire; factor analysis	Shopping process involved (12) Choice optimising (18) Shopping process apathetic (20) Apathetic (10) Economic (31) Nondescript (9)
Lesser and Hughes 1986	Head of household	Female – 55% Male – 45%	6,808	Telephone interview; Q-factor analysis	Inactive (15) Active (13) Service (10) Traditional (14) Dedicated fringe (9) Price (10) Transitional (7) Convenience (5) Coupon saver (5) Innovator (4) Unclassified (8)
AGB 1987	Housewives	Female – 100%	Panel members	Questionnaires; cluster analysis	Caring and conscientious (20) Indifferent (21) Old fashioned (15) Healthy brigade (20) Hedonist (23)
Cullen 1990	Principal household shopper	Female – 75% Male – 25%	2,484	Postal questionnaire; factor analysis	Shopping affect (n/a) Economic (n/a) Apathetic (n/a) Shopping snob (n/a)
Kirk-Smith and Mak 1992	Financial services users	Mixed – unspecified	2,630	Questionnaire; factor analysis	Uninvolved (9) Pleasurists (23) Conserving carers (22) Belongers (24) Confident modernists (22)

IN A LAND FAR, FAR AWAY

Faced with the recent rise of trolley rage, we can in classic Hegelian fashion ('the Owl of Minerva takes flight at dusk') attempt to make retrospective sense of the phenomenon. We can concoct all manner of pseudo-psycho-socio-anthropo 'explanations', such as the pace of modern life, increased traffic congestion, the decline of good neighbourliness, violence on television, availability of video nasties and splatter movies, water fluoridation, coffee drinking, constrictive underwear, *fin de siècle* fever, extra-terrestrial activity, an artefact of newspaper 'silly-season' hoopla or, most plausibly perhaps, increased male participation in routine shopping expeditions (a comparative rarity in Stone's day), coupled with the accompanying masculinisation – the 'macho-fication' – of a hitherto feminised domain (Davies and Bell 1991).

Irrespective of hindsight insight, it is our belief that the tragic events in Darlington raise a number of important issues for consumer and marketing research. In the first instance, it is noteworthy that the trolley-rage syndrome was identified, not by cutting-edge consumer researchers, but by investigative newspaper reporters and front-line retailing practitioners (Everitt 1995; Tedre 1995; Thorpe 1996). While this may not come as a surprise to postmodern commentators such as Richard Rorty (1989) or Keith Tester (1993), who contend that literary genres like journalism, comic books and the novel offer more meaningful representations of human behaviour than the learned cogitations of ivory tower academics, it nonetheless remains an indictment of our sub-discipline, with its supposed expertise in, understanding of and sensitivity to consumption-related activities.

A second disconcerting implication is the simple fact that we have been aware of anti-shopping shoppers since the mid-1950s, yet this particular category of consumer has never been subject to detailed investigation. Granted, this academic neglect is partly attributable to the managerial thrust of much consumer research, in that the pursuit of reluctant or recalcitrant shoppers is considered rather less attractive – from a retail management standpoint – than attempts to tempt recreational shoppers, impulsive shoppers, compulsive shoppers, sybaritic shoppers and the like. (Ironically, a preliminary study undertaken by the authors suggests that antipathetic shoppers are comparatively price insensitive and, hence, a more profitable target market than individuals hailing from the 'expert shopper' end of the consumption spectrum.) Be that as it may, compared to the enormous intellectual resources we have devoted to 'shopaholics' and their manifold variants (d'Astous 1990; Elliott 1994; Valence *et al.* 1988), our comprehension of 'shopaphobic' consumers is woefully inadequate. Indeed, even if this appalling oversight were redressed in light of the Darlington incident, our academic endeavours seem forever condemned to fall into the too-little-too-late category.

The third, and in some ways the most profound, implication of the shopping catastrophe in Co. Durham pertains to methodological and epistemological issues. Part of the reason that we researchers have been caught unawares by the rise of trolley rage is the continuing predominance of the positivistic mind-set, with its emphasis on neutrality, objectivity, disinterestedness and emotionlessness. The fact, for example, that 48 per cent of people 'dislike waiting' at crowded checkouts, is perfectly legitimate in itself (East *et al.* 1994), but such findings – unfailingly reported in unadorned modes of expression – serve seriously to underplay the sheer depths of emotion that checkout hold-ups are now known to engender. True, the emotional side of the shopping experience has attracted the attention of several interpretive or post-positivist consumer researchers (a disreputable group of individuals, on the whole, who seem to spend most of their time playing peek-a-boo among the anorexic ruins of postmodernism). However, it is fair to say that the bulk of these studies concentrate on the hedonic, pleasurable side of consumer behaviour (Hirschman and Holbrook 1982; Holbrook and Hirschman 1982), or the negative consequences of having too much of a good thing (Hirschman 1992; O'Guinn and Faber 1989), or indeed the ascetic, puritanical thrill that comes from successfully resisting temptation (Babin *et al.* 1994; Hoch and Loewenstein 1991). When it comes to some people's outright dislike – their sheer hatred – of shopping, the consumer research cupboard is disconcertingly bare.

THERE LIVED A LONELY YOUNG WOMAN

The tragic events outside a Darlington supermarket, which warranted a single paragraph on the back page of the newspaper of record, thus symbolise the state of marketing and consumer research in general and the shopper typology literature in particular. This is not the place to make unseemly comparisons between the academic corpus and the corpse in the car park; between that awful outpouring of shopping-induced emotion and the emotional repression that characterises scholarly endeavour; between the man helping police with their inquiries and the lines of inquiry being adopted by consumer analysts; between the death of a retired businessman and the demise of an approach to business research that, to put it at its most charitable, is long past the age of retirement. Nor, for that matter, is it proper to attempt to draw parallels between the dreadful Darlington incident, which was considered an insignificant, almost unnewsworthy item, and the inconsequential, uninfluential character of most published marketing and consumer research (in the eyes of practitioners and policy makers, at least). It may be more befitting to regard our prefatorial supermarket story as a turning point, a new beginning, a symbol of the way forward for marketing and consumer research, rather than a mark of past mistakes, misdemeanours and misrepresentations.

In this respect, it is intriguing that we – and the media even more so – automatically describe the trolley-rage incident as a 'story'. Storytelling is one of the key features, if not *the* key feature of the latter-day post-modern turn within the academy. According to Hutcheon (1989: 54), for example, postmodern culture is 'essentially novelistic'. For Waugh (1992: 1), 'it carries with it wherever it goes the idea of "telling stories"'. Simpson (1995) describes the postmodern penchant for anecdote, aphorism, auto-biography, conversation, confessional and vignette as nothing less than an 'epidemic of storytelling'. McHale (1992: 4) maintains that 'story in one form or another, whether as object of theory or as the alternative to theory, seems to be everywhere'. And, none other than the diagnostician of the postmodern condition, Jean-François Lyotard (1989: 153), contends that 'the intelligentsia's function should not be to tell the truth and save the world, but to will the power to play out, listen to and tell stories'.

Storytelling, of course, can hardly be described as a recent invention. As Barthes (1977) rightly notes,

> The narratives of the world are numberless ... narrative is present in myth, legend, fable, tale, novella, epic, history, tragedy, drama, comedy, mime, painting (think of Carpaccio's *Saint Ursula*), stained glass windows, cinema, comics, news item, conversation ... narrative is present in every age, in every place, in every society; it begins with the very history of mankind and there nowhere is nor has been a people without narrative. All classes, all human groups, have their narratives, enjoyment of which is very often shared by men with different, even opposing, cultural backgrounds. Caring nothing for the division between good and bad literature, narrative is international, trans-historical, transcultural: it is simply there, like life itself.
>
> (Barthes 1977: 79)

Indeed, Jameson (1981: 13) goes so far as to make the essentially essen-tialist suggestion that 'the all-informing process of *narrative* is the central function or *instance* of the human mind.'

Just as humankind's storytelling propensity goes back to the very dawn of history, so too stories about storytelling are very long established. The tale is often told, for instance, that Aristotle staked a reasonable claim to be the first narratologist when he suggested, in the *Poetics*, that a play must have a beginning, middle and end. He also drew an important distinc-tion between 'story' and 'plot'; that is, between the events to be recounted and the way in which they are portrayed. A variation on this dichotomy (known as *fabula* and *sjuẑet*) was central to the work of the Russian Formalists, who did much to promote the study of narrative in the early years of the twentieth century (Berger 1997; Gibson 1996; Martin 1986; Tambling 1991). Narratology has since burgeoned into a thriving sub-disci-pline, which culminated (arguably) in the celebrated structuralist analyses of Propp, Greimas, Todorov, Genette and Lévi-Strauss among others. To cite but a couple of examples: Propp's (1958) famous study of a hundred Russian fairy tales found that, under the plethora of story-specific details, a limited number of basic plot elements were identifiable. Although no single story contained all thirty-one elements, these functions always occurred in an inviolate, preordained sequence. Lévi-Strauss (1968: 228), likewise, felt moved to formulate a universally applicable 'formula' for the structure of myths, albeit he prudently prefaced this 'law' with those time-honoured academic get-out clauses – 'approximate formulation' and 'need to be refined in the future'.

Despite the antiquity of the storytelling impulse and the enormous literature that now exists on the nature of narrative, it is not unreasonable to suggest that it is only within the past few years that storytelling has escaped its lit-crit. confinement. But broken out it most certainly has. As the merest glance across the extant intellectual landscape readily reveals, a literary transformation has occurred in all manner of academic disciplines, disciplines that traditionally orientated themselves towards the hard sciences – economics (McCloskey 1994), sociology (Chaplin 1994), anthropology (Benson 1993), politics (Horton and Baumeister 1996), geography (Brosseau 1994), psychology (Murray 1995), psychiatry (Phillips 1993), philosophy (Krell 1996), history (Callinicos 1995), legal studies (Posner 1995), media studies (Taylor and Saarinen 1994), organisation studies (Jeffcutt 1993) and education (Coles 1989). Indeed, it has been argued that the continuing popularity of the physical sciences is predicated, as much as anything, upon the astonishing storytelling skills of Stephen Jay Gould, Richard Dawkins, Roger Penrose and the veritable horde of latter-day scientific popularisers-cum-proselyters (Brockman 1995).

WHO DIDN'T LIKE SHOPPING

In our postmodern world of *petit recits*, it is perhaps not surprising that contemporary consumer research has drunk deeply and often from the storytelling well. In the early 1980s, for example, Levy (1981) contended that marketing researchers could use literary theory to help investigate the stories that consumers tell about products. To this end, he conducted six in-depth interviews, during which the informants were encouraged to recount family anecdotes concerning food preferences, and from which Levy was able to identify the various Lévi-Straussian myths – origin, emergence, migration, etc. – that inhered in these consumption-inflected narratives. In a similar vein, Durgee (1988) argued that the interview transcripts from the celebrated Consumer Behaviour Odyssey could be examined from a narratological perspective. Working on the definitional assumption that 'stories' have (a) a beginning, middle and end, (b) one or more protagonists, (c) obstacles to be surmounted, (d) improbable occurrences, (e) a degree of suspense over the outcome and (f) some sort of underlying moral message or homily, he succeeded in identifying over

300 such narratives in the Odyssey field-notes and classified them according to clearly identifiable stages of the consumption process.

In continental Europe, furthermore, Floch (1988) has interrogated the interview protocols of 400 French hypermarket shoppers and, in a *tour de force* of semio-storytelling literary explication, used them to help develop a new store layout, one which was radically different from the traditional arrangement of right-angles, grid-lines and serried ranks of monotonous display racks. Heilbrunn (1996), likewise, has employed the principles of narratology to examine the nature of the relationship between consumer and brand. Drawing upon Propp's seminal analysis of plot structure, he highlights how the four basic stages of the narrative chain – acquisition of competency, contract, performance and sanction – can be applied to ongoing contacts between the buyer and his or her preferred brand. In line with Propp, he argues that the various narrative functions need not occur in each and every purchasing occasion (straight re-buy situations, presumably, obviate the necessity for competency acquisition), albeit Heilbrunn also maintains – contra Propp – that the functions may fail to unfold in the same, preordained sequence.

Significant though the foregoing studies are and ample though the literature on consumer storytelling now is (Brown 1997), the foremost academic exponent of narratology remains Barbara B. Stern, a consumer researcher trained in literary theory. In addition to her pioneering analyses of advertising narratives (Stern 1991, 1994), she has undertaken a detailed investigation of the myths and rituals embedded within the annual Thanksgiving festival. Drawing upon an extant database of interview protocols (Wallendorf and Arnould 1991), Stern demonstrated that the events in each consumer story could be interpreted in terms of Northrop Frye's (1971) famous four-fold classification of narrative forms: *comedy* (joyful or happy occurrences); *tragedy* (sadness or wisdom related); *romance* (nostalgic, the way things were) and *irony* (tales with a twist in the tail). When combined with evidence from Thanksgiving-orientated advertising treatments, it was abundantly clear that 'even though consumer respondents do not set out to create works of literature, their stories do contain plots that are traceable to mythoi found in the oldest works of western culture' (Stern 1995: 184).

On a broader scale, moreover, the field of marketing and consumer research is literally replete with research techniques and findings that are rooted in narrative. Consider, for instance, the growing use of projective procedures, such as the TAT (thematic apperception test), which specifically require respondents to 'tell a story' about the behaviours under investigation (Aaker and Stayman 1992; Day 1989; Hassay and Smith 1996; Sherry *et al.* 1993, 1995). The critical incident technique, beloved by academics from the services marketing end of the spectrum, is highly literary in ethos, as is the analogous dramaturgical metaphor (Bitner *et al.* 1990, 1994; Czepeil 1990; Deighton 1992; Fisk and Grove 1996). Textual tropes suffuse the study of scripts, schemata and frames in memory (Alba *et al.* 1991; Baddeley 1990; Mick 1992); the relationship marketing literature is littered with quasi-evangelical organisational parables of the 'I was lost but now I'm found' variety (Heskett *et al.* 1994; Kanter 1994; McKenna 1992) and it is hard to conceive of more overtly fabulous artefacts than the countless case studies that punctuate each and every chapter of each and every marketing textbook. Indeed, it is profoundly ironic that Harvard Business School, having stuck with their renowned case study method throughout the whole of the 'modern' marketing era, should be debating its abandonment at the very time when storytelling is back in postmodern fashion (Lataif 1992; Linder and Smith 1992; Mintzberg 1992; Mitroff and Churchman 1992).

BUT THEN ONE FINE DAY

Another technique predicated on chronicle is the controversial 'subjective personal introspection' procedure, espoused by a number of leading consumer researchers. In essence, this involves the researcher reflecting on and analysing his or her own personal experiences pertaining to the topic under consideration and bringing them together in the form of an extended autobiographical essay. Although 'autoethnographies', as they are sometimes known, remain comparatively few in number, the procedure has been applied to the study of pastimes, collecting activities, sporting achievements, aesthetic appreciation, sexual proclivities, near-death experiences and shopping behaviours for both convenience and comparison goods (Gould 1991; Hirschman 1990, 1991; Holbrook 1986, 1987, 1995; Lehmann 1987; Pollay 1987; Reid and Brown 1996a, 1996b; Rose 1995). Variants on the methodology, what is more, have been employed with some enthusiasm and not a little success in propinquitous academic domains such as psychology, sociology and anthropology (Clandinin and Connelly 1994; Ellis 1991; Hixon and Swann 1993; Richardson 1994). In fact, it has become something of a cult in Literary and Cultural Studies, where the latter-day rise of 'autobiographical' or 'confessional' criticism – possibly as a reaction against the author-erasing excesses of post-structuralism – is very strongly marked and generating considerable intellectual excitement (Simion 1996; Veeser 1996).

Intellectual excitement, however, is not the expression that springs automatically to mind when the introspective corpus of consumer research is examined. On the contrary, the emergence of personal introspection as a potential research technique has proved highly controversial. So much so, it appears to have precipitated a deep schism within the ranks of the interpretive research community, a community that has only just succeeded in establishing itself as a credible counterweight to the positivistic orthodoxy. Although a number of voices have been raised in opposition (Campbell 1996; O'Guinn 1996; Uusitalo 1996), the foremost critics of introspection are Wallendorf and Brucks (1993). In a wide-ranging, not to say devastating, assessment, they contend that 'researcher introspection', as practised by Gould, Holbrook and several others, suffers from severe methodological shortcomings pertaining to: the time period concerned (i.e. the temporal relationship between the experiences being reported and the time of report); data specificity (the danger of generalised inferences rather than reports of specific instances); documentation (the extent to which introspections are recorded in a form accessible to others); sampling (how 'representative' is the introspector?); analysis (impossibility of establishing the necessary di-stance between informant and researcher); and the overall appropriateness of the procedure (why use introspection when other, less controversial, options are available?). For Wallendorf and Brucks, at least, the inadequacies of researcher introspection are so profound that the technique has little to recommend it, except as a means of accomplishing other, non-scholarly, essentially narcissistic, lamentably exhibitionist ends. Such studies, they conclude 'make for fun reading but may mislead readers if not based on sound, carefully thought-out and articulated methods' (Wallendorf and Brucks 1993: 356).

Needless to say, the champions of introspective approaches to consumer and marketing research have responded robustly to this challenge. Drawing upon an impressive body of supporting literature, ranging from rhetoric and romanticism to neo-pragmatism, Holbrook (1995, 1996) posits that personal introspection comprises the ultimate form of participant observation. While it is not without weaknesses, like all research methods, introspection provides a number of practical advantages in relation to fieldwork (easy), access (unrestricted), ethics (no formal accountability) and so on. In a similar vein, Gould (1995) contends that Wallendorf and Brucks's attempt to discredit introspection is both premature and unnecessarily restrictive. The technique offers depths of insight that are simply unobtainable from more established research methods. It focuses on rich and specific aspects of one particular consumer's life, benefits from the informant's incomparable self-awareness and is thus capable of contributing significantly to the theory building process. Indeed, in an otherwise critical assessment of introspection, as promulgated by Holbrook in particular, Campbell (1996) concedes that

> introspection is a legitimate method of inquiry open for use by any researcher or scholarly investigator, no matter what their discipline. To reject it out of hand on the pretext that it is 'unscientific' strikes me as particularly churlish if only because it should be obvious that the study of a wide range of phenomena is necessarily dependent on such an activity. Those who wish to investigate topics as various as backache, daydreaming, nostalgia, creativity and mystic enlightenment are all in the first instance dependent on reports that derive from introspection. To accept that such data are indispensable when originating

from 'subjects' but to deny it any value when it originates from 'researcher as subject' has always seemed to me to be a peculiarly inconsistent standpoint.

(Campbell 1996: 100)

An alternative, and in many respects much more radical, defence of introspection involves the abandonment of any aspiration to scientific status. As a consequence of its acknowledged lack of reliability, validity, objectivity and suchlike, researcher or personal introspection simply cannot qualify as a scientific method. However, this does not mean that the procedure is uninsightful. Quite the reverse. When judged by appropriately aesthetic criteria, such as those outlined in Table 4.2, the introspective essay comes into its own. Like the works of art that they undoubtedly are, well-written introspective accounts succeed in capturing the world in a grain of sand. They reverberate. They dazzle. They evoke an epiphanic 'A-ha, that rings true, *that's* the way it is' response in the reader (Bachelard 1994; Calvino 1986; Kundera 1988;). Introspections, in other words, do not represent the 'truth' in any absolute, neo-positivistic sense (an ambition that is unattainable in any event), but they are not necessarily unreliable, invalid or untrue either, at least not in aesthetic terms. While introspection can be justified on 'scientific' grounds, the very act of doing so concedes too much to the critics. It presupposes that scientific criteria are the most appropriate – in fact the only – criteria that can be applied or brought to bear upon the subject. This is simply not the case.

Energetic as the defenders of introspection undoubtedly are, and disparate though their attempted vindications have been, perhaps the most fundamental shortcoming of Wallendorf and Brucks's critique is the simple fact that certain aspects of it rely on personal introspection, the very procedure they rule out of court! Thus, when discussing the technique's alleged lack of distance between researcher and introspector, they assert – without any supporting evidence – that 'social scientists are likely to find it difficult to develop an etic interpretation of data about themselves' (Wallendorf and Brucks 1993: 351). As this statement can have been derived only from personal introspection on the authors' part, it must be deemed unacceptable according to their own evaluative criteria. More to the point, there is some evidence from the aesthetic domain which suggests that Wallendorf and Brucks's introspectively derived concerns about 'di-stance' are either mistaken or precipitate. Introspection, remember, is an important aspect of literary endeavour and, for some authors at least, the attempted separation of author and self (Rimbaud's *je est un autre*) is central to the creative process. As the postmodern author, Paul Auster (1995) brilliantly observes,

the more deeply I descended into the material, the more distanced I became from it. In order to write about myself, I had to treat myself

Table 4.2   Differences between scientific and artistic approaches to research

Criteria	Science	Art
Mode of representation	Formal statements; literal language	Non-literal language; evocative statements
Appraisal criteria	Validity paramount; unbiased methods of data collection and analysis; conclusions supported by evidence	Persuasiveness paramount; seek illumination, penetration and insight; arguments supported by success in shaping concepts
Point of focus	Concentrates on overt or expressed behaviour (which can be recorded, counted and analysed)	Concentrates on experiences and meanings (observed behaviour provides springboard to understanding)
Nature of generalisation	Extrapolates from particular to general; randomly drawn sample is deemed representative of universe and statistically significant inferences drawn about latter from former	Studies single cases and the idiosyncratic, but presupposes that generalisations reside in the particular, that broad (if not statistically significant) lessons can be learnt from the unique
Role of form	Results reported in neutral, unembellished manner (third person, past tense) and according to a standard format (problem, literature review, sample, analysis, implications)	Avoidance of standardisation; form and content interact; meaning of content determined by form in which it is expressed
Degree of licence	Factual emphasis; little scope for personal expression or flights of imaginative fancy	Subjective orientation; imaginative self-expression both permitted and expected
Prediction and control	Aims to anticipate the future accurately, thus enabling or facilitating its control	Aims to explicate, thereby increasing understanding; less algorithmic than heuristic
Sources of data	Standardised instruments, such as questionnaire surveys or observation schedules, used to collect data	The investigator is the principal research instrument and his or her experiences the major source of data
Basis of knowing	Methodological monism; only formal propositions provide knowledge (affect and cognition separate)	Methodological pluralism; knowledge conveyed by successful evocation of experience in question (affect and cognition combined)
Ultimate aims	Discovery of truth and laws of nature; propositions taken to be true when they correspond with the reality they seek to explain	Creation of meaning and generation of understanding; statements seek to alter extant perceptions about the world

Source: Adapted from Eisner 1985

as though I were someone else ... The astonishing thing, I think, is that at the moment when you are most truly alone, when you truly enter a state of solitude, that is the moment when you are not alone anymore, when you start to feel your connection with others ... In the process of writing or thinking about yourself, you actually become someone else.

(Auster 1995: 106–7)

HER FAIRY GODFATHER APPEARED

Irrespective of the cut and thrust of the introspection debate, it is clear that the decision 'to introspect or not to introspect?' is likely to remain controversial for the foreseeable future. There is no reason, however, why variants on the subjective personal introspection technique cannot be employed. Wallendorf and Brucks, after all, identified several different types of introspection in addition to the controversial self-report (researcher introspection) process. These comprise: *guided introspection*, where people other than the researcher are asked to introspect or think aloud about themselves and the resultant information is gathered as data; *interactive introspection*, where the researcher helps others introspect and, through a two-way sharing of experiences, enriched introspective insights emerge; *syncretic introspection*, a composite category involving introspective procedures that combine or fail to distinguish clearly between the procedures employed (combining researcher with informant introspections, for example); and, finally, *reflexivity within research*, where the researcher reflects on his or her participation in, relationship to and possible contamination of the data gathering process.

In the belief that personal introspection, for all its shortcomings, can provide meaningful information on consumption behaviour, the authors conducted a large-scale introspective exercise. A group of fifty-five, final year, undergraduate business studies students (53 per cent female; age range 20–30; mean 21.6 years) was asked to write extended autobiographical essays on any aspect of their personal shopping behaviour. Although the students had some familiarity with the shopper typology literature and standard qualitative research techniques, they had not been exposed to any published examples of subjective personal introspection. The students, moreover, were given no guidance or hints concerning the type of shopping expedition or expeditions to be described (everyday shopping, gift giving, Christmas shopping or whatever). They were merely invited, in the classic, primary school, what-I-did-on-my-holidays mode of discourse, to reflect on themselves as shoppers, to think about their own shopping experiences, to examine their emotional reactions, to evaluate their likes and dislikes, to contemplate the pleasures and pains of consumption, and to describe them in an expressive manner. In short, to write a composition on shopping.

Clearly, this approach does not fit into any of the five categories of introspection outlined by Wallendorf and Brucks. It is essentially researcher introspection writ large, albeit with a leavening of guided introspection. Hence, it suffers from many of the procedure's purported methodological flaws – memory effects, event selection, non-specificity and so on. Whether these are exacerbated or eradicated by the comparatively large sample size is an open question, the answer to which probably depends, as much as anything, on the extent of one's sympathy for the introspective approach. Set against this, however, it must be acknowledged that this compositional format is not dissimilar to the 'storytelling' process that inheres in analogous research methods – projective techniques, critical incident technique, narrative analysis and the like. The essential difference is that the introspective stories are written down rather than recounted to an interviewer. As Derrida (1976) makes clear, the western intellectual tradition has traditionally – and mistakenly – privileged speech over writing, what he terms *phonocentrism*. While tales told in a face-to-face situation may seem 'purer' or 'truer', thanks to the *metaphysics of presence* (the very corporeality of the speaking subject), they are not better than, nor preferable to, those communicated in writing. If anything, the reverse is the case, since the written version involves an extended process of personal reflection and self-interrogation, which arguably provides a deeper insight into human behaviour than even the longest of long interviews. More to the point perhaps, such spoken tales are invariably textually reproduced, mediated and transmitted in the course of the research process – interview transcripts, content analyses, written reports, published papers, etc. – and are thus irrevocably infected by writing, the very thing they are privileged over and have sought to suppress.

Given the comparative 'openness' of the essay writing guidelines, the students' ruminations exhibited considerable freedom, not to say richness, of expression. The introspections averaged 1,826 words (*s.d.* 635), which compares very favourably with the 250 and 400 word *maxima* reported by Rook (1985) and Hassay and Smith (1996) respectively, and pertained to a wide variety of shopping situations ranging from the trials and tribulations of the typical grocery store visit to the sybaritic delights of weekend shopping sprees in London or Dublin. In the majority of cases, the accounts concentrated on a single, specific shopping trip (75 per cent), with approximately one-third of the total being Christmas or special occasion related (e.g. wedding, birthday, new baby, etc.). The bulk of the reported expeditions involved the purchase of clothing and/or footwear, either for the essayist or their partner, though a small but significant number referred to errands, directed browsing and, that seemingly perennial pastime, 'shopping for nothing in particular'. Almost half of the trips were undertaken by car; approximately two-thirds involved other people, the principal accompanists being parents, siblings, acquaintances and, above all, boyfriends or girlfriends; brand names, as might be expected, were frequently and freely mentioned, as were the names of retail organisations. The maximum number of cited shops was fifteen (mode seven) and, unsurprisingly perhaps in light of the composition of the sample, Levi's and Benetton proved to be the most frequently named brands.

AND SAID THE MAGIC WORDS

In many respects, the most interesting aspect of the students' introspective accounts was their marked lack of enthusiasm for shopping. Around three-quarters of the sample reported some negative feelings or experiences, albeit the extent of resentment ran all the way from absolute abhorrence (24 per cent), through predominantly negative (25 per cent) to favourably inclined with irritating elements (25 per cent). Obviously, this incidence of ostensible distaste cannot be divorced from the nature of the sample. Students are notoriously strapped for cash and the manifold attractions of consumer society are denied them in the main. What's more, as a substantial proportion of the reported behaviours referred to Christmas shopping, with all its inherent stresses and strains, negative experiences are perhaps more prominent in this particular batch of introspective accounts than they would otherwise be. The sample, moreover, may have been slightly 'male-heavy', in that men, albeit a rapidly growing component of the consumer population, remain somewhat less shopping-orientated and considerably more shopping-averse than females. Likewise, the antipathy in the accounts may reflect the fact that many of the informants are *comparatively* inexperienced shoppers (living away from home for the first time, at a transitional life stage when personal appearance is particularly salient, etc.) and perhaps more uncomfortable than most with their manifest marketplace maladroitness.

Be that as it may, the introspections are remarkable for their sheer depth of emotional expression, not to say turmoil. The compositions are replete with words like 'angry', 'frustrated', 'vexed', 'irritated', 'anguish', 'torture', 'gutted', 'disgusted', 'detested', 'fed-up', 'ordeal', 'flustered', 'bothered', 'dread', 'hatred', 'horror' and 'annoyed'. Phrases of the 'about to explode', 'done my head in', 'got to get out', 'panic attack', 'blind fury', 'severely pissed-off', 'can't take any more', 'blow a fuse', 'approaching meltdown', 'losing the head', 'the final straw' and 'never again!' variety are a virtual commonplace. And references to 'nightmare', 'recurring nightmare', 'complete nightmare', 'worst nightmare', 'ultimate nightmare', 'absolute nightmare' and 'Nightmare on High Street' experiences are the rule rather than the exception.

On the basis of the introspective essays, two emotional states – one essentially inner directed and the other outer directed – are particularly salient. The former, embarrassment, is perfectly illustrated by the following mortifying incidents involving female shoppers:

The total button is activated and the cashier's uninterested voice drones out, '£52.67 please'. My eyes shoot open in an instant and I can feel the heat of my embarrassment cover my face in a flash. Immediately, I realise why the phrase 'I wish the ground would open up and swallow me' was coined. My feelings range from downright embarrassment to panic to humiliation, as I sheepishly explain to the cashier that I've only got £38.75.

(female, 21)

She had lifted a pair of Levi's off the shelf and asked me what I thought of them. When no response was forthcoming, she turned around to see a complete stranger standing behind her with a puzzled look on his face. Needless to say, by the time I saw it, her face was red. I thought this was all very amusing but she failed to see the funny side for a while.

(male, 22)

So, I did an about turn to leave the shop; but to my utter embarrassment my umbrella triggered off the alarm mechanism. My face fell as the army of staff advanced toward me. Futile, as I had no bags to search. I eventually marched off in high dudgeon, and thankfully immersed myself in the traffic flow heading into Marks and Spencer.

(female, 22)

The latter emotion, anger, is also much in evidence, as revealed by the explosive reactions of two tired and weary shoppers: the first on discovering that, thanks to her little sister's recalcitrance, the family's 150-mile round trip to Belfast had been in vain; and the second on being forced to indulge his girlfriend's predilection for browsing in greeting-card shops

I find the others leaving Dunnes Stores – empty handed. Then Joanne [little sister] makes her statement, 'I told you that the trousers and shirt I want are in Ultimate in Dungannon [home town].' I stare at her in utter disbelief. Then I lose my head. I shout at her and tell her I'm never taking her shopping again and then declare the whole day a total waste of time. By this time the shops are closing, so I'm furious. I go off to the car in a huff and don't speak to anyone until we get out of the city.

(female, 21)

The main thing on my mind as we left the sports shop was to keep Aideen away from the card shop, as she would read every card in the shop, stopping now and again to say, 'read this, isn't it lovely?' … I almost succeeded. I nearly had her by the shop when she broke ranks and was away like a bullet, through the entrance and had a card in her hand before I could do anything. Oh no, my worst nightmare has come true and at this stage of the day it *was* my worst nightmare. Next it was, 'Barry, come over to you read this.' 'Yes, Aideen, what is it?' (really enthusiastic). *Jingle Bells* on in the background and people pushing past each other to get a better look at the cards on view. Aideen was holding a rather large card with a winter scene on the cover. 'Isn't this lovely?' and she handed the card to me. I took a quick glance at the cover, read the first few words and handed it back. 'Yes, it's lovely.' Who cares? Then I asked who she was going to get it for and she turned and told me she was just looking, as she already had all her cards. This was the straw that broke the camel's back. I just felt like exploding. I was not going to last much longer.

(male, 22)

For the most part, however, the essayists endeavour to keep their emotions in check. It would appear that lips are constantly being bitten, ten is routinely counted up to and, beneath the polite surface of 'sorrys', 'pardons' and 'excuse mes', an inferno of frustration, irritation, exasperation and, above all, suppressed or unexpressed hostility rages.

As I was walking back to the holiday apartments with my girlfriend, after another gruelling and fruitless shopping expedition in that revolting heat, the only thing that made me feel better was the reflection that, had I had a gun on me, I would by now have shot at least three people.

(male, 22)

I was seated in the no-smoking section and just as I started to eat, a woman at the table beside me lit up a cigarette and eagerly smoked away at it, without any consideration for anyone else in the no-smoking section. I would have asked her to put it out, but just didn't have the nerve. I finished my meal and left quietly, throwing her a dirty look as I walked past her.

(female, 21)

After I had left I could hear myself telling those assistants what I thought of them. I felt like telling them that they were being paid to serve me. I was shown no courtesy whatsoever and was extremely annoyed. I realise now that I should have complained to someone in charge but at the time I was tired, hungry and had a sore head and just wanted to go home and put my feet up.

(female, 22)

When we walk outside again to join the stampede, I receive a whack on the leg from someone's bag and am almost tripped by a pram. The mother then says, 'Oh, I'm sorry.' I turn around and reply politely, 'That's okay', but deep down I think, I just wish people would watch where they are going and not walk along with their eyes shut!

(female, 22)

In addition to the sheer depth of emotion that shopping experiences engender, and the process of constant self-control that they necessitate, the volatility of the informants' emotional states is striking. As we shall see, perfectly ordinary shopping expeditions can quickly degenerate into hellish ordeals, from which there is no escape. Conversely, a disappointing day can be rescued, and the shopper transported to a state of acquisitional euphoria, by the most minor acts of consuming courtesy or shopping accomplishment, such as a friendly shop assistant or getting a bargain. Indeed, it is clear from the essays that, contra the extant academic literature which seeks to identify, classify and enumerate distinctive 'types' of shopper, the students' shopping orientations are not clear cut or stable, but highly contingent, situation specific and the outcome of a host of interacting factors. Many of the informants specifically refer to themselves as a complex, mutable amalgam of shopper 'types'.

> One word could not describe the type of shopper that I am. I am not only compulsive but also impulsive, erratic and indecisive. I am a mixture of different types of shopper rolled into one.
>
> (female, 21)

> In general I would say that I am an apathetic shopper, an economic shopper, an ethical shopper and finally a personalising shopper. Therefore, if Stone were to use me as an example in his research, he could not classify me into just one of these categories, because my attitudes towards shopping and my shopping behaviour change extensively depending upon the item which I am looking for, who it is for, the type of weather it is, my shopping companion, how busy the shops are etc.
>
> (female, 21)

For our present purposes, however, these contingencies and multiple shopping 'selves' can be summarised in terms of Belk's (1975) famous five-category framework of situational consumer behaviour – *physical surroundings, social surroundings, task definition, antecedent states* and *temporal perspective* – though it must be emphasised that, in practice, the categories are neither clear-cut nor independent. The framework (which was not imposed upon but emerged from the data) merely provides a convenient means of structuring our extended discussion.

SHOP 'TIL YOU DROP

As might be expected, and as the academic literature suggests, the physical surroundings of the retailing environment have a significant impact upon the character and quality of the shopping experience (Bitner 1992; McGoldrick 1990; Pieros and McGoldrick 1993). Badly designed or poorly laid out stores are particularly off-putting, as are overpowering smells, substandard signage and oppressive heat.

The Globe and The Reject Shop suffered the same problem – there was no indication of where in the shops they had put anything. They both seemed to be very mixed up. For example, in The Reject Shop there were shelves of glasses displayed in three different parts of the store, which made shopping there very confusing for me.

(male, 22)

The shop is bunged, hordes of people everywhere, hot and sweaty and hard to move. The truth be told, there were only about 40 people in the store but as the store layout is so appalling in Easons, this is what it felt like. Whoever designed the aisles really needs a good size nine boot up the kyber.

(male, 23)

As I walked through the door I felt immediately suffocated by the strong smell of perfume which greeted my arrival. On any normal day this would have been enough to put me back out of the shop. However, perfume was the sole reason that I had gone into the shop, as this was my intended present for my sister.

(male, 22)

I love going into clothes shops like Top Man and Parks. The one fault all clothes shops have is that when I am trying on clothes, the shops are too warm and stuffy and it is very unpleasant. I break out in a sweat and feel trapped. I always end up saying, 'Why did I do that when I know what will happen?' I just keep forgetting. I get into a fluster and that makes it worse.

(male, 21)

No less irritating is retailers' choice of in-store music, which is either the wrong type, old-fashioned, too loud, over-familiar or crassly commercial. Their predilection for relocating the merchandise without warning, especially in supermarkets, is guaranteed to drive certain consumers into a bullet-spitting frenzy. Window displays are considered indicative of the calibre of shopping experience to be found therein, as are fixtures and fittings. Carrier bags, furthermore, are a constant source of frustration. They are too small, too heavy, too painful on the fingers and palms, too liable to burst open without warning and, not least, an all too easily decoded signifier of the downmarket shops patronised by the undiscerning.

While standing waiting for my turn, the grim realisation dawns on me that the chronic Daniel O'Donnell song that was playing leads to yet another chronic croon in his dulcet tones. My worst nightmare has come true and I can't escape the Daniel O'Donnell compilation tape until I have finished my shopping. What an incentive to move quickly – who is responsible for this dire taste in music?

(female, 21)

I frantically run up and down the aisles, running round in circles. Typical, they have moved all the stuff around again. I hate the way they change everything around so you can't find anything. It is so frustrating.

(female, 22)

Where will I go first? I looked in a few windows and thought, 'Oh no, I'm in trouble.' If there is nothing in the windows there will be nothing in the shop and that's the way things go.

(female, 21)

Our trip begins with a bee-line to American Madness, one of two retail outlets where I prefer to buy jeans and whose plastic bags are 'cool' to be seen with. I have found these bags also come in handy in times of sheer desperation, when I have found myself in 'not so cool' shops such as Chicago and Playgirl, as I can disguise my purchase in a trendier bag and just hope nobody I know has seen me coming out of the shop.

(female, 22)

Of all the elements of the physical environment, however, perhaps the most frustrating are changing rooms and shopping trolleys. Communal variants of the former are universally reviled and, even when individual cubicles are provided, these are unfailingly small, cramped and overheated, with trick mirrors, a dearth of pegs and curtains that conspire to leave a yawning gap, through which passing voyeurs can catch a less than titillating glimpse of threadbare underwear, unshaven legs and unsightly rolls of fat. It is little wonder that many people buy clothes without trying them on, even though a wardrobe full of ill-fitting and unworn outfits is the inevitable outcome.

When shopping for clothes I might look around for hours and chat about clothes till I am blue in the face, but when it comes to trying them on in the shop I tend to be in and out of the changing rooms in 5 seconds. It seems strange but I have a kind of fear of changing areas. It's like the curtain doesn't pull the whole way across, I might have smelly feet without shoes on and I more times than not start to feel intense heat and sweat like mad. I don't think I can get my original clothes on quick enough, no matter how nice the new ones are. I can take a guess and say I bought a lot of clothes without actually seeing them on me in the shop!

(male, 21)

Fortunately, most of the cubicles were empty and I had the opportunity to try several before finding one where the curtains aspired to cover more than 70 per cent of the gap. A single hook was thoughtfully provided on which to hang my coat, jumper, jeans and the yet to be purchased suit. My own clothes were consigned to the floor. With a gap of about two inches either side of the curtains, I felt but failed to look like a Chippendale with stage fright. Then, thankfully, it was all over and two discoveries had been made. The jacket was too small and the trousers too big. I couldn't go through it again. A larger jacket and smaller trousers were chosen, then I approached the till.

(male, 22)

The things that sort of exasperate me about shopping include ... changing rooms that are communal (who wants to see my grotesque body?), are too small (I have acquired countless bruises while trying to demolish minuscule cubicles), have curtains that must have shrunk in the wash and I am convinced that the mirrors are different from the one in my bedroom, because I certainly look different in them.

(female, 20)

Similarly, shopping trolleys are demonstrably an alien species intent on the slow but steady extermination of the shopping population through an epidemic of twisted backs, bruised ankles, crushed feet and coronary thrombosis induced by decades of raised blood pressures. It is generally acknowledged that trolleys have minds of their own, make decisions on the route to be followed around the store and develop psychosomatic ailments like wobbly, dead or squeaky wheel, but only after entering the retail establishment (such symptoms are *never* exhibited in the car or trolley park). What's more, they obstinately refuse to be de-coupled from their companions, even when the requisite monetary deposit is inserted, and on taking possession of certain vulnerable categories of consumer – the old and the young in particular – they are especially dangerous. They slow down, speed up, won't stop, veer suddenly, block aisles and ram innocent bystanders amidships. Like bucking broncos, trolleys have to be broken and often physically abused before deference, docility and a sense of direction are established, restored or imparted.

Right, here goes – quick check to see if I have cash and a pound coin for the trolley. These stupid trolleys never work as I try a few and finally find one that didn't require the consumption of three Weetabix to push it.

(female, 23)

When I put the £1 coin in the slot for the trolley, it would not release. By this time, I was getting angry and could not wait to get home and put my feet up. I went to a different trolley and thankfully this one released. When I got into the supermarket to do the shopping, I found that the trolley I had picked would not wheel in a straight line, but I persevered with it, as I could not be bothered going outside to change it. As more groceries are put into the trolley, it gets heavier and harder to steer. I wished then that I had changed it. I tried desperately to dodge old women and women with screaming babies in prams who think that they own the supermarket, as they occupy the whole breadth of the shopping aisles ... Time after time, I become more tempted to bang into them with my trolley to make them realise that they are not the only people in the supermarket. The only thing that stops me is the fact that I know how sore a bump with a trolley can be, as some silly mothers let their children wheel the trolley and they bang into everything.

(female, 21)

We eventually get our trolley and it seems to be quite co-operative. As soon as we enter the supermarket, the trolley begins to squeak and yes, you've guessed it, the wheels have minds of their own, oblivious and uninterested in what way I may wish to go – Oh no, we've hired the trolley from Hell! As we stand and plan our route of attack, I receive a sharp dig in the ankles from a trolley being badly navigated by a granny with a semi-satanic grin on her face. 'Sorry', she mutters, then off she shuffles ... The next stop is the meat counter. As we go towards our destination, the trolley from Hell seems to have its own ideas and veers off in the direction of the cereal display. Just missing by inches, we gently persuade the trolley to come round to our way of thinking by giving it a good hard kick. I do not know if this treatment did the trolley any good but it sure made me feel better.

(female, 21)

Retail, we are often informed, is detail and it is only to be expected that the above issues – combined with colour schemes, clean toilets, lighting effects, display racks, doorways, flooring materials, ticketing systems, etc. – are noted by and loom large in the minds of consumers. However, the introspective essays also indicate that the overall atmosphere or gestalt of retail establishments is negatively or positively responded to by the informants. A general, almost indefinable, sense of liking or disliking, of comfort or discomfort, of belonging to or excluded by, of being in or out of place is very strongly marked.

I always judge a shop by its appearance and only if it looks like 'me' will I enter.

(female, 20)

As she wandered about looking at the latest 'fashion' offered by Next, I stood nodding approval now and again, but beside this I felt somewhat out of place. She picked, I paid, only too gladly. Anything to return to the comfort of the street.

(male, 20)

We eventually reach Roger's, which is probably my favourite shopping destination and where I buy most of my clothes ... I feel more comfortable as I browse through the selection of clothing within this environment, as the sales person never seems to take much notice of you, however doing so in a nice way. Due to this comfortable feeling, I tend to take more time to browse and to try on clothes.

(male, 22)

Everything about this store makes me feel paranoid and gives me knots in my stomach, more severe than anything I've ever experienced before. This may sound like a gross exaggeration but take it from me, the term 'in-store atmospherics' takes on a whole new meaning and suddenly meeting Freddie in the land of Nod is a credible alternative.

(female, 22)

This sense of feeling welcomed or cold-shouldered by a store, affected as it is by the perceived price, selection, exclusivity, range and depth of merchandise, gives rise to a virtually instantaneous assessment of an outlet's suitability or otherwise and the associated decision to patronise or bypass. The same is true of the merchandise itself, footwear and clothing in particular, which is expected to 'catch the eye' of the consumer. As Rook (1985) has demonstrated, an instant, magnetic, almost animal attraction – love at first sight – seems to prevail in the lonely hearts column of consumption. And when the magic isn't there, even the most well-stocked and appointed outlets are dismissed as 'having nothing' or with some variation on the old line, 'there was nothing in the shops'.

I made my way through the crammed maze to the portable CD section, in a small section of the store, and looked at the selection they had on offer. This on the whole was very limited and to be honest it looked as if it had just been thrown onto the chipboard shelves. Straight away, I knew I wasn't going to purchase anything here.

(male, 21)

Walking through the doors of this shop was really like stepping out onto a building site . . . I glanced at the barren rails and quickly realised that I was wasting my time here.

(female, 22)

First port of call was River Island, no particular reason, it just happened to be one of the first clothes shops that I passed. A surprise then that I found exactly what I was looking for. Well, not exactly. To be honest, it wasn't even close. But it was too late, I was in love.

(male, 22)

We wander into the first shop, Principles. I browse around but unfortunately nothing catches my eye, not even any possibilities. Not a good start, I think to myself . . . However, as soon as I walk through the door of Brazil, a brown jacket on display screams out for my attention, assuring me that it would match my skirt.

(female, 22)

SO SHE SHOPPED AND SHE SHOPPED

The personification that characterises shopper–shop and customer–product relationships is remarkable enough in itself, but it is reinforced by the comparative impersonality of person–person interactions and the generally anti-social nature of the social surroundings. One of the most distasteful aspects of the reported shopping experiences is other people, both en masse and individually. Crowds of 'bloody people', none of whom look where they are going, are especially hateful, as is the associated hustle and bustle, pushing and shoving and all-round chaos and disorder (Eroglu and Machleit 1990). Busy shops are described as 'cattle markets'; an irrational mob mentality seems to reign; panic attacks are narrowly averted or succumbed to; and a fight or flight propensity is all too apparent (the fighters scratch and elbow with the best of them, whereas the flighters retire from the fray and wait, usually with a cup of coffee or cigarette, for the crowds to subside).

> After that, we went to Index near Cornmarket, which was packed full of people of all sorts, in what was a cramped and very hot atmosphere, in what could only resemble a cattle market which was doing my head in. So, after choosing a suitable razor for her brother, we proceeded to the front desk which was crammed full of people grabbing their goods and then pissing off as soon as they could, to get out of the bollocks of a mess they were standing in. It was a mad scramble, with people from all backgrounds going absolutely mad.
>
> (male, 23)

> Looking at the crowds that were swarming through the store, I knew that this was not the place for me. What could I do? I spent two minutes in the store and then had to get the hell out of the place before someone ran over the top of me in a panic to reach the counter.
>
> (male, 20)

> They say good things come in small packages, but when you find yourself in what feels like a herd of cattle and behaves in a similar fashion, somehow those words of wisdom lose their value and provide no consolation whatsoever. However, I've discovered a wonderful defence mechanism when I find myself in a situation where crowds are inevitable. I define it as the art of shoving, and find it very effective indeed!
>
> (female, 20)

There is, admittedly, a lighter side to the exhausting shopping scrum, most notably the elaborately choreographed ritual of avoidance and mis-read side-steps that ensues when head-on collisions seem inevitable, but the general rule appears to be that no matter what direction you are headed, the majority of people are going the other way.

When I eventually arrived at The Games Zone, I was pleasantly surprised that I had avoided the Droitwich Street Dance. In this street dance the two partners approach from opposite directions and try politely to get out of each other's way. They step to the left, step to the right, apologise, left again, right again and bump into each other, and this is repeated as often as unnecessary.

(male, 23)

On our way there I notice yet again that everyone who goes shopping in the centre of town must be blind, except me. This is the only explanation I can fathom for people walking straight toward me, with myself always being the one to take evasive action in order that I'm not trampled to death. This phenomenon is something which I have observed over many years and something that really pisses me off.

(male, 22)

Regarding pedestrian flow, the only type of flow I seem to encounter when shopping is that which is going in the opposite direction to me. I feel like I'm fighting a force field in order to break through the barrier to space – open space.

(female, 21)

Seething though this mass of shoppers undoubtedly is, it is not undifferentiated. On the contrary, it is composed of constituent parts, some of which are more lethal than others. The least-wanted list is many and varied, though old age pensioners, courting couples, parents with children and diverse street people ride high in the rankings of numerous informants. Pensioners are too slow, too deliberate, too cantankerous, too judgemental or just too old to be allowed to roam freely, while courting couples are too much in love with being in love for some onlookers.

And finally . . . it's Supergran steering her little 'shopper on wheels' at an unbelievably slow pace. Has she stopped or is she still moving? Only one way to go – forward. I carefully go to overtake her, trying not to disturb or disrupt her. But, no, at the most awkward moment in time, Supergran decides that she shall take off too, right across my runway. Bang. One injury. Supergran's shopper basket. 'Youngsters today, you have no respect.' 'I'm very sorry, it was an accident. I didn't mean to . . .' 'No respect whatsoever. In my day . . . blah, blah, blah.' Please God, no. I really could not bear another 'In my day, children knew their place' speech. How am I going to escape from the grasp of Supergran the storyteller?

(female, 21)

I do not know how anybody else feels but one of my biggest dislikes is courting couples when I go shopping. They are everywhere – holding hands, smiling, batting their eyes at one another, licking one another's tonsils, as if there is no tomorrow. Boys kissing girls, girls kissing boys, boys kissing boys and girls kissing girls – it is enough to make you throw up. There is a time and a place for everything. High streets and shopping centres should ban these individuals, or throw a sack over them.

(male, 21)

Parents, similarly, seem to think that the sun rises and sets on their disobedient children; act as though the streets and footpaths are for their own exclusive use (and woe betide anyone who disagrees); refuse to control their loathsome offspring when they are tormenting everyone within earshot or sticky-fingered grabbing distance; and, when they do institute the necessary disciplinary measures – or, conversely, capitulate to their unreasonable demands – merely succeed in compounding rather than resolving the problem.

Top of my [hate] list is parents, especially mothers, with prams. They think they have the right to walk straight ahead and that myself, and every other shopper, has to move and twist their way around *them*. If I don't move for them and accidentally collide with them, I can be 100 per cent sure I will get tutted at and told to 'watch where I am fucking going'. They think they own the footpaths.

(male, 21)

I always feel sorry for the poor mothers who have to cope with screaming kids that are trying to demolish the sweets at the counter. I hate spoilt wee brats that throw temper tantrums in public.

(female, 21)

Placing them in my rather cumbersome basket, I made my way to the check-out. At the end of the aisle I heard a mother brashly scold her son for demanding sweets and she suggested that he 'shut his bake'. I am sure the wails of the child could be heard all the way up to lingerie.

(female, 22)

The streets, in fact, appear to be lined with collectors, vendors, barkers and hucksters of all sorts, who are as one in their desire to fleece the unwary shopper. Our essayists, fortunately, are cognisant of their wiles, ploys and sales pitches, and resolve not to be waylaid or duped.

Save the whales? Not today, thank you. Save me please from the vultures trying to claw every last penny out of me. Today, there is no chance. I shall not be pressurised. I am on a mission and am on my way.

(female, 21)

As always, the entrance to Castle Court shopping centre is carefully guarded by the demons of the rattling tin. As I tactfully avoid this request for money, probably for skateboards for the disabled or some worthless political organisation or even worse a student organisation, I do wonder how much of my money would have gone to the so-called needy anyway.

(male, 23)

I barely walk a few steps when I have a collection box pushed into my face for some charity appeal, the name of which I am unable to read. Almost grudgingly, I fumble in my pocket for a few coins.

(female, 22)

Alongside the overall madness of the marketplace, with its socio-pathic-cum-mendicant sub-groups, there is a more specific anti-social side to the social surroundings. This pertains to the incomprehensible, inexplicably infuriating and utterly bizarre behaviours of individual consumers (McGrath and Otnes 1995). These are the people who cause delays when everyone else is in a hurry, who imperiously block the aisles with their shopping trolleys or coven of confidants, who can't make up their minds, who push and shove but don't apologise, who are unspeakably rude, nosy or unfriendly and who not only have more money and less taste than the essayists, but also turn out to be the very people they least want to meet – ex-girlfriend, old school teacher, next-door neighbour, estranged relative, etc. – albeit the ritual of avoidance occasionally involves both parties.

As the store had only opened at the start of the week, it appeared to be still suffering from what I would call the 'curious shopper syndrome'. No!, let's be honest!, it's the Nosy Bastard Problem. You know the sort, the assholes with no intention of, perish the thought, actually buying anything. No!, they're there to further infuriate those of us trying to make purposeful progress through the store.

(male, 22)

Every Friday night I faithfully set the alarm for eight a.m., with the intention of being in town for nine. The reason for this early start is that Cookstown is descended upon by a horde of farmers' wives and their children (of which at least ten per cent will be wearing shell suits) ... One thing that is typical of [these] housewives is that they are unbelievably nosy. They spend most of their time looking into other people's baskets and talking to themselves as they go round the shop. I refuse ever to end up like this.

(female, 21)

Unfortunately, whilst making my way from the start to the finish of the supermarket, I undoubtedly will encounter at least one of my aunties, to whom I no longer speak, but then every family has its squabbles. These encounters typically involve both parties pretending to be extremely interested in the items on the lower shelves.

(female, 21)

Needless to say, the crucible of these hateful personal encounters is the
checkout queue, although queues for changing rooms, toilets, car parks
and delicatessen counters are almost as horrid. Apart from the well-
known, frequently observed and extremely irritating, yet almost inevitable,
fact that the 'other' queue always moves faster, a prolonged period of
close personal contact with ill-mannered, ill-bred and occasionally
malodorous individuals is an exercise in endurance that many shoppers
prefer not to undergo. Checkout psychosis is redoubled when the store is
badly laid out, the tills are understaffed, idle shop assistants look on, other
shoppers abuse the unwritten code of checkout conduct, such as paying
by personal cheque, and, as often as not, by the fact that the person one
wants to avoid at all costs is immediately in front or behind.

> Messages gathered, I face another dilemma – checkout queues. Which
> queue should I join? I feel due to having only six items, the 'ten or
> less' is my best bet. Bad move. As I stand at the 'express checkout', I
> cannot help but notice that every single other queue seems to be moving
> at a much faster pace than my own. Trolleys of goods are being scanned
> at a heightened pace, leaving the 'baskets only' eating their dust.
>
> (female, 21)

> Now came the fun bit, trying to pay for the goods and leave. The queue
> stretched half way up the middle aisle and to say it was moving slowly
> would be a gross understatement. There were children in front of me
> crying about getting home in time for Christmas and the old lady behind
> was asking for volunteers to witness her last will and testament.
>
> (male, 22)

> We finally make the choice of checkout, taking our position in the
> queue which seems to be moving the quickest. Surprisingly enough
> though, as soon as we join the queue, the other checkouts seem to
> move quicker than ours, which appears to have come to a standstill.
> Why does this not surprise me?! There is just one person to go. Hooray!
> We wait with bated breath, it's nearly our turn, the prospect of leaving
> this hell-hole is near. The woman's goods are totalled, it's time for her
> to pay, a minute from now we'll be unpacking our goodies. Suddenly,
> a cheque-book is slammed on the counter. CHRIST!!! Why can't people
> pay by cash? It's so much quicker, I mean this is the era of Switch.
> The processing of the cheque seems endless and I start to develop quite
> evil tendencies towards the woman in front of me. She moves away
> with her trolley of goods, escaping her unknowing death – narrowly.
>
> (female, 21)

Reaching the head of the queue is no relief either, since this is the point
when things *really* start to deteriorate. Payment proves problematical, the
tills have temper tantrums, other, more attractive merchandise is spotted
but can't be obtained without leaving the queue, or something untoward

occurs which either means having to go through it all again or succeeds only in antagonising the people behind. Rather than cope with such hostility and torment, it is hardly surprising that many people prefer not to make a purchase if a long wait is in prospect or simply choose to take their custom elsewhere.

By the time Sharon and I reached the front we went to one of the two tills in operation, and the cause of the hold-up became apparent. The checkout system was not your straightforward, electronic-point-of-sale scanner, but instead a computer system which required codes from each item to be entered manually. Fine for stock control and other management objectives, but not a lot of good to the discerning Christmas shopper.

(male, 22)

I went to the cash desk to pay for my dress. The person behind the counter looked very worried. 'We are having a few problems with the till,' she said, 'it should only take a few minutes to fix.' Great, it could only happen to me, I thought! Ten minutes had passed and the four people who had congregated around the till still could not get it to work. Why do I like shopping so much, I thought to myself? One of the assistants behind the counter suggested that everyone in the queue should go to the back cash point and pay. I got to the back of the shop eventually, after dodging the crowds. When I got to the cash desk it seemed that all the customers who were behind me before were now in front of me.

(female, 21)

To be honest, I have lost count of the number of times that I have found something in a shop that I consider to be perfect for someone, then looked at the queues, set it back down and walked out of the shop. I love looking around shops, and shopping in general, but I will have to admit to having pet hates, one of which is standing in long queues. Another reason for this is that I get so bored standing waiting in inexorably long queues, that I gaze around the shop, lo and behold, there is the perfect present for Aunt Matilda. But, there is no way on this earth that I am leaving this queue, which by this time has stretched twice around the shop, to get the item. This must be the ultimate frustration, and I will end up saying to myself, 'I just cannot be bothered. I'll get her a pair of tights!'

(female, 20)

If queues at checkouts and analogous points of consumer congestion are generally regarded with a degree of resigned fatalism – when things move unexpectedly quickly, it is a wonderful, life-enhancing bonus – there are two social imponderables of paramount importance. Indeed, it is no exaggeration to state that the overall outcome of a shopping expedition often hinges on sales assistants and shopping companions. The former, in the main, are a major source of consumer discontent (Thompson *et al.* 1989, 1990). They are either excessively pushy, alighting on the hapless shopper before he or she has had a chance to take stock of the stock and come to a tentative decision, or they are utterly indifferent to the customer's plight, preferring to chat among themselves rather than perform the duties for which they are paid.

> The first shop I entered was a local men's clothing retailer named Fosters for Men. I'd heard of its reputation of having pushy sales staff but this was laughable. As I entered, I felt like I was being watched by hungry beasts who were ready to pounce on their prey. Every item I stopped to check the price or material of, I heard a voice behind me saying, 'That's good looking', or something to that effect. I just shrugged these remarks off.
>
> (male, 21)

> Within about thirty seconds of standing in the video section I was approached by a member of staff to enquire if I needed any help ... However, as I hadn't had time to have a look around properly and I also wanted to go to Laser, I rejected the offer of help ... In the few minutes I spent looking through the videos, I was approached two more times by staff enquiring if I needed any help. The first time I was asked was fine, but to be asked again two more times in such a short space of time was maddening ... At this point I was afraid of what I might say to the next member of staff who came anywhere near me. Up until now I had been very civilised in my refusals of help, but couldn't guarantee a polite response in the near future. I decided to leave.
>
> (female, 21)

> I approached the till. In most cases this would indicate that I wished to make a purchase. Not so here. The two female assistants were deep in conversation with a male colleague – obviously important business, but I declined to listen. By this time a combination of extreme heat in the shop, and a throbbing head, had caused me to begin sweating profusely. I could feel a panic attack coming on. I set the items on the counter. This got a response. One of the female assistants had decided to serve me, and not before time.
>
> (male, 22)

> We decided that we would wait a while before we did what little shopping was needed, so we went to get a coffee and a doughnut. The staff of this shop were, in a word, uninterested. They gave the impression of people who did not want to be there. They seemed to be afraid of smiling in case their faces cracked. One girl in particular gave me a look of disgust whenever I wished her a happy Christmas. We drank our coffee in double quick time and decided that it would be safer

to chance the large queues than to face the wrath of those in the coffee shop.

(male, 22)

In extreme cases, sales assistants are downright rude, deliberately obstructive, especially when handling enquiries, and are endowed with a supercilious stare that succeeds only in making shoppers feel uncomfortable, unfashionable or simply unworthy of the august establishment.

After what seemed like ages queuing I finally got served. Trust me to get the unpleasant assistant. There was no greeting whatsoever. NEXT, was all she roared. No smile or cheerful look, just a grumpy little worker who couldn't bother herself to even try to look pleasant, even if she didn't feel it. I got my Chicken Sandwich meal and strawberry milkshake, some of which was dripping down the side of the cup, in a not so pleasant or polite manner. I really felt like telling the 'grump' where to shove her food, but I was that hungry and it smelt quite nice, I couldn't wait to scoff it down. I therefore bit my tongue and counted to ten as I waited for my change.

(female, 21)

Eventually, after coming under the scrutiny of the resident security man, I attracted the attention of a sales assistant. Obviously coming to the end of her shift, the air of annoyance transcended the gap between us. Pretending not to have heard the exasperated sigh, I question her about the blue-striped shirt that I wanted to buy for my father. 'Are there any in the back store?' I suddenly realised that my fingers were crossed and hoped that the assistant with attitude, has not noticed. 'Nah!' This word reverberated from her gum, clod mouth, 'all we have is what's out on the shelves.' As she called her departure to her presumed supervisor, utter disgust flowed through my veins. I felt like dragging her to the store and making her look; at least to humour me.

(female, 22)

Buying petrol is a big walled emptier, where I am concerned. As I live in the country, there is only one local petrol pump and it is run by an old hag of a woman. I go there if I am really stuck. She is a really nice person – a nicer person you couldn't hit with a brick. I had the misfortune last week to stop for petrol at her establishment. I put £3 in the car, as I believe she gives short measures. I went in and said '£3' to her. She said sarcastically, 'Is that all?' With that I threw the money on the counter and left, hoping I would never need her petrol again.

(male, 21)

We head on up towards Corn Market and into Propaganda, a shop which I am not terribly fond of. This is due to the fact that everyone who works here is kitted out, head to foot, in about £700 worth of designer gear.

For some reason, when I am in their presence, I come over all inferior. I am not alone in this feeling, as I have conferred with my friends on this matter, who I also find experience 'Propaganda paranoia'.

(male, 22)

When they do deign to serve the undeserving, moreover, shop assistants are of little help, since their product knowledge is often limited or non-existent, their sales patter is risibly clichéd and the advice they disburse is driven more by the prospect of a sale, and the resultant commission, than the needs of the customer. Hence, it is usually resisted, discounted or treated with scepticism and contempt.

A stop-off in Dixons proved as useful as I had expected. 'Do you stock 3DO games?', I enquired. To which the assistant replied, 'Huh . . . don't think so, what is it?' I should have known better than to try there. They didn't know what it was but I'll bet they could have sold me a bloody guarantee for it!

(male, 23)

By this time I had been in a number of stores and I was getting very pissed off at the shop assistants coming up to me and saying, 'Can I help you?' 'No, I'm just looking', even though at this stage I felt like saying something else.

(male, 20)

Just as we set off to return the shirt to its appropriate place on the rack, a sales assistant spots us . . . and sees his chance for a handy sale. Have you ever noticed that they never seem to bother you until you find something for yourself and then they appear as if from nowhere to assure 'sir' that he has made an excellent choice? Today, I ain't in the mood. Anyway, he's nothing but a snotty-nosed school kid, probably only hired for the Christmas rush and knows no more about clothes retailing than dental surgery. 'I like this shirt but I can't find chinos to match.' 'Has sir looked on the rail?' Ahaa!, I thought, why didn't I think of that? Of course I looked on the rail you jumped up little twat, I thought to myself.

(male, 22)

'Excuse me, I was wondering would you have any short, black, plain skirts?' 'Well, we have blue, red, green . . .' 'Yes, thank you, but you see I need black.' 'Did you know that this season's colour is red? Very classy, very trendy, everyone should have one.' 'Yes, that may be, but . . .' 'This would be gorgeous on you.' A red and blue polka-dot skirt is thrust into my hand. She tells me to try it on and she'll give me her honest opinion. She's not after the sale, of course not, she really wants to help.

(female, 21)

In fairness, many of the essayists are cognisant of and sympathetic towards the unpleasant lot of the shop assistant – underpaid, overworked and maltreated by management and customers alike. There is no doubt, what is more, that encountering a competent, enthusiastic or attractive shop assistant can loosen the purse strings or open the wallet of even the most jaded consumer. Nevertheless, sales clerks are widely regarded as more of a hindrance than a help. So much so, that the worm occasionally turns and retribution is exacted by acts of deliberate shopping subversion, of consumer retaliation, of retailing revenge (see Elliott *et al.* 1996).

> Walking to the cash point I am suddenly hit by a feeling of relief. The queue is relatively small and I purchase the product within a couple of minutes. I am now in a good mood compared to an hour earlier. The sales person is stressed out. She has probably been doing the same old shit all day and wants to get home. For a moment I feel quite sorry for her but then I remember that she is getting paid for it.
>
> (male, 21)

> While browsing in every store, I always hear an assistant approaching me. I think to myself, super, smashing, great, time to play the interested consumer. 'Can I help you?', they always ask. This statement gives me the shits. I wish someone would devise a new way for assistants to ask if they could help me. They are most likely thinking the same thing about me because of my answer, 'No, I am only looking.' Just as they are about to leave me I will go, 'Ah, do you see this boot, do you have it in a nine?' I have no intention of buying boots, I just love wasting their time because, after all, that is what they are there for. I try the boots on, walk around in them and then go back to the assistant, smile and say, 'Thank you, I will be back later.'
>
> (male, 21)

> On one occasion, whilst walking round the Foyleside wearing shell-suit bottoms and a rugby polo shirt, I spied a shirt I liked in Parks. Parks is very expensive but I thought 'what the hell!' So I walked casually into Parks and over to the shirt. Whilst looking at the shirt I could see some of the staff in Parks look at me as if I was a tramp who had just walked in off the street. It was there and then that I would no longer purchase the shirt although I liked it and even though it was in my price range. Therefore I made up my mind to annoy the staff as much as possible. There were designer label jeans costing £79.99 which I decided to try on; I tried various different sizes so they would have to fetch clothes from the shelves to the fitting rooms. Then I decided I would need shoes to match my jeans so I tried on different sizes until I found a pair I liked. Both the jeans and the shoes totalled £125, so as the assistant and I walked towards the till, her thinking she had

made a great sale, I informed her I had left my cheque book at home and could not pay for the clothes and promptly left.

(male, 20)

The relationship between consumers and their shopping companions is equally ambivalent. On the one hand, a second opinion is often welcome when difficult decisions have to be taken about certain product categories – expensive household goods, for instance. What's more, when the accompanist is a parent – and, therefore, footing the bill – their presence is especially welcome, as are their opinions, on occasion.

> Shopping is a pleasure when it is a social event . . . It is nice to be in the company of friends because we can help each other decide on which items suit us and which don't.
>
> (female, 20)

> Anytime I shop for myself, and it is clothes I am buying or looking for, I always go by myself first of all and then when actually spending the money on the garment I take somebody with me. This more than likely comes from a look of non-approval from the second party, as I usually make a lot of rash decisions on clothes or shoes that are allegedly 'in fashion' at that time.
>
> (male, 21)

> Although the assistant was helpful, she would have told me anything to get a sale. That's where I needed my mum. I liked the jacket but I had to choose between five skirts. With mum's critical nature, we managed to eliminate four of them. We decided on a long, black velvet skirt, with a black top and red jacket . . . All the items were placed on the counter and I thought, after this, I will have to sit in for the next year. Here it comes. Shit. £394.00. Help. Danger alarms were flashing in my head. Thankfully mum came to the rescue and says, 'I'll pay for that, otherwise you will be going nowhere to be able to wear them.'
>
> (female, 22)

On the other hand, shopping expeditions can quite easily be waylaid, frustrated or quite simply ruined if the wrong person or persons are in attendance. A prime example of this involves friends who tag along, even though they have no real desire to shop and quite quickly get bored, tired, impatient or, as often as not, a combination of all three. Worse still, for some people at least, is shopping with mother. Not only does she think she knows what's best for her (grown up) children and has simply no conception of the going rate for goods, but also she unfailingly insists on patronising the most downmarket or unfashionable establishments and actively endeavours to embarrass her offspring on every conceivable occasion.

My first mistake was deciding to go to Dublin with two people who were not going shopping. Never go shopping with people who do not want to shop. They only hold you back as well as getting on your nerves.

(female, 21)

Oh no! My mother had spotted Dunnes Stores better value. My mum is a real bargain hunter, which means she keeps showing you awful clothes at £2.99 and saying how nice they would look on you. We finally leave Dunnes an hour later, we bought a pair of cord trousers for two pounds less than their original price.

(female, 22)

To cut a long story short ... I had to go ahead with the unthinkable, shopping with my mother. After finding a suitable place to park the car, we headed for the Richmond Centre. I just hoped no-one would see me. I would get some stick from the boys. These were but a few thoughts going through my head, as I proceeded through the main entrance, keeping my head down in an effort to avoid eye contact with anyone. I was on the look-out for a pair of jeans and a shirt that will help me attract my 'dream woman' tonight at the local disco. If anything was to work in my favour, it was the fact that, if I had gone alone, I would not have got a lot of money to spend. I had a strategic plan formulated. It was to trail my mother around the most expensive shops, in order to make her realise that the days of buying a shirt and jeans for fifteen pounds were well and truly over ... On to Next. It was here that I fell in love with a beige sweater. I asked the shop assistant was there any XLs left, from whom I got a swift reply, 'No, sorry, it's just what we have on the shop floor.' This was just my luck, the first thing I saw and actually liked, there was none left. Leaving the store, my mother noticed that there was the same jumper in the shop window display (you know how it is, they miss nothing). So, in she walks, bold as brass, and requests if someone could check what size the garment was on display. Reluctantly, one of the sales staff followed the command. After knocking a few things down, and stumbling back on to the shop floor, the sweater was indeed an extra large. Apologising for the trouble she had gone to, I gladly accepted the sweater and proceeded to the cash desk, with the intention of buying it after all the commotion. Laying it on the counter, mum inspected the item for any flaws. At this stage, I wanted to crawl into a hole and die. The inevitable happened, there was a stitch, or something, out of place. I ground my teeth and said, in an oh-so-softly voice, 'Mum, it doesn't matter, I want the top. Come on.' Her next sentence was the final straw, 'Is there any chance of getting a couple of pounds off?' Once I heard those words, I walked out of the shop and sat on a bench opposite the store. I just didn't need this, as my head was bouncin' from the night before. A few minutes later, I saw a beaming face through the congested flow of shoppers. 'Gerard, I got 10 per cent off. You see, you would just have taken it.' That made her day. That £3.50 seemed a lot more to a woman, who goes out of her way to unintentionally embarrass you, but you have to love them.

(male, 21)

Worst of all, however, is the boyfriend or girlfriend, albeit for completely different reasons. Men, it seems, simply cannot comprehend the female shopping psyche, which requires them to examine every single item of merchandise in every single shop, before making a purchase in the very first one they visited – several hours previously. Men, moreover, are merely required to nod dumb approval, act as unpaid native bearers for the manifold shopping trophies and stand resolute outside women's changing rooms, or in the lingerie department, whilst magenta with self-consciousness and mortification.

> I found a shiny silver dress. I went into the changing room and tried it on. He said it looked great and I agreed with him that I really liked it as well. Just as he was beginning to look relieved and surprised that it had only taken me one hour to find a dress that suited me, I realised that it creased very easily and told him that I wanted to look around some other shops in case 'there was anything nicer somewhere else.' 'How many times have I heard that before?' moaned my boyfriend. He knew he was in for a day of torture.
>
> (female, 21)

> First on the agenda was something for her mother. Would it be a handbag?, a watch?, something to wear? Dilemmas, dilemmas. The result was that we went from shop to shop, to and fro for about an hour and a half, because Paula could not decide what would be most suitable for her mum, all of which was frustrating me to an unbelievable level. Paula ... is a typical female shopper who likes to irritate me by dragging me into every possible shop, asking ME what her mum would like. I mean, it is just an impossible situation, which totally angered me. And this was just trying to get something for her mum!
>
> (male, 23)

> After a while ... I noticed she had not many bags and I commented on this ... to which she replied, saying that she liked such and such a skirt, etc., so let's go back to that shop again. I asked her why she didn't buy it in the first place and she answered, 'What if I had bought it and found something nicer later?' But she hadn't and everything she did like she didn't find anything nicer, so it all began again. 'Let's go back to this shop.' So once again I was getting trailed round women's shops. I was left standing outside changing rooms myself and strange women in their bare feet would come out from behind the curtains and look at me as if I was some sort of pervert. I thought I was the only

person who would feel like this, but I met another man abandoned outside the changing cubicles and he had the same feelings as myself.

(male, 22)

Women, conversely, are lumbered with a masculine shopping albatross, who tries to distract them from the task in hand, steers them away from shops that have to be visited, refuses to queue, won't take advice, acts like a spoilt child if he doesn't get his way, is prone to irrational temper tantrums, constantly stops for caffeine, nicotine or alcoholic infusions and who labours under the delusion that shopping can be carefully pre-planned, conducted in no time at all and executed with military precision. Indeed, they even believe that their own shopping behaviours exhibit these traits.

My boyfriend came into town with me that day, not to add an opinion, just to hold the money. It was in one leather jacket shop that I tried on a beautifully fitted, military-style jacket. I knew even before I put it on that it had far too many buttons and stripes on it for my liking. After all, I did not want people saluting me when I came into a room ... I knew he was disappointed that our shopping trip had not come to an early end. 'Next stop, Top Shop,' I delighted in telling him, safe in the knowledge that he hated the place. I found it a challenge to get him inside this female frenzy of a clothes shop, instead of outside with the other, pitiful males. I triumphed that he could 'hack it', only on my account.

(female, 21)

Flanked by a protesting James, who is either on the verge of murder or exploding, I try to calm him down with those three soothing, tender words, 'Oh shut up!' Sensing another outburst, I dive into the shop, select and pay for the jacket and appear before James has realised I've gone! 'WHY COULDN'T YOU HAVE DONE THAT TWO HOURS AGO?' Here we go again, the usual rant, 'We could have been out of here in five minutes! When I go shopping I get what I want in one shop and go home – inside half an hour. You have to go into every shop and then back to the first one and pick the first thing you saw. We could have been home ages ago!' Are all men the same? Why is it they have to apply this macho, chauvinistic image to everything? Men are better at this. Men are better at that. We can do our shopping in five minutes!

(female, 23)

AND SHE SHOPPED AND SHE SHOPPED

No matter how much of a help or hindrance sales assistants prove to be, or how extortionate the price of shopping with mother, individual consumption experiences are mediated by the task in hand. Unsurprisingly perhaps, certain shopping tasks, certain sorts of shop and certain types of shopping trip are much less appealing than others. Routine grocery shopping is intrinsically unrewarding and running errands for other people is unspeakably vile, as are expeditions precipitated by special events, such as a party, wedding, christening, dinner, job interview, birthday, and, above all, Christmas (Fischer and Arnold 1990; Otnes *et al.* 1993). Apart from the ever-present problems of crowds, queues, out-of-stock situations and so on, Christmastime entails buying presents for friends and relatives, all of whom already have everything they'll ever need. Thus, not only is it an almost impossible task in the first place, but also it is an ordeal that often goes unrewarded, since the recipient rarely appreciates the Herculean effort that went into acquiring their perfect gift in the first place. True, some people enjoy the Yuletide marketing milieu – buying presents for children is especially rewarding – but for many people Christmas shopping is troublesome at best and sheer torture at worst.

> It's the same old story, one week before Christmas Day and not one present has been bought for anyone. I usually leave the shopping to my sisters for the rest of the family and grand-parents, but this year they are busier than ever and I have been talked into buying the worst present of all – my mum's. In recent years, my mum has been notoriously hard to buy for as she has already got so much, but this year the job has been made much easier as she has given us one serious hint – a foot-spa for her aching feet. This sounds like an easy task but it turned into a living nightmare.
>
> (male, 21)

> Following a quick, desperate scurry around the shop, I came across a new style of sets, little colour co-ordinated sets with mini-bottles of bath products and little soaps, which were set on a cardboard base, covered in plastic wrapping, in a matching-coloured design, tied at the top with ribbon. Exactly what I was looking for (and at the all-important student-friendly price). After some serious contemplation, I decided on the white musk set (if only my friend could even begin to appreciate the agonies of shopping I went through to buy this gift!).
>
> (female, 27)

> Christmas is a time for giving and weary feet, a time to rejoice in the good things to eat. It is a complex period that involves a variety of emotions. And I love it. The queues, the crowds, the food, the calories, the non-availability of items that you would not normally even think of looking at, never mind purchasing. Apart from the fact that it is Christmas Eve and you still have not bought your dad anything!
>
> (female, 20)

> After finishing up, I made my way to Hanna's Toy Shop. I must admit, I rather enjoyed it myself . . . Finally she decided on a bright pink doll's house. It was certainly her colour, hardly the size of her little hand and

two little characters to go along with it. The attendant was delighted by her choice and commented what a pretty girl she was. The smile on her face spelt glorious triumph. It was well worth the peace and calm. My only regret was why I hadn't come here first.

(female, 21)

There is, of course, a positive side to the Xmas extravaganza and that is being on the receiving end of familial largesse. In this respect, the self/other distinction is of paramount importance. Whereas shopping for others is often an ordeal – even for individuals partial to purchasing *per se* – shopping for oneself is usually quite enjoyable, even at Christmastime (Thompson *et al.* 1990). This propensity is reinforced when certain, highly salient product categories are involved (e.g. jeans, video-recorders and popular music), albeit their perceived importance makes the final decision all the more difficult.

I really hate Christmas shopping. I think my problem stems from the fact that I'm spending money on other people. When heading for Royal Avenue I was trying to think, did my brother get me anything last year?, and if he didn't I'm not going to bother to get him anything. It's a different story if I'm buying something for myself, I automatically become more interested. I usually end up buying the members of my family things I like, not really things they would like.

(male, 21)

Shopping, well to me it can be a pleasurable or absolutely frustrating experience, all depending on whether I am in pursuit of products for my own personal satisfaction or of a gift for a friend or relation. When, and may I say not too often, I have substantial funds in which I can satisfy my own needs and wants for clothing and pleasure, I can spend hours upon hours touring and exploring Belfast city.

(male, 21)

It's that dreaded time again, my jeans are on their last legs and our long and steady relationship must come to an end. My loyalty to them however is infinite and I will find a place for them in the back of my wardrobe. You never know when they will come in handy! The back of my wardrobe holds many mysteries of which C.S. Lewis would be proud ... This may seem like a digression but there is method in my madness as it shows how important clothes are to me, and the problems I attempt to describe are those surrounding the purchase of 'new jeans', which I would liken to finding a new best friend.

(female, 22)

Decision taking dilemmas are not confined to high-involvement, high-risk goods, however. On the contrary, many of the essays refer to the difficulties of deciding what to buy, not least among the more mundane categories of merchandise. Interestingly, this indecision is often blamed, at least in part, on the unnecessary proliferation of products that characterises the contemporary marketing system – having too much to choose from – or the fact that they are unwitting, easily manipulated dupes, in the mendacious thrall of multinational capital.

> Now we're looking at nappies. I've never come across anything so baffling than the stay-dry, comfy-leg, elasticated-waist, double sticky-sided, midi, maxi, mini, midi-maxi, mini-midi variations in probably the most objectionable items associated with babycare. Whatever happened to small, medium and large? Isn't this taking market segmentation to its extremes? They even come in different colours – pink bunnies for girls and blue for boys. PLEASE!
>
> (female, 22)

> I became aware of the existence of [household cleaning] products after I became a student (the time our flat was in danger of being declared a health hazard). Now, I know that they are essential, but is it really necessary to have such a vast selection of the things? I mean, you can only use one at a time and surely they all do the same thing anyway, don't they? Like, why is there not a 'simple' sign giving valuable information such as 'suitable for removing a year's grease off the cooker', or 'one simple application will remove all sauce/gravy/ink etc. etc. stains off all finishes' and 'spray once to allow normal inhalation of air to recommence'. Or more importantly simplify everything and have one, and one only, multi-purpose cleaner.
>
> (female, 20)

> I've always had a problem since I was a child myself of deciding what to buy, whether it be sweets, clothes, shoes or even what to watch on video. I can't just go in and buy and leave, no not me. Every factor has to be weighed up before the final decision can be made. Even the most simple things like which shampoo to use. Like the ad. goes, just wash and go, but me I have to read every label and smell every scent, consider all cost. Why is shopping so hard or is it just me that makes it hard? . . . I put it down to a number of things which seem to constantly drift into and out of my head. People, displays, ads, every little thing seems to affect me as a shopper, maybe that's the way 'they' want us to think when it comes to what we buy . . . I just seem to be a brainwashed, unthinking consumer which has so many choices programmed into the simplest of decisions that I just seem to be unable to cope.
>
> (male, 21)

Contrariwise, many informants describe an heroic internal struggle between the hedonistic and ascetic sides of themselves, between the overwhelming desire to have, to possess, to spend, to indulge and their ever-present, ever-prudent, ever-nagging consciences, which remind them that bank accounts are overdrawn, wardrobes already full of clothes and the number of calories in cream cakes, crisps and bars of chocolate. In short, between their Calvinistic and CalvinKleinistic inclinations.

As I limp off with my war wounds, the battle of savoury versus sweet begins. We bypass the healthy and sensible food aisles with amazing ease and proceed to fill the trolley with twiglets, crisps, family bags of wine gums and jelly babies etc. etc., so fast that I think even Dale Winton of *Supermarket Sweep* would be impressed.

(female, 21)

I caught sight of a pair of jeans, just what I was looking for. After holding them up, I decide against them. Besides, I've already paid a fortune for my dress and if I don't stop buying I won't be able to get my shoes. The smell of fresh baking wafts past me, making me feel hungry. Just looking at those delicious eclairs and lemon pies, makes the calories pile on. No, I won't be tempted or I'll ruin my lunch.

(female, 21)

After returning from my holidays, I swore that I would do my utmost to avoid the torture of shopping, which is after all arguably a form of organised looting and pillaging. I was more convinced than ever that shopping was put before us to encourage greed, invite acquisitiveness and a hunger for possession, not to mention the must-have mania. However, a few weeks later the shopping needs were beginning to bite. The ink cartridge on my computer had seen better days, I needed to buy a suit for one of those dreadful job interviews and the rest of my family had gone on holiday, which meant that I needed to do some food shopping. Another shopping ordeal was looming ... As I pondered on this thought, the phone rang. It was my friend Bob. He sensed the anguish in my voice. 'What could be the matter Brian, you poor soul?' 'Bob, I can't take it any more, I'm afraid I've got a terminal dose of the shopping heebie-jeebies.'

(male, 22)

Bad as the eternal internal struggle and the shopping heebie-jeebies can prove to be, it seems that a successful shopping trip, where some or all of the objectives are accomplished, compensates for even the most horrendous experiences along the way. The very worst shopping expeditions, by contrast, seem to occur when an ostensibly routine matter, such as picking up one's purchases, turns out to be much more problematical than expected. Indeed, it is no exaggeration to state that perceived success or failure is the single most important influence upon the tenor of the essayists' introspective accounts.

As I made my way over to the collection point, which was indicated by a sign somebody's child must have made in play school, I remember thinking this looks worse than hell, and I was not to be proved wrong.

Once there, I stood around like a spare part for a while until this gentleman asked me for my receipt, which I gave him, and he told me to wait a minute until the item was brought down from the store. This man wore a red Santa hat and as I stood there I thought it was just like Santa Claus (as he was a fat bastard) and his little helpers, as members of staff brought in packages from the stores, with everyone praying their item was in the next batch to be brought in. After about ten minutes, my CD player arrived and I went to Santa Claus and told him it was mine. After he searched for the receipt, which surprisingly he could not find, he looked at me in a dubious way. I told this person I had given him the receipt and thankfully he remembered my face and explained that he must have given the receipt to somebody else. As he gave me the CD player with a bag, that he knew and I knew it would never fit into, I explained I wanted a receipt. Santa did not enjoy this statement and tried his best to forget about it, but this was a matter of principle and I would not let him forget. Eventually, he told me to go to the till and he would contact the girl and tell her about the problem and she would give me a manual receipt. I stormed off to the tills and stormed up to the front of the queue, much to the disgust of many queuers. I didn't care at all and if anybody had complained I would have shoved the CD player down their throat – sideways. Eventually, the girl noticed me and I explained the problem. The girl wrote me out a manual receipt and she told me she was sorry about my trouble and I went on my way. Walking out of Dixons, I told myself I would never go back and this was further enhanced when I tried to put the CD player in the bag that Santa Claus had given me. It must have been a fucking joke as the bag was barely big enough to hold a CD itself.

(male, 21)

Failure, of course, comes in many shapes and forms – available goods turn out to be the wrong colour, size, shade, fit, brand, model, specification, price, etc. – though 'near misses' are especially frustrating. These are situations where the fit, colour or match is almost but not quite right, every size is stocked *except* the one that is required, the last item was sold only half-an-hour beforehand (and replenishment, naturally, will take several weeks), the merchandise is held in the shopper's local branch (which was earlier bypassed in favour of the 'better choice' at the main outlet) and, when a purchase is eventually made, the exact same item is spotted in another shop, at a substantially lower price, or something even better suddenly materialises.

[Having] fought my way into Next, I spied in the corner what appeared to be red dresses. But what reds! Could I really see myself in snarling scarlet, acid orange with a hint of puce or livid ketchup? Shielding my eyes from the glare, I groped my way out of the store.

(female, 22)

The story of my life at present is ... 'Sorry but', 'We ran out of stock yesterday', 'We don't seem to stock your size sir.' But just why do they not have my size, or stock that particular item? Oh!, but why?, tell me why? Is it not a simple request to have every item, in every size, in every flavour, all of the time?

(male, 21)

The last straw is generally going into a shop, seeing something I want, and they don't have it in the right size. Perhaps a well meaning shop assistant will say, 'Our Ballymena branch also stocks these!!' It is like a scene out of a horror film, I feel like screaming and instead I have to smile, say thank you, all the while thinking what a waste of time this has been.

(female, 20)

I began to look through the skirts and the first one I saw was the long satin skirt that I had bought in the Belfast branch just before Christmas. It cost me £35 then and I didn't want to look at the price, but unfortunately I did. It was only £16 in the sale. I was raging, but that's what you get when you buy clothes in the month of Christmas. So I left this shop straight away in fear I would see something else that was reduced and I had paid more for it.

(female, 21)

The fault that I find most often with my behaviour is that I can become obsessive about a particular garment, or whole outfit, buy it, and then walk ten yards down the mall and see something I prefer. This has happened quite a few times.

(male, 21)

In these impossible circumstances, many consumers are inclined to blame themselves for the failings of the marketing system, to rationalise the situation in terms of their own physical and psychological defects, to dramatically lower their initial, impossibly ambitious expectations, to patronise retail outlets they wouldn't normally contemplate, to buy something – anything! – just to render the effort worthwhile, to offset their abject failure with some sort of token purchase or, not least, to ruefully reflect on the fact that they have managed to spend all their money without buying anything they intended to. Where did it all go?

Feeling relieved that I had bought something, I decided to resume my quest for the red dress or any dress at this stage. A promising window display at Dorothy Perkins enticed me into the store ... Several dresses later I came to the conclusion that a tub of Slimfast would be a much wiser purchase, as I did not possess the traditional hour-glass figure so essential for the fashion design of the moment. To console myself, I purchased a pair of sleeper earrings. Clearly, at a price of £2.99 they were most definitely not sterling silver.

(female, 22)

After such a harrowing experience we need a boost, so we decide it's to be in the shape of a ten-glass bottle of vodka. Walking towards the car park we make the final decision of the day. Let's go home and do what children do best without parental control. In other words, get well and truly pissed and throw one mother of a party!!!

(female, 21)

The journey home was spent trying to calculate just what we spent our money on. It was one of those cases where you think that you have nothing to show for the money you spent, then you try to think, what did I do with it?

(male, 21)

I had walked around enough for one day and just wanted out of there. I would have been happy to buy anything, just to have something for the day's shopping.

(male, 20)

Success, conversely, invariably occurs when it is least expected. The very best, most precious acquisitions are made when idly browsing with nothing specific in mind (Thompson *et al.* 1989, 1990). Triumph, moreover, can be and often is wrested from the very jaws of shopping disaster. Indeed, just as failure brings its own reward, in the shape of compensatory consumption, so too successful shopping expeditions can stimulate additional, celebratory expenditure, often of a consumable variety.

The reason why I get such a kick from impulsive shopping is that you never suspect what you might buy, also I don't have to prepare a shopping list. All the items that I have bought from impulsion are still my favourite items of clothing. I suppose it was a case of love at first sight. Products that I buy from impulse give me great satisfaction and I can never wait to get home and show them off.

(male, 21)

I wandered from rack to rack, picking up and leaving down, hoping I would come across something spectacular – but to no avail ... Then, after fitting on about half a dozen pairs of shoes, just when I was out of luck, the lady handed me the most elegant pair of black suede sandals. They were perfect. Great, there's £5 off as well. It's not like me to pick a bargain.

(female, 21)

Our relationship dwindling, we walk nonchalantly to the next shop ... I go through the same motions as before, 'too long', 'too short', 'too tight' but then I succeed and find a pair that are 'just right'. I walk out of the changing room triumphant and my friend, noticing my giddy expression, joins with me in my euphoric mood, happy in the knowledge that the ordeal is over. I pay for the jeans in cash, wishing I had a credit card to annoy the 'too trendy' shop assistant, but relish the fact the some day people like that will be working for me. We leave the shop and go to relax in Roscoffs, where a coffee for us is the order of the day. Just as the theatre was the place to be seen in Alexander Pope's time, this is the place to be seen in our time.

(female, 22)

It is fair to say, however, that for many informants the most enjoyable, most rewarding, most successful part of a shopping trip is when it is over. The sheer relief of leaving the last shop, buying the final present, getting into the car/bus/taxi, not to mention the mid-trip *thought* of doing so, is what sustains copious tired, weary and frustrated consumers, and gives them the strength to struggle on. When the shopping gets tough, the tough get going home.

I get to the point where I just do not want to go on anymore, perhaps I have 'shopped 'til I dropped'. At any rate all I want to do is get a seat. So I will go in for a cup of tea, which never seems to revive me even though I put such faith in it. Usually once I reach this stage, I am not far from throwing in the towel and going home ... Who cares about Christmas anyway? All I want to do is go home and have a long relaxing bath.

(female, 20)

Great, I thought, that's it finished, free, and all the rest. However, no-one had thought of warning me of what was to come next; twenty-five minutes we waited on that taxi, and then the tube wouldn't lift his ass off the seat long enough to either load or unload the shopping. Who cares? It's all over and I survived.

(male, 22)

Trying to extract myself from the incoming hopefuls, I shoved my way out of the store. To the unsuspecting eye I was indeed a hardened shopper. I was no longer the victim but toughened through experience. The will to get home gave me a spurt of vitality. The energy which I have been denied all day came to me in a rush like no drug could offer. Happy with the knowledge that, although not completed, there was now a serious dent in my shopping.

(female, 22)

I love the feeling of driving out of the car park, having everything finished, as other poor sods have yet to start. Home sweet home. At least one handle on one of the bags is sure to break whilst bringing the groceries into the house. Never mind, at least it's over for another week.

(female, 21)

UNTIL SHE EXCEEDED HER CREDIT LIMIT

Just as shopping expeditions are often evaluated retrospectively, in terms of 'successful' or 'unsuccessful' outcomes, so too they are influenced, at least in part, by consumers' antecedent states. Unsurprisingly perhaps, perceived financial status is particularly important in this regard. Shopping is an entirely different undertaking when there is money in the bank account, a long-awaited pecuniary windfall finally materialises or, best of all, someone else is paying, than when the coffers are running low, numerous demands are competing for strictly limited resources and sponging on one's friends is no longer feasible or tolerated. From the introspective accounts it appears that the arrival of a salary or grant cheque acts as the green light for a serious shopping splurge, whereas the end-semester/month absence of wherewithal precipitates parsimony, general belt-tightening, the embarrassed patronisation of cheaper shops and reluctant recourse to rather less exclusive brand names than usual. A dialectic of shopping celibacy and promiscuous purchasing thus obtains.

> When I have just received my grant cheque and I have money in the bank, for a change, it is enjoyable to go on a shopping spree with my friends. I feel that this is because we all have got money in the bank and now we know that if we see something that takes our fancy we can most probably purchase it.
>
> (female, 20)

> It was January 1996 and I had firstly completed my exams and secondly received my student loan. As my bank account was therefore extremely healthy I decided to purchase something sensible rather than waste it away. I finally decided on a video recorder.
>
> (female, 21)

> Bacon collected and it's a left turn up the biscuits aisle. I must admit to being a bit ignorant of prices on regular purchases when it is daddy's money I'm spending. When it's my own shopping I look at every price, making a mental calculation of the likely total.
>
> (female, 21)

> Presently I am wearing Dunnes Stores underwear, but I know if my financial situation was reversed I would not hesitate to pop out to the shops and slip on a pair of Calvin Klein undies, feeling like James Dean, and that would give the girlfriend something to smile about.
>
> (male, 21)

Interestingly, however, it seems that being flush with funds is not necessarily unproblematic, since ill-considered, not to say mistaken, acquisitions are often made, difficult buying decisions have to be agonised over and the money that is burning a hole in the proverbial pocket is all too liable to be foolishly squandered or frittered away. Likewise, an empty wallet does not always precipitate a thrifty turn. On the contrary, penury is quite capable of inducing an air of fatalistic abandon, a sort of irrational 'I'm broke but what the hell' bravado. Indeed, it is one of the ironies of late twentieth-century consumer society that whenever people have money to spend they can find nothing in the shops, while the most covetable items by far are invariably spotted when the financial cupboard is completely bare.

> Clothes shopping is very important to me at the moment due to the fact that I have the money to get the things I want due to my part time job. I can walk past a shop window and half the time say, 'I can afford that, so why not?' Looking back, I wish I was poverty stricken after some of the things I bought and worse, actually wore.
>
> (male, 21)

> Sometimes if finances are poor I will curtail my shopping activities, though in other instances I take the attitude, I am broke anyway so it won't make much difference. A ready-cash deficit will mean that I am more likely to look for bargains and special offers. It has happened in the past that I have been quite flush but there has been nothing to buy ... Now I don't know, but every time I am in the mood for shopping, I dash off to the nearest shop, cash in hand, only to find that there is nothing to buy. Maybe the shops don't want to sell to me.
>
> (female, 20)

> The best kind of shopping for me is saving up one or two months' wages and then embarking on a spending spree, buying everything that catches my eye. Oh yes, the feel-good factor. I love going into Belfast with two or three hundred pounds to spend and buy what I like. Unfortunately this is not always the case. I've lost count of the number of times when I've went shopping with the best intentions of spending lots of money, only to arrive home with nothing more than a management magazine (which invariably lies beside my bed, unread, until the next edition arrives) and a sense of defeat. Then there are times when I go with the sole intention of buying very little, yet I arrive home – after raiding the bank account – with numerous items of clothing, several new records, and several other items which will ultimately be forgotten about once the initial 'I need/want this' feeling wears off.
>
> (male, 22)

Paralleling, and partly mediated by the perceived pecuniary position, is the consumer's extant physical and mental state. As Saturday is the traditional shopping day and Friday night is party night (for this group of informants, at least), many of the introspectionists refer to the difficulties of shopping while feeling the worse for wear – hungover, tired, bleary-eyed, unshaven, groggy, poorly slept, etc. – or having foolishly consented to go shopping while under the influence. Others deliberately resist the temptation to over-indulge the night before, thereby ensuring that some 'serious shopping' can be done, although it appears that best laid plans gang aft a-gley when one's acquaintances turn out to be inveterate party animals.

> The idea of hitting Cookstown's high street with Sharon, her mother and her brother's two year old son, does not appeal to me at the best of times, but with only seven shopping days left to Christmas and a hangover that felt like I had fallen off the top deck of a speeding bus and into the path of a freight train, the prospect was terrifying.
>
> (male, 22)

> Five o'clock Friday evening, Brian my boyfriend and myself arrived in Connolly Station. The Talbot Guest House was first on the list. A quiet evening was had. We dined within walking distance of the guest house and had a few drinks in the bar of the Gresham Hotel on O'Connell Street. I didn't fancy the following day shopping with a whopper of a hangover, so heads hit the pillow early.
>
> (female, 21)

> The train arrived in Dublin just in time for us to carry out our dutiful student roles of going for a few drinks before bed, and a full day's shopping in front of us, or should I say, me. What a great night! Seven a.m. and the hustle and bustle of the streets of Dublin had already begun. Wrecked as I was, I managed to peel myself from the bed and crawl to the shower to wake myself up. One hour later I was ready to go . . . Unfortunately I was the only person up and my friends showed no signs of moving. I decided it was up to me to move them, which they finally did – not before taking some headache tablets in preparation for spending the day shopping with me.
>
> (female, 21)

In these circumstances, it is not altogether surprising that many shopping expeditions are undertaken in a temper which, if not exactly foul, is certainly less than good. Moods, however, are remarkably malleable (Dawson *et al.* 1990; Gardner 1985; Snodgrass *et al.* 1988) and can change according to all sorts of contingent, well-nigh trivial, circumstances – the weather, a bargain, busy streets, attractive passers-by, being served, pleasant shop assistants, new stock, filling up a shopping trolley, the restorative powers of a cup of coffee or, in 'hair of the dog' extremis, alcoholic beverages.

> Chore shopping tends to be stressful and tedious and I find that in this frame of mind I encounter more little annoyances like prams and buggies invading my space, bad mannered people who would rather walk over me than around me and long queues, where the checkout operator seems to be on a go-slow.
>
> (female, 20)

By now there was a sprinkling of rain and I thought to myself perhaps the elements were creating a sympathetic background to complement my dampened mood.

(female, 22)

After piling the trolley with all my favourite goodies, I smile and think things are looking up. I experience a certain feel-good factor, knowing I have purchased the products I will enjoy most.

(female, 21)

The snow was still falling and I hated the thought of walking to the top of Grafton Street in slush. My dream day of shopping was quickly turning into a disaster. The snow would keep stopping and starting and everyone was dashing in and out of the shops to escape it. I was beginning to feel very uncomfortable, but I was not going to let the snow ruin the rest of my day. I began picking up quite a few bargains, even if they didn't fit me. I thought some of my sisters would get a turn out of them. Again in one of the snowfalls I ran into a shop by the name of Pamela Scott. The sale inside was excellent and I said to myself that I wasn't leaving without finding something I liked. I must have spent half an hour in the shop. Some of the clothes were beautiful and I enjoyed browsing around them. The shop assistants were so pleasant. One assistant in particular was wearing a jumper that I liked. She knew that I was watching her and she approached me to see if I was OK. I commented that her jumper was lovely and we began chatting about the usual, clothes and the sales. She accompanied me to the rail which the jumpers were on and was pleasant in leading me to the changing rooms that were upstairs. While I was trying on the jumper she went about looking for something to wear with it. She showed me trousers and skirts that matched the jumper and gave me her opinion on which suited me the best. She gave me her full attention which indicated to me that training of the staff was a major factor in the success of the store. Usually during sale times the shop assistants are not very helpful and can sometimes be very ignorant. In this shop assistant's eyes I was the customer and she was there to satisfy me. I eventually bought the jumper and a pair of trousers to match and I think it was the first purchase that I was actually pleased with so far in the day.

(female, 21)

However, if there is one antecedent event capable of transforming even the most amenable, easy-going consumer into a cantankerous, foul-mouthed marketing misanthrope, it is travelling to the designated shopping area. Buses and trains are unfailingly late, slow, prone to stop at every hole in the hedge en route and crammed full of unspeakable others with their bizarre outfits, bad manners, filthy habits and ill-bred children.

The bus pulls up. Number 38. Something going in my favour? No, not a chance of that. This was the 'slow boat'. Great, the scenic route to Belfast (I was going on a tour of every town between Newry and Belfast). Oh, how I was filled with excitement, a forty-five minute journey that was now going to take nearly two hours.

(male, 21)

The train has arrived in Ballymena. People are getting on and off. Oh my God, what is that? As my dear old mum would say, she looks like a 'beatnik'. I wonder what she thinks of me? Does she find my Levi's, Benetton jumper and boots as repulsive as I find her clothes? Thank God we are all different.

(female, 22)

The next thing I knew I had caught the train to Coleraine, after trying to persuade her to shop in Derry. So there I was in the train and still very tired, a sore wrist and tortured by two little brats who kept running up and down the train carriage shouting and singing unnoticed by their father, who just continued reading the paper.

(male, 22)

Motor cars are equally stressful, since driving into town is an exercise in unending frustration, a precursor of Purgatory, the nearest thing to Hell this side of the grave. It comprises a constant round of slow-coaches ahead, maniacs behind, know-it-all back seat passengers, queues on the motorway, queues for the multi-storey, queues behind idiots who don't know how to park and people who steal one's space without so much as a by your leave.

The first encounter I had was with an old man, who was driving at forty miles per hour and could I get past him? No. When there was a straight bit of road, there was always sure to be cars coming to keep me behind him and when we were driving on a corner, where I could not see if there were any cars coming, there was not another vehicle in sight until there was another straight bit of road. Damn! I wished that I could have driven over the top of him or that I had a rocket launcher to blast him out of the way. But, with time, I managed to get past him ... I arrived in Coleraine safely and now it was time to go shopping, or so I thought. I had to sit for fifteen minutes in a queue of traffic waiting to get into the car park. The sign at the entrance of the car park said 'car park full'. Just brilliant!

(female, 21)

My eyes are sore from concentrating on the road and my temper is fraying, as I've got three back-seat drivers, none of whom have a licence between them. Still, I've got money and those shops are beckoning.

(female, 21)

Approximately forty-five minutes later, we arrive at the shopping complex and start the tiresome task of trying to find a parking space on a Saturday morning, not easy may I add. Our luck seems to be in as we spot a space on the horizon, calling for us to park in it. Suddenly, out of nowhere, a burgundy Mercedes with a fat, balding owner appears and steals our prime spot. He reverses in and with a smug grin on his fat face gives us the 'birdie', which I return with great affection. NOT! The air within the car turns blue with verbal delicacies as we try to find an alternative parking space.

(female, 21)

It also involves 'bloody women drivers', 'bloody men drivers' and 'bloody boy racers' who can turn on a sixpence, not to mention double yellow lines, curmudgeonly traffic wardens, poorly lit parking decks, disconcerting stair-wells, the joys of circulating endlessly in search of a space and not having enough change for the pay-and-display machines.

My Saturday morning grocery shop starts as soon as that alarm clock goes off. So early, just because Wellworths' car park is minutely small, without a proper traffic flow system. I hate car parks that have dead ends, causing me to reverse or do a three point turn, while some smartass nineteen-year-old boy in a Nova ... takes great pleasure in watching my embarrassment at having to do a nine point turn in my small car. It is an annoying fact of life that some men will always be better at parking than some women and don't they know it.

(female, 21)

Driving a car around a busy main street can be a harrowing experience, though I feel that the stress is lessened if there is someone else there to talk to. Also, in Ballymena the main parking area is a multi-storey car park. This can be daunting to enter as it is usually dark and unfriendly and in general I do not feel comfortable walking alone in them.

(female, 20)

As we arrive in the centre of Belfast we come across the first obstacle of the day, that of finding a parking space ... I turn into the streets, but to my dismay there is not one free space. I then start feeling dizzy as I drive around in circles, losing count of the number of times I have driven past the Ulster Hall ... Then, as I turn into a street for the umpteenth time, my eyes light up when my mum yells out, 'There's one!' and when I look I see an easy end space and sigh with relief that I don't need to parallel park. However, when I park the car my heart sinks as a horrible thought comes into my head. Do we have any change to get a ticket from the pay-and-display machine?

(female, 22)

Driving, furthermore, necessitates dealing with car park attendants who switch on the 'Full' sign when spaces are still available, who charge an exorbitant daily rate when tickets are accidentally lost, who demand payment for three whole hours when it's just one miserable minute over two and who insist on the exact change, *or else*.

Last Friday, I waited twenty minutes for a space in this car park. There were only four cars in front of me and I could see at least ten empty spaces and he had the cheek to light up the 'Full' sign on the way in. Shopping in Coleraine is usually limited to two hours for me. Why? Because after two hours the price of the car park space doubles. I feel like Anneka Rice running from one shop to another, trying to be inside the deadline.

(male, 21)

To my utter rage I discovered that I had mislaid my car parking ticket and a grunting attendant in the kiosk charged me for the full daily rate, something like three or four pounds. 'Happy Christmas to you, sir', I bellowed out the window. I drove out of Belfast, tired and disappointed.

(female, 22)

As we headed out of the car park towards the NCP attendant in his little booth, I realised that I didn't have any change. When I handed over the ticket to the attendant and was duly asked to pay the amount, I handed over a ten pound note. The attendant took a look and proceeded to tear strips off me, shouting about the correct fucking change and how I was holding up the rest of the motorists behind me. At this point I replied with a stream of equally colourful language, while my girlfriend sat beside me telling me to shut up, instead of at least backing me up or producing the correct change. When we eventually left the car park with wheels spinning, my temper had moved into the red face with bursting headache stage and stayed like that until we were halfway down the motorway.

(male, 30)

While there is no doubt that if Nietzsche were alive today, he would doubtless explain such behaviours in terms of the will to park, the foregoing transportation-induced traumas pale by comparison with their *anticipated* state (Bitner 1992; Grossbart *et al.* 1990; Thompson *et al.* 1990). Knowing that the traffic jams will stretch for miles, that no spaces will be available, that queue jumping, parking tickets and road rage will be the order of the day, as well as the inevitable fact that the shops will be overcrowded and overheated, that sales assistants will be unfailingly surly or inept, that checkout queues will be endless, that the best bargains will have long gone, that one's shopping companions will be recalcitrant at best and incorrigible at worst, are in certain respects even *worse* than the real thing. For many consumers, the plot, story-line, trajectory – call it what you will – of a shopping expedition is preordained, predictable, always already written, as it were, and its subsequent unfolding is assessed in accordance with this anticipated schema.

> Another Christmas. Oh no, this means another day beating about Belfast doing Christmas shopping. The very thought of it does my head in.
>
> (male, 21)

> I jump into my car and begin my journey picking up a friend en route for moral support and guidance. She is dreading the trip as much as I, as she would describe me as a 'fussy shopper'.
>
> (female, 22)

> A trip to the city will be in order. That of course will mean fighting through hordes of people and driving around for ages to find a parking space. Christmas is a wonderful time of year – the bright lights, the festive feeling in everyone's hearts – but it is the worst time of year to go into the city centre. Well, bugger that, I just have to go in anyway.
>
> (male, 23)

> It is a Saturday and I am driving into Belfast with my mum, hoping to find a new outfit for myself. I have mixed feelings about the day ahead. The thought of getting a new outfit was exciting but was it going to turn into one of those typical shopping trips when I cannot find anything? Then mum starts complaining that I am too fussy and begins to point out to me the most hideous looking clothes, which to be honest I would not be seen dead in.
>
> (female, 22)

> It was a Sunday morning, I was very bored and I'd been thinking about my video all weekend. I suddenly decided to go over to the Abbeycentre to have a look. Just as I was about to leave I thought that I was maybe rushing into it and decided to wait until I could go into Belfast city centre to shop around. Once again the boredom set in and I began considering the movies I could watch when I bought the video. Nothing was going to prevent me from my shopping trip to the Abbeycentre ... The first part of the journey seemed to take forever. I began imagining how disappointing it would be now if I had to come home empty-handed.
>
> (female, 21)

Such pre-purchasing expectations, suffice it to say, are relative concepts, which differ markedly from person to person, time to time, situation to situation, store to store and trip to trip. Nevertheless, from the intro-spective accounts, it appears that each individual purchasing episode is embedded within a broad, but by no means stable (contra the traditional typology literature), shopping predisposition. Thus, it is not unusual for the 'shopaphobics', those with very low or antipathetic expectations, to

be pleasantly surprised when a trip proves less nightmarish than anticipated. The 'retailiacs', on the other hand, those who venture forth with
high hopes, a spring in their step, a clear idea of what they want and
money in their pockets, are liable to be more disappointed than most
when things go awry.

> After enduring this torture, the last thing I needed was some Caribbean
> gentleman forcing jewellery and T-shirts down my throat. Nonetheless,
> to my surprise, at one particular stall I was impressed by the range of
> T-shirts on offer. Had a combination of 'trolley rage', the revolting heat
> and the young man's 'hard sell' got the better of me? Maybe so. My
> girlfriend proceeded to purchase an Adidas T-shirt and I invested in
> two Reebok T-shirts of apparently good quality.
>
> (male, 22)

> He also stated, as they always do, that this was an excellent product
> and a great buy. While making my decision I thought, though I hate
> to admit it, that this person was actually quite helpful, but I thought it
> would be nice for once if they told you this product was shit and to
> definitely purchase something else.
>
> (male, 21)

> I walked to the ladies-wear department and there it was, the dress of
> all dresses! A warm, crimson chiffon creation with layer upon layer of
> quality textile, flowing from a fitted satin bodice, soft to the touch and
> pleasing to the eye. Feeling euphoric, I sprinted to the first assistant
> that I could find and asked her to fetch my size. She apologetically
> informed me that 'those dresses are out of stock love, try Sprucefield.'
> Gutted, I reluctantly returned the dress to its rail and meandered down
> the escalator to the food hall.
>
> (female, 22)

> Disaster struck early on Saturday morning. I jumped out of bed bursting
> with energy, pulled back the curtains and all I could see was SNOW.
> Yes, it was snowing. The flakes that fell on the window-ledge were as
> big as the palms of my hand. I really felt like crying. Of all weekends
> it has to snow the weekend I come to Dublin to do a bit of shopping.
>
> (female, 21)

> Short, plain black skirt. Well, that should be easy enough to find. The
> clothes shops will be bulging with skirts, a plain black one will be no
> problem ... Numerous shops later and still no black skirt. I am about
> to surrender. Today is not my day. Then I see, tucked away in a corner,
> my last port of call. I go in to find myself in a shop which strongly
> resembles a disco, apart from the fact that it sells clothes instead of
> drink. Music blares around the shop, while bright lights dazzle you.
> However, it does have potential. Yes, I have arrived. Rows and rows

of skirts in every style, size, shape and colour! In front of my eyes, there it is, my little black skirt.

(female, 21)

There is more to this sense of pre- and post-trip depression – or, on occasion, euphoria – than the consumers' (in)ability to accomplish the tasks they set themselves prior to departure. The retailing labours, Augean though they sometimes prove (especially at Christmastime), are not just about working one's way through a shopping list, mental or otherwise. On the contrary, it is clear from the essays that very strong fantasy elements are involved. Just as some marketing misanthropes fantasise about the nightmare experiences that await them, so too many consumers are prone to elaborate pipe-dreams about the transformative powers of the products that they hope to acquire, or have just acquired – how well/sophisticated/glamorous/seductive they will look, the admiring glances/members of the opposite sex they are sure to attract, the hours of pleasure they will derive from their new video, CD, computer game, etc. and the look of joy on a friend or relative's face when they unwrap that special, carefully selected gift.

It makes me feel really good when I put something on in a changing room and suddenly I am someone different for a few minutes.

(female, 21)

Finally dragging myself away from the inspired images of myself walking along a beach at sunset with deep reddish-brown shades of silk flowing with my movements, I ended up in the aromatherapy section.

(female, 27)

'Why don't you try them on', she said. Looking in the direction of my male friend, I got a nod and a smile at this last remark. Well, why not? I won't get another chance I guess, so I make my way to the changing rooms. It felt more like I was walking into a different era – out of a shop into a western! I pushed my way past what there was of the swinging doors and tried on my latest selection of clothing . . . I decided to do a bit of the Cindy Crawford by strutting my stuff out on the shop floor, although I felt more like John Wayne as I pushed the swinging doors once again.

(female, 20)

Next stop Boots. Hmmm, I never realised that Boots sold infant toys. They had cute little motor toys and bath toys, among others, which, of course, I had to test out for possible Xmas presents for my nephew, Caelan. I could just imagine the beaming excitement and stunned amazement on his (deceptively) angelic little face at some of those toys. Well, it would be necessary for me to play with – I mean – check out toys in other shops before I could choose the ideal toy.

(female, 27)

Such fantasising, admittedly, is partly an artefact of the introspective research procedure, which explicitly encourages the essayist to reflect on their reflections, yet it remains powerful for all that and helps us comprehend the sheer depth of emotion involved. As Campbell (1987, 1995), Holbrook and Hirschman (1982), Rook (1987, 1988) and Sherry *et al.* (1995) have argued, daydreaming has long been and remains an important element of the consuming impulse.

FELL DEEPLY INTO DEBT

Another crucial aspect of these retailing-related reveries concerns their ontological status and, indeed, the ontological status of shopping expeditions *per se*. Now, it cannot be denied that such behaviours unfold in real time. Retail outlets, department stores and shopping centres are unquestionably patronised; actual purchases are made, information is gathered and social exchanges transpire; people indubitably pause to reflect for a few moments on the progress of the trip thus far; and shopping trophies are borne home in triumph or, more often than not, relief. Many of the essayists, what is more, specifically refer to the very real temporal pressures that impinge upon their shopping expeditions – oversleeping, lateness, delays, interruptions, diversions, dilatory shopping companions, long queues, lazy sales assistants and any number of looming deadlines ranging from the threat of a parking ticket when the time limit expires, through the need to start work in less than fifteen minutes and the desire to get home in time for a favourite television programme, to the fact that a friend is getting married the very next day and the wedding gift has not yet been bought (see Iyer 1989; Park *et al.* 1989; Thompson 1996).

> All I want to do is get this over and done with – the sooner I get through the damn door the sooner I get home. Does it not occur to people that Danni is falling passionately in love in tonight's episode of *Neighbours*.
>
> (female, 23)

> It was a disaster from the very start. Instead of meeting her at her own house and getting a Citybus into the centre, we foolishly decided to make our own way into Belfast and then meet at that fateful time of noon, outside the jewellers opposite the City Hall. Well, that was the plan, because I managed to get into town for that time, with absolutely no sign of Paula. To say I was pissed off would be an understatement because I was standing on my own in the pissing rain looking into a jewellers window for 20 minutes ... Paula eventually arrived looking as if she was dragged backwards through a bush by a herd of wild cavemen and my query of 'Where the hell were you?' was greeted by 'Shut the fuck up. You won't believe what happened to me.' The story started to unfold, as she was waiting for a bus, a car drove over

a puddle and soaked her, then the bus she got on was diverted from its original route and thus the reason why she was late.

(male, 23)

As we stand in the queue at the checkouts, mum asks, 'What time was on the ticket?' 'I think it was 4.50', I reply as I look at my watch and realise it is 4.40, only ten minutes left. Then, the person in front takes out her cheque book to pay for about four items. Mum and I look at each other in disgust. When we finally pay for the groceries, we raced onto the escalator laden down with bags on either hand, only to come to a sudden halt by a woman standing with her basket which we were unable to pass for what seemed like an eternity yet was only 30 seconds.

(female, 22)

By the same token, and notwithstanding the positive side to time pressures (in so far as they can help overcome chronic procrastination and serve as an excuse for terminating tedious social encounters), the introspective accounts do exhibit elements of liminality, of otherworldliness, of being betwixt and between (Belk *et al.* 1989; Sherry 1990). Thus, time and space are experienced in a highly distorted fashion. Time expands exponentially when delays or disruptions are encountered and contracts dramatically when the marketplace endorphins kick in.

I glanced up at the clock on the town hall, aware of how much shopping I had to do. With this in mind, I hastened my step . . . No time to dander. I gaze longingly at each shop window as I pass, wishing I had more time, but knowing I hadn't.

(female, 21)

To my abhorrence I saw my old headmistress heading my way. I tried to duck, but to no avail, she had spotted me and was making a beeline to me. 'Merry Christmas Pauline', she almost sang in her shrill, operatic tones. I couldn't believe that she still mixed me up with my best friend and I thought the better of correcting her. After exchanging pleasantries for what seemed like one hundred years, I managed to break away and fought my way into Next.

(female, 22)

Once I actually do get near the till, nothing aggravates me more than being stuck behind someone whose limit on their cheque card is less than the amount on the cheque which they have just written. The assistant then has to phone the bank to check if it is okay to accept the cheque. This seems to take an eternity.

(female, 20)

Unfortunately for the members of my family, time was running out and I had just spotted the Manchester United Store. We had a field day in there. It was like letting a bull loose in a china shop and, if you haven't guessed it by now, yes I am a United fan. I spent what seemed ten minutes wading through posters, framed pictures, videos, etc. but was actually just over an hour. How do you spend an hour in the one shop? It is not usually like me to do that.

(male, 21)

Space is equally mutable, since the merest walk across a busy mall can feel like 'a gruelling marathon', shops become so big they are literally 'unending', crowds number in their multi-millions, no less, and, when expectations are high, world famous shopping streets (like film stars) turn out to be smaller than expected. As noted earlier, a nightmare nether-world – a marketing dystopia – can and does materialise at the flick of a Switchcard.

The floors of Debenhams were heaving with 'women in packs' chatting among themselves and paying no heed to anyone. My quiet night of browsing turned into a living nightmare. There were women bombarding me in all directions, hitting me with their bags and baskets, while babbling to each other. Anyone would have thought they owned the place. It was nearly enough to make me turn on my heels and walk straight back out and head for home. I could not believe this was happening.

(female, 20)

Stumbling through the huge crowd of Christmas shoppers I began to get rather irritated. Then it began to rain, sorry not rain, pour. I strug-gled into Castle Court past those at the door seeking cover from the elements. Making my way upstairs the Christmas spirit was noticeable but to be honest I was past that stage. All I wanted to do was buy this bloody present and get home. I walked into Index and saw that the queues were more or less the same size as those in Argos. The day was turning tragic. I looked at the Index catalogue and discovered a quite reasonably priced foot-spa at £34.99. Success? I jotted down the catalogue number of the item and was more or less pushed into the first available queue by the Index shopping mob. I stood in that queue for the guts of twenty or thirty minutes but it felt longer.

(male, 21)

The shop assistants, complete with 'mumsie' look stare at me with hard-ened eyes. They're thinking 'Intruder'. 'Escape', is screaming through my head . . . I storm past mummy shop assistant one and nearly break my neck on what resembles a bean-bag on wheels. Mummy shop assis-tant two sniggers and my brolly catches on something as I hurry towards the exit. I turn around to find my bizarre friend stooping over a scat-tered carton of nursing bras ready for the shelf . . . My heart is pounding and my throat is so dry that I can only mouth the word 'sorry' at the shop assistants, already decided on the malefactor. Claire goes off to price the Bendy Bugle (of *Rainbow* fame) that we saw on the way in and I edge away from the two motherly beings. It was as if they knew Claire was 'one of them' and I was an unalterable infiltrator polluting their aseptic environment with anti-baby vibes.

(female, 22)

Set against this, an Elysium of consuming euphoria is also within easy reach, whether it be the 'Garden of Eden' that is the frozen food section, an Aladdin's Cave stuffed with treasures from the pseudo-orient, the 'temple of paradise' that is electrical equipment stores or, quite simply, another place where everyday cares and worries are left behind. In fact, it is not unusual for informants to find themselves 'floating' around, 'suspended' above, 'sucked' into and 'pulled' towards certain shops, restaurants, displays, merchandise, collectibles and hitherto 'forbidden worlds' (Rook 1985).

After our fix of slander and social intrusions we usually 'hit' the shops. Some magnetic force would guide us effortlessly through the trendiest stores in the centre of town such as Next, Top Shop, Dorothy Perkins and Principles, with the inevitable cessation – the perfume counter at Boots.

(female, 22)

I have been told frequently that I am a very irritating person to shop with simply because I go off into a world of my own. Nobody can give me advice because I have my own 'wee' ideas in my head. My girl-friend can back me up on this one, rather unwillingly I'm sure, because all the time she is constantly screeching into my ear, 'Wait for me!'

(male, 21)

Swerving past the queues of trolleys at the butcher shop, I just can't resist a quick glance at Masquerade next door. Masquerade is a delight-fully small space rather than a shop, with fascinating bits and pieces. Sensual aromatherapy oils, scented candles, floating candles, burners, vases, miniature clocks and coveted silver jewellery are all carefully aligned into this Pandora's Box. I snatch a quick smell from the erotic Ylang Ylang (purported to be an aphrodisiac). Encapsulated, I drift into Wellworths. Is there such a thing as an aphrodisiac for shopping I wonder.

(female, 23)

There was only one thing for it, I would have to enter the forbidden world of The Body Shop. Drifting on a sea of scent, I picked up a green basket, fooling myself that it was not really necessary for the one item that I was going to buy. Lots of unusual-shaped soaps and bath pearls were the first things to greet me and naturally I had to show my appreciation of such items by individually examining them and smelling them. Somehow a silver-grey, moon-shaped soap and pale pink star-shaped bath pearls found their way into my basket.

(female, 27)

A closely related aspect of the introspective accounts is the shopping environment's ostensible, not to say remarkable, ability to catapult the informants back in time (Sherry 1990). Again and again, the essays refer to being transported back to their childhood or, more precisely, a golden age of childhood, a kind of paradisiacal pre-pubescent state where shopping was easy, goods were plentiful, money no object and parents unfailingly on hand to make the right decisions. Unsurprisingly perhaps, the 'trigger' for many of these retrospective fantasies turns out to be toy shops, though for some consumers at least the very act of 'going shopping' calls forth the inner child. For other shoppers, their present-day consumer behaviour is strongly influenced by events – both good and bad – that occurred in their formative years (Olsen 1995). Oedipus shops!

After we managed to battle our way through the crowds on the streets, we reached Leisureworld. Standing outside the store we could hear the sounds of games being experimented with by over-indulgent parents – sounds that would bring out the long-gone child of even the coldest of hearts.

(male, 22)

Have you ever experienced the delight of entering the Walt Disney Store in Belfast? Staff are dressed colourfully, portraying the image of my childhood, and you are greeted with a welcoming smile. It touches my heart to see so many young children being able to have fun and enjoyment in a store with so much character and appeal. Stores like this give me satisfaction, I can enjoy a shopping trip without spending one single penny. I can enter the Disney Store and see the world from a different view, trouble free, all as one having fun. As a child Mickey Mouse was my hero and with a couple of extra pounds jingling in my pocket, I would usually end up purchasing a pen, poster or whatever is financially affordable. To this day my childhood behaviour reflects me. Now as a 22 year-old male, I wear a Mickey Mouse character watch.

(male, 21)

My estranged companion makes her way to the exit and awakens me with a well-practised, motherly, 'Keep up!' The years fall off me and I follow in reverence, dithering behind in fear of getting a 'clip behind the ear' ... I feel about six again and I'm overcome with an urge to scream, 'I want my mummy!!!'

(female, 22)

I am the original lone shopper. I prefer to shop alone. This I blame on my childhood when my mother treated me as the daughter she never had, dragging me round endless clothes shops in search of the eternal bargain. Far from putting me off shopping, it actually encouraged me, although I now prefer to drag myself around at my own pace.

(male, 22)

'Do you want to go to Miss Selfridge to try on the hats there? They have some really wacky ones.' Of course the answer was yes, [though] I wondered why in hell I have this fixation for trying on hats. As we crossed over to Miss Selfridge, I remembered the multi-coloured bobble hat that I had seen there and had become slightly attracted to, and needed to try it on one more time. perhaps I did not dress up enough as a child, I thought to myself. However, it was too late to ask why. We had already entered the shop and were heading for the hat section, when I heard myself saying, 'I love trying on hats.' 'I know', my friend replied.

(female, 21)

If, in an admittedly contrived attempt at synthesis, the introspections had to be summarised in a single word, that word would probably be 'quest'. The majority of these tales from the crypt of consumption are premised on a search – sometimes successfully realised, oft-times a frustrating exercise in under-achievement – for something other, something else, something better, something above and beyond the present, be it a perfect party dress, a 'just right' gift, a more attractive self, an eco-friendly world, a romantic encounter or, as often as not, the sheer relief of surviving the ordeal, of coming unscathed through the valley of the shadow of debt. True, this overarching theme cannot be dissociated from the storytelling task with which the informants were charged (the journey metaphor is as structurally homologous to 'going shopping' as it is to any other processual domain – life, knowledge, enlightenment, etc.). Nevertheless, like all quests in the chivalric tradition (Liveley and Kerven 1996), the introspective essays consist of encounters with good and evil, triumph and disaster, digressions and diversions, challenge and response, temptations to be resisted, grails to be pursued, amusing or pacific interludes, recalcitrant companions, shopping centre sirens, the Scylla of credit versus the Charybdis of cash and, as shall be demonstrated elsewhere, all manner of enchanting or thaumaturgic occurrences. The 'magic of the mall' (Goss 1993) really does exist, for these informants at least, in both black and white permutations.

AND LIVED UNHAPPILY EVER AFTER

It is tempting to conclude this chapter on the above magical note, with a sort of textual disappearing act, as it were. Where did they go? Who cares? What's next? However, the norms of traditional academic discourse require us to bring together (summary), reflect on (discussion), apologise for (limitations) and suggest improvements to (future research) the approach articulated herein. Rather than follow such a time-worn scholarly schema, we simply wish to make the following key points. First, it is clear from the introspections that shopping orientations are rather more contingent and situation specific than has traditionally been assumed. Although, as the extant typology literature indicates, consumers may possess an overall sense of liking or disliking shopping, or certain types of shopping, it is apparent that these feelings are remarkably fluid, depending as they do on a host of fluctuating, if not entirely arbitrary environmental, social and antecedent circumstances.

Second, the essays highlight some of the more aversive aspects of shopping. While we have long been aware of the 'existence' of the so-called apathetic shopper, and the 'dark side' of consumer behaviour generally, hate-to-shop shoppers have been somewhat neglected hitherto. However, the recent rise, or rather labelling, of 'trolley rage' indicates that the issue is in need of serious investigation. Certainly, the introspections indicate that many people would prefer to drop shopping than shop 'til they drop, albeit such an option is unavailable in most cases. We have to shop whether we like it or not – and some of us don't!

Third, the findings demonstrate the potential of the introspective research procedure. Maligned though it often is – rightly in some respects, wrongly in others – the sheer calibre of the students' shopping representations and the remarkable depth of insight they provide, indicates that the technique has been dismissed too readily. Granted, the validity of our consumer chronicles cannot be scientifically demonstrated; the Truth of such compositional exercises is uncertain; and many readers, especially those with a weakness for excruciating puns, will doubtless dismiss the foregoing fabulations as a 'con'. Yet established qualitative techniques also suffer from many of the self-same shortcomings, albeit these tend to be obscured by the 'metaphysics of presence', the entirely unwarranted presupposition that speech is superior to writing, that fabulation is a poor relation of confabulation. Why, to reiterate Campbell's (1996) challenge, do we accept that introspective data are indispensable when originating from 'subjects' but deny them any value when they come from 'researcher as subject'?

A final point, and one that enables us to conclude with an extended quotation which illustrates (a) the utility of the introspective procedure, (b) the aversive side of shopping and (c) the sheer contingency of consumer behaviour, pertains to the all-important fact that the above treatment was necessarily compartmentalised. For the purposes of exposition, the content of the essays was presented in terms of Belk's famous, five-category 'situational' framework – physical surroundings, social surroundings, task definition, antecedent states and temporal perspective. In practice, of course, all these elements interact, sometimes working together, sometimes cancelling out and, on occasion, precipitating a nightmare situation where everything that can possibly go wrong with a shopping trip does go wrong – in spades! When it comes to shoppers on the verge of a nervous breakdown, this one's got it all.

I don't mind going shopping as long as I'm shopping for myself. I can happily wander around on my own as I know exactly what I want before I start. But I hate going shopping with my girlfriend who has to get into every ladies' shop – and more.

Things started off quite well that day. I followed her around the various shops, wading through the rails of clothing, stopping every now and then for her to pick something off a rail, hold it up to herself, and then look to me for some sort of sign of approval. This ritual would go on until she had an armful of clothes, then it was off to the changing rooms while I waited for her to appear every five minutes to ask me what I thought. I would try and look interested, complimenting her on how well she looked in the outfit, but after half a dozen more shops I was trying to sound more convincing in the hope that she would take my word for it and buy the bloody thing, but she wasn't to be fooled. Saying that the outfit didn't feel right on her and that she knew another shop that she could try.

So off we headed again, hand-in-hand, with me trying to reassure her that I really did like the last outfit that she had tried on, only to be told to put out the cigarette I had just lit. I wouldn't have minded that much, only it was the first one I had smoked since we had left home.

We walked for what seemed like hours from shop to shop and then back again, and I hadn't had a chance to look for a suit for myself but that didn't seem to matter. My girlfriend then dropped the bombshell. When she had found the dress that she wanted she would need a pair of shoes to match. 'Shit!' We would have to walk from one end of Belfast to the other again. I started to realise how my dog Ben must feel when I drag him along on the lead when he doesn't really want to go.

We entered another ladies boutique and went through the same procedure of looking through the rails of clothes with me nodding approval like one of those miniature dogs you sometimes see in the back window of a car. Then it was off to the changing rooms with me standing like a sentry outside waiting while she tried on the various outfits.

The changing rooms in this particular store just happened to be positioned right at the back of the store smack bang in the middle of the lingerie department. I wouldn't have minded, only, where I was standing there were ladies parading in and out past me with handfuls of knickers and bras giving me funny sideways glances. The sight of ladies with their underwear in their hands didn't annoy me as I had a business of my own which stocked among other things the same type of ladies underwear, and I was used to them asking me for all shapes, colours and sizes. But standing in the middle of these ladies I started to feel very uncomfortable and imagined that all eyes were fixed on me as if I was some sort of Peeping Tom. I said to myself that this was it. I wasn't going into any more shops to stand around like a wet lettuce while my girlfriend tried on clothes that she seemed to have no intention of buying. When she emerged from the changing room with that look on her face that meant that we would have to look elsewhere for the long black dress, I gave one of those eyes-half-closed, teeth-gritted looks that you give when you are extremely pissed off with someone, and she duly gave me one back. I knew from that moment that the rest of the day was going to be a disaster, and that is exactly what it turned out to be.

I suggested that maybe we could get a cup of coffee and something to eat, but that was the wrong suggestion. We would have to get the dress before we did anything else. At this stage in the proceedings I was walking about ten paces behind my girlfriend who had broken into what can only be described as a gallop. When I eventually caught up with her she had a face like a bulldog chewing a wasp and started to give me my second public warning of the day. At this point I didn't care about getting myself a suit. I just wanted her to get the dress so that we could get the hell out of Belfast.

And so, with total disinterest I followed my girlfriend around a few more shops until eventually she had satisfied herself that every shop that could possibly have done what she wanted had been visited, and so we headed back to one of the first that we had been in at the start of the day. At this point our conversation consisted of two words, yes and no, but I was prepared to give it one last go as we entered through the front door of Jigsaw for the second time. Our first visit had been a friendly shopping experience with very friendly staff greeting us with a smile and asking if they could be of assistance.

This time around the reaction seemed to be quite the opposite. The staff didn't smile or ask us if they could help. They were more interested in standing around talking among themselves and sniggering. When my girlfriend had made her choice and asked if they would have it in her size the assistant looked directly at the clock on the wall which showed the time as being ten past five, twenty minutes before closing time. I made a comment to my girlfriend that maybe we should let them keep the dress and look elsewhere, just as the assistant came back from looking for the correct size and informed us that that particular dress had sold really well and that there were only two left, and neither was the size that my girlfriend wanted. We were just about to leave the store when my girlfriend spotted the dress among other clothes on a rail, and upon closer inspection found it to be the correct size. I immediately looked around at the assistant, who turned and started to make herself busy by tidying the clothes on a rail. At this point I really wanted to let rip with a well-rehearsed string of verbal abuse, but decided that it wouldn't read that well on a charge-sheet if the worst came to the worst and the assistant decided that she needed the help of the 'boys in blue' to calm the situation. And so, I thought the best course of action would be for my girlfriend and myself to leave the shop minus the dress. But no! My girlfriend had other ideas. As I headed for the door expecting her to follow, she made a beeline for the changing room with the dress slung over her arm. At this point I was outside in the street mouthing obscenities to myself and feeling a real prick, convincing myself that I would definitely not be going to the wedding. When my girlfriend appeared from the changing room kitted out in the long black dress, she wagged me to come in and take a look, but there was no chance. I shouted to her that I would meet her back at the car, turned on my heels and walked off.

I was sitting in the car for about ten minutes thinking just how fast our relationship was going downhill when she arrived holding a Jigsaw carrier bag smiling from ear to ear. She jumped into the car and proceeded to tell me how well the dress had looked on and that she would have to get a pair of shoes to match. I couldn't believe it. Gone was the bulldog and the wasp features replaced by a butter wouldn't melt in the mouth look. I pointed out that we had spent so much time looking for the bloody dress I hadn't had a chance to look for a suit for myself. This didn't seem a real problem to her, and she suggested that we could come down to Belfast another day to look for a suit. At this point the shit really hit the fan. I told her that the wedding invitation was worse than getting a bloody summons, and that I definitely wouldn't be going, so she may make other arrangements ...

Needless to say, I went back on my word and attended the wedding, and surprisingly enough we had a really good day. My girlfriend in her new black dress and me in my nearly new suit. But at the end of the day we would never go through a nightmare shopping experience again like it, or at least not together anyway, as we decided shortly after that to go our separate ways.

(male, 30)

REFERENCES

Aaker, D.A. and Stayman, D.M. (1992) 'Implementing the concept of transformational advertising', *Psychology and Marketing*, 9, 3: 237–253.

AGB (1987) *Lifestyles Report*, London: Audits of Great Britain.

Alba, J.W., Hutchinson, J.W. and Lynch, J.G. (1991) 'Memory and decision making', in T.S. Robertson and H.H. Kassarjian (eds) *Handbook of Consumer Behavior*, Englewood Cliffs, NJ: Prentice Hall, 1–49.

Auster, P. (1995) *The Red Notebook and Other Writings*, London: Faber & Faber.

Babin, B.J., Darden, W.R. and Griffin, M. (1994) 'Work and/or fun: measuring hedonic and utilitarian shopping value', *Journal of Consumer Research*, 20, March: 644–656.

Bachelard, G. (1994 [1958]) *The Poetics of Space*, trans. M. Jolas, Boston, MA: Beacon.

Baddeley, A. (1990) *Human Memory: Theory and Practice*, Hillsdale, NJ: Erlbaum.

Barthes, R. (1977 [1968]) 'Introduction to the structural analysis of narratives', in R. Barthes, *Image, Music, Text*, trans. S. Heath, London: Fontana, 79–124.

Baudrillard, J. (1995 [1991]) *The Gulf War Did Not Take Place*, trans. P. Patton, Bloomington, IN: Indiana University Press.

Belk, R. (1975) 'Situational variables and consumer behavior', *Journal of Consumer Research*, 1, December: 157–164.

——, Wallendorf, M. and Sherry, J.F. (1989) 'The sacred and the profane in consumer behavior: theodicy on the Odyssey', *Journal of Consumer Research*, 16, June: 1–38.

Bellenger, D.N. and Korgaonkar, P. (1980) 'Profiling the recreational shopper', *Journal of Retailing*, 56, 3: 77–92.

Benson, P. (ed.) (1993) *Anthropology and Literature*, Urbana, IL: University of Illinois Press.

Berger, A.A. (1997) *Narratives in Popular Culture, Media and Everyday Life*, Thousand Oaks, CA: Sage.

Bitner, M.J. (1992) 'Servicescapes: the impact of physical surroundings on customers and employees', *Journal of Marketing*, 56, April: 57–71.

——, Booms, B.H. and Mohr, L.A. (1994) 'Critical service encounters: the employee's viewpoint', *Journal of Marketing*, 58, October: 95–106.

——,—— and Tetreault, M.S. (1990) 'The service encounter: diagnosing favorable and unfavorable incidents', *Journal of Marketing*, 54, January: 71–84.

Brockman, J. (1995) *The Third Culture: Beyond the Scientific Revolution*, New York: Simon & Schuster.

Brosseau, M. (1994) 'Geography's literature', *Progress in Human Geography*, 18, 2: 333–353.

Brown, S. (1997) *Postmodern Marketing Two: Telling Tales*, London: International Thomson Business Press.

Callinicos, A. (1995) *Theories and Narratives: Reflections on the Philosophy of History*, Cambridge: Polity.

Calvino, I. (1986 [1982]) *The Uses of Literature*, trans. P. Creagh, San Diego, CA: Harcourt Brace.

Campbell, C. (1987) *The Romantic Ethic and the Spirit of Modern Consumerism*, Oxford: Blackwell.

—— (1995) 'The sociology of consumption', in D. Miller (ed.) *Acknowledging Consumption: A Review of New Studies*, London: Routledge, 96–126.

—— (1996) 'Romanticism, consumption and introspection: some comments on Professor Holbrook's paper', in R.W. Belk, N. Dholakia and A. Venkatesh (eds) *Consumption and Marketing: Macro Dimensions*, Cincinnati, OH: South-Western, 96–103.

Chaplin, E. (1994) *Sociology and Visual Representation*, London: Routledge.

Clandinin, D.J. and Connelly, F.M. (1994) 'Personal experience methods', in N.K. Denzin and Y.S. Lincoln (eds) *Handbook of Qualitative Research*, Thousand Oaks, CA: Sage, 413–427.

Coles, R. (1989) *The Call of Stories: Teaching and the Moral Imagination*, Boston, MA: Houghton Mifflin.

Cullen, C.W. (1990) *Shopping as Entertainment: Implications for the Shopping Centre Manager*, University of Stirling: Institute for Retail Studies.

Czepeil, J.A. (1990) 'Service encounters and service relationships: implications for research', *Journal of Business Research*, 20, 1: 13–21.

Darden, W.R. and Ashton, D. (1975) 'Psychographic profiles of patronage preference groups', *Journal of Retailing*, 50, 4: 99–112.

d'Astous, A. (1990) 'An inquiry into the compulsive side of "normal" consumers', *Journal of Consumer Policy*, 13, 1: 15–31.

Davies, G. and Bell, J. (1991) 'The grocery shopper – is he different?', *International Journal of Retail and Distribution Management*, 19, 1: 25–28.

Dawson, S., Bloch, P.H. and Ridgway, N.M. (1990) 'Shopping motives, emotional states and retail outcomes', *Journal of Retailing*, 66, Winter: 408–427.

Day, E. (1989) 'Share of heart: what is it and how can it be measured?', *Journal of Consumer Marketing*, 6, 1: 5–12.

Deighton, J. (1992) 'The consumption of performance', *Journal of Consumer Research*, 19, December: 362–372.

Derrida, J. (1976 [1967]) *Of Grammatology*, trans. G.C. Spivak, Baltimore, MD: Johns Hopkins University Press.

Durgee, J.F. (1988) 'Interpreting consumer mythology: a literary criticism approach to Odyssey informant stories', in M.J. Houston (ed.) *Advances in Consumer Research*, 15, Provo, UT: Association for Consumer Research, 531–536.

East, R., Lomax, W., Willson, G. and Harris, P. (1994) 'Decision making and habit in shopping times', *European Journal of Marketing*, 28, 4: 56–71.

Eisner, E. (1985) *The Art of Educational Evaluation: A Personal View*, London: Falmer.

Elliott, R. (1994) 'Addictive consumption: function and fragmentation in postmodernity', *Journal of Consumer Policy*, 17, 2: 157–179.

——, Eccles, S. and Gournay, K. (1996) 'Revenge, existential choice and addictive consumption', *Psychology and Marketing*, 13, 8: 753–768.

Ellis, C. (1991) 'Sociological introspection and emotional experience', *Symbolic Interaction*, 14, 1: 23–50.

Eroglu, S.A. and Machleit, K.A. (1990) 'An empirical study of retail crowding: antecedents and consequences', *Journal of Retailing*, 66, Summer: 201–221.

Everitt, A. (1995) 'It's shopping rage! Don't get mown down or beaten up in the rush – know thine enemy', *Sunday Mirror Magazine*, 10 December: 22.

Fischer, E. and Arnold, S.J. (1990) 'More than a labor of love: gender roles and Christmas gift shopping', *Journal of Consumer Research*, 17, December: 333–345.

Fisk, R.P. and Grove, S.J. (1996) 'Applications of impression management and the drama metaphor in marketing: an introduction', *European Journal of Marketing*, 30, 9: 6–12.

Floch, J-M. (1988) 'The contribution of structural semiotics to the design of a hypermarket', *International Journal of Research in Marketing*, 4, 2: 233–252.

Frye, N. (1971) *Anatomy of Criticism: Four Essays*, Princeton, NJ: Princeton University Press.

Gardner, M. (1985) 'Mood states and consumer behaviour: a critical review', *Journal of Consumer Research*, 12, December: 281–300.

Gibson, A. (1996) *Towards a Postmodern Theory of Narrative*, Edinburgh: Edinburgh University Press.

Goss, J. (1993) 'The "magic of the mall": an analysis of form, function and meaning in the contemporary retail built environment', *Annals of the Association of American Geographers*, 83, 1: 18–47.

Gould, S.J. (1991) 'The self-manipulation of my pervasive, perceived vital energy through product use: an introspective-praxis perspective', *Journal of Consumer Research*, 18, September: 194–207.

—— (1995) 'Researcher introspection as a method in consumer research: applications, issues and implications', *Journal of Consumer Research*, 21, March: 719–722.

Grossbart, S., Hampton, R., Rammohan, B. and Lapidus, R.S. (1990) 'Environmental dispositions and customer response to store atmospherics', *Journal of Business Research*, 31, 2: 225–241.

Hassay, D.N. and Smith, M.C. (1996) 'Fauna, foraging and shopping motives', in K.P. Corfman and J.G. Lynch (eds) *Advances in Consumer Research*, 23, Provo, UT: Association for Consumer Research, 510–515.

Heilbrunn, B. (1996) 'In search of the hidden Go(o)d: a philosophical deconstruction and narratological revisitation of the eschatological metaphor in marketing', in S. Brown, J. Bell and D. Carson (eds) *Marketing Apocalypse: Eschatology, Escapology and the Illusion of the End*, London: Routledge, 111–132.

Heskett, J.L., Jones, T.O., Loveman, G.W., Sasser, W.E. and Schlesinger, L.A. (1994) 'Putting the service-profit chain to work', *Harvard Business Review*, 72, March–April, 164–174.

Hirschman, E.C. (1990) 'The day I almost died: a consumer researcher learns some lessons from a traumatic experience', in E.C. Hirschman (ed.) *Research in Consumer Behaviour*, 4, Greenwich: JAI Press, 109–123.

—— (1991) 'Secular mortality and the dark side of consumer behavior; or, how semiotics saved my life', in R.H. Holman and M.R. Solomon (eds) *Advances in Consumer Research*, 18, Provo, UT: Association for Consumer Research, 1–4.

—— (1992) 'The consciousness of addiction: toward a general theory of compulsive consumption', *Journal of Consumer Research*, 19, September: 155–179.

—— and Holbrook, M.B. (1982) 'Hedonic consumption: emerging concepts, methods and propositions', *Journal of Marketing*, 46, Summer: 92–101.

Hixon, J.G. and Swann, W.B. (1993) 'When does introspection bear fruit? Self-reflection, self-insight and interpersonal choices', *Journal of Personality and Social Psychology*, 64, 1: 35–43.

Hoch, S.J. and Loewenstein, G.F. (1991) 'Time-inconsistent preferences and consumer self-control', *Journal of Consumer Research*, 17, March: 492–507.

Holbrook, M.B. (1986) 'I'm hip: an autobiographical account of some musical consumption experiences', in R.J. Lutz (ed.) *Advances in Consumer Research*, 13, Provo, UT: Association for Consumer Research, 614–618.

—— (1987) 'An audiovisual inventory of some fanatic consumer behaviour: the 25-cent tour of a jazz collector's home', in M. Wallendorf and P.F. Anderson (eds) *Advances in Consumer Research*, 14, Provo, UT: Association for Consumer Research, 144–149.

—— (1995) *Consumer Research: Introspective Essays on the Study of Consumption*, Thousand Oaks, CA: Sage.

—— (1996) 'Romanticism, introspection and the roots of experiential consumption: Morris the Epicurean', in R.W. Belk, N. Dholakia and A. Venkatesh (eds) *Consumption and Marketing: Macro Dimensions*, Cincinnati, OH: South-Western, 20–82.

—— and Hirschman, E.C. (1982) 'The experiential aspects of consumption: consumer fantasies, feelings and fun', *Journal of Consumer Research*, 9, September: 132–140.

Horton, J. and Baumeister, A.T. (eds) (1996) *Literature and the Political Imagination*, London: Routledge.

Hutcheon, L. (1989) *The Politics of Postmodernism*, London: Routledge.

Iyer, E.S. (1989) 'Unplanned purchasing: knowledge of shopping environment and time pressure', *Journal of Retailing*, 64, Spring: 40–57.

Jameson, F. (1981) *The Political Unconscious: Narrative as a Socially Symbolic Act*, London: Methuen.

Jeffcutt, P. (1993) 'From interpretation to representation', in J. Hassard and M. Parker (eds) *Postmodernism and Organisations*, London: Sage, 25–48.

Kanter, R.M. (1994) 'Collaborative advantage: the art of alliances', *Harvard Business Review*, 72, July–August: 96–108.

Kirk-Smith, M. and Mak, E. (1992) 'A consumer typology for the UK financial services market', in J. Whitelock (ed.) *Marketing in the New Europe and Beyond*, MEG Annual Conference Proceedings, Salford: Salford University.

Krell, D.F. (1996) *Nietzsche: A Novel*, Albany, NY: State University of New York Press.

Kundera, M. (1988) *The Art of the Novel*, trans. L. Asher, London: Faber & Faber.

Lataif, L.E. (1992) 'Debate – MBA: is the traditional model doomed?', *Harvard Business Review*, 70, November–December: 128–129.

Lehmann, D.R. (1987) 'Pumping Iron III: an examination of compulsive lifting', in M. Wallendorf and P.F. Anderson (eds) *Advances in Consumer Research*, 14, Provo, UT: Association for Consumer Research, 129–135.

Lesser, J.A. and Hughes, M.A. (1986) 'Towards a typology of shoppers', *Business Horizons*, 29, 6: 56–62.

Lévi-Strauss, C. (1968 [1958]) *Structural Anthropology*, trans. C. Jacobson and B.G. Schoepf, Harmondsworth: Penguin.

Levy, S.J. (1981) 'Interpreting consumer mythology: a structural approach to consumer behavior', *Journal of Marketing*, 45, Summer: 49–61.

Linder, J.C. and Smith, H.J. (1992) 'The complex case of management education', *Harvard Business Review*, 70, September–October: 16–33.

Liveley, P. and Kerven, R. (1996) *The Mythical Quest: In Search of Adventure, Romance and Enlightenment*, London: British Library.

Lyotard, J-F. (1989) 'Lessons in paganism', in A. Benjamin (ed.) *The Lyotard Reader*, Oxford: Blackwell, 122–154.

McCloskey, D.N. (1994) *Knowledge and Persuasion in Economics*, Cambridge: Cambridge University Press.

McGoldrick, P. (1990) *Retail Marketing*, London: McGraw-Hill.

McGrath, M.A. and Otnes, C. (1995) 'Unacquainted influencers: the role of strangers in the retail setting', *Journal of Business Research*, 32, 3: 261–272.

McHale, B. (1992) *Constructing Postmodernism*, London: Routledge.

McKenna, R. (1992) *Relationship Marketing: Own the Market Through Strategic Customer Relationships*, London: Century.

Martin, W. (1986) *Recent Theories of Narrative*, Ithaca, NY: Cornell University Press.

Mick, D.G. (1992) 'Levels of subjective comprehension in advertising processing and their relations to ad perceptions, attitudes and memory', *Journal of Consumer Research*, 18, March: 411–424.

Mintzberg, H. (1992) 'Debate – MBA: is the traditional model doomed?', *Harvard Business Review*, 70, November–December: 129.

Mitroff, I.I. and Churchman, C.W. (1992) 'Debate – MBA: is the traditional model doomed?', *Harvard Business Review*, 70, November–December: 134–136.

Moschis, G.P. (1976) 'Shopping orientations and consumer uses of information', *Journal of Retailing*, 52, 2: 61–70, 93.

Murray, K.D. (1995) 'Narratology', in J.A. Smith, R. Harré and L. van Langenhove (eds) *Rethinking Psychology*, London: Sage, 179–195.

O'Guinn, T. (1996) 'The romantic arbiter: a comment on Holbrook', in R.W. Belk, N. Dholakia and A. Venkatesh (eds) *Consumption and Marketing: Macro Dimensions*, Cincinnati, OH: South-Western, 83–86.

—— and Faber, R.J. (1989) 'Compulsive buying: a phenomenological exploration', *Journal of Consumer Research*, 16, September: 147–157.

Olsen, B. (1995) 'Brand loyalty and consumption patterns: the lineage factor', in J.F. Sherry (ed.) *Contemporary Marketing and Consumer Behavior*, Thousand Oaks, CA: Sage, 245–281.

Otnes, C., Lowrey, T.M. and Kim, Y.C. (1993) 'Christmas shopping for easy and difficult recipients: a social roles interpretation', *Journal of Consumer Research*, 20, September: 229–244.

Park, C.W., Iyer, E.S. and Smith, D.C. (1989) 'The effects of situational factors on in-store grocery shopping behaviour: the role of store environment and time available for shopping', *Journal of Consumer Research*, 15, March: 422–433.

Phillips, A. (1993) *On Kissing, Tickling and Being Bored*, London: Faber & Faber.

Pieros, C.P. and McGoldrick, P.J. (1993) 'Modelling the effects of atmospherics in major shopping centres', in P.J. McGoldrick and G. Davies (eds) *ESRC Seminars: Research Themes in Retailing*, Manchester: Manchester Business School, 1–33.

Pollay, R.W. (1987) 'The history of advertising archives: confessions of a professional pac-rat', in M. Wallendorf and P.F. Anderson (eds) *Advances in Consumer Research*, 14, Provo, UT: Association for Consumer Research, 136–139.

Posner, R.A. (1995) *Overcoming Law*, Cambridge, MA: Harvard University Press.

Propp, V. (1958 [1928]) *Morphology of the Folktale*, trans. L. Scott, Austin, TX: University of Texas Press.

Reid, R. and Brown, S. (1996a) 'Square pegs, round holes and shopper typologies: an introspective examination', in M.J. Baker (ed.) *2021 – A Vision for the Next 25 Years*, MEG Conference Proceedings, Glasgow: University of Strathclyde.

—— (1996b) 'I hate shopping! An introspective perspective', *International Journal of Retail and Distribution Management*, 24, 4: 4–16.

Richardson, L. (1994) 'Writing: a method of inquiry', in N.K. Denzin and Y.S. Lincoln (eds) *Handbook of Qualitative Research*, Thousand Oaks, CA: Sage, 516–529.

Rook, D.W. (1985) 'The ritual dimension of consumer behavior', *Journal of Consumer Research*, 12, December: 251–264.

—— (1987) 'The buying impulse', *Journal of Consumer Research*, 14, September: 189–199.

—— (1988) 'Researching consumer fantasy', in E.C. Hirschman and J.N. Sheth (eds) *Research in Consumer Behaviour*, 3, Greenwich, CT: JAI Press, 247–270.

Rorty, R. (1989) *Contingency, Irony and Solidarity*, Cambridge: Cambridge University Press.

Rose, D. (1995) 'Active ingredients', in J.F. Sherry (ed.) *Contemporary Marketing and Consumer Behavior*, Thousand Oaks, CA: Sage, 51–85.

Sherry, J.F. (1990) 'A sociocultural analysis of a midwestern American flea market', *Journal of Consumer Research*, 17, June: 13–30.

——, McGrath, M.A. and Levy, S.J. (1993) 'The dark side of the gift', *Journal of Business Research*, 28, 2: 225–244.

——,—— and —— (1995) 'Modanic giving: anatomy of gifts given to the self', in J.F. Sherry (ed.) *Contemporary Marketing and Consumer Behavior*, Thousand Oaks, CA: Sage, 399–432.

Simion, E. (1996 [1982]) *The Return of the Author*, trans. J.W. Newcomb and L. Vianu, Evanston, IL: Northwestern University Press.

Simpson, D. (1995) *The Academic Postmodern and the Rule of Literature: A Report on Half-Knowledge*, Chicago: University of Chicago Press.

Snodgrass, J., Russell, J. and Ward, L. (1988) 'Planning, mood and place-liking', *Journal of Environmental Psychology*, 8, 3: 209–222.

Sunday Times (1996) '"Trolley rage" kills shopper', *Sunday Times*, 13 October, Section 1: 28.

Stern, B.B. (1991) 'Who talks advertising? Literary theory and narrative "point of view"', *Journal of Advertising*, 20, 3: 9–22.

—— (1994) 'Authenticity and the textual persona: postmodern paradoxes in advertising narrative', *International Journal of Research in Marketing*, 11, 4: 387–400.

—— (1995) 'Consumer myths: Frye's taxonomy and the structural analysis of consumption text', *Journal of Consumer Research*, 22, September: 165–185.

Stone, G.P. (1954) 'City shoppers and urban identification: observations on the social psychology of urban life', *American Journal of Sociology*, 60, 1: 36–45.

Tambling, J. (1991) *Narrative and Ideology*, Milton Keynes: Open University Press.

Taylor, M.C. and Saarinen, E. (1994) *Imagologies: Media Philosophy*, London: Routledge.

Tedre, R. (1995) 'Suddenly, spectacularly, losing your cool is all the rage', *Observer*, 15 October: 14.

Tester, K. (1993) *The Life and Times of Post-modernity*, London: Routledge.

Thompson, C.J. (1996) 'Caring consumers: gendered consumption meanings and the juggling lifestyle', *Journal of Consumer Research*, 22, March: 388–407.

——, Locander, W.B. and Pollio, H.R. (1989) 'Putting consumer experience back into consumer research: the philosophy and method of existential-phenomenology', *Journal of Consumer Research*, 16, September: 133–146.

——,—— and —— (1990) 'The lived meaning of free choice: an existential-phenomenological description of everyday consumer experiences of contemporary married women', *Journal of Consumer Research*, 17, December: 346–361.

Thorpe, V. (1996) 'Shop assistants get anti-violence video as "store rage" soars', *Independent on Sunday*, 22 September: 10.

Uusitalo, L. (1996) 'How to study imaginary aspects of consumption', in R.W. Belk, N. Dholakia and A. Venkatesh (eds) *Consumption and Marketing: Macro Dimensions*, Cincinnati, OH: South-Western, 87–95.

Valence, G., d'Astous, A. and Fortier, L. (1988) 'Compulsive buying: concept and measurement', *Journal of Consumer Policy*, 11, 4: 419–433.

Veeser, H.A. (ed.) (1996) *Confessions of the Critics*, New York: Routledge.

Wallendorf, M. and Arnould, E.J. (1991) '"We gather together": consumption rituals of Thanksgiving Day', *Journal of Consumer Research*, 18, June: 13–31.

—— and Brucks, M. (1993) 'Introspection in consumer research: implementation and implications', *Journal of Consumer Research*, 20, December: 339–359.

Waugh, P. (1992) *Postmodernism: A Reader*, London: Edward Arnold.

Westbrook, R.A. and Black, W.C. (1985) 'A motivation-based shopper typology', *Journal of Retailing*, 61, 1: 78–103.

Williams, R.H., Painter, J.J. and Nicholas, H.R. (1978) 'A policy-oriented typology of grocery shoppers', *Journal of Retailing*, 54, 1: 27–42.

5 Exploring the *différance*

A postmodern approach to paradigmatic pluralism in consumer research

Craig J. Thompson, Eric J. Arnould and Barbara B. Stern

EXECUTIVE SUMMARY (AS IF ...)

The embrace of pluralism in consumer research raises a myriad of philosophical and methodological questions concerning the relationships among different paradigmatic orientations and their respective knowledge claims. The terms of this embrace have been scripted in modernist terms that privilege research narratives expressing consensus and convergence while rendering problematic those narratives reporting on dissensus and conflicts of interpretations. We argue that this predisposition toward a logic of convergent validation has denuded critical pluralism of its radical, status quo challenging properties. Our discussion draws from Derrida's concept of *différance* to show that the systematic exploration of paradigmatic diversity can be used to create a reflexive disciplinary conversation about consumer behaviour. This conversation would be attuned to the panoply of social and theoretical interests that are marginalised by any one paradigmatic account. A postmodern logic is developed that highlights the narratological underpinnings of research paradigms and the dynamic of inclusion/exclusion that operates in their research narratives. This postmodern approach revitalises the widely discussed Kuhnian concepts of paradigms, Gestalt switches, and incommensurability and provides a powerful alternative logic for conceptualising paradigmatic pluralism in consumer research. We also discuss how a postmodern conception of pluralism can foster inter-paradigmatic dialogues that contribute to enriched theoretical accounts of consumption phenomena and offer a more reflexive alternative to ritualised statements of limitations. Of course, we could be lying about all of this. This chapter could well be almost anything: a secret message from another galaxy, a pornographic story, a tortured voice emanating from the lunatic fringe of academe, or some combination of them all, kind of like those perverse postmodern double coded alliterative narratives that Stephen Brown writes. The only way that you'll ever know the real 'Truth' is to read on . . . .

We must enter into a concrete historical condition and study the categories of a specific thought and a specific language. Only on this condition will we avoid arbitrary stands and speculative solutions.

(Derrida 1982: 181)

You know the difference between a real science and a pseudoscience? A real science recognises and accepts its own history without feeling attacked.

(Foucault 1988: 11)

NOTES ON THE MARGINS

As the end of the millennium approaches, we can nostalgically recall the 'good ole days' of consumer research practice. Yes, those were the days when bitter, acrimonious debates flourished in our literature and a deep, seemingly irrevocable ideological divide separated different paradigmatic camps. Those in the post-positivist/post-structuralist/post-modernist/post-comprehensible camp (hereafter the 4 Post-Ps) drew inspiration from the Romantic image of being a troupe of broadminded, emotionally attuned, aesthetes struggling to emancipate a field that had been seized by an oppressive, dogmatic, Orwellian, body snatching, phallocentric regime. In dialectical relief, those in the empiricist/traditionalist/but-don't-you-dare-call-me-a-positivist camp rallied around the neo-Comtean image of the 'true scientist'. Paradoxically, their narratives were often the richest in poetic imagery as they provided a near holographic, Technicolor with Dolby® surround-sound representation of a titanic battle between the tireless defenders of truth, reason, and the achievements of western civilisation and the rampaging hordes of Nietzsche quoting, Marxist loving, nihilist espousing, sophist worshipping, morality defying, reason refuting *RELATIVISTS*. And of course you know what **that** means. It means they are a bunch of Nietzsche quoting, Marxist loving, nihilist espousing. . . .

Today, a far more prosaic discourse pervades the field. In place of these allegorical tales of good versus evil, we now offer platitudes about the value of diversity and breathless endorsements of pluralistic research whereby the many, equally valid paradigmatic views can converge upon a 'richer', 'deeper', 'fuller' (and other perspectival metaphors ad infinitum) understanding of consumption phenomena. Yes, things have definitely taken a turn for the worse.

Have we lost our minds, you ask? Have we fallen off the postmodern divide? How could anyone doubt that the embrace of 'multiple ways of knowing' ushers the dawning of a glorious new episteme in which a diverse array of consumer researchers join in the march toward unified and definitive knowledge?

Well, dear reader, such is the nature of ideology: it banishes certain lines of discourse and counterarguments into the realm of the unspeakable. So brace yourselves, we dare to speak against this new world intellectual order. This kinder, gentler, pluralistic discourse and its convergent-based logic of methodological pluralism offers a case in which the implications of a postmodern episteme are oppressed and delegitimatised by the still dominant (dare we say hegemonic?) voice of modernism.

We have now reached the point of the chapter where *you* the reader begins to look impatiently for the 'hook' that provides a compelling and concise description of the chapter's objectives and analytic logic. However, this paper traffics in postmodern pretensions. (Or maybe it's just a pretentious postmodern paper. It's so hard to tell sometimes.) In any event, our 'hook' must be ironic and the logic of our analysis must be presented in an obtuse manner using ponderous quotes like these:

> Postmodernism is a cross-disciplinary trend encouraging sensitivity to differences and tolerance of the incommensurable. This trend challenges the hold of 'specific totalising visions' and the 'general paradigmatic style of organising research' over 'fragmented scholarly communities'.
>
> (Sherry 1991: 551)

> The use of triangulation should again assuage those who may be concerned that advocates of alternative methods embrace reality relativism. There would be absolutely no reason to triangulate if researchers genuinely believed that rival multiple realities were incapable of comparison and evaluation.
>
> (Hunt 1991: 42)

Here's the irony. We agree with Hunt (sort of). Here's the hook. Consumer research cannot pursue a postmodern vision of paradigmatic pluralism while also adhering to the modernist logic of convergent realism and its methodological offspring 'triangulation' (e.g. Lincoln and Guba 1985). This malproductive juxtaposition of antithetical positions correlates almost perfectly to disjunctures between philosophical views and methodological practices found in the many clarion calls for postmodern consumer research.

In their general philosophical preludes, those endorsing a postmodern approach express an epistemological position similar to that described in the preceding quote from Sherry (see Belk *et al.* 1988; Hirschman and Holbrook 1992; Holt 1991; Hudson and Ozanne 1988; Thompson 1990). However, the implementation of such epistemological claims invokes a very different narrative. The postmodern call for polyvocality in our research narratives, the exploration of difference, and the importance of creating localised accounts of meaning is displaced by a modernist axiology emphasising singular representations of reality, narratives proclaiming the progressive accumulation of knowledge, and preference for totalising analyses and theories. For example, Sherry (1991), in keeping with a postmodern ethos (e.g. S. Brown 1995; Lyotard 1984; Rabinow 1986; Rorty 1979), waxes poetic about the value of 'polyvocal' scholarly discourses among different paradigmatic approaches. Furthermore, he applauds a version of the incommensurability thesis holding that fundamental and informative differences exist among paradigmatic approaches. However, Sherry still offers 'triangulation' as one of the primary directions for future postmodernist consumer research. Hence, differences are expected to converge upon a singular corpus of meanings. Whither polyvocality?

On the modernist stylisation of postmodernist discourse

This tension between postmodern and modernist predilections is not simply a matter of a logical inconsistency. Rather, it reflects several institutional factors that have structured the diffusion of postmodern discourse into consumer research field. Many of the resulting disparities can be traced to the concessions that arose from advancing postmodern discourses in a field where the modernist episteme is institutionalised in a multitude of largely taken-for-granted research values, core assumptions, and practices. Accordingly, the juxtaposition of postmodernist and modernist values served a politically pragmatic purpose by positioning alternative research methods in terms more palatable to the mainstream consumer research community (see Belk 1991).

This mixed discourse also reflects the prominent role that 'technocratic' rationality (Habermas 1972) plays in the discourses of consumer research (e.g. S. Brown 1995; Murray and Ozanne 1991). Modernist values and research logics are designed to serve technocratic interests (Grimes and Rood 1995). The appeal to technocratic interests predisposes consumer research narratives toward particular modernist goals and contributions, such as developing a more effective apparatus for knowledge gathering and/or generating findings that allow consumer behaviours to be situated in an explanatory matrix. Hence, when 'postmodern' consumer researchers sought to address the 'so what?/now what?' question – which has an irritating tendency to arise after fifteen or twenty pages of soaring philosophical prose – their methodological answer more often than not rings familiar: convergent realism, consensus, and triangulation across multiple perspectives.

Our perspective is that the resulting transformation of postmodernism from radical fringe to mainstream acceptability presents a form of *stylisation* in which alternatives to conventional norms and assumptions are comfortably assimilated to a technocratic cultural code (Ewen 1988). Stylisation insulates a cultural status quo from radical challenges by transforming threatening counter-cultural meanings and practices into a marketable form (or fashion) more palatable to mainstream consumption. Historians of pop culture may recall that the once subversive practice of rock 'n' roll (and its counter-cultural affiliation with black and working class white youth) entered the white American mainstream using bizarre stylising tactics, such as having Pat Boone cover Little Richard's *Tutti Frutti*.

Hence, we have the striking analogical relationship: Pat Boone is to Little Richard as Naturalistic Inquiry is to 'Postmodern Consumer Research': a striking parallel whose implications are clearly beyond the scope of this chapter. Oh all right, we're not sure what it all means either. Let's try another analogy, shall we?

This now 'stylised' paradigmatic pluralism is analogous to the logic of multi-method convergence exemplified by traditional approaches to construct validation (Campbell and Fiske 1959) and procedures for establishing trustworthiness advanced by modernist strains of ethnomethodologies (Hirschman 1986; Lincoln and Guba 1985; Wallendorf and Belk 1989). Not surprisingly, pluralistic consumer research has often been advocated as a powerful means to generate networks of convergent propositions about consumption phenomena (Belk *et al.* 1988; Hunt 1991; R.J. Lutz 1989; McQuarrie and Mick 1992; Sirsi *et al.* 1996). This incompatibility between this appeal to a convergent logic and postpositivist proposals regarding the multiplicity of social realities is the target of Hunt's (1991) critique of logical inconsistency.

A key normative assumption underlies this conceptualisation: convergence is the optimal and hence preferred epistemological outcome. As a case in point, two distinct paradigmatic approaches converging upon mutually corroborative conclusions is seldom characterised as troubling or potentially problematic. Rather, convergent findings are invariably regarded as signifying increased trustworthiness (or validity) (R.J. Lutz 1989; Wallendorf and Belk 1989). Thus, paradigmatic pluralism becomes yet another manifestation of that age-old parable, the blind men and the elephant.[1] To slightly paraphrase this language game, there is an extant 'phenomenon' that researchers, who cannot see the whole, attempt to comprehend in a piecemeal fashion. Forever doomed to an always partial understanding of the elephant (e.g. that measurable, palatable reality), the researchers argue insatiably over whose methodological 'grasp' offers the more valid knowledge. The pluralistic moral is that this problem of 'incommensurate' knowledge claims could be resolved if the researchers would not argue about who has the 'right' understanding and instead 'triangulate' their limited grasps to get a better 'feel' for the whole.

In Wittgensteinian terms (1953), it is through the 'conjuring trick' of implicitly evoking four quintessential modernist assumptions that this rhetorical construction appears to be self-evident and (rationally)

[1] Critical Interlocutor (CI): AHA! You're using a sexist metaphoric image. This discussion seems awfully inconsistent for a paper to be endorsing *différance*, which I know is a 'code' word for male-bashing, tree hugging, Birkenstock wearing, tofu eating, vegan fascist, Nietzsche quoting, Marxist loving, nihilist espousing, sophist worshipping, morality defying . . .

The Authors Who Speak As One, for now (US): We know, we know. In this case, the masculine reference is quite appropriate because the dominant tradition of consumer research has been steeped in a patriarchal conception of science (See Bristor and Fischer 1993; Hirschman 1991, 1993). You'll have to excuse us for now, our tofu burgers are done.

undeniable. First, is the implicit assumption that a transcendental (or God's eye) view is attainable; in the structure of the parable, there is an implicit observer who sees the whole from an omnipotent perspective that encompasses other limited perspectives. The second assumption is that a true and complete understanding of the object-ive world can be obtained by using a wide range of methods to discover and describe the various parts of a finite whole. The third assumption is that 'conflict of interpretations' should be ultimately situated in a totalising narrative whereby differences are transformed into a mutually corroborative and logically consistent system of propositions. The fourth, and perhaps most pivotal assumption, is that the true characteristics of the object exist independently from the 'methods' by which it is understood. As such, different methods can converge on exactly the 'same' phenomenon, albeit from different perspectives.

Through this stylised epistemological discourse, paradigmatic pluralism has been re-inscribed in the hegemonic 'cultural code' of modernist consumer research. This code sanctions convergence, agreement and a unified order while portraying divergence, discordance and fragmentation as fundamentally problematic. In this context, convergence is prima facie evidence that different research approaches are 'in touch' with, at least some, aspects of object-ive reality whereas the presence of divergence needs to be 'rationally' explained in order to be accepted. Hence, we have a paradox: this modernistic conception of methodological pluralism re-affirms a commitment to a unified meta-perspective rather than advocating a critical exploration of diversity among paradigmatic constructions of consumer phenomena. As noted by Foucault (1980), such a modern discourse 'disciplines' social life by authorising knowledge claims that arise from convergent accordance. While such disciplining reduces conflict, it implicitly subjects the complexity of social phenomena to the domination of formalised rules, tactics of simplification (such as the endorsement of parsimony as a definitive research value) and an established language of conform-ation.

So, consumer researchers joyfully consume a stylised postmodernism-lite: its radical edges softened, its bite tamed, its mind altering properties defused, its kick decaffeinated, its punch watered down, its sugar, sodium, fat and cholesterol contents lowered, well you get the idea. If consumer research's postmodern discourses had not become stylised and technora-tionalised, the accepted aims of pluralistic consumer research would not be a repackaging of modernist objectives. Rather, paradigmatic pluralism would aspire to heighten sensitivity to differences of interpretations, to ensure that less conventional and/or entrenched perspectives have a voice in scientific dialogue and to explore the vast network of understudied social dynamics and marginalised social interests that emerge in the practices of consumer culture. This 'other' pluralism would be a self-reflexive undertaking whereby the tensions and dialogues among different perspectives always harbour the potential for transforming consumer research conventions and practices (Habermas 1972; Joy 1991).

This difference in epistemological orientation can be illustrated by considering the meaning that convergence would assume if consumer researchers aspired toward diversity. In conventional research terms, pluralistic convergence would become analogous to findings that support the null hypothesis. Consumer researchers would thus feel compelled to explain why and how their differing methodological/theoretical paradigms could arrive at a similar understanding. In this 'null' case, convergence among different research approaches would be experienced as a disappointing outcome that merely re-presented a shared understanding. More importantly, such convergent 'validation' could signal conformity to an entrenched set of disciplinary beliefs or an over-arching socio-cultural narrative. A reflexive concern would then arise over which socio-cultural narratives were precluded from having a voice in the convergent account and the social implications of that preclusion.

What's the *différance*?

To speak differently about the disciplinary functions of paradigmatic pluralism, postmodern consumer researchers first need to resist the technocratic interest and develop research strategies and logics of analysis that speak to critical (Habermas 1972) and self-reflexive interests (also see Murray and Ozanne 1991). Let us first start by discussing the critical interests and its relationship to the concept of praxis (Eagleton 1991; Hetrick and Lozoda 1994).

By analysing the cultural matrix of social, economic, and political interests which are implicitly reflected in paradigmatic knowledge claims (Bourdieu 1990; Foucault 1980; C. Lutz 1993; Schatzki 1993), the pursuit of the critical interest reconfigures the social constructivist agenda – specifying the co-constituting relationships existing between research paradigms and their attendant knowledge claims (e.g. Anderson 1986; Gergen 1985; Peter and Olson 1989) – in terms of praxis: that is, analyses which reveal conflicts and struggles among dominant and marginal narrative positions and that offer strategies for transforming consumer research practice. An underlying assumption to this claim to praxis is that research narratives indirectly and directly represent and sustain power relationships among various social interests. Hence, implicit to 'a scientifically detached' research narrative is an implicit alliance and privileging of particular socio-cultural and political interests that relate to issues such as the social legitimation (or dislegitimation) of ethnic and sexual identities, gender politics, class conflicts, the power/resistance dynamic between marketers and consumers, tensions between transnational capital and local socio-economic structures, and power relationships between 'First World' and 'Third World' nations.

By reflexive interests, we refer to social scientists' efforts to interrogate and represent in their research narratives, their constructive role in the knowledge construction process (Joy 1991; Woolgar 1988). Reflexive narratives strive to identify the institutional alignments, theoretical commitments, narrative conventions and socio-cultural beliefs that comprise the social matrix in which research narratives are formulated (Ashmore 1989; Bourdieu 1990; Woolgar 1988; Woolgar and Ashmore 1988). For this type of reflexive analysis, we believe that focusing on the points of convergence among different research paradigms is likely to reproduce rather than to challenge these meta-conventions.

Our postmodern conceptualisation of paradigmatic pluralism argues for elucidating the knowledge claims of consumer research in a language of *différance*: a term originally coined by the philosopher Jacques Derrida (1976) and subsequently developed by a number of postmodern theorists pursuing his deconstructionist approach (Norris 1991). As noted by Hekman (1990), *différance* and the conventional term difference are not distinguishable when uttered verbally. It is only in their graphical written form that this subtle distinction can be realised. In this manner, the concept of *différance* reinforces Derrida's effort to resist privileging speech over writing: a convention which he deemed to be a major historical theme of western philosophy. Derrida's emphasis on writing (and hence narrative) coheres with our own interest in analysing the knowledge claims offered by a given consumer research paradigm as a play of well-established narrative conventions, rather than as the result of a methodology that is unproblematically reported in the objective language of science.

Différance is a complex term whose meaning offers a fusion of the English verbs differ and defer (Hekman 1990). The first aspect relates to the semiotic insight that the meaning of a given sign is always defined by its differences to other signs in a linguistic system. For example, the meaning of 'woman' cannot be grasped unless one understands this gender term's socio-historical contradistinctions to 'man'. This semiotic conception can then be extrapolated to understand the narrative conventions and interpretive predilections of a research paradigm. In the broader field of the social science literature, research paradigms are not autonomously self-defined entities; rather, their nature is constituted and understood in relation to other research orientations.

To illustrate this point (in a postmodern way), let us offer a pastiche of historical examples culled from various social science disciplines and intellectual traditions. For completely arbitrary reasons, let's start with psychology. The turn of the century rise of behaviourism in American psychology arose in contrast to the 'mentalism' of the introspectionist school and 'the stream of consciousness' tradition associated with William James (see Pollio 1982). Throughout the 1940s, 1950s and 1960s, the Gestalt school (Kohler 1947), the early information processing approach

(Miller *et al.* 1960) and the resurgent humanistic school of psychology (Wann 1964) all defined themselves in contrast to the then dominant behaviourist movement. Turning to the continental tradition, structuralism (in historical and anthropological analysis) defined itself in contrast to Husserlian phenomenology and existentialism (Dreyfus and Rabinow 1982). Marxist social theory defined itself in contrast to the phenomenologists (geez, nobody wanted to be like those guys!) and various strains of Weberian and Schutzian sociology. In terms of contemporary debates, feminist theory has defined itself against the broadly defined spectre of patriarchal social science and phallocentric reason (Fraser 1989; Lloyd 1989). Postmodernists have long defined themselves against the project of modernity (Firat and Venkatesh 1995). And last but not least, modern empiricists (Hunt 1989) have defined themselves against (the rampaging hordes of Nietzsche quoting, Marxist loving, nihilist espousing, sophist worshipping, morality defying, reason refuting) *RELATIVISTS*.

The sense of defer which also contributes to the meaning of *différance* interjects a temporal dimension into this deconstructive logic. For Derrida (1976), meaning is a 'constant flickering' across an entire chain of signifiers whose nature is constantly transforming over time (i.e. diachronic dynamism) and whose synchronic form can never be comprehended in a single moment. As such, understanding of the system is perpetually being deferred to future moments. This notion of deferral then implies that the analysis of *différance* articulates differences-which-make-a-difference while also recognising that the analysis is (1) never exhaustive in scope; and (2) that the identified differences are comprehended retrospectively through the very narrative that articulates them. Accordingly, the analysis of *différance* is always contingent on a perspective situated in the present moment and it is always in process. Hence, paradigmatic pluralism directed at an analysis of *différance* does not aspire to a final, totalised view of the research field and its constituent assumption: rather, such an undertaking provides one moment of reflexive insight that can be further developed through a future play of differences.

In articulating our position, we will revisit certain philosophical issues that have been previously discussed in the consumer research (e.g. Anderson 1986, 1989; Arnold and Fischer 1994; Belk *et al.* 1988; Holbrook and O'Shaughnessy 1988; Hudson and Ozanne 1988). By considering these issues in relation to the postmodern emphasis on diversity, their endorsement of paradigmatic pluralism can be situated in the context of several important postmodern constructs: the dynamic of inclusion/exclusion that operates in paradigmatic representations of social reality, the shaping influence that narrative conventions exert on paradigmatic representations, and strategies for creating reflexive accounts (and learning from reflexivity). Our analysis speaks to more conventional research interests by explicating how more encompassing and enriched theoretical models can be attained through the exploration of paradigmatic diversity.

We draw also upon recent developments in the philosophy of science and social theory that clarify and enrich Kuhn's original proposals regarding the nature of a research paradigm (Bourdieu 1990; Rorty 1979; Woolgar 1988). These works are used to develop a narratological conception of research paradigms and to articulate a narrative strategy for utilising diversity that does not rely on the logic of convergent validation. Our rationale is that the logic of convergence inevitably marginalises or excludes voices differing from the dominant ones. In conventional terms, convergence discourages innovation and encourages the maintenance of the disciplinary status quo. In contrast, we propose that postmodernism offers a logic of pluralism that better utilises the diversity among paradigms to redress research limitations, expand sensitivity to the different theoretical and societal voices who should have a 'say' in a given analysis, and finally generate more complex theoretical models of consumer phenomena.

Our proposal for a postmodern paradigmatic pluralism also resonates with a movement in moral philosophy that seeks to create productive social and scholarly dialogue while also respecting diverse interests (Benhabib 1992; Rorty 1989). This philosophical movement is particularly attuned to the current socio-political context as nearly every institution in American society – political, educational, economic, legal, and marketing – is having to address the implications of diversity (West 1994). The conceptual parallel to pluralistic consumer research lies in the dynamics precipitated by distinct groups (often marginalised ones such as ethnic minorities, religious minorities, feminists, gays and the physically challenged) seeking greater voice in social discourse and a broader acceptance of their interests. The challenge for a pluralistic society – and for a pluralistic discipline – is to foster public discourses that acknowledge and benefit from these diverse social voices and interests without becoming fractionated into isolated and potentially antagonistic communities.[2]

[2] CI: I'm not impressed in the least. You're simply trying to establish the credibility of your account by appeal to external authorities, Foucault, Derrida, Benhabib, Rorty, blah, blah, blah. This is a very tiresome rhetorical ploy. But let's get down to brasstacks. I protest my position in the footnotes. This tactic is marginalisation of the highest order.

US: *In citing these theorists, we are simply acknowledging some of the major influences on our thinking. We neither intend nor expect that these references per se will establish the credibility of our proposals. Anyway, we have a citation somewhere that says it's okay to appeal to external authorities. As for your positioning in the text, postmodernists argue that the 'margins' are the centre of the text. So you see, the prominence of our voice in this narrative actually places us in a marginal position whereas your voice, being in the all too easily skipped over footnotes, stands as the centrepiece of the chapter. Really, that is as plausible an interpretation of Derrida as any.*

CI: I have certain friends who might take this postmodern 'death of the author' business rather seriously, if you know what I mean.

US: *Your chain of signifiers is coming through loud and clear. Look, we wish that you could be positioned more prominently in the text but alas dire space restrictions have been imposed upon us by a repressively hegemonic constellation of domineering strategies and devious Lacanian motives (i.e. the editors). How about if we represent your voice in a boldface type? That is very noticeable.*

POSTMODERN PARADIGMATIC PLURALISM (oops, we're short one P!)

From convergent realism to interpretive communities

Although the tenets of postmodernism should undermine the field's faith in multi-method convergence upon an extant reality, they are new entrants into the consumer research literature; a field where the logic of 'convergent realism' has long functioned as a powerful metanarrative. In its 'classic' form, this metanarrative presumes that scientific research is structured by the following conditions: (1) 'reality' is composed of a finite network of objective (theory-independent) properties; (2) scientific knowledge is a body of gradually accumulating verified linguistic propositions that map (more or less) accurately the objective properties; (3) a given research study contributes to the common body of knowledge by analysing a manageable component of the larger reality; (4) adherence to the scientific method enables these limited efforts to build cumulatively and to eventually form a unified and mutually corroborative system of knowledge; (5) the research community is united by a commitment to **the** scientific method and the ideal of an all-encompassing 'totalised' perspective upon reality (Rorty 1979). Figure 5.1 presents the classic model of scientific research that follows from these assumptions.

Figure 5.1 characterises conceptions of social scientific research prior to Kuhn (1970) and others who advocate a social constructivist view of scientific knowledge (Anderson 1986; Hudson and Ozanne 1988; Sherry 1991). These developments engendered a more fragmented conception of social science research. Rather than presenting a unified perspective, the scientific enterprise is portrayed as multi-perspectival marked by fundamental paradigmatic differences among major questions, central problems, and metaphoric models (Rorty 1989).

However, the lingering legacy of the classic modernist portrayal of *science* can be seen in contemporary interpretations of the implications of paradigmatic diversity. According to this modified 'post-Kuhnian' claim, methodological paradigms are uniquely attuned to specific facets of the totalised reality. Conversely, each paradigm is assumed to systematically overlook some major component of the larger reality. Figure 5.2 models a post-Kuhnian conception of scientific research.

In this second model, post-positivist methods contribute to a totalised view of reality by providing 'alternative perspectives' or different

[2] *continued*

CI: Well, this might work. But I demand that you explain to the readers why they should put up with this alternative narrative form gambit in the first place.

US: Well, Woolgar (1988) says it is of the utmost importance that narratives seeking to represent reflexive analyses disrupt normal modes of reading. We're actually a little fuzzy about why he believes this but you gotta admit, dialogical interruptions are about as narratively disruptive as it gets.

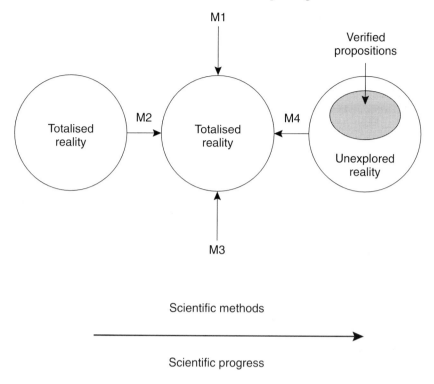

M = specific research method used to attain convergence

Figure 5.1   Pre-Kuhnian model of scientific research

methodological 'lenses'; epistemological metaphors that remain tied to the modernist ideal of a totalised perception of an extant reality (Poster 1989). Triangulation functions as a post-Kuhnian metaphor for applying different research approaches to a single phenomenon in order to achieve a more complete representation of it. Convergence among the different approaches is then interpreted as evidence that each approach has captured at least some of its essential characteristics. In consumer research, this logic is expressed in the many proposals that note, and/or actively pursue, the potential benefits offered by triangulating across methodological paradigms (Arnould and Price 1993; McQuarrie and Mick 1992; Mick and DeMoss 1990; O'Guinn and Faber 1989; Sirsi *et al.* 1996; Wallendorf and Belk 1989).

This modernist reformulation obscures a major Kuhnian insight that research paradigms function as broad-based interpretive frameworks, generated by a community of researchers, that shape understanding of the phenomenon being explored. Accordingly, a methodological analysis of a consumer phenomenon situates a complex array of social events and

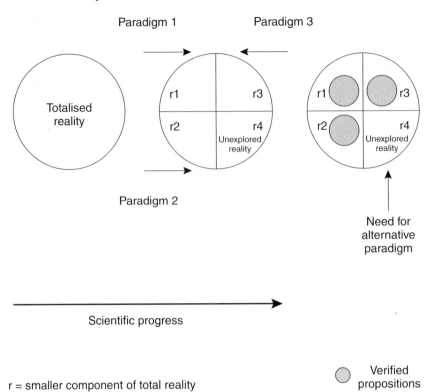

Figure 5.2   Post-Kuhnian model of scientific research

relationships within a scripted system of 'codifying' terms, techniques of measurement and documentation, strategies of analysis and representation and rules of legitimation. This codification not only highlights certain aspects of social reality as central, but also frames the analysis in terms of specific assumptions, beliefs and values. In this way, reification reduces the complexity of social reality to a particular narrative construction of it. Further, certain theoretical discourses (and the social interests they represent) can come to dominate other equally viable narrative scripts (see Hetrick and Lozada 1994; Murray and Ozanne 1991).

An important thread of the postmodern contention is that narrativity is an enabling condition for the scientific representation of social phenomena and that paradigmatic narratives manifest not only philosophical assumptions but also implicit political and ideological commitments (Rosaldo 1989; Sherry 1991; White 1987). Narrativity is defined as the 'rule-governed ways in which human beings (re)fashion their universe', with emphasis on 'the *way* in which the medium is used to present the *what*' (Prince 1982: 524). The implication being that the content of the narrative is fundamentally shaped by the conventions of narrative form – such as the familiar voice of third-person narration or the preference for a linear, rather than circular, chronological ordering of events (Stern 1993). Although the traditional tendency is to regard narrative form as a merely 'stylistic' consideration, postmodern theorists have shown that these narrative preferences embody a multitude of predispositions following from the social and theoretical position of the author(s) (H.R. Brown 1993). These theorists further propose that each research paradigm functions as a narrative subculture organised around tacit agreements regarding core assumptions about phenomena of interest, questions worthy of investigation, acceptable methodological procedures, and criteria for plausible (or non-plausible) interpretations of data.

This narratively based conception of the research paradigm meshes with Foucault's (1972) conception of 'discursive practices', that is, narrative systems that provide logics for creating, identifying, analysing and organising statements that can be classified as legitimate knowledge claims (also Dreyfus and Rabinow 1982). Participants in the paradigm (both as readers and writers) come to expect and even to demand that these taken for granted narrative conventions (or genres of storytelling) be present in a 'credible' research report (Pratt 1986). This emphasis on narrative convention, interpretive community and socio-cultural positions calls attention to the political and class-based interests that are latent to any form of social scientific theorising (H.R. Brown 1993; Denzin 1994; Rabinow 1986; Rosaldo 1989; White 1987).

A postmodern conceptualisation of narrative function (and power) provides a more philosophically viable post-Kuhnian model of paradigmatic pluralism. As Rorty (1979) notes, Kuhn's original analysis of scientific paradigms was constrained by his reliance on terms and metaphors steeped in the traditional dichotomy between objectivity and subjectivity. By rejecting the objectivist metaphysic, Kuhn's proposals often adopted a subjectivist tone – such as the claim that researchers in different paradigms 'see' different realities – that has long roused critical ire. However, recent philosophical developments provide a language to reformulate Kuhn's insights in terms that more effectively conceptualise the sources of paradigmatic diversity and that do not evoke subjectivist connotations.

Here, Kuhn's metaphor of the 'Gestalt switch' is particularly relevant. His original conception of this process was ambiguous, having two distinct meanings. The meaning that has captured the most attention connotes a subjectivist claim that researchers committed to different paradigms 'see' different and incommensurate realities. The other meaning of Kuhn's 'Gestalt switch' has gained much less attention, even though it foreshadowed recent developments in the philosophy of science. Here, 'paradigm' refers to a researcher's idealised model of the research process (Kuhn 1970), or in psychological terms, an exemplar-based category (G. Lakoff

1987). For example, researchers whose ideal of scientific inquiry is a controlled experiment are likely to judge many forms of post-positivist research as poor examples of scientific research.

In this second meaning, the 'Gestalt switch' refers to a change in the ideal of scientific inquiry that guides a particular research community. This meaning of the Gestalt switch directly relates to Kuhn's broader claim that a paradigm represents a series of tacit agreements, among a community of researchers, on the questions deemed interesting and/or significant, relevant theories and definitions of phenomena, and the range of plausible explanations. A research community's idealised image of the research situation is situated within a broader set of narratives that create a shared context of meaning and interpretive frame-of-reference. Accordingly, a more robust account of the Gestalt switch would need to focus upon the narratological nature of a research paradigm, not only an image of the idealised research situation, but also common literatures and strategies for writing and reading research reports.

Fish's (1980) conception of the interpretive community offers such an account. His account was originally developed to explain the differences in interpretations of literary texts that arose among different schools of literary criticism. Fish extended the post-positivist insight that a given text has multiple (as opposed to singular) meanings by providing a more systematic explanation of how different interpretations are constructed through the acts of reading and writing (see Radway 1991). Critical to this conception is that these acts are not idiosyncratic but, rather, they are communal ones grounded in shared conventions of reading and accepted rhetorical and interpretive strategies. Therefore, interpretive communities

> must be studied in terms of textual encoding [for] every … text, no matter how 'modern' or 'unconventional,' contains some indication of the artistic and/or cultural codes it is affirming, reaffirming, or 'playing' with (playing against).
>
> (Suleiman 1980: 21)

The conceptualisation of research paradigms as a communal undertaking rekindles an important theme of continental philosophy: a philosophical tradition that, prior to Kuhn's analysis of scientific revolutions, had largely been ignored in American academic circles due to its incompatibility with the modernist model of the scientific enterprise:

> Cognition is the most socially conditioned activity of man and knowledge is the paramount social creation. The very structure of language presents a compelling philosophy characteristic of that community and even a single word can represent a complex theory.
>
> (Fleck (1935) *The Genesis and Development of a Scientific Fact*, quoted in Douglas 1986: 12)

In this rediscovered 'postmodern' conceptualisation, the key differences between paradigms derive from the narrative history in which a given method is situated. As such, paradigmatic boundaries are defined by the joint considerations of interpretive frameworks, narrative justifications and the methodological procedures that can be logically justified within this narrative history (e.g. recognised literature bases, legitimised research procedures and conventionalised strategies of representation). Finally, research paradigms are not self-contained entities. Within the larger context of the consumer research discipline, each must acknowledge certain meta-conventions regarding appropriate topics of investigation, standards of rigour, and logics of justification (such as the logic of convergence).

Figure 5.3 illustrates this narratological conception of research paradigms. At the base, consumer behaviour 'phenomena' are portrayed as a multiplicity of social relationships situated in a shared context of cultural knowledge (Berger and Luckmann 1967). The context provides culturally agreed-upon standards for determining whether a particular event or circumstance represents a good exemplar of a cultural category (G. Lakoff 1987). Thus, social science narratives presuppose everyday cultural knowledge in order to formulate intelligible research problems, questions and definitions of phenomena.[3]

In terms of this postmodern framework, paradigmatic narratives manifest a dynamic between inclusion and exclusion (or marginalisation). Through this dynamic, certain cultural assumptions and social interests assume a primary position in the account while others are (explicitly or implicitly) ignored or rendered as a marginal concern (hooks 1992). Thus, each paradigm manifests unique theoretical narratives that address but a subset of the range of research issues that could be intelligibly defined as dimensions of a given consumer phenomenon. For example, the information processing tradition emphasises 'internal' psychological processes and cognitive structures. This paradigm tends to exclude from theoretical consideration structural relationships among socially determined roles or the ritualised, dramaturgical and aesthetic aspects of consumer behaviour: all important constructs in ethnographic narration. By contrast, ethnographic consumer research presumes the ontological priority of the culturally constituted life-world and tends to exclude consideration of constructs referring to internal cognitive processes and structures.

[3] **CI: Ah ha! You're capitulating to the visual metaphor by offering a picture of your narratological model?! Have you not just spent pages and pages lamenting the horrors of totalising, Cartesian representational strategies? Seems that I have caught you in yet ANOTHER philosophical contradiction. Oh, what a tangled web you postmodernists weave.**

US: We are invoking a conventionalised Cartesian representational strategy by presenting an iconic model of our framework. But since we're using this presentation mode for the purpose of subverting it we figure it's OK in an ironic, postmodern sort of way. Also, Eric gets a real charge out of playing with his new-fangled graphical software package. You know, us postmodernists always choose immediate sensory gratification over staid, cerebral abstractions.

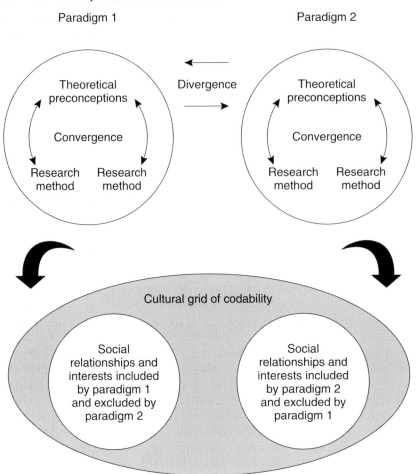

Figure 5.3   Post-positivist model of scientific research

The dynamic of inclusion/exclusion is perhaps most clearly revealed when critical voices identify specific social interests who have been seldom represented in standard consumer research narratives (e.g. feminist, Bristor and Fischer 1993; Hirschman 1993; addicts, Hirschman 1992; gay, Peñaloza 1996; Wardlow 1996; homeless, Hill 1991; Hill and Stamey 1990; Third World, Arnould 1989). From a postmodern perspective, this narrative process is neither inherently positive nor negative. Rather, it is an inevitable concomitant of the choice of one way of telling as opposed to another. Each set of narrative conventions provides a distinctive framework for reducing the complexity of the world and making it more readily comprehensible. However, a dilemma arises when an interpretive community fails to recognise the framing functions of dominant paradigmatic narratives and/or its exclusionary tendencies (Fraser 1989). Postmodern theorists suggest that this occurs when a paradigmatic community is predisposed to view shared conceptions about methodological rigour or definitions of key problems as unquestioned givens rather than as culturally based interpretations.

The dilemmas posed by scientific analyses that deny their status as socially contingent interpretations have been concretely demonstrated by a multitude of feminist critiques. As noted by Jaggar (1991)

> We should not forget that much of the achievement of feminist scholarship, in a number of disciplines, over the past twenty years has consisted precisely in identifying various forms of male bias concealed within apparently gender-blind assumptions or conceptual frameworks. Pretending that social distinctions and privileges do not exist is usually equivalent to perpetuating them.
>
> (Jaggar 1991: 96)

Feminist researchers have repeatedly demonstrated that scientific texts (particularly those in the medical and social science fields) have presumed culturally defined masculine interests and characteristics as the universal norm. As such, biological and social science research have consistently 'converged' on findings that formulate gender differences as a 'lack' or 'inadequacy' on the part of women. Hence, intrusive scientific interventions have often been prescribed to restore 'normalcy', even though these normative standards may have little or no relevance to the lived experiences and/or cultural situations of women (Daly 1978; Ehrenreich and English 1979; Gilligan 1982; Keller 1989; Rothman 1989; Sayers 1986). These patriarchal, and sometimes blatantly misogynist, assumptions, and their many inequitable socio-cultural effects, went largely unacknowledged until the divergent voices of feminist scholarship articulated their pervasive influence on the scientific discourses (see Epstein 1988).[4]

By diverging from accepted perspectives and assumptions, feminist scholarship has articulated implicit power relationships structuring scientific narratives, enhanced cultural sensitivity toward gender biases, and has contributed to an alternative system of research values, theoretical concepts, goals, and methodological orientations that reflect – rather than marginalise or dominate – culturally defined feminine interests (Gavey

[4] **CI: This discussion all maddeningly abstract. Give me some specific examples of what you're talking about here?**

US: Fair enough. This view of the woman as being fundamentally 'other' is particularly evident in the medical and psychiatric fields where research has consistently 'converged' on findings that formulate gender differences as feminine deviations that must be controlled or cured (Crawford and Marecek 1989; Daly 1979; Epstein 1988; R. T. Lakoff 1990). A litany of intrusive scientific interventions, ranging from institutionalisation to clitoridectomies to estrogen therapy, has been prescribed to restore women to states of 'normalcy,' even though these normative standards have often had detrimental consequences to their well-being and/or cultural situations (Daly 1978; Ehrenreich and English 1979; Gilligan 1982; Rothman 1989).

1989; Harding 1989). In this way, feminist research has not only enhanced cultural sensitivity toward gender biases, but also expanded the scope of 'legitimate' scientific understanding.

The case of feminist scholarship demonstrates that exploring the key divergences among research traditions is particularly necessary given the finite nature of human (and hence scientific) understandings. In this spirit, Rabinow offers the more general commentary about scientific narratives and their implicit interpretive conventions: 'all interpretations, most especially those that deny their status as interpretations, are only possible on the basis of other interpretations, whose rules they affirm while announcing their negation' (Rabinow 1986: 255).

In sum, it is not possible to anticipate all the alternative interests that are precluded from a given paradigmatic framework of interpretation. Rather, the comprehension of these inclusions and preclusions (and their ramifications) is developed over time through concrete comparisons to alternative accounts. The resulting play of differences provides an enriched comparative perspective for specifying the implicit assumptions that distinguish among research approaches, assessing how these assumptions result in different knowledge constructions, and more thoroughly evaluating the consequences on scientific knowledge that result from the exclusion of specific cultural and/or theoretical interests in scientific discourse.

NARRATIVE STRATEGIES FOR 'DOING' *DIFFÉRANCE* VIA PARADIGMATIC PLURALISM

Postmodernists, of course, prefer engaging in matters of practice rather than offering abstract philosophical reflections. Well, that is not quite the case. Postmodernists actually prefer to write interminable philosophical treatises on how we all need to stop all this philosophising and just get on with matters of practice. So, perhaps in this section, we are boldly entering into an age of post-postmodern consumer research. In any event, we want to discuss in interminable philosophical detail two narrative strategies for conducting pluralistic consumer research in terms of *différance*. These narrative strategies offer two (but certainly not the only) ways by which paradigmatic pluralism can serve reflexive and critical interests. Well, enough of this narrative foreplay; on with the 'practice'!

Specification of paradigmatic boundaries

This narrative strategy follows from the 'differ' connotation of *différance* which draws from the semiotic insight that the meaning of a sign (or term) is defined by its differences to other signs in the linguistic system (Mick 1986; de Saussure 1966). As applied to our postmodern framework, the implication is that the nature of a paradigm is most clearly revealed by contrast to other paradigmatic orientations. Narrative framings are recognised *as* assumptions when placed in contrast to other narratives that script the phenomenon in terms of different paradigmatic assumptions and, thereby, give priority to very different theoretical voices and social interests (Benhabib 1992; Gergen 1991).

In consumer research, the value of such comparative contrasts has been demonstrated by Anderson's (1986) critical relativist comparison among positivist consumer research programmes, Sherry's (1991) review of the diverse traditions participating in consumer research's interpretive turn, and at more macro-level of contrast, Hirschman's (1993) use of a masculine/feminine ideological dichotomy to classify specific consumer research studies. However, pursuing the semiotic implications of these paradigmatic contrasts calls attention to an avenue of inquiry not discussed by these previous considerations. Specifically, the systematic exploration of paradigmatic differences offers a means to – in Kuhnian terms – invigorate the process of normal science without necessitating a 'revolutionary' change in the narrative tradition of a given paradigm.

The semiotic analogy implies that the relationships between specific research paradigms and the general field of consumer research discourse are parallel to those existing among signs in a semiotic network. Accordingly, the differences (and even points of conflict) between paradigms are constitutive and meaning creating, rather than being a source of encapsulation and polemical stagnation. In contrast to Hunt's (1991) metaphoric claim that the assertion of paradigmatic differences creates *walls* that stop debate and freeze positions, we counter that these differences function as oppositional polarities that energise the research process. Importantly, these energising dialogues do not require all parties to adopt the same research criteria, goals or even narrative formulations of consumer phenomena. Supporting this claim, however, requires a consideration of the broad historical conditions that underlie the development of paradigmatic diversity in consumer research (and the social sciences at large).

The history of social science research has been structured by a family of fundamental contrasts, such as that between Romanticism – emphasising emotional and aesthetic experience – and Rationalism – emphasising formalised processes of logical reasoning – and the Cartesian dichotomy between mind (mentalist frameworks) and body (behaviourist frameworks) (e.g. Keller 1989; Rorty 1979). These and other meta-binaries have precipitated innumerable critiques, rebuttals, adaptations and attempts at synthetic solutions. Implicit to all research paradigms are conceptual and methodological legacies that have arisen from this philosophical genealogy. Thus, the phrase 'encapsulated paradigms' (e.g. Anderson 1986), while not a misnomer, obscures that these 'macrostructures' have been shaped by a play of diversity among earlier foundational frameworks: a dynamic that continues to shape research in the present and that could be further facilitated by more explicit and systematic considerations of paradigmatic diversity.

The specification of paradigmatic boundaries can enrich the network of constructs and research domains that are represented in the consumer research literature by sensitising participants in its constituent interpretive communities to specific theoretical and/or cultural interests that have been marginalised by their established meta-conventions. An important demonstration of this process is offered by the initial Romanticist calls to broaden the conceptual and methodological horizons of the field to encompass experiential, symbolic and aesthetic dimensions (Hirschman and Holbrook 1982; Holbrook and Hirschman 1982). In recent years, consumer researchers have used this narrative strategy to recognise specific socio-cultural (as opposed to conceptual) interests that have been under-represented or ignored (Bristor and Fischer 1993; Hill 1991; Hill and Stamey 1990; Joy 1991; Murray and Ozanne 1991). In so doing, these researchers and others often demonstrate the marginalised interest's significance to the consumer research community. Thus, the presentation of paradigmatic difference creates a narrative space for the expression of alternative voices and expands parochial definitions of 'mainstream' or relevant consumer research issues and topics.

However, this 'space' exists within the field of hegemonic narrative conventions and must constantly be defended against pressures to return to the traditional exclusionary norm (Williams 1994). In this regard, the diversity of the post-positivist paradigms has enabled certain core theoretical ideas (the importance of cultural symbolism, experientialism, social constructivist models of knowledge) to be expressed in different vernaculars (such as symbolic interactionism, semiotics, ethnomethodologies, hermeneutics and phenomenology) and to become thoroughly established in the narrative history of the field (Hirschman and Holbrook 1992; Sherry 1991).

Dialogical Retextualisation

Retextualisation refers to a process in which one research narrative is reformulated in light of another paradigmatic orientation and the pattern of exclusions that this dialogue reveals. This process stands as a postmodern counterpart to a replication study which pursues the traditional empiricist question of whether a set of findings can be reproduced by different researchers using similar methods. In contrast, retextualisation revisits an existing set of research propositions but focuses on the different issues, social positions and cultural interests that would be voiced by a different paradigmatic narrative.

Conceptually, this process mirrors the deconstructionist insight that the act of critical writing creates new meaning. As such, a deconstructive critic is not revealing the 'essence' of a literary text, but instead is creating a new textual meaning (Culler 1982). As applied to pluralistic research, the implication is that dialogue among different paradigms creates a new interpretive text that provides a different way of understanding the data (in terms of its collection, analysis and presentation) and the consumer phenomenon that has been explained. This strategy lends itself to metaphors, such as an ongoing conversation, that imply an ongoing transformation of established narrative boundaries (Benhabib 1992; Rorty 1989).

In contrast to the Kuhnian conception of a total disciplinary 'revolution', retextualisation requires negotiation among delimited narrative conflicts in consumer research discourse. The innovations inspired by these dialogues can provide significant contributions such as offering an explanation of anomalous phenomena or resolving entrenched problems facing a given research community. Thus, the ongoing conversation among diverse research paradigms offers a conceptual (as well as empirical) means to continuously advance the cause of theory development by engendering more inclusive and innovative explanations of consumer phenomena. However, the development of a more inclusive account should not be regarded as an inherent progression toward absolute knowledge or totalising truth. Rather, it simply offers a novel narrative to be considered, analysed and eventually reformulated by the various interpretive communities existing within consumer research.

From a postmodern orientation, dialogical retextualisation injects a healthy degree of incredulity into the research process by calling attention to the dynamic and contingent nature of even the most well-supported theoretical propositions. Rather than being supported or falsified, theory is always on the way toward a new formulation, whose developmental course is only partially driven by intra-paradigm empirical confrontations among 'competing' frameworks. The other transformative source is the play of diversity in which dialogues among different paradigmatic orientations identify interests and issues that had been excluded or marginalised in existing theoretical models.

One example of this type of dialogical retextualisation is offered by Hirschman's (1993) Marxist reading of a study by Thompson, Locander and Pollio (1990). The Thompson *et al.* study offered a phenomenological account of the 'lived' experiences of consumer choice reported by a sample of stay-at-home mothers. As Hirschman writes (1993),

> feminist standpoint epistemology may be used to detect some shortcomings in the Thompson *et al.* (1990) study. For example, the use of an all-male research team may have limited the discernment of ideological constraints on these female consumers' freedom of choice. For example, why were their husbands never mentioned in housework or child-care? Did these women never question their choice to live primarily in the role of the homemaker? Were they, in fact, victims of patriarchal hegemony and false consciousness, persons who, as Eagleton (1991) described them, had learned all too well that women should not seek more in life?

> (Hirschman 1993: 549)

Pursuing these questions and offering a comprehensive materialist analysis of these women's experiences of 'free choice' would have then highlighted a range of social issues related to class and gender dynamics that were left unsaid in the psychologically focused narrative paradigm of phenomenological consumer research.

An excellent and more fully developed example of feminist retextualisation is offered by Calàs and Smirich's (1991) deconstruction of 'seminal' works in the management literature on leadership. Rather than adopting a Marxian perspective that focuses on economic relationships in the manner suggested by Hirschman, Calàs and Smirich draw from the French post-structuralist tradition of feminist theory that is identified with theorists such as Julia Kristeva (1986) and Luce Irigaray (1985). This tradition of feminist theory emphasises the carnality of human existence, non-phallocentric conceptions of erotic pleasure (i.e. *jouissance)* and the politics of gender identities and sexual pleasures. Calàs and Smirich's retextualisation of the leadership literature highlights a multitude of sexualised themes which are not voiced in the formal texts. They suggest that this literature portrays leadership in an organisation as a game of seduction in which the leader attempts to engender in others a desire and a longing that can be satisfied only through faithful attachment to the leader. In terms of the alternative reading, leadership is the exercise of libidinal energy by an essentially narcissistic masculine figure. They further note that this literature conveys a homo-erotic subtext related to the patriarchal social structure characteristic of many organisational settings.[5] Finally, this feminist retextualisation enabled Calàs and Smirich to articulate an alternative feminised, maternal model of leadership that differed in several key respects from the traditional, masculinised/phallocentric models.

In the consumer research literature, one of the most extensively developed examples of retextualisation is offered by Stern (1995), who retextualised the texts of Wallendorf and Arnould's (1991) ethnography of American families' Thanksgiving stories and practices in terms of a literary paradigm. Using Northrop Frye's typology of mythoi, Stern analysed the structures of the stories reported by the informants in the Wallendorf and Arnould study and called attention to patterns of gender conflicts, psychological tensions and strategies for creating happy endings that were not explicitly addressed by Wallendorf and Arnould's ethnographic framing. By adopting a narrative paradigm that invoked an

---

[5] **CI: I was afraid of this. Give you postmodernists an inch and ... Well, I must rise up in protest! I forcefully insist that this stream of reasoning must be ejected from the chapter. I will not let you diminish the sizeable accomplishments of this fertile theoretical framework. Besides, this whole discussion is making me feel rather, uh, uncomfortable.**

US: So, does this mean that you don't want us to present our retextualisation of Hunt's (1983) **Marketing Theory** *using 'Spartacus' as the framing text?*

CI: Absolutely NOT! All criteria of scientific adequacy would shrink at the mere thought of such a narrative intercourse.

institutional analysis (or critique) such as Eagleton (1991), an even wider array of marginalised conflict narratives (related to class, gender and ethnicity) could have been given voice.

Dialogical retextualisation also has direct implications for another important modernist convention of social science discourse: the preference for parsimonious explanation. Rather than being a logical necessity, we suggest that parsimony is an aesthetic criterion that reflects a modernist conception of theoretical elegance and a desire for maximally efficient predictive power (Anderson 1986, 1989; Rorty 1979). Whereas the modernist project is to reduce complex social phenomena to a more parsimonious set of explanatory constructs, the postmodern project is to construct a more inclusive consideration of the conceptual and social diversity within an issue, through 'maximal comparison' (Sherry 1991) or some such device. Whereas the criterion of parsimony serves the goals of control and prediction, a postmodern approach aims at enriching understanding of contextual complexity, embedded layers of meanings, the multi-faceted nature of social experiences, and finally, the narratological contingencies of research.

The postmodern aesthetic is not about satisfying some Le Corbusier-like quest for an idealised rational form offering the most parsimonious 'constructs follow explanation' analysis. On the contrary, a postmodern design aesthetic manifests a critical stance through parody, juxtaposition, and reappropriation; it does not privilege one stylistic (i.e. paradigmatic) form over another; it allows many types of expressive, creative, symbolic forms to emerge (Meamber 1995). In sum, a postmodern aesthetic prefers a 'messy vitality' to an obvious or imposed unity (Venturi 1966: 22). What could be more fun than that?

Beyond ritualistic statements of limitations and reflexive confessionals

A topic of particular relevance to our narratological conception paradigmatic diversity is the ubiquitous statement of limitations. As Wells notes (1993: 493), these statements assume a ritualistic quality in scientific narration: 'if taken seriously, the limitations would invalidate the findings. It is surprising to outsiders that the authors then go on to state broad general conclusions – as though the limitations had vanished upon being confessed.' Expanding on Wells's point, these statements serve an even broader ritualistic function. By stating the specific limitations to a study, researchers demonstrate allegiance to the ideal of attaining a totalised view of reality. Thus, the self-confessed 'limitations' reinforce the ideal of unified community of researchers who use their methodological skills to build more complete knowledge. While these ritualised statements may help to foster a sense of solidarity and commitment to common ideals, they do so by invoking a largely unreflexive conception of research limitations (Woolgar 1988). The conventional reference is to intra-paradigm limitations such as sample size, research setting, method(s) of measure, tool(s) of analysis, failure to consider intervening variables or rival theoretical explanations.

These statements tend not to critically explicate the socio-cultural and paradigmatic viewpoints that frame the account or to address those which have been excluded from narrative representation. In this way, methodological limitations are delimited within a field of socio-cultural and theoretical precepts, but do not go so far as to question the narrative field itself. One means to make statements of limitations something more than a ritualised expression is to explicitly identify and explore the contingent relations between the research narrative and its narratological underpinnings (Joy 1991). Toward this end, it is becoming more common-place for researchers to openly acknowledge their theoretical and social positions in the research narrative (Bristor and Fischer 1993; Joy 1991). In these terms, the statement of limitations (or more accurately a statement of narrative preconditions) might take a form such as 'this narrative was constructed by a western, male, upper middle-class, heterosexual, speaking as a classical economist.'

However, this type of reflexivity itself offers little more than a ritualised postmodern confessional unless systematic linkages between the identified preconditions and the structure of the research narrative are developed (Bourdieu 1990). In this spirit, we contend that the more challenging and informative task of reflexivity is to critically assess the communal (or paradigmatic) conditions of the research narrative rather than simply specifying the social position of the author(s). On this point, the following passage from Bourdieu and Wacquant (1992) is particularly informative:

> reflexivity does not entail the reflection of the subject [researcher] on the subject ... What has to be constantly scrutinised and neutralised, in the very act of the construction of the [research] object, is the collective scientific unconscious embedded in theories, problems, and categories of scholarly judgment ... It follows that the subject of reflexivity must be the social science field in toto. Thanks to the dialogic of public debate and mutual critique, the work ... is not carried out by its author alone but by the occupants of all the antagonistic and complementary positions which constitute the scientific field.
>
> (Bourdieu and Wacquant 1992: 40)

The necessity for this type of paradigmatic reflexivity (and exploration of 'limitations') follows from the inclusion/exclusion dynamic manifest in any narrative. Awareness of this dynamic implies that reflexive statements of limitations must do more than acknowledge that a set of findings may not generalise to other research settings and populations or that they are globally related to the researcher(s) life history. Rather, these statements would explore the manner in which the researchers' paradigmatic orientation framed the 'phenomenon' in terms of specific theoretical and social interests and provide some insight into how excluded paradigmatic narratives would provide a fundamentally different understanding.

We also note that concerns over reflexivity often manifest certain assumptions about how readers respond to the text. A useful commentary on this underlying assumption is offered by LaTour (1988) who states:

> For many writers [on reflexivity], the main deleterious effect of a text is to be naively believed by readers. Readers have this bad habit they say of being immediately taken in by any story and being led to believe that there is something out there which is the referent of the text and which corresponds to the text.
>
> (LaTour 1988: 166)

Although LaTour's passage oversimplifies the concerns of 'many writers', its primary thesis remains relevant. That is, many of the stylistic elements of reflexive narratives are directed at dissuading readers from a 'realist' interpretation of the text. To the extent that readers become familiar with (and apply) an anti-foundational logic, however, this concern becomes less relevant. For example, such readers would interpret omniscient narration as a literary device rather than as a voice of absolute objectivity and so on. In the context of a postmodern framework, then, the interest in reflexivity should not be motivated by a concern that one's text might be 'naively' believed. Rather, the motivation should derive from a recognition that one can never escape the authority of authorship and that authorship always entails the privileging of certain values and the marginalisation and exclusion of others.

This self-reflexive understanding of consumer research's preferred methodological orientations has several desirable outcomes: it can provide enhanced critical insights into assumptions formerly taken for granted; it can increase sensitivity to the subtle influences of class-based, ethnocentric and gender-biased conceptions; it can enrich the scope of intellectual dialogues; and it can continually challenge and revitalise the status quo by interjecting anomalous evidence and unconventional perspectives into mainstream discourse.

(A SIMULACRA OF) A FURTHER CONVERSATION WITH OUR CRITIC

(CI): Where to begin? Your article is a veritable refutation-fest. Well. let's start with my favourite philosophical bugaboo: the imprecise and hence meaningless use of a term. You have really missed the mark here with your ill-defined and overly elastic conception of a paradigm. You slip from a discussion of the usual dimensions (axiology, epistemology, ontology) to a discussion about representing the interests of marginalised groups. The relationship between the two is tenuous to say the least and a logical nonsequitur to say a bit more.

(US): You had us worried for a moment. Fortunately, the natural language philosophers such as Austin and the later Wittgenstein pretty much slew this philosophical chimera of the 'precise definition'. Except for a few remarkably anachronistic supporters of the correspondence theory of meaning, there really is not much debate in philosophical or linguistic circles that the meaning of a term is contingent upon its use in a given context (see G. Lakoff 1987; Rorty 1979).

Our discussion reflects the multi-faceted meaning that 'paradigm' now assumes in the social sciences. Our particular usage places twin emphasis on exemplar-based categories (e.g. a socially shared image of the scientific method) and their co-constituting relationship with interpretive communities. We argued that this usage is worthwhile because it reformulates the meaning and research implications of the incommensurability thesis. To clarify our position, the connections between research interests and socio-cultural-political interests are certainly complex and seldom exhibit a one-to-one correspondence. But we have never been talking about isomorphic relations. What we are saying is that understanding these dynamics of narrative inclusion/exclusion can not be done by an analysis of a paradigm's theoretical interests alone. Rather, it must address the institutional factors (such as the legacy of patriarchy and western imperialism) that constitute the social matrix in which social science narratives are formulated (see among others Alarcon 1994; Benhabib 1992; H.R. Brown 1993; Butler 1990; Fraser 1989; Gilligan 1982; Haraway 1991; Lugones and Spelman 1983; Pratt 1986; Rosaldo 1989; Strathern 1987; White 1987).

CI: Whatever. Look, I was simply being magnanimous. I began with an easy criticism to spare you a little embarrassment. But now the time has come to mercifully put an end to your tortured logic and strained rationales (not to mention your impenetrable prose). Your 'argument', for lack of better word, implies that cross-paradigmatic triangulation is the cornerstone of consumer research these days. Well, this is hardly the case. Researchers are more concerned with convergent validity as an intra-paradigm problem. Second, your proposals about *différance* are all very old news. This is exactly what has always been done in the social sciences. A classic example is the variety of synthetic work, such as Weber's, that arose when Durkheim's structural-functionalist paradigm was contrasted with Marx's critical materialist perspective. So, Hasta la vista baby!!!

US: Sorry, but we're not terminated that easily. To usurp a phrase from Sherry (1991) who commandeered it from who knows where, our position steers between the Scylla of unreflexive normal science conventions and the Charybdis of dialectical synthesis. We argue that paradigmatic pluralism should be used in the service of exploring the narratological 'differences that would make a difference' in the conduct of consumer research. We agree that convergent validation is best treated as a within paradigm problem. However, our point is that this epistemological logic is often extended to discussions of cross-paradigm research. What we are trying to do is provide an alternative conceptual model for thinking about critical pluralism. As for the sociological troika, it seems to us that these three thinkers shared a common-world-view, as evidenced by their modernist predilections for totalising theory, taxonomy and evolutionism. More to the point, our version of critical pluralism is clearly directed toward a different purpose and has a different goal than creating a synthetic account.

We are contending that critical pluralism – if one takes social constructivism seriously – implies a play of differences and the analysis of these differences can be used for more than an exercise in deconstructive criticism (insert references to incomprehensible French writers here). A divergence-focused critical pluralism can provide new insights into the nature of a research paradigm's mode of knowledge construction and into the specific consumer phenomenon it represents.

CI: Indeed, sophistry is the last refuge to which a postmodernist will flee. Let me remind you there was a time when you all would have burned at the stake for speaking such heresy. Those were the days! We could really refute disagreeable arguments with kindling, fire and screams of agony! Oh, but where was I? Face it, there is nothing interesting to be learned by showing that different research approaches have different ways of representing reality. The only interesting case is when these different modes of representations converge upon a common set of relationships. At that point, we can be assured that our platoon of methodologies have cornered 'the beast' and that its true nature has surrendered to the irresistible forces of science.

US: Ah, the 'will to power' does have seductive qualities doesn't it? However, we beg to differ with this 'macho science' portrayal. Convergence across different paradigmatic approaches does not mean that a singular reality has been captured. What it tells you is that different research approaches have been situated in a higher order network of assumptions and meta-norms that are tacitly embraced by a broadly defined research community. For example, Peñaloza (1994) argues that consumer research has seldom questioned the binary of masculine/feminine and therefore, has consistently failed to recognise that consumer identities often transgress this taken-for-granted boundary. Bristor and Fischer (1993) and Hirschman (1991) have shown that a masculinist language replete with images of warfare (e.g. targeting), domination, and sexual metaphors (e.g. market penetration) lies at the heart of marketing theory. Murray and Ozanne (1991) have argued that the texts of mainstream consumer research have, for the most part, excluded consideration of the substantial differences in power and social interests that exist between individual consumers and marketers. Hence, convergence among paradigmatic functions to reproduce, rather than challenge, the dynamic of privileging and marginalising narratives that hold a hegemonic position in a given research community.

CI: Much ado about nothing. Certain points-of-view get marginalised because most people in the research community to which you refer teach in business schools. Their research naturally reflects the interests of those paying the bills. Marketing researchers tend to serve 'capitalist interests'. If these pragmatic motives bother you so much, why don't you all go and do consumer research in the other social science fields where these 'marginalised' interests are advanced and leave the capitalist pursuits to us real marketers?

US: Always the tempest. To read or not to read consumer research done by marketing professors – that seems to be the question. (Sorry readers, but CI started it.) The problem of marginalisation has moved to centre stage in many other fields. This is a truly multi-disciplinary movement in which critical scholars have strongly challenged their particular discipline's canonical voice for privileging particular socio-cultural positions at the expense of all others. They have demonstrated that including other voices can alter taken-for-granted paradigmatic assumptions and open new avenues of social scientific theorising (e.g. Butler 1990; Gilligan 1982; hooks 1989; Keller 1989; Kristeva 1986; Said 1978; West 1994 to name just a few). So, these issues have implications for all social science fields that study consumer phenomena. Furthermore, this research community – due to its multi-disciplinary, multi-paradigmatic form – is ideally positioned to be one of the most innovative social science fields in regard to the development of postmodern applications of pluralistic research.

CI: Not so fast. You talk a pretty good game about doing research but all you offer is a recipe for infinite regress. Your proposals for hyper-reflexive analyses is a Pandora's box that promises nothing but an endless series of reflections on the reflections about whose interests aren't being 'voiced' in the text. Since you refuse to accept the epistemological bedrock and sense of finality offered by convergent accord, all you have left is futile exercise in the ceaseless exploration of *différance*. Who, pray tell, would have the time and energy for doing such research? I've had just about enough of all your postmodern polysyllabic poppycock!!!!

US: Great alliteration. Mind if we use that in the chapter?

CI: Just like a postmodernist. Trying to dodge an irrefutable criticism by changing the subject. Well, all those effete French intellectuals might have let Derrida get away that kind of foolishness but it won't work here.

US: We admit that the infinite regress problem has sometimes thwarted reflexive analysis. But this doesn't have to be the case. Many of the 'problems' are tied to an inability to escape the auspices of the visual metaphor and the related modernist idea that science can not proceed unless it is in touch with some bedrock of absolute rules and criteria that tell us when the job is done. Well, let's switch metaphors. The fact that one can choose to talk about anything does not preclude the possibility of having meaningful conversations, right? Well, the mere availability of an infinite number of deconstructive positions does not preclude researchers from placing specific goals and limits on their reflexive undertakings. For example, a researcher might choose to confront one variant of the empiricist paradigm with one variant of the humanities paradigm to show a specific pattern of inclusions and exclusions. Now, the resulting analysis could be subsequently contested by, say, a conflict-focused neo-Marxian paradigm. However, this situation does not refute the formerly marginalised voices that would be identified nor the new pattern of insights generated.

CI: Ah ha! Sounds to me like you have just indulged a 'modernist' impulse by suggesting that the analysis of *différance* does in fact offer a superior account because it somehow presents 'more' voices than had previously been acknowledged. Sounds to me like that nasty ole modernist narrative about the progressive accumulation of knowledge. It is just as I suspected. Your 'postmodern' approach to paradigmatic pluralism is premised on a self-refuting logic. Consider yourself falsified.

US: This is all very embarrassing. We never expected you to turn the rhetorical tables on us. But, we have been expecting this familiar tu quoque *argument that is invariably levelled at proposals that espouse a skeptical or relativistic stance toward science's presumed epistemological foundations (e.g. Ashmore 1989). (For further elaboration on this critique see Hunt's 'All the World's Miseries Are Caused By Self-Refuting Relativists')*

CI: Hold on there! Professor Hunt is a fine scholar who has never written such a paper, at least not yet.

US: You're quite right. So sorry. We're still getting our bearings after your rhetorical turn. We promise to pay penance; 'Praise Popper'. But back to your objection. First off, we do not claim that a postmodern approach to paradigmatic pluralism stands exempt from the phenomena it identifies (e.g. latent social interests, paradigmatic commitments, narrative privileging and marginalization of social and theoretical voices, etc.). As with any reflexive undertaking, the processes being reported are also mirrored in the act of reporting. Our formulation of paradigmatic pluralism as a critical analysis of différance *does aim to raise awareness of sedimented narrative conventions by challenging established conventions of writing and reading. However, our whole approach is predicated on the metaphor of dialogue and conversation, which implies that any written account is an always-contingent one that is open to revision and reformulation. You interpreted our position in terms of the modernist ethos of epistemological progress. Our claim is that the exploration of diversity creates different narratives of understanding that enrich the vocabulary by which consumer researchers can represent consumption phenomena. A richer, more complex dialogue does not mean, however, that an interpretive community has progressed toward a totalising language of truth.*

CI: No, no, no. You don't understand. Some narrative conventions must be treated as sacrosanct lest we plunge into chaos and anarchy. Science cannot become a prescription for existential angst. I have no desire to stare down the epistemological abyss that you propose. If you want to go ahead and saw off the branch that you are sitting on, fine by me. I'll stay right here nice and secure in the tree of knowledge with its roots solidly planted in a firm epistemological ground.

US: Oh come on, live a little. Do some 'extreme' epistemology. A wild plunge into the Derridian quagmire can be quite invigorating. Why it's the next best thing to a Mountain Dew commercial. [For those who are not familiar with the paragon of consumer culture, these commercials feature the Dew Dudes – a bunch of twenty-something adventurers and extreme sports enthusiasts 'who have been there and done that' and for whom only a swig of Mountain Dew can generate any sense of excitement. Boy will this footnote look dated in a few years, if not a few months.]

CI: Yes it will. That's the problem with you postmodernists. You're just a fleeting series of commercial fads. For your information, I am a Coca-Cola drinker. That's a True beverage secure in its tradition and based on a timeless, never changing secret formula. It will never seem dated like the 'Dew Dudes' or your own 'extreme' postmodern epistemology.

US: Oh yeah? What about the New Coke débâcle?

CI: Well, that's what they did you see. One night, a bunch of relativist philosophers got the idea. They hatched a diabolical scheme to relativise Coca-Cola. 'Cause, they knew that Coca-Cola was not just a brand. No! It was the very Archimedean point upon which the western intellectual tradition stands! And you know what else? Captain Queeg, he was right. They all should have been hanged for mutiny. They'd all read Nietzsche too, the whole scurrilous lot of them.

US: Hey, are you OK? The Caine Mutiny stuff is kind of postmodern so we'll let that go without comment. But, your counter-arguments, conspiracy theories and fear of relativists seem to be – well, how can we put this tactfully? – uh, paranoid and delusional.

CI: Very tactful indeed. But you make an interesting point. Oh wait, there it is, my super fast-acting double strength Prozac. Please pardon me for a moment. I'll just mix up a dose right here in my Coke Classic – can't beat the real thing you know – and *voilà*!!! I feel better already and with no bitter after taste. Sorry about all that. I gotta tell you I've been looking for my medication ever since I misplaced them on a hunting trip down to Texas. Found them just in the nick of time though.

Anyway, I'll grant your thesis that there are no absolute foundations that undergird our claims to truth. However, this doesn't change the pragmatic requirements for doing consumer research without being overcome by despair and a sense of futility. Consumer researchers *need* to act as though their narratives are supported by an unquestionable and irrefutable canon of truth-confirming procedures and rationales. Only in this way can we merrily go about our business of making incremental refinements in theories that have no relevance outside the narrow confines of our heavily rationalised and always denied paradigmatic parochialism.

US: *We fully concur that underneath all the complex rhetorical gestures of philosophical objections and refutations to the implications of postmodernism is a profound case of Cartesian anxiety* and *very pragmatic (and understandable) fears about changing the rules of a language game that has served us all so well for so long. In fact, we couldn't have stated this point better if we had written it ourselves.*

However, we are neither asking consumer researchers to give up the 'game' nor demanding that they relinquish their own paradigmatic voices. We had hoped that a paper arguing against the quest for developing totalising visions would not imply to anyone that a single study must *do anything. Since this doesn't seem to be the case, let us reiterate our basic premises. Lots of researchers have argued that it is beneficial to use multiple perspectives to triangulate upon a convergent reality. Of course, calls for multi-perspectivalism do not imply that triangulation should be required for every specific research study. Now, we have been arguing that another useful application of paradigmatic pluralism is to identify paradigmatic boundaries by analysing divergent voices and to explicate processes of marginalisation and exclusion latent to any research narrative.*

The metaphor we have in mind is something like an ongoing ratcheting process. That is, a pluralistic analysis of a research narrative would lead to a more inclusive reformulation that in turn could become the target of yet another analysis that identifies another pattern of inclusions/exclusions. In the abstract, there would seem to be no limit to the number of such analyses that could be undertaken, for that which is included, the 'said' of a text, is finite while that which is excluded, its unsaid realm, is infinite. However, analyses are never undertaken in the abstract. Rather, they are motivated by specific problems and issues that are (or can be) shown relevant to the interests of a research community. Hence, the recognition that one can never say everything does not preclude the possibility of having meaningful discourse about specific issues and marginalised voices and of exploring the implications that follow from this specific pattern of inclusions/exclusions. As noted by Schatzki (1993), struggles against hegemony – whether in the realm of theoretical discourse or political practice – are always 'local': a specific form of resistance that contests a particular hegemonic structure.

CI: OK, I get the idea: one conversation, one conflict, one struggle, one narratological transformation at a time. 'The path makes the work', isn't that what Heidegger said? So, your epistemology won't end my career and it might even make things a bit more interesting. But answer me this. What if I want to engage in this conversation but on my modernist terms rather than yours? What if I really believe that my language game is really the only one that offers any hope for intellectual and moral progress? Doesn't your postmodernist model – while singing the praises of diversity – preclude my voice from the conversation? I fear that an unintended consequence of your proposal is a new orthodoxy of politically correct consumer research.

US: A postmodern approach to paradigmatic pluralism can accommodate a voice that proclaims an absolutist position; unlike an absolutist narrative per se, *however, the postmodern narrative positions this absolutist voice within a cacophony of differing positions. Despite our differences, we have no desire to silence you. In fact, we would be happy to participate in another book chapter where our roles reversed. You can provide the voice of the primary text and we'll be the marginal voice in the critical footnotes. Of course that would require another volume. Oh, Stephen, Darach . . .*

CI: At last, a sensible proposal. Oh, what the heck. I'll confess to seeing some value to your position. I think there is something worthwhile to be gained by exploring the *différance*. But . . . you're still a bunch of Nietzsche quoting, Marxist loving, nihilist espousing, sophist worshipping, morality defying, reason refuting RELATIVISTS.

POSTSCRIPT (Yahoo! The missing P)

Postmodernists have an irritating habit of always first talking about what they are not talking about. No reason to change at this late stage of the game, is there? So, our approach does not say that convergence is prima facie evidence of validation or that divergence among research approaches is indicative that validity is lacking. To the contrary, we have 'argued' (and yes CI we are stretching the meaning of this term) that convergence among paradigmatic approaches should be treated sceptically for it may signify an implicit or explicit conformity to one particular set of theoretical and cultural narratives. Second, divergences among paradigmatic approaches is not a 'problem' but an opportunity to understand how fundamentally different core assumptions, conceptualisations, conventions and research interests have shaped texts that codify knowledge claims. The articulation of these differences involves specifying ways that underlying assumptions of different research traditions lead to diverse understandings; assessing the practical consequences that ensue from diverse accounts; and clarifying the different frameworks by means of which different postpositivist approaches address or ignore common phenomena.

By exploring and articulating these paradigmatic differences, consumer researchers gain a more informed understanding of the many ways that methodologically validated knowledge is always contingent upon underlying socio-cultural assumptions and beliefs that privilege certain cultural interests over others. This self-reflexive understanding of the discipline's preferred methodological orientations has several desirable outcomes: it can provide enhanced critical insights into assumptions formerly taken for granted; it can increase sensitivity to the subtle influences of ethnocentric and gender-biased conceptions; it can enrich the scope of intellectual dialogues; and it can continually challenge and revitalise the status quo by interjecting anomalous evidence and unconventional perspectives into mainstream discourse.

As a closing, self-reflexive statement, we acknowledge that a deconstructive logic has provided the conceptual foundation for our approach to critical pluralism in consumer research. As such, the deconstructive voice was implicitly elevated to a position of authority in narrative. We justify this rendering by proposing that a deconstructive logic encourages the community of consumer researchers to view its body of knowledge in a more humble and self-critical fashion. We hold that the integrity of our research community is best served by a willingness to critically deconstruct our 'collective unconscious'. That is, our agreed-upon conventions regarding what problems are important, what theories warrant continued testing, what narrative forms are deemed to signify good scholarship and, finally, what social interests are to be served by the research community (also see Bourdieu and Wacquant 1992). A deconstructive logic serves this important reflexive task and, in so doing, recalls an insight noted long ago by the philosopher who perhaps first characterised the emerging spirit of postmodernism. After all, we are a bunch of, well you know:

> What therefore is truth? A mobile army of metaphors, metonymies, and anthropomorphisms; in short, a sum of human relations which become poetically and rhetorically intensified, metamorphosed, adorned and, after long usage, seem to a nation fixed, canonic and binding.
>
> (Nietzsche 1873: 180)

ACKNOWLEDGEMENTS

There are a number of supportive and helpful colleagues, friends and family toward whom we could extend many thanks. However, the inescapable social phenomenon of *guilt by association* necessitates that we remain very discreet about these matters. We had thought about changing the names to protect the innocent but then we would only impugn those who just happened to share the hyperreal pseudonyms. So, you all know who you are and we extend our deepest thanks to each of you. Most importantly, we promise not to reveal your joyously fragmented identities to anyone else.

REFERENCES

Alarcon, N. (1994) 'The theoretical subject(s) of this bridge called my back and Anglo-American feminism', in S. Seidman (ed.) *The Postmodern Turn*, Cambridge: Cambridge University Press, 140–152.

Anderson, P.F. (1986) 'On method in consumer research: a critical relativist perspective', *Journal of Consumer Research*, 13, September: 155–173.

—— (1989) 'On relativism and interpretivism: with a prolegomenon on the Why question', in E.C. Hirschman (ed.) *Interpretive Consumer Research*, Provo, UT: Association for Consumer Research, 10–23.

Arnold, S.J. and Fischer, E. (1994) 'Hermeneutics and consumer research', *Journal of Consumer Research*, 21, June: 55–70.

Arnould, E.J. (1989) 'Toward a broadened theory of preference formation and the diffusion of innovations: cases from Zinder Province, Niger Republic', *Journal of Consumer Research*, 16, September: 239–267.

—— and Price, L.L. (1993) '"River Magic": extraordinary experience and the service encounter', *Journal of Consumer Research*, 20, June: 24–46.

Ashmore, M. (1989) *The Reflexive Thesis*, Chicago: University of Chicago Press.

de Beauvoir, S. (1952) *The Second Sex*, trans. H.M. Parshley, New York: Vintage.

Belk, R.W. (1991) 'Epilogue: lessons learned', in R. W. Belk (ed.) *Highways and Buyways: Naturalistic Research from the Consumer Behavior Odyssey*, Provo, UT: Association for Consumer Research, 234–238.

——, Sherry, J.F. and Wallendorf, M. (1988) 'A naturalistic inquiry into buyer and seller behavior at a swap meet', *Journal of Consumer Research*, 14, March: 449–470.

——, Wallendorf, M. and Sherry, J.F. (1989) 'The sacred and the profane in consumer behavior: theodicy on the Odyssey', *Journal of Consumer Research*, 16, June: 1–39.

Benhabib, S. (1992) *Situating the Self: Gender, Community, and Postmodernism in Contemporary Ethics*, New York: Routledge.

Berger, P. and Luckmann, T. (1967) *The Social Construction of Reality*, New York: Penguin.

Bourdieu, P. (1990) *In Other Words: Essays Toward a Reflexive Sociology*, Cambridge: Polity Press.

—— and Wacquant, L.J.D. (1992) *An Invitation to Reflexive Sociology*, Chicago: University of Chicago Press.

Bristor, J.M. and Fischer, E. (1993) 'Feminist thought: implications for consumer research', *Journal of Consumer Research*, 19, March: 518–536.

Brown, H.R. (1993) 'Modern science: institutionalization of knowledge and rationalization of power', *The Sociological Quarterly*, 34, Spring: 153–168.

Brown, S. (1995) *Postmodern Marketing*, London: Routledge.

Butler, J. (1990) *Gender Trouble: Feminism and the Subversion of Identity*, New York: Routledge.

Calàs, M.B. and Smirich, L. (1991) 'Voicing seduction to silence leadership', *Organisation Studies*, 12, 4: 567–602.

Campbell, D.T. and Fiske D.W. (1959) 'Convergent and discriminant validation by the multitrait-multimethod matrix', *Psychological Bulletin*, 56, March: 81–105.

Crawford M. and Marecek, J. (1988) 'Psychology reconstructs the female: 1968–1988', *Psychology of Women Quarterly*, 13, June: 147–165.

Culler, J. (1982) *On Deconstruction: Theory and Criticism after Structuralism*, Ithaca, NY: Cornell University Press.

Daly, M. (1978) *Gyn/Ecology: The Metaethics of a Radical Feminism*, Boston, MA: Beacon.

Denzin, N.K. (1994) 'The art and politics of interpretation', in N.K. Denzin and Y.S. Lincoln (eds) *Handbook of Qualitative Research*, Thousand Oaks, CA: Sage, 500–515.

Derrida, J. (1976) *Of Grammatology*, trans. G. Spivak, Baltimore, MD: Johns Hopkins University Press.

—— (1982) *Margins of Philosophy*, trans. A. Bass, Chicago: University of Chicago Press.

Douglas, M. (1986) *How Institutions Think*, Syracuse, NY: Syracuse University Press.

Dreyfus, H.L. and Rabinow, P. (1982) *Michel Foucault: Beyond Structuralism and Hermeneutics*, Chicago: University of Chicago Press.

Eagleton, T. (1991) *Ideology*, London: Verso.

Ehrenreich, B. and English, D. (1979) *For Her Own Good: 150 Years of the Experts' Advice to Women*, Garden City, NY: Anchor.

Epstein, C.F. (1988) *Deceptive Distinctions: Sex, Gender, and the Social Order*, New Haven, CT: Yale University Press.

Ewen, S. (1988) *All Consuming Images*, New York: Basic Books.

Featherstone, M. (1991) *Consumer Culture and Postmodernism*, London: Sage.

Firat, A.F. and Venkatesh, A. (1993) 'Postmodernity: the age of marketing', *International Journal of Research in Marketing*, 10, August: 227–251.

—— and —— (1995) 'Liberatory postmodernism and the reenchantment of consumption', *Journal of Consumer Research*, 22, December: 239–267.

Fish, S. (1980) *Is There a Text in This Class: The Authority of Interpretive Communities*, Cambridge, MA: Harvard University Press.

Fleck, L. (1979 [1935]) *The Genesis and Development of a Scientific Fact*, Chicago: University of Chicago Press.

Foucault, M. (1972) *The Archaeology of Knowledge*, New York: Pantheon.

—— (1980) 'Truth and power', in *Power/Knowledge*, Colin Gordon (ed.) New York: Pantheon, 109–133.

—— (1988) *Technologies of the Self*, L.H. Martin, H. Gutman, and P.H. Hutton (eds) Amherst, MA: University of Massachusetts Press.

Fraser, N. (1989) *Unruly Practices: Power, Discourse, and Gender in Contemporary Social Theory*, Minneapolis, MN: University of Minnesota Press.

Gavey, N. (1989) 'Feminist poststructuralism and discourse analysis', *Psychology of Women Quarterly*, 13: 459–475.

Gergen, K.J. (1985) 'The social constructionist movement in modern psychology', *American Psychologist*, 40, March: 266–275.

—— (1991) *The Saturated Self: Dilemmas of Identity in Contemporary Life*, New York: Basic Books.

Gilligan, C. (1982) *In a Different Voice*, Cambridge, MA: Harvard University Press.

Grimes, A.J. and Rood, D.L. (1995) 'Beyond objectivism and relativism: descriptive epistemologies', in W. Natter, T.R. Schatzki, and J.P. Jones III (eds) *Objectivity and its Other*, New York: Guilford, 161–178.

Habermas, J. (1972) *Knowledge and Human Interest*, London: Heinemann Educational.

Haraway, D.J. (1991) *Simians, Cyborgs and Women: The Reinvention of Nature*, New York: Routledge.

Harding, S. (1989) 'Feminist justificatory strategies', in A. Garry and M. Pearsall (eds) *Women, Knowledge, and Reality: Explorations in Feminist Philosophy*, Boston, MA: Unwin Hyman, 189–202.

Hekman, S. (1990) *Gender and Knowledge*, Cambridge: Polity.

Hetrick, W.P. and Lozada, H.R. (1994) 'Constructing critical imagination: comments and necessary diversions', *Journal of Consumer Research*, 21, December: 548–558.

Hill, R.P. (1991) 'Homeless women, special possessions, and the meaning of "Home": an ethnographic case study', *Journal of Consumer Research*, 18, December: 298–310.

—— and Stamey M. (1990) 'The homeless in America: an examination of possessions and consumption behaviors', *Journal of Consumer Research*, 17, December: 303–321.

Hirschman, E.C. (1986) 'Humanistic inquiry in marketing research: philosophy, method, and criteria', *Journal of Marketing Research*, 13, August: 237–249.

—— (1991) 'A feminist critique of marketing theory: toward agentic and communal balance', in J.A. Costa (ed.) *Gender and Consumer Behaviour*, Salt Lake City, UT: University of Utah Press, 324–340.

—— (1992) 'The consciousness of addiction: toward a general theory of compulsive consumption', *Journal of Consumer Research*, 19, September: 155–179.

—— (1993) 'Ideology in consumer research, 1980 and 1990: a Marxist and feminist critique', *Journal of Consumer Research*, 19, March: 537–555.

—— and Holbrook, M.B. (1982) 'Hedonic consumption: emerging concepts, methods, and propositions', *Journal of Marketing*, 46, Summer: 92–101.

—— and —— (1992) *Postmodern Consumer Research: The Study of Consumption as Text*, Newbury Park, CA: Sage.

Holbrook, M.B. and Hirschman, E.C. (1982) 'The experiential aspects of consumption: consumer feelings, fantasy and fun', *Journal of Consumer Research*, 9, September: 132–140.

—— and O'Shaughnessy, J. (1988) 'On the scientific status of consumer research and the need for an interpretive approach to studying consumption behavior', *Journal of Consumer Research*, 15, December: 398–402.

Holt, D.B. (1991) 'Rashomon visits consumer behavior: an interpretive critique of naturalistic inquiry', in R.H. Holman and M.R. Solomon (eds) *Advances in Consumer Research*, 18, Provo, UT: Association for Consumer Research, 57–62.

hooks, b. (1989) *Talking Back: Thinking Feminist, Thinking Black*, Boston, MA: South End Press.

—— (1992) *Black Looks: Race and Representation*, Boston, MA: South End Press.

Hudson, L.A. and Ozanne, J.L. (1988) 'Alternative ways of seeking knowledge in consumer research', *Journal of Consumer Research*, 14, March: 132–140.

Hunt, S.D. (1983) *Marketing Theory*, Homewood, IL: Irwin.

—— (1989) 'Naturalistic, humanistic, and interpretivist inquiry: challenges and ultimate potential', in E.C. Hirschman (ed.) *Interpretive Consumer Research*, Provo, UT: Association for Interpretive Consumer Research, 185–198.

—— (1991) 'Positivism and paradigm dominance in consumer research: towards critical pluralism and rapprochement', *Journal of Consumer Research*, 18, June: 32–44.

Irigaray, L. (1985) *This Sex Which is Not One*, trans. C. Porter, Ithaca, NY: Cornell University Press.

Jaggar, A.M. (1991) 'Feminist ethics: projects, problems, and prospects', in C. Card (ed.) *Feminist Ethics*, Lawrence, KS: Kansas University Press, 78–107.

Joy, A. (1991) 'Beyond the Odyssey: interpretations of ethnographic writing in consumer behavior', in R.W. Belk (ed.) *Highways and Buyways: Naturalistic Research from the Consumer Behavior Odyssey*, Provo, UT: Association for Consumer Research, 216–233.

Keller, E.F. (1989) 'Feminism and science', in A. Garry and M. Pearsall (eds) *Women, Knowledge, and Reality*, Boston, MA: Unwin Hyman, 175–188.

Kohler, W. (1947) *Gestalt Psychology*, New York: New American Library Press.

Kristeva, J. (1986) *The Kristeva Reader*, T. Moi (ed.) New York: Columbia Press.

Kuhn, T.S. (1970) *The Structure of Scientific Revolutions*, Chicago: University of Chicago Press.

Lakoff, G. (1987) *Fire, Women and Dangerous Things: What Categories Reveal About the Mind*, Chicago: University of Chicago Press.

Lakoff, R.T. (1990) *Talking Power: The Politics of Language*, New York: Basic Books.

LaTour, B. (1988) 'The politics of explanation: an alternative', in S. Woolgar (ed.) *Knowledge and Reflexivity*, London: Sage, 155–176.

Lincoln, Y.S. and Guba, E.G. (1985) *Naturalistic Inquiry*, Beverly Hills, CA: Sage.

Lloyd, G. (1989) 'The man of reason', in A. Garry and M. Pearsall (eds) *Women, Knowledge and Reality: Explorations in Feminist Philosophy*, Boston, MA: Unwin Hyman, 111–128.

Lugones, M.C. and Spelman, K.V. (1983) 'Have we got a theory for you! Feminist theory: cultural imperialism and the demand for the women's voice', *Hypatia, Women's Studies International Forum*, 6, 6: 578–581.

Lutz, C. (1993) 'Social contexts of postmodern cultural analysis', in J.P. Jones III, W. Natter and T.R. Schatzki (eds) *Postmodern Contentions: Epochs, Politics and Space*, New York: Guilford, 137–163.

Lutz, R.J. (1989) 'Positivism, naturalism, and pluralism in consumer research: paradigms in paradise', in T.K. Srull (ed.) *Advances in Consumer Research*, 16, Provo, UT: Association for Consumer Research, 1–8.

Lyotard, J.F. (1984) *The Postmodern Condition: A Report on Knowledge*, Minneapolis, MN: University of Minnesota Press.

McQuarrie, E.F. and Mick, D.G. (1992) 'On resonance: a critical pluralistic inquiry in advertising rhetoric', *Journal of Consumer Research*, 19, September: 180–197.

de Man, P. (1989) *Critical Writings, 1953–1978*, L. Waters (ed.) Minneapolis, MN: University of Minnesota Press.

Meamber, L.A. (1995) 'Symbols for self-construction: product design in postmodernity', in B.B. Stern and G.A. Zinkhan (eds) *AMA Educators' Conference: Enhancing Knowledge Development in Marketing,* Chicago: American Marketing Association, 529–534.

Mick, D.G. (1986) 'Consumer research and semiotics: exploring the morphology of signs, symbols, and significance', *Journal of Consumer Research*, 13, September: 196–213.

—— and Buhl, C. (1992) 'A meaning-based model of advertising experiences', *Journal of Consumer Research*, 19, December: 317–338.

—— and DeMoss, M. (1990) 'Self-gifts: phenomenological insights from four contexts', *Journal of Consumer Research*, 17, December: 322–332.

Miller, G.A., Galanter, E. and Pribram, K. H. (1960) *Plans and Structures of Behavior*, New York: Adams-Bannister-Cox.

Murray, J.B. and Ozanne, J.L. (1991) 'The critical imagination: emancipatory interests in consumer research, *Journal of Consumer Research*, 18, September: 129–144.

Nietzsche, F. (1964 [1873]) 'Truth and morality in their ultramoral sense', in *The Complete Works of Friedrich Nietzsche*, O. Levy (ed.) New York: Gordon.

Norris, C. (1991) *Deconstruction: Theory and Practice*, London: Routledge.

O'Guinn, T.C. and Faber, R.J. (1989) 'Compulsive buying: a phenomenological exploration', *Journal of Consumer Research*, 16, September: 147–157.

Ozanne, J.L. and Hudson, L.A. (1989) 'Exploring diversity in consumer research', in E.C. Hirschman (ed.) *Interpretive Consumer Research*, Provo, UT: Association for Consumer Research, 1–9.

Peñaloza, L. (1994) 'Crossing boundaries / drawing lines: a look at the nature of gender boundaries and their impact on marketing research', *International Journal of Research in Marketing*, 11: 359–379.

—— (1996) 'We're here, we're queer, and we're going shopping: a critical perspective on the accommodation of gays and lesbians in the U.S. marketplace', in D.L. Wardlow (ed.) *Gays, Lesbians, and Consumer Behavior*, New York: Harrington Park Press, 9–42.

Peter, J.P. and Olson, J.C. (1989) 'The relativist/constructivist perspective on scientific knowledge and consumer research', in E.C. Hirschman (ed.) *Interpretive Consumer Research*, Provo, UT: Association for Consumer Research, 24–28.

Pinch, T. and Pinch, T. (1988) 'Reservations about reflexivity and new literary forms: or why let the Devil have all the good tunes', in S. Woolgar (ed.) *Knowledge and Reflexivity*, London: Sage, 178–197.

Pollio, H.R. (1982) *Behavior and Existence*, Monterey, CA: Brooks/Cole.

Poster, M. (1989) *Critical Theory and Poststructuralism*, Ithaca, NY: Cornell University Press.

Pratt, M.L. (1986) 'Fieldwork in common places', in J. Clifford and G.E. Marcus (eds) *Writing Culture: The Poetics and Politics of Ethnography*, Berkeley, CA: University of California Press, 27–50.

Prince, G. (1982) *Narratology: The Form and Functioning of Narrative*, Berlin: Mouton.

Rabinow, P. (1986) 'Representations are social facts: modernity and post-modernity in anthropology', in J. Clifford and G.E. Marcus (eds) *Writing Culture: The Poetics and Politics of Ethnography*, Berkeley, CA: University of California Press, 234–261.

Radway, J. (1991) *Reading the Romance: Women, Patriarchy, and Popular Literature*, 2nd edn, Chapel Hill, NC: University of North Carolina Press.

Rorty, R. (1979) *Philosophy and the Mirror of Nature*, Princeton, NJ: Princeton University Press.

—— (1989) *Contingency, Irony, and Solidarity*, Cambridge: Cambridge University Press.

Rosaldo, R. (1989) *Culture and Truth: The Remaking of Social Analysis*, Boston, MA: Beacon.

Rothman, B. (1989) 'Women, health and medicine', in M.J. Freeman (ed.) *Women: A Feminist Perspective*, Mountain View, CA: Mayfield, 76–86.

Said, E. (1978) *Orientalism*, New York: Pantheon.

de Saussure, F. (1966 [1915]) *Course in General Linguistics*, trans. W. Baskin, New York: McGraw-Hill.

Sayers, J. (1986) *Sexual Contradictions: Psychology, Psychoanalysis, and Feminism*, London: Tavistock.

Schatzki, T.R. (1993) 'Theory at bay: Foucault, Lyotard, and politics of the local', in J.P. Jones III, W. Natter and T.R. Schatzki (eds) *Postmodern Contentions: Epochs, Politics and Space*, New York: Guilford, 39–64.

Sherry, J.F. (1991) 'Postmodern alternatives: the interpretive turn in consumer research', in T.S. Robertson and H.H. Kassarjian (eds) *Handbook of Consumer Behavior*, Englewood Cliffs, NJ: Prentice Hall, 548–591.

Sirsi, A.K., Ward, J.C. and Reingen, P.H. (1996) 'Microcultural analysis of variation in sharing of causal reasoning about behavior', *Journal of Consumer Research*, 22, March: 345–372.

Stern, B.B. (1993) 'Feminist literary criticism and the deconstruction of ads: a postmodern view of advertising and consumer responses', *Journal of Consumer Research*, 19, March: 556–566.

—— (1995) 'Consumer myths: Frye's taxonomy and the structural analysis of consumption text', *Journal of Consumer Research*, 22, September: 154–164.

Strathern, M. (1987) 'An awkward relationship: the case of feminism and anthropology', *Signs*, 12, Winter: 270–292.

Suleiman, S.R. (1980) 'Introduction: varieties of audience-oriented criticism', in S.R. Suleiman and I. Crosman (eds) *The Reader in the Text: Essays on Audience and Interpretation*, Princeton, NJ: Princeton University Press, 3–45.

Thompson, C.J. (1990) 'Eureka! and other tests of significance: a new look at evaluating qualitative research', in M.E. Goldberg, G. Gorn and R.W. Pollay (eds) *Advances in Consumer Research*, 17, Provo, UT: Association for Consumer Research, 25–30.

——, Locander, W.B. and Pollio, H.R. (1990) 'The lived meaning of free choice: an existential-phenomenological description of everyday consumer experiences of contemporary married women', *Journal of Consumer Research*, 17, December: 346–361.

Venturi, R. (1966) *Complexity and Contradiction in Architecture*, New York: Museum of Modern Art.

Wallendorf, M. and Arnould, E.J. (1991) 'We gather together: consumption rituals of Thanksgiving Day', *Journal of Consumer Research*, 18, June: 13–31.

—— and Belk, R.W. (1989) 'Assessing trustworthiness in naturalistic consumer research', in E.C. Hirschman (ed.) *Interpretive Consumer Research*, Provo, UT: Association for Consumer Research, 115–132.

Wann, T.W. (ed.) (1964) *Behaviorism and Phenomenology: Contrasting Bases for Modern Psychology*, Chicago: University of Chicago Press.

Wardlow, D.L. (1996) 'Introduction', in D.L. Wardlow (ed.) *Gays, Lesbians, and Consumer Behavior*, New York: Harrington Park Press, 1–8.

Wells, W. (1993) 'Discovery-oriented consumer research', *Journal of Consumer Research*, 19, March: 489–504.

West, C. (1994) 'The new cultural politics of difference', in S. Seidman (ed.) *The Postmodern Turn*, Cambridge: Cambridge University Press, 65–82.

White, H. (1987) *The Content of the Form: Narrative Discourse and Historical Representation*, Baltimore, MD: Johns Hopkins University Press.

Williams, R. (1994) 'Selections from *Marxism and Literature*', in N. Dirks, G. Eley and S.B. Ortner (eds) *Culture/Power/History*, Princeton, NJ: Princeton University Press, 585–608.

Wittgenstein, L. (1953) *Philosophical Investigations*, New York: Macmillan.

Woolgar, S. (1988) 'Reflexivity is the ethnographer of the text', in S. Woolgar (ed.) *Knowledge and Reflexivity*, London: Sage, 14–34.

—— and Ashmore, M. (1988) 'The next step: an introduction to the reflexive project', in S. Woolgar (ed.) *Knowledge and Reflexivity*, London: Sage, 1–11.

6 Post-structuralism and the dialectics of advertising

Discourse, ideology, resistance

Richard Elliott and Mark Ritson

INTRODUCTION

Post-structuralism is not a single entity, but a loose collection of assumptions, concepts and perspectives which focus on three key themes: language and discourse; power and ideology; conflict and resistance. Although it is often described as developing in France in the 1960s, principally with the work of Barthes, Derrida, Foucault and Lacan, its roots are really in Marx and neo-Marxists such as Gramsci, Adorno and Althusser. Far from being superseded by postmodernism, post-structuralism is currently being further developed by the work of Giddens, Bourdieu, Billig, Laclau, Rorty and Fairclough in a range which extends from the broadest of social theory through a reconstruction of political economy to critical discourse analysis.

Here we shall not be limiting ourselves to the rather outmoded negativity of the Derridian impossibility of decision between competing meanings, but will retain a commitment to a *critical* analysis of discourse which rejects the (a)political vacuum of postmodernism. What distinguishes post-structuralism from postmodernism is that post-structuralism views all reality as historically, socially and culturally specific yet does not deny the importance of the material as well as the symbolic. This gives rise to social theories which attempt to account for both the individual's material condition and specific experience but at the same time locate the individual in a politicised social setting of power, conflict and resistance. This position has been termed neo-structuralism, interpretive structuralism and even post-structuralist structuralism (Morrow 1994).

Crucially, this framing of post-structuralism is not pessimistic but retains the belief that individuals can achieve (limited) freedom of action and sustain a (fragile and imaginary) integrated self. In contrast, 'the post-modern is a condition which operates as if post-structuralism were true' (Parker 1992: 70) and postmodernism fails to adequately theorise the dynamics of the construction of meaning and to embrace the depth of human symbolic experience. The postmodern is an experience of signification in which 'each and every thing is equally invested with meaning'

(Lash 1988: 312) and can thus be argued to be of little empirical utility in consumer research (*pace* Firat and Venkatesh 1995). Post-structuralism on the other hand, through the methodologies of deconstruction, critical ethnography and discourse analysis, provides powerful tools for empirical studies guided by articulated conceptual models. This holds out the possibility of changing the human condition through the 'awakening of consciousness and socioanalysis' (Bourdieu 1990: 17).

Here, we shall first examine language and discourse and the ensuing problematic perspective on the social, the self, freedom and choice before developing a post-structuralist analysis of advertising which attempts to confront the complexity of the subject in terms of both ideological power *and* consumer resistance.

Language and discourse

The one essential defining factor across all approaches to post-structuralism is the central role played by language in the construction of the self and of the social world. Language is viewed as both reflecting reality and constituting reality in a dialectic dynamic. This entails the assumption that the self is not genetically determined but is socially constructed and produced across a range of discursive practices where meaning is a constant site of struggles for power (Weeden 1987). Discourse is defined here as a system of statements that constructs an object, supports institutions, reproduces power relations and has ideological effects, and is realised through texts. Texts are 'delimited tissues of meaning' that can be reproduced in any form that can be subjected to interpretation (Parker 1992: 6). Although individuals 'imagine' that they are the authors of their discourse and in control of its meaning (Weeden 1987: 31), discourse is largely socially and ideologically constructed. However, the social practices of discourse are in a dialectical relationship with social institutions and although individuals are constrained by their position in orders of discourse, they are also enabled to act creatively within the discursive frame (Fairclough 1989). Social practices draw upon discourse types but do not mechanically reproduce them, so there is a gap between objective social space and representations of that space which become 'a site for symbolic struggles that transform the real by renaming it' (Collins 1993: 127).

Multiple meanings are inherent in post-structuralism, and we prefer to reject Foucault's (1972) insistence on the inescapable power of language and its deterministic unity. We prefer Barthes' description of language's inevitable 'overflows, leaks, skids, shifts, slips' (Barthes 1977: 69). This freedom for language (and the individual) is evident in the lack of a unitary discourse found in empirical studies of everyday conversation where 'people frequently argue with each other, and often aloud with themselves' (Billig 1996: 15). In their social practices individuals are faced with 'ideological dilemmas' as to how to categorise information into the multiplicity of alternative schemas they possess (Billig *et al.* 1988: 3). This indeterminacy of meaning and relative freedom of the individual to escape from 'regimes of truth' has been related to consumption through Bourdieu's theory of social practice as 'necessary improvisation' in symbolic fields (including consumption) (Bourdieu 1977). Consumption as a social practice is a dynamic and relatively autonomous process which involves the symbolic construction of a sense of self through the accumulation of cultural and symbolic capital.

However, to paraphrase Marx: although we make our own history, we do not do so in circumstances of our own choosing. Symbolic freedom is severely constrained by social structure and by ideological limits to that which we are able to imagine. Discourse is socially determined through relationships of power extending through class and society. But this is not a uni-directional process as discourse also constructs social structures in a dialectical relationship, and individual acts of symbolic creativity are socially constitutive in that they cumulatively restructure orders of discourse (Fairclough 1989).

We shall now explore the dialectic between ideological control and oppositional freedom through an analysis of the powerful commodity-text of advertising and the countervailing opportunities for symbolic resistance through polysemy and active resignification of meaning by subcultural practices.

THE POWER OF THE COMMODITY-TEXT: ADVERTISING AS IDEOLOGY

The origin of ideology stems from an acceptance that ideas, and more specifically those ideas relating to society as a whole, do not emerge autonomously in each individual member of that society but have had a centre of formation, irradiation, dissemination and persuasion (Gramsci 1971). This 'centre of formation' represents an axis of power which attempts to create and maintain a superior position within society by constraining and controlling the ideas that individuals hold. Crucial to the subjugating role of ideology is the inability of those which it influences to become aware of the original source or purpose of the ideas which influence them. It becomes impossible for those influenced by ideology to recognise that influence, 'if ideology knew itself it would instantly cease to be so' (Eagleton 1991: 60). Karl Marx regarded ideology, specifically the ideology propagated by the bourgeoisie and accepted by the working class, as an essential prerequisite of the asymmetrical class system which characterised western society. In the Marxist perspective the concept of ideology came to be of central importance as a means of explaining how the dominant class remained in power through the control and imposition of their 'ruling ideas' (Scannell *et al.* 1992: 1). Ideology became the way in which Marx explained both the fact that the working class continued to be exploited and the observation that 'the ideas of the ruling class are in every epoch the ruling ideas' (Marx and Engels 1970: 64). By ensuring that the ideas of the bourgeois were both dominant but simultaneously invisible it was possible for the working class to be exploited without recognising their exploitation. The direct result of ideology is that the 'stabilising tendencies' (Marcuse 1964: 105) conveyed through ideology by the ruling classes ensure the continuation of an inherently unfair class-based society. The subservience of the working classes is continued not because of their lack of consciousness of their position within society but because that consciousness is based, through ideology, on falsity.

> Ideology is a process accomplished by the so-called thinker consciously, it is true, but with a false consciousness. The real motive forces impelling him remain unknown to him; otherwise it simply would not be an ideological process. Hence he imagines false or seeming motive forces.
>
> (Marx and Engels 1965: 49)

Marx saw his work as a 'critical tool' which could expose the misleading falsity of bourgeois ideology, awaken the working class from their false consciousness and in doing so emancipate society from the inequalities of a class-based system (Martin 1981b). The traditional Marxist approach to ideology was developed by the work of Gramsci and Althusser who, while continuing to accept the influence of ideology on class-based relations, also accepted that such influence formed part of a much wider political context and recognised that ideology could be utilised by any power regardless of the nature or basis from which that power was derived. Ideology has since been extended into the representative realm by Bourdieu's theory of 'symbolic violence' which describes the imposition of systems of symbolic meaning which achieve domination through the 'complicity' of the dominated (Bourdieu 1991: 51). Regardless of the particular power base which a specific ideology attempts to support with the process of 'ideologising', the practice of ideology itself must invariably centre on a specific set of strategies and methods. Ideologies are essentially the facilitating force which permits a small, select group with a particular political agenda to influence a much wider, diverse section of the population.

For ideology to be successful it must ensure that society's consciousness remains within the 'ideological contours' (Lull 1995: 21) which favour the power base of its sponsor. The actual process of controlling consciousness is therefore directly related to the control of the meanings which individuals attach to different objects. Ideology works, at a primary level, on the semiotic plane by controlling the meaning of each individual sign as it is interpreted. The interpretation of signs produces meaning and these various interpretive acts form the basis for each individual's construction of 'reality'. A study of the way in which ideology works therefore becomes

Learning Resources Centre

a study of the ways in which meaning can be harnessed and used to establish and sustain relations of domination through the ongoing process of producing and receiving symbolic forms (Thompson 1990).

IDEOLOGICAL STRATEGIES

Ideological strategies vary from power base to power base and from context to context. Therefore no list can claim to be an exhaustive taxonomy of ideological strategies (Eagleton 1991). However, several general ideological strategies do emerge as effective mechanisms for maintaining or creating societal power. Six key strategies are now explored:

- legitimisation
- universalisation
- unification
- fragmentation
- naturalisation
- enlightened false conciousness

Legitimisation

If a power is to exert a dominating influence on society its authority must be accepted by that society as representing a group whose interests should be observed. Legitimacy ensures not only that individuals will accept their domination by a particular group but also through that acceptance that the questioning of such domination will remain 'inaccessible to analysis and public consciousness' (Habermas 1970: 99). The actual process of legitimisation involves the representation of authority in symbolic terms (Thompson 1990). Specifically an individual power base is associated, through ideological coding, with a particular source of inherent societal authority derived from any one of three areas which Weber (1979: 215) identifies as 'pure types': rational or legal authority to issue commands; traditional authority where authority is granted; and charismatic authority.

Universalisation

The process of universalisation ensures that a particular power does not loom 'embarrassingly large' (Eagleton 1991: 56) on the horizons of the society it dominates. If a power were to draw attention to the fact that it had suddenly taken control, such attention would invariably lead to society questioning its dominance. Universalising a power therefore entails a process of symbolic stretching, attempting to associate the power with an authority which spreads over contexts of time and space. In relation to time it is clearly of vital importance to show that the dominant power has maintained its influence and position throughout history. For a particular group to be dominant for only a part of history is to accept that their dominance has in some way been contrived. Thus the goal of ideology is to portray a particular group as being dominant throughout time. Similarly, a cognate process applies to spatial contexts. The ideological strategy of universalisation emphasises the presence of a power in every time and every setting and in doing so suggests its dominance exists without challenge.

Unification

A less subtle but equally effective ideological strategy is to unify society behind a particular system of thought and thus ensure that challenges to the dominant order can be controlled and thus avoided (Tetzlaff 1992). Again this strategy is initiated at the symbolic level where a shared code leads to a homogeneous interpretation of reality which in turn ensures that the dominant order can control and thus avoid challenges to the existing relations of power. Unification as an ideological strategy is particularly successful if it can unify society behind a belief or interest which in some way serves not only to unite society but also to unite them *behind* the extant dominant power. Thus ideology must 'engage significantly with the wants and desires that people already have' (Eagleton 1991: 15).

Fragmentation

The alternative ideological strategy to unification behind a dominant power is not by unifying individuals in a collective, but by fragmenting those individuals and groups that might be capable of mounting an effective challenge to dominant groups (Thompson 1990). Ideology's purpose in fragmentation is to represent the oppositional forces within society as being disparate and unworthy of support in their challenge to the dominant powers within society.

Naturalisation

The strategy of naturalisation involves ideology attempting to instil in society the beliefs and values of a dominating power as being natural and self-evident. In effect successful naturalisation goes beyond any other ideological strategy because it ingrains the dominant power within society at the level of common sense and thus beyond the level of consciousness or awareness (Fiske 1990). The ideological goal of naturalisation is not simply to avoid awkward questions which may challenge the societal authority of a particular group but to transfer that group's power into the subconscious where its existence is accepted tacitly and without question or challenge (Williamson 1978). Bourdieu's concept of the 'habitus' (Bourdieu 1977: 80), as the common unconscious which influences a group's perception of the world and each individual's social practices, represents a structure which ideology must infiltrate in order to naturalise a particular power base. For ideology to be successful it must naturalise the presence of a power base through the 'orchestration of the habitus' (Bourdieu 1977). Thus the acceptance of a particular dominant force in society shifts from history to nature; and its presence within society, the individual's life world and social practices are completely and implicitly accepted. The concealing effect of naturalisation enables a particular ideology to maintain a powerful influence while simultaneously preventing those it influences from noting its effect. In this way a dominant power becomes part of what Bourdieu calls 'the doxa' which represents 'an adherence to relations of order which, because they structure inseparably both the real world and the thought world, are accepted as self-evident' (Bourdieu 1979: 471). When a power becomes fully naturalised its position within society becomes unquestionable and its loss of power seems impossible. The threat from opposing ideologies and power-bases is diminished because 'a ruling ideology does not so much combat alternative ideas as thrust them beyond the very bounds of the thinkable' (Eagleton 1991: 48).

Enlightened false consciousness

One of the crucial elements of ideological effect can be related to its apparent invisibility to those it influences. In Marx's classic definition, 'Sie wissen das nicht, aber sie tun es' ('they do not know it, but they are doing it'). With the advent of more complex, cynical individuals within society the ideological prerequisite of invisibility becomes increasingly difficult to maintain; 'ideology is supposed to deceive; and in particular in the cynical milieu of postmodernism we are all too fly, astute and streetwise to be conned for a moment by our own official rhetoric' (Eagleton 1991: 15). The more cynical members of society are thus increasingly able to hold up the attempts at ruling ideology and meet them with everyday banality and ridicule. However, despite this apparent ability to see through the invisibility of ideological manipulation, ideology continues to affect the cynical individual by performing a 'negation of a negation' (Zizek 1989: 30), openly announcing its manipulative intent but continuing to influence society through an enlightened false consciousness. Awareness of the presence and source of ideology only contributes a false sense of freedom if the end result of such awareness does not alter one's behavioural response.

ADVERTISING AS IDEOLOGY

Advertising has long been linked to the concept of ideology. From the original work of the Frankfurt School through to contemporary cultural theory, advertising has taken its place among other forms of mass-communication as a 'site for ideological action' (Bourne 1981: 53). This ideological nature relates to the combination of symbolic messages with a rhetorical function, for advertisements are never ideologically impartial: 'treating meaningful activities as raw materials to be *re-worked* into signs in the interest of maximising commodity sales inherently locates advertisers in the field of ideology' (Goldman 1992: 85).

Aside from combining meaning with a particular vested interest, advertising can be more generally classed as ideology in the sense that it provides a particular representation of reality (Dyer 1988) which is slanted or skewed in the sense that this representation can be construed as being false or misleading (Leiss *et al.* 1990). This attempt at producing an apparently misleading conception of reality has led many cultural theorists to classify advertising as a mechanism for the 'systematic moulding of consciousness' (Gabriel and Lang 1995: 16).

The control of meaning and the imposition of particular codes for preferred interpretations of advertising symbolism establish advertising as a prime ideological instrument. But to what degree can this symbolic control be connected with the larger political distribution of power to which all ideological systems must in some way contribute? Does advertising utilise the ideological strategies of legitimisation, universalisation, unification, fragmentation, naturalisation, enlightened false consciousness and if so, in what ways and in whose favour are such strategies oriented? Each of the six ideological strategies is now explored in relation to advertising. Clearly, analogous to the basic ideological model, not every strategy will be utilised in every advertising campaign. Different combinations of ideological strategies will be present in different advertising campaigns.

Legitimisation

Possibly the most crucial ideological role for advertising is to legitimise the consumer's activities for him or her and thus allow society to acknowledge the authority of consumption without guilt, suspicion or resistance. Advertising ideology legitimises the consumption of products through the association of the commodity form with established, legitimate social structures of authority. Advertising continually defends the 'treasured relations' of society and in doing so maintains an 'ideology of corporate-capitalist legitimacy' (Goldman 1992: 88). Through its portrayal and defence of existing structures of authority advertising ideology attempts to gain a surrogate authority for its own product and consumption in general. Three examples of such legitimisation through association illustrate this function of advertising ideology.

A first surrogate authority which advertising ideology transfers to products is the aspirational nature of society. Every individual and social group has aspirations for the future. These aspirations, particularly in the achievement-orientated culture of America, represent a healthy influence on society, an influence which is appropriated by advertising ideology. In effect, advertising draws a semantic parallel between the presence and influence of society's hopes (socially accepted as a natural and legitimate influence on individuals) and the consumption of products. For example in ads dripping with images of achievement and aspiration, Gillette ('The Best a Man Can Get') interpellates the consumer with the conjoined image of future success and a branded good. It is as legitimate for the individual to aspire to many of these images (successful romance, successful work, successful friendship) as it is to desire and use the Gillette product. To deny this implicit connection would be to deny our hopes and aspirations for the future.

A second surrogate authority is gleaned from the family. As with aspiration, families represent a powerful yet legitimate influence on individual lives. Indeed the authoritarian influence of family on individual decisions must surely represent the most commonly experienced example of power encountered within society. Advertising celebrates this influence, and in doing so, simultaneously associates its product with this important source of authority. For example, in the famous Oxo advertisements the legitimate authority of the family structure which is portrayed within the long-running series of ads is conferred onto the product through their shared location within the frame of the ads. The Oxo product and the family are seen as equally legitimate elements of everyday life.

A final example of advertising's adoption within surrogate structures of authority can be drawn from the original Weberian types of authority and legitimisation. In particular the use of the celebrity endorser represents a classic utilisation of the Weberian 'pure type' of charismatic authority where legitimisation is derived from an individual with 'supernatural, superhuman, or at least specifically exceptional powers' (Weber 1979: 238). The positive influence that celebrity endorsers, such as Paul Newman or Claudia Schiffer, bring to an ad is that their symbolic meanings are transferred to the product which in turn signifies these positive associations in the mind of the consumer. In all three examples advertising ideology associates particular brands and, over time, consumption itself with established sources of authority commonly experienced by the consumer in their life world. In doing so advertising ideology legitimises the brand by reflecting in its portrayal in television and press advertising the meanings associated with these other more traditional societal influences.

Universalisation

Advertising ideology attempts to universalise consumption and consumer goods. In every ad execution the reality portrayed is one dependent on and inclusive of products. 'Because ads are so pervasive and our reading of them so routine, we tend to take for granted the deep social assumptions embedded in advertisements. We do not ordinarily recognise advertising as a sphere of ideology' (Goldman 1992: 1). The end result of continual and pervasive portrayals of a reality predicated by consumption is to effectively universalise consumer goods within society and to render consumption an omnipresent element of existence (Pollay 1986). By effectively universalising consumption within society individuals are denied the ability to contrast their current life world with one in which consumption does not maintain such an extensive influence.

Unification

Advertising often appeals to the consumer by highlighting his or her individuality (Solomon 1996) and thus any attempt to unify the market into a homogeneous mass contradicts the instrumental need to value the individual over society. Advertising is able to appellate the individual subject and simultaneously unify the market behind its product through the application of pseudo-individualism which represents a method for achieving these two goals simultaneously (Goldman 1992). In effect, the ad manages to target the individual subject on a mass-mediated level, that is, without specifically identifying which subject within its audience it is targeting: 'appellation, then, gives us imaginary blinkers in preventing us from looking sideways and recognising other people, contiguous to us; it only allows us to see forwards, into the ad' (Williamson 1978: 155). The result is an advertising ideology which bases its enduring appeal on the individual choice of consumers and emphasises the individuality and freedom of their lifestyle while simultaneously unifying the market behind a particular brand and unifying society behind the act of consumption.

Fragmentation

Advertising 'does not have a monopoly in the symbolic marketplace' and this competition for structural control of society has resulted in advertising utilising a strategy of fragmentation against the 'archetypal institutions of social control' (Schudson 1984: 246). Advertising ideology has gradually undermined these institutions in order to implicitly support the role of consumption in organising the life world of the consumer. Not only has consumption managed to define the good life but it has 'come to supplant religion, work and politics as the mechanism by which social and status distinctions may be established' (Gabriel and Lang 1995; 8). As consumption has increasingly dominated society, these more traditional infrastructural institutions have seen their role and influence in society increasingly undermined (Tharp and Scott 1990). While the decline of traditional institutions is often seen as an event which occurred independent of the rise of consumption in society, some social theorists attribute this decline to advertising, consumption and strategies of infrastructural fragmentation. 'It is important to underscore the role of advertising in accelerating this collapse of meaning. The decline of symbolic structures of meaning outside the self has been a central process in the development of a consumer culture' (Lears 1983: 4). The effect of infrastructural fragmentation on the individual is ironic. Individuals were liberated from the traditional domination and controlled meaning systems of the ideological state apparatus conceptualised by Althusser, but the apparent freedom from institutions such as the church or the family was merely a 'pseudo-emancipation' (Lasch 1978: 140) as the individual was freed from one ideological code to be influenced by another, that of consumption ideology in the form of advertising.

Naturalisation

Advertising ideology naturalises particular brands by implicitly positioning those brands as automatic inclusions in everyday existence. Through the naturalisation of brands in the consciousness of the consumer, these products are established at the level of common sense, signifying their intended meanings at an unquestionable level. Thus rather than questioning the arbitrary semantic relationship that exists between ice-cream and sex or carbonated soft drinks and youthfulness the consumer accepts these meanings as the 'real, natural foundations of everyday life' (Goldman 1992: 34). This acceptance leads to a blurred distinction between the natural reality of the life world and the manufactured naturalisation created by advertising ideology. In extreme cases this divide between the natural world of the consumer and the naturalised world of advertising can have a number of wide-ranging consequences. In the much publicised marketing disaster of Nestlé milk substitute for example, the natural breast milk of mothers was replaced by artificial formula with tragic consequences for many families in Kenya (Leiss *et al.* 1990). Advertising ideology had naturalised artificial milk to such an extent in Kenya that it replaced the natural substance it originally imitated. While such an example is both emotive and extreme it does offer a clear illustration of the naturalising effect of advertising ideology on product consumption.

Advertising ideology is able to achieve this effect through 'the naturalising function of denotation' (Barthes 1993: 24). While the connotative meanings signified in an ad are open to numerous interpretations (Dyer 1988), the denotative meaning, that is the photograph in the press ad or the images in the TV ad, appear to represent reality in a singular, incontestable way. The apparent reality of the advertising image is the key to understanding its naturalising function. Instead of recognising the ad as a 'cultural representation' of reality, ads appear to reflect reality itself (Mick 1986). Rather than recognising that the denotative meaning of the ad, like its connotative meaning, has been manipulated the consumer perceives the photograph to represent a badge of truth. The end result of the process is inherently ideological. The denotative sign naturalises the connotative sign (Dyer 1988) and the favourable meaning of the ad is interpreted at the level of common sense where the consumer is far more likely to accept such overtly controlled meaning transfer without challenging it. Advertising ideology, through its naturalising function, renders its meanings both influential and invisible, the perfect ideological combination (Schudson 1984).

Enlightened False Consciousness

Despite ideological strategies such as naturalisation and legitimisation, the influence of advertising is often recognised and opposed by the consumer. Advertising ideology engenders enlightened false consciousness in the mind of the consumer as a means of acknowledging this awareness while maintaining its ideological influence. In effect, advertising perpetrates a semantic 'double bluff' by incorporating criticism or 'by showing up the ad system as rather dishonest and silly' (Dyer 1988: 135). While such self-criticism may appear counter-productive to advertising ideology's basic agenda of influence, such 'self awareness' actually performs an 'essential self-validating function' (Williamson 1978: 172). By becoming 'reflexive' a particular ad can distance itself from the identified influence of advertising and in doing so add ideological power to its own influence.

By creating enlightened false consciousness advertising ideology is able to absorb the challenges to its authority by a particular social group and thus nullify any limitation those challenges could have placed on the persuasive power of the current ad. By drawing attention to the apparent obviousness of advertising and consumer goods the ad appears to apply a reverse ideological strategy (Cook 1992) when in fact the overall result of such a strategy is to continue to persuade and influence the consumer. By applying 'tongue-in-cheek' (Wernick 1991: 69) executions, undercut with a strategic 'knowing wink' (Goldman 1992: ch. 8), advertising ideology is able to wipe the slate of consciousness clean and begin the process of ideology anew with the new 'enlightened' consumer.

ADVERTISING AS SUPER-IDEOLOGY

The ideological analysis of advertising reveals a definitive fit between the ideological forms identified throughout the social sciences and the influence of advertising. It would, however, be a mistake to conclude simply that advertising does represent an essentially ideological influence on society. In fact it can be argued that advertising is *the* ideological force of late capitalism, a super-ideology that surpasses any other ideological force from this or any other historical period. Six main factors support this proposition. First, we must recognise advertising's semiotic richness and concentrated rhetorical form. Unlike many other forms of mass communication which may also contribute ideological influences, advertising's purpose, its instrumental 'raison d'être' (Wernick 1991: 25), derives from its ability to change attitudes. As such, advertising represents the most effective communicative method for changing the beliefs, values and interpretations of society. It was by no means a random act which led Barthes to select an ad for his seminal semiotic analysis of the 'rhetoric of the image' (Barthes 1993: 15). For Barthes, advertising as a media form was 'frank' in the sense that it represented such a concentrated attempt to semantically influence the reader/viewer.

Second, this rhetorical symbolic content is combined with repetition and omnipresence. No other medium in history has concentrated strategically on repeating its message until its presence becomes an abstraction, maintaining an influence, 'without consumers being able to identify the antecedents of the processes responsible for that influence' (Janiszewski 1988: 207). Advertising meanings are repeated to such a degree that over time they begin to form part of the consumer's 'assumptive worlds' (Lull 1990: 15). This repetitive format is complemented by advertising's omnipresence throughout society, advertising occupies our TV screens, our newspapers and even overlooks the streets through which we walk. This pervasive nature ensures that the influence of advertising ideology remains constant throughout the vagaries of day-to-day life and, like a constant background hum, anaesthetises us to its presence (Goldman 1992). While ideologies throughout history have attempted to conceal their presence and their influence over society no ideology has ever attained such influence yet with such anonymity. This apparent contradiction between influence and invisibility is illustrated by the fact that despite the general recognition that advertising does affect society, most individuals continue to believe that advertising does not influence *them* (Pollay 1986).

Third, advertising constitutes a unique ideological representation of reality. Media portray the world in two different ways. They either attempt to represent the world factually with the burden of truth and impartiality restricting their ideological influence, as in news reporting for example (Jensen 1990). Or alternatively, a medium actively ideologises reality and represents the world in a fictional but analogous way, as in situation comedy for example (Grote 1983). Thus each genre of media must locate itself ideologically according to its structural limitations (Feuer 1992). A trade-off is made between fact and ideology and all media are constrained somewhere on this continuum. Advertising, however, uniquely combines the apparent representation of everyday reality with an overtly ideologised account of that reality. Advertising portrays reality-as-lived against reality-as-possibly-lived with the consumer good as the connecting step. By portraying these idealised accounts of reality alongside a representation of actual reality, advertising ideology is able to combine the power of truth with the influence of ideology. Advertising is both fictional and factional and thus a force of unique ideological potency.

Fourth, the presence of multiple levels of advertising influence also contributes to advertising's super-ideological status. There are many examples of media which work on an instrumental/superficial level while simultaneously influencing its audience ideologically. For example film is thought to have a greater influence on the ideological level if it also simultaneously entertains the individual on an explicit hedonistic level (Altman 1984). While a concealing level of instrumentality is not unique to advertising ideology, what is unique is the fact that in advertising's case that instrumental level is *itself* inherently ideological. Film is constrained, as an ideological influence, by its instrumental need to entertain because the ideological message it contains must fit within the contours of the entertainment function it explicitly performs. In the case of advertising, however, no such limitation exists. Persuasion, rhetoric, influence, suggestion, seduction – these are the watchwords of advertising in its explicit function as an ideological influence in the domains of the consumer and the market. There are no non-ideological instrumental contours to limit advertising ideology's effect. Advertising's explicit instrumental orientation uniquely legitimises the operation of advertising as 'concentrated ideology' (Myers 1986: 100) within society.

Fifth, advertising ideology works in a different way from every other form of social ideology used by institutions such as the church, the state or school (Wernick 1991). Whereas these institutions 'combine social control with a cultural dimension' advertising constitutes an entirely cultural/symbolic influence (Schudson 1984: 246). The advantage of advertising ideology over its alternative, institutional forms is that advertising does not move the consumer towards a particular social order but rather to the gratification of self through existential decisions. There is no social order to conform to in the consumption of advertising and the brand, simply the freedom to exercise one's right as a sovereign consumer (Sinclair 1987). The simple fact that so many new products fail in the market reflects this emphasis on consumer discrimination; 'no religion could tolerate a rejection rate of 80 or 90 per cent of what it has to offer' (Fiske 1989a: 14). That the freedom which advertising and consumption confer is an illusory freedom is unimportant if this illusion is not observed by the consumer (Elliott and Ritson 1995). Advertising is not ideology in the service of a particular social order, but ideology in the service of the asocial order of the self. It is this choice and this individualism which elevates advertising ideology beyond the influence of more traditional, socially orientated ideologies and confers on it the status of super-ideology.

A final point, and perhaps the most powerful, is a consideration of the effects of advertising on society in the relatively short space of time which it has occupied. Advertising ideology has drastically reshaped the structure and consciousness of every individual on the planet. This statement is not a hyperbolic attempt to inflate the influence of advertising on society, it is a simple reflection of the fact that no other ideological form in history has influenced so many individuals in such a short space of time. Stop. Right now. Look up. Shift your focus from this chapter and gaze around the cultural space in which you are currently located. Office, bedroom, park, aeroplane. We guarantee that the fruit of advertising ideology will be readily apparent to you! The usurpation of the bastions of societal infrastructure, the introduction of consumer culture, the increased emphasis on materialism, the global reach of consumer goods, the institutionalisation of the brand in daily life – these developments and many more stand testament to the dramatic transitions which advertising ideology has effected in under a century of activity; transitions possible only with the influence of a super-ideology.

In summary advertising is not a form of ideology, it is *the* form of ideology which now surpasses and supplants all others. In the promotion of the commodity sign, advertising ideology has far outdone itself, expanding out from the domain of the consumer and refracting out into the furthest reaches of societal structure. Advertising is ideology and what's more it is an ideology with a power and influence beyond any other.

THE CONTERVAILING POWER OF THE READER: ADVERTISING POLYSEMY AND SUBCULTURAL PRACTICES

We might now seem to have reached the conclusion that texts of any kind, and in particular the commodity-text of advertising, have the power to alter and control a reader's interpretation of reality; texts 'read' their readers (Martin 1981a: 8). The meanings contained in the text are activated through the act of reading to transform the way that readers construct their interpretation of reality. In this way the ideological code contained within a text becomes influential in making sense of the phenomena of the reader's everyday life. This perspective, however, represents only half of the interpretive process because just as the text has the power to alter the meanings held by the reader, simultaneously the reader has the power to alter the meanings of the text. By concentrating on the textual aspects of interpretation structuralist approaches relegate the experiences and activity of the reader to a minor theoretical role (e.g. Stern 1989, 1994). The theoretical focus of structuralism concerns itself with the meanings of the text, as a result these theories are guilty of the 'fallacy of internalism' (Thompson 1990: 105). This fallacy leads to a serious explanatory flaw in structuralist theories of interpretation. If the text's structure is all-powerful, if the text does indeed 'read' the reader, if we all engage in 'perfectly transparent communication' (Hall 1973: 136), why does our everyday experience suggest a continual emphasis on varied interpretive strategies and differing semantic results? For example the majority of the working class in Britain regularly read papers which contain overt right-wing ideology yet the majority of this large demographic group continue to vote Labour (Eagleton 1991). Similarly structuralist theories cannot account for the fact that even in countries where every media source was ideologically controlled by the state, that control could not prevent the popular revolutions which occurred (Lull 1995). In relegating the role of the reader to an ancillary position behind that of the text structural theories inaccurately represent the actual process of interpretation. In the synaptic moment of interpretation there is a climacteric movement from the 'crystalline' text to the 'actualised' text (Eco 1979: 7). In this shift from the realm of the text to the realm of the reader the original author loses control of the text; his or her control is now superseded by the interpretive power of the reader. The encoded text with all its semantic certainty now lays itself open to the decoding of the reader (Hall 1973). As much as the author would prefer the reader to adopt the intended meaning of the text, such passive transference is highly unlikely. As Fiske (1990: 164) notes, 'reading is not akin to using a tin opener to reveal the meanings of the message'.

The shift in power from text to reader has formed a central element of recent developments in fields as diverse as literary theory, cultural studies and communication theory. This movement essentially represented a 'paradigm shift' in the theoretical conceptualisation of interpretation. The relationship between the text and the reader is not a mutually exclusive one, rather each works as an antagonistic force on the other (Fiske 1987). In effect the reader-orientated approach to interpretation relies on an 'essential dependency' (Radway 1984) between the reader and the text. There are 'dialectic relations between concrete experience and mediated meaning' (Murdock and McCron 1976: 204), and it is as a dialectic that the interpretive process is best understood.

POLYSEMIC TEXTS AND HETEROGLOSSIA

With the acceptance that readers were active in their interpretation of textual meaning came the equally radical implication that texts were now 'the site of potentially differential readings' (Moores 1992: 142). In the seminal encoding/decoding model the text provides a code to guide its interpretation but that code is matched by the application of the reader's own interpretive code. The semantic distance between the two codes dictates the degree to which a reading will vary from the intended meaning of the text. The optimum communication event is classified as 'perfectly transparent communication' which relies upon the matching of codes between encoder and decoder. If these codes differ then alternative interpretive results are produced by the reader and these meanings contrast with the intended, preferred meanings of the author. As a result the text, caught between the intended and actualised codes of the encoding/decoding model, can be conceptualised as polysemic; in that several interpretations coexist as potentials in any one text, and may be actualised differently by different audiences, depending on their interpretive conventions and cultural backgrounds (Jensen 1990).

Heteroglossia (Bakhtin 1981) is the situation of a subject 'surrounded by a myriad of responses he or she might make at any particular point, but any one of which must be framed in a specific discourse selected from the teeming thousands available' (Holquist 1990: 69). The major implication of polysemy and heteroglossia for authors and broadcasters alike was that they could no longer assume that the reader/viewer would always emerge from the chaos of the heteroglossic moment with the intended meaning (Morley 1980). That intended meaning was only one semantic option available to the reader, thus instead of the passive acceptance of the intended meaning the author had to strive to ensure that the text would maintain its meaning through the semantic challenges of the interpretive process. Followed to its extreme, the conceptualisation of television or any other medium as polysemic suggests that a complete conceptualisation of the meanings of a text is impossible. It is confounded by the 'blankness' and 'semiotic chaos' (Tetzlaff 1992) of a mass audience, its members each subjectively producing individual meanings of an almost infinite range.

In practice (rather than in theory) the interpretation made by the reader will be limited in two crucial ways. First, polysemy is limited by the text; some texts are more polysemic than others in that they confer a greater heteroglossic range. Second, the reader represents a polysemic limitation in that rather than arriving at a unique, totally idiosyncratic meaning, the reader will subjectively interpret the text but the end result will be a meaning which is very similar to other individuals' subjective interpretation of the same text. These individuals form a group called an interpretive community. These two limitations, textual and contextual, are now explored in turn.

Textual limitations to polysemy: open and closed texts

While heteroglossia and polysemy do indeed represent a wide diversity of freedom for the reader, that freedom exists within a framework of alternatives which the text can partly 'delimit'. Thus rather than their own personalised, interpretive infinity, readers select from 'a limited number of possible readings' (Blumler *et al.* 1985: 260). In de Certeau's (1984: 174) elegant metaphor, readers are 'nomads' travelling across 'fields they did not write'. While metaphorical nomads are free to move in any direction, they are still continually conscious that their movements are constrained and restricted by the land upon which they travel. The text cannot control the reader any more than the ground can direct the nomad; polysemy ensures this is semantically impossible. The text can, however, in a dialectical twist, ensure that the concept of polysemy is constrained and to some degree controlled. The essential tension between the text and the reader continually characterises the process of interpretation. Thus while the author can not control the meaning which the reader ascribes to the text, he or she can attempt to construct the text in such a way that it guides the reader towards the intended, preferred meaning. If a text operates 'definitive boundary conditions' (Radway 1995: 334) which constrain the readers and guide them towards one, unisemantic conclusion to the exclusion of all other alternatives it can be classified as being a 'closed' text. If a text allows or positively encourages interpretive freedom and thus stimulates polysemic outcomes it can be classed as 'open'. Confusingly open texts are far more likely to be read in a manner which the author has anticipated (Eco 1979). In contrast closed texts, because of their attempts to transport the reader down one particular semantic path without any subjective deviation, often encourage and empower alternative reading strategies which result in alternative meanings that differ greatly from those originally intended by the author.

Contextual limitations to polysemy: interpretive communities

Even if, despite having established its theoretical impossibility, a text was open to an infinite polysemic array of meanings the end result of its interpretation by a mass audience would still not result in a range of n meanings, where n is the total number of individuals present in that audience. The reason for this restriction can be traced to the audience and the interpretive limitations they place on the polysemic text. Even with an infinitely polysemic text the reader would invariably interpret that text's meaning within a 'framework of similarity' to his or her peers (Fiske 1987: 81). The reason for this similarity relates to the inherently social nature of interpretation. While the individual brings his or her own subjective repertoire to a particular interpretive act, it is a repertoire shaped in 'particular social-historical contexts' (Thompson 1990: 218). The social nature of interpretation 'delimits' the heteroglossic potential of a reading in much the same way as open and closed texts exercise a degree of limitation on the polysemic text. The readers' connection to their 'social position' ensures that their subjective interpretation will often match or correspond with other readers' interpretations of the same text. Thus interpretive communities are formed.

It is important to note that these communities are far removed from the rigid cultural groupings into which society is traditionally divided. For example, an African-American belongs to one group, a working-class individual to another. The concept of interpretive communities transcends these static boundaries as readers take up their membership of different social groups on a continual, ever-changing basis dependent on the particular interpretation at hand. The end result of interpretive communities is a radically different conceptualisation of the media audience; a continually shifting series of interpretive segments who possess only one common denominator, the shared 'interpretive conventions' (Radway 1984: 11) with which they approach a particular text. These interpretive conventions provide a significant limitation to the polysemic potential of the text.

SUBCULTURES AND SEMIOTIC OPPOSITION

The concept of subculture originated with the work of Cohen (1955) and his seminal study of youthful delinquents in Chicago. In Cohen's research the particular delinquent subculture he explored was a group of adolescents who distinguished themselves from the mainstream (mass) culture which dominated their milieu, through the adoption of alternative vocabularies, beliefs and dress codes (Cohen 1955). The subordinate status of the subculture empowers the group to seek to reject the mass-cultural symbolic systems, and thus to become 'symbolically distinct' (Fitzgerald 1992: 112) from its 'parent culture' (Clarke 1975: 13). Indeed the need to develop a different semantic identity and then maintain that difference, the concept of *ethnogenesis* (Roosens 1992) forms the instrumental core of the subculture's semiotic activity. Specifically the subculture attempts to attain 'oppositional significance' (Clarke 1975: 13), readily identifiable semantic distinctions from the mass-culture that surrounds them. The desire to identify a semiotic difference in their identity runs parallel to the need to attain power within the society which the subculture inhabits. For all subcultural groups societal power is, for a variety of differing reasons, denied to them. Specifically the subculture perceives itself to be powerless to control the generation and attribution of meanings within society. This powerlessness impacts upon the autonomy and identity of its members. This lack of power cannot be immediately rectified in the material realm of their day-to-day lives; they remain a disenfranchised, powerless minority and an escape from this position is unlikely (Fiske 1989b). In the semiotic realm, however, such cultural amendment is possible. The subculture takes the meanings of the mass-culture, those meanings which they feel ostracise, alienate and exploit them, and re-signifies them in order to make them simultaneously belong to the group and also reflect the group's combined rejection of the mass-cultural milieu. Regardless of the specific method used by the subculture, the semiotic motivation which lies behind the act remains the same; the transformation of a mass-culture's semiotic phenomena into something new, radical and different. The more everyday and 'normal' the sign is, the more taken-for-granted in the mass-cultural milieu of mainstream society and thus the more attractive it becomes as a subcultural object of transformation. The more a sign represents the powerful majority, the more it also presents a possible site of subcultural distinction if it is transformed. Thus the most grounded symbolic phenomena become the most eagerly appropriated. 'Dwelling, moving about, speaking, reading, shopping, and cooking are activities that seem to correspond to the characteristics of tactical ruses and surprise: clever tricks of the "weak" within the order established by the "strong"'(de Certeau 1984: 174).

The use of the terms 'strong' and 'weak' suggests that subcultural activity contributes to the ideological struggle for societal power. The power of texts propagates a particular ideology which controls society through the instigation of a particular code that influences the interpretation of meaning and as a result, consciousness. In addressing the power of the audience, and in particular the power of the subculture, it is possible to see the antagonistic influence of an alternative code which is exercised by the reader in direct opposition to the one encoded into the text by the author. The application of ideological codes within society, particularly when viewed in Gramscian terms, transforms the staid depiction of the text into a 'battlefield' (Gramsci 1971: 377) as the dominant codes of the powerful clash for control with the oppositional codes of the subcultures operating within that society. The subculture attempts to apply its own code to a particular text, 'invert' the dominant cultural meanings of society (Jenkins 1992) and thus escape the ideological 'effects' of the mass-media. Thus despite the total hegemonic dominance of the media, a subculture can still resist this ideology through their active re-signification of a particular text or commodity. 'In order to project style it became necessary to appropriate the commodity, then to redefine its use and value and finally to locate its meaning within a totally different context' (Hebdige 1975: 93). This subcultural re-signification of tangible symbolic phenomena is defined as 'bricolage', an activity which involves the 'reordering and recontextualising of objects to communicate fresh meanings' (Clarke *et al.* 1975: 53). Possibly the most famous example of this re-signification of cultural objects was the punk subculture of the late 1970s. Punks were the 'bricoleurs par excellence' (Moores 1993: 136) of the subcultural milieu because their almost total rejection of the traditional, mass-cultural code empowered them to the furthest extremes of oppositional tactics.

Subcultures represent a stage beyond the interpretive community. Not only will a subcultural group share a particular interpretive approach which results in a shared meaning from a cultural text but also as a group they will actively observe the intended meaning of the text before rejecting it in favour of their own radically different interpretation. Just as the punk subculture recognised the dominant meaning of a lavatory chain before inverting and re-signifying that meaning, some subcultures choose to practise intangible transformations on dominant interpretations. Rather than selecting a commodity as the object for bricolage they reject the need for any tangible shell and simply utilise the dominant meanings attached to a particular mass-cultural interpretation. In the quest for a subcultural identity, these interpretations of the parent culture are appropriated and re-signified in a radical manner. When Aboriginals read a popular comedy programme on television in a way which contrasts with the dominant ideology that the programme attempts to convey (Fiske 1987) or when a group of middle-class, mid-western women attempt to read a particular genre of books in an unusual and unintended way (Radway 1984), these disparate subcultural groups are semiotically distancing themselves from the dominance of mass-culture through their alternative, oppositional interpretations of cultural texts.

Youth subcultures

The subcultures of youth are a particularly active oppositional force within most mass-cultures. There are a number of reasons for this activity. First, the period of life known as youth or adolescence represents a peculiarly alienated stage in the development of the self. The adolescent individual is caught between rejecting the culture of childhood and opposing the responsibilities of adulthood. This 'antagonistic relationship with the social order' (Clarke *et al.* 1975: 35) represents the empowering motivation to oppose and re-signify the meanings of the 'grown-up', adult world. A second reason for youth subcultural activity results from the fact that in youth contexts leisure, fashion, music and consumption prove to be particularly important elements and it is in these contexts that oppositional tactics can prove to be the most easy to adopt and effective (Murdock and McCron 1975). Third, because young people are often preoccupied with every aspect of their appearance to others (Murdock and McCron 1975) they often show strong urges to blend into tight, social groups in which their apparent self-consciousness is 'protected' within the group. In effect the self-consciousness nature of the adolescent forms a subcultural 'glue' which cements the tight interpersonal relationships characteristic of subcultures. Finally Willis (1990) has empirically explored the symbolic context characterised by late modernity which he represents as a unique semiotic challenge to today's youth. He cites such societal changes as the increasingly mundane nature of young people's work, increased media projections of stereotypical youth templates, the decline of structural guidance from institutions and the loss of contact with the artistic elements of society. All of these societal changes constrain the adolescent need to be creative and to experiment and as a result youth subcultures develop around the concept of 'symbolic creativity' (Willis 1990: 7). In effect the powerlessness described earlier and common to all subcultures is particularly felt in youth subcultures and as a result individuals are empowered to be symbolically creative with many different forms of commodity and medium.

In recent history this intense symbolic creativity has been particularly aimed at the tangible semantic object and in particular the commodity form (Muncie 1981). As a conspicuous sign of the meanings held by mainstream, adult society the consumer good has rich semiotic potential and has found its way into a wide variety of youth subcultural contexts. Subcultures of youth clearly represent a rich and commonly occurring semiotic phenomenon. In particular their explicit need to draw attention to their differences from other youth subcultures and their parent culture means that their subcultural activity is relatively open to identification and exploration.

Gay subcultures

While many gay men and lesbians choose to exist within the mass-cultural realm, sealing themselves within the 'private subcultural space' (Creekmur and Doty 1995: 2) of the closet, many others openly display their identity to the 'straight' majority. The progression from the latter to the former, the seminal 'coming out of the closet', clearly represents an important semiotic relocation from mass-cultural to subcultural identity. Like other groups, the gay subculture uses the re-signification of mass-cultural meanings as a vital source of subcultural ethnogenesis (Roosens 1992). However, because of the covert, partly invisible nature of the gay identity, 'the subculture that dare not speak its name', the emphasis in gay bricolage has been firmly placed on the purely symbolic, intangible phenomena of the media rather than the tangible commodity form. In youth subcultures the conspicuous quality and declaratory function of commodities make them ideal subcultural fodder; 'Look at me, look what I am doing to this safety pin, look how different I am, I am a punk.' With gay subcultures, located as they often are within an overtly homophobic milieu, the semiotic emphasis of their re-signification switches from the tangible to the intangible realm. While the act of re-signification itself and the semiotic agenda that motivates it retain the same oppositional, subversive appeal this activity now exists in a far more covert and internal context. As a result gay subcultures have constructed their identities around the application of oppositional reading strategies which produce 'alternate explications' from the mass-cultural, straight interpretations which dominate and denote society (Becker *et al.* 1995). Indeed no other subculture has so overtly institutionalised its own oppositional reading strategies, recognising their particular style of reading and the interpretations it produces as 'camp'. Camp literally represents a 'gay code' which provides the interpretive basis for an alternative decoding of text which has been encoded largely by and for an overtly straight culture.

ADVERTISING POLYSEMY

Consumer meanings, much like literary meanings, are open to interpretation and just as authors attempt to guide the reader towards a preferred outcome, so the producer of consumer meanings (the capitalist author) attempts to ensure that the consumer derives a particular meaning from a particular commodity or service. While the production and promotion of consumption meanings falls within the authorial influence of encoding practices, the decoding activity of the consumer ensures that in many instances rather than passively accepting these intended meanings consumers are active in their interpretations. As with any form of communication the ad can provide only the semiotic elements; it is the consumer who must assemble these various abstract images and sounds into a meaningful whole within the interpretive realm.

Advertising as a text, with its rich array of symbolic imagery, is replete with connotative signs. Because the connotative sign represents the primary site for renegotiation, advertising represents an overtly polysemic text. Similarly the attempts by advertisers to semantically 'connect' with their target market by portraying images and issues within the execution that are familiar to the audience also increases the polysemic potential of advertising. In effect the advertising audience display 'expanded repertoires' (McCormick and Waller 1987: 204) which enable them to select from a relatively large heteroglossic range when interpreting advertising messages. Aside from the expanded repertoires of the audience and the semantically open connotative nature of the advertising text, several other factors also prove influential in rendering advertising as polysemic. The ad may entertain, frighten, inform but the only possible authorially sponsored conclusion is purchase (Allen 1992). This fact is well known by the consumer and it can result in increased scepticism during reading (Ford *et al.* 1990) which in turn serves to shift the interpretation of a particular ad away from the dominant and towards the oppositional. The very act of purchase which resonates so richly throughout the advertising text, can act as a stimulus to perform an oppositional reading.

Another polysemic factor is the behaviour of the consumer/viewer during reading. Literary texts are usually consumed in an particular time and spatial context which has been devoted to the reading act (Radway 1984). This interpretive context is less intense, but equally deliberate, in the case of television reception (Buckingham 1993). In the case of advertising, however, the text is unique in that it exists in a non-sponsorial interpretive context, i.e. it is the only occasion when readers have not actively committed themselves to the reading act but are nevertheless being asked to engage in it. In fact the presence of ads in between texts that the reader *has* selected may increase the oppositional context of advertising interpretation. Aside from the semantic dislocation between encoder and decoder, audiences are often also physically distant and active during television advertising (Kitchen and Yorke 1986). This activity can clearly impede the impact of a preferred reading. What is the probability that a viewer will decode the intended meaning of an ad while interpreting it from another room, bathing a small child for example?

All of these factors can contribute to the variable semantic results which the consumer derives from the advertising text, and a number of recent studies provide empirical evidence of advertising's polysemic status (Elliott *et al.* 1993, 1995; Mick and Buhl 1992). Polysemy is a potentially fatal threat to a successful advertising campaign because it prevents the producer from getting intended meanings across to the target market and as such offers a significant limitation to a campaign's effectiveness and consequently a brand's future success in the market. The acknowledgement that an ad's meaning can be attributed to its target audience's own interpretation is not a magical solution to the strategic threat posed by the polysemic properties of advertising. Indeed this acknowledgement actually leads the advertiser into the 'hell of advertising connotation'

(Mick and Politi 1989: 85) where the freedom to interpret advertising meanings can engender semiotic chaos in the tightly defined target market. Despite the hopeful encoding attempts by the advertiser, the relatively weak semantic weight of the advertising text combined with the interpretive strength of the advertising audience combine to ensure that, irrespective of the best efforts of the advertiser in attempting to restrict the consumer to their intended meaning, the balance of power in the interpretive struggle between ad and consumer lies with the latter.

An admixture of various textual, reader and contextual factors combine in the interpretation of advertising to suggest that advertising represents a rich polysemic source of meanings. Indeed such is the power of the advertising audience over the text that it could be argued that advertising represents a far more polysemic form than either its literary or televisual counterparts. Such a statement, if correct, brings us to a startling conclusion. Although advertising represents *the* classic ideological text because of the power of its connotative codes to locate the reader in a particular subject position, we can now portray the advertising audience as equally prominent in its contextual power to utilise alternative, oppositional codes in interpreting the text and resisting its ideological power. These two conclusions are not mutually exclusive. In the general interpretive process both text and reader can be powerful simultaneously. In the case of advertising interpretation, despite its passive, rather staid portrayal in consumer research texts, we may be witnessing the semantic clash of the Titans.

ADVERTISING SUBCULTURES

The rich resource of commodity meanings which originate in consumer goods, services and promotional activity has come to dominate the symbolic worlds of many members of western society leading to the development of a 'consumer culture'. It has already been established that the more accepted, central and secure a position that a particular sign occupies in the dominant culture, the more attractive it is to the various subcultures attempting to distance themselves from their parent culture through bricolage. As consumption meanings continue through the period of late capitalism to prove an ever more important semiotic resource to the mass-cultural majority, one side-effect of this trend, apart from a string of Baudrillardian nightmares, is the increased adoption of commodity-signs by disaffected subcultures attempting to transform these meanings and thus simultaneously transform their own identity. Essentially the formula of subcultural activity is identical to that described earlier; the only alteration is the choice of commodities and consumer behaviour as the arbiter of subcultural identity. Thus the commodity, shaped by powerful capitalist forces, signifies the dominant, mass-cultural meanings of society, yet 'the pleasures and meanings offered by the plenitude of goods in shopping malls are multiple, and bear the dominant ideology while offering considerable scope for cultural manoeuvre within and against'(Fiske 1989a: 35). This signified meaning, like any other in the semiotic relationship between signifier and signified, is not fixed perpetually in a semiotic embrace; the signifying object can be freed and replaced with an alternative meaning. As a result a huge array of commodities is appropriated by subcultural groups, as the re-signified commodities become 'neo-tribe paraphernalia' (Bauman 1992: 25) which unite the members of the subculture. Despite the fact that this critical, resistive motivation is commonly accepted as being the *raison d'être* for subcultural groupings this critical dimension is sadly missing from extant definitions of consumption subcultures (e.g. Schouten and McAlexander 1995).

The specific consumer behaviour that forms the basis for these subcultural tactics can consist of a number of different activities. The above definition leaves the actual 'consumption activity' very open in defining consumption subcultures. Aside from the subcultural activity centred around the tangible phenomena of consumer goods the case must also be made for consumption subcultures which utilise the intangible elements of consumption phenomena. Despite the initial need for tangible commodities, the inherent core of subcultural activity (the semantic nectar at the core of the commodity flower) is the sign value of the commodity in mass-cultural society. Advertising is a cultural product in its own right and as a cultural product it is 'no more immune to subversion, evasion or resistance than any other strategic force' (Fiske 1989b: 32). Because theories of advertising from both practitioner and academic sources have maintained a linear progression in the movement of 'advertising effect' (De Groot 1980: 52) they have ignored this possible reversal of advertising causality (Lannon and Cooper 1983), so that 'the valorization of advertising awaits acknowledgement of the truth that advertising does not exploit consumers, but, rather, that consumers exploit advertising' (Fowles 1996: 161).

In subcultural contexts the individual operates a radical, oppositional code which literally inverts the dominant code present in the ad (Ozanne and Murray 1996). The interpreted meaning of the ad differs from the intended meaning of the advertisers not because of differences in repertoires or distractions in the reading context but because the advertising subculture wants, *needs*, to read it aberrantly. A number of examples illustrate the social practices of advertising subcultures. When the UK Government ran the infamous 'Heroin Screws You Up' campaign the ads were stolen and then used as posters by the very subculture the ads had set out to destroy (Davidson 1992). Rather than accept the advertising code and its intended meanings which attempted to negate the glamorous image of heroin, the heroin-using subculture directly reversed the meanings and used the campaign as a celebration of their way of life and nihilistic outlook. Similarly when New Age Travellers invaded and occupied a site in London owned by the brewers Guinness they decided to name the camp 'Pure Genius' (Montefiore 1996). By using the brewer's most famous advertising strapline the travelling subculture reversed the causality of advertising ideology and used it to manipulate the original author of the ads. In a final example of subcultural consumption, a small group of lesbian activists used the brand identity of IKEA furniture stores as raw materials for their demonstrations in 'Gay Pride' marches and in the construction of their group identity (Ritson and Elliott 1996). In these examples the advertising text is appropriated, re-signified and then utilised as a key subcultural resource in the 'struggle' (McCormick and Waller 1987: 195) for cultural meaning on the ideological 'battleground'.

THE NEW DIALECTICAL IMAGINATION

The valorisation of symbolic forms by the individuals who produce and receive them, whether it be by the ascription of economic value by being constituted as a commodity which has value in the market, or by the ascription of value as symbolic capital, is commonly accompanied by the 'conflict of symbolic valorisation' (Thompson 1990: 155). In the case of mass communications such as advertising, the viscous meaning in the text is subjected to individual readings and to elaboration in social contexts where the social reality of the group and self is compared with the consumption-based mythology of advertising before a contextualised meaning is interpreted (Ritson and Elliott 1995). The seminal work of the Frankfurt School in developing Critical Theory (Jay 1973) has not been eclipsed but has gained renewed importance with the recognition of advertising as a potent ideological force. However, Horkheimer's and Adorno's rather pessimistic account of the ability of the individual to resist imposed meanings must be adjusted in the light of polysemy and oppositional social practices. For even if we only imagine freedom, imaginary concepts can have real effects.

REFERENCES

Allen, R.C. (1992) 'Audience-oriented criticism and television', in R.C. Allen (ed.) *Channels of Discourse, Reassembled*, 2, London: Routledge, 101–137.
Altman, R. (1984) 'A semantic/syntactic approach to film genres', *Cinema Journal*, 23, Spring: 14–15.
Bakhtin, M. (1981) *The Dialogical Imagination*, Austin, TX: University of Texas Press.
Barthes, R. (1977) *Roland Barthes*, London: Macmillan.
—— (1993) 'The rhetoric of the image', in A. Gray and J. McGuigan (eds) *Studying Culture*, London: Edward Arnold, 15–27.
Bauman, Z. (1992) *Intimations of Postmodernity*, London: Routledge.
Becker, E., Citron, M., Lesage, J. and Rich, B.R. (1995) 'Lesbians and film', in A. Creekmur and A. Doty (eds) *Out in Culture: Gay, Lesbian and Queer Essays on Popular Culture*, London: Cassell, 25–43.
Billig, M. (1996) *Arguing and Thinking: A Rhetorical Approach to Social Psychology*, Cambridge: Cambridge University Press.

Billig, M., Condor, S., Edwards, D., Gane, M., Middleton, D. and Radley, A. (1988) *Ideological Dilemmas: A Social Psychology of Everyday Thinking*, London: Sage.

Blumler, J.G., Gurevitch, M. and Katz, E. (1985) 'Reaching out: a future for gratifications research', in K.E. Rosengren, L.A. Wenner and P. Palmgreen (eds) *Media Gratifications Research: Current Perspectives*, London: Sage.

Bourdieu, P. (1977), *Outline of a Theory of Practice*, trans. R. Nice, Cambridge: Cambridge University Press.

—— (1979) *Distinction*, trans. R. Nice, London: Routledge.

—— (1990) *In Other Words: Essays Towards a Reflexive Sociology*, Cambridge: Polity.

—— (1991) *Language and Symbolic Power*, Cambridge: Polity.

Bourne, G. (1981) 'Meaning, image and ideology', *Form and Meaning* 1, 4, Milton Keynes: Open University Press, 37–66.

Buckingham, D. (1993), *Children Talking Television: The Making of Television Literacy*, London: Falmer.

Clarke, J., Hall, S., Jefferson, T. and Roberts, B. (1975) 'Subcultures, cultures and class', in S. Hall and T. Jefferson (eds) (1991) *Resistance through Rituals*, London: Routledge, 9–74.

Cohen, A.K. (1955) *Delinquent Boys: The Culture of the Gang*, New York: Free Press.

Collins, J. (1993) 'Determination and contradiction: an appreciation and critique of the work of Pierre Bourdieu on language and education', in C. Calhoun, E. LiPuma and M. Postone (eds) *Bourdieu: Critical Perspectives*, Cambridge: Polity.

Cook, G. (1992) *The Discourse of Advertising*, London: Routledge.

Creekmur, A. and Doty, A. (1995) 'Introduction', in A. Creekmur and A. Doty (eds) *Out in Culture: Gay, Lesbian and Queer Essays on Popular Culture*, London: Cassell, 25–43.

Davidson, M.P. (1992), *The Consumerist Manifesto: Advertising in Postmodern Times*, London: Routledge.

de Certeau, M. (1984) *The Practice of Everyday Life*, trans. S. F. Rendall, Berkeley: University of California Press.

De Groot, G. (1980) *The Persuaders Exposed*, London: Associated Business Press.

Dyer, G. (1988) *Advertising as Communication*, London: Routledge.

Eagleton, T. (1991) *Ideology*, London: Verso.

Eco, U. (1979) *The Role of the Reader: Explorations in the Semiotics of Texts*, Bloomington, IN: Indiana University Press.

Elliott, R. and Ritson, M. (1995) 'Practicing existential consumption: the lived meaning of sexuality in advertising', in F. Kardes and M. Sujan (eds) *Advances in Consumer Research*, 22, Provo, UT: Association for Consumer Research, 740–746.

——, Eccles, S. and Hodgson, M. (1993) 'Re-coding gender representations: women, cleaning products, and advertising's "new man"', *International Journal of Research in Marketing*, 10: 311–324.

——, Jones, A., Benfield, A. and Barlow, M. (1995) 'Overt sexuality in advertising: a discourse analysis of gendered responses', *Journal of Consumer Policy*, 18, 2: 71–92.

Fairclough, N. (1989) *Language and Power*, London: Longman.

Feuer, J. (1992) 'Genre study and television', in R.C. Allen (ed.) *Channels of Discourse, Reassembled*, 2, London: Routledge, 138–160.

Firat, A.F. and Venkatesh, A. (1995) 'Liberatory postmodernism and the reenchantment of consumption', *Journal of Consumer Research*, 22, 3: 239–267.

Fiske, J. (1987) *Television Culture*, London: Routledge.

—— (1989a) *Reading the Popular*, London: Routledge.

—— (1989b) *Understanding Popular Culture*, Boston, MA: Unwin-Hyman.

—— (1990) *Introduction to Communication Studies*, 2nd edn, London: Routledge.

Fitzgerald, T.K. (1992) 'Media, ethnicity and identity', in P. Scannel, P. Schlesinger and C. Sparks (eds) *Culture and Power*, London: Sage, 112–136.

Ford, G.T., Smith, D.B. and Swasy, J.L. (1990) 'Consumer skepticism of advertising claims: testing hypotheses from economics of information', *Journal of Consumer Research*, 16, March: 433–441.

Foucault, M. (1972) *Archaeology of Knowledge*, London: Tavistock.

Fowles, J. (1996) *Advertising and Popular Culture*, London: Sage.

Gabriel, Y. and Lang, T. (1995) *The Unmanageable Consumer*, London: Sage.

Goldman, R. (1992) *Reading Ads Socially*, London: Routledge.

Gramsci, A. (1971) *The Prison Notebooks*, London: Lawrence & Wishart.

Grote, D. (1983) *The End of Comedy: The Sit-Com and the Comedic Tradition*, Hamden, CN: Shoestring.

Habermas, J. (1970) *Towards a Rational Society*, London: Heinemann.

Hall, S. (1973) 'Encoding/decoding', in S. Hall, D. Hobson, A. Lowe and P. Willis (eds) *Culture, Media, Language*, London: Routledge, 128–138.

Hebdidge, D. (1975) 'The meaning of mod', in S. Hall and T. Jefferson (eds) (1991) *Resistance through Rituals*, London: Routledge, 87–98.

Holquist, M. (1990) *Dialogism: Bakhtin and his World*, London: Routledge.

Janiszewski, C. (1988) 'Preconscious processing effects: the independence of attitude formation and conscious thought', *Journal of Consumer Research*, 15, September: 199–209.

Jay, M. (1973) *The Dialectical Imagination: A History of the Frankfurt School and the Institute for Social Research, 1923–1950*, Boston, MA: Little, Brown.

Jenkins, H. (1992) *Textual Poachers: Television Fans and Participatory Culture*, London: Routledge.

Jensen, K.B. (1990) 'The politics of polysemy: television news, everyday consciousness and political action', *Media, Culture and Society*, 12: 57–77.

Kitchen, P.J. and Yorke, D.A. (1986) 'Commercial TV breaks: consumer behaviour and new technology – an initial analysis', *European Journal of Marketing*, 20: 40–53.

Lannon, J. and Cooper, P. (1983) 'Humanistic advertising', *International Journal of Advertising*, 2: 195–213.

Lasch, C. (1978) *The Culture of Narcissism*, New York: W.W. Norton.

Lash, S. (1988). 'Discourse or figure? Postmodernism as "regime of signification"', *Theory, Culture and Society*, 5, 2/3: 311–336.

Lears, T.J. (1983) 'From salvation to self-realization', in R.W. Fox and T.J. Lears (eds) *The Culture of Consumption*, New York: Pantheon.

Leiss, W., Kline, S. and Jhally, S. (1990) *Social Communication in Advertising: Persons, Products and Images of Well Being*, London: Routledge.

Lull, J. (1990) *Inside Family Viewing: Ethnographic Research on Television Audiences*, London: Comedia.

—— (1995) *Media, Communication, Culture*, Oxford: Blackwell.

McCormick, K. and Waller, G.F. (1987) 'Text, reader, ideology', *Poetics*, 16, 1: 193–208.

McCracken, G. (1989) 'Who is the celebrity endorser? Cultural foundations of the endorsement process', *Journal of Consumer Research*, 16, December: 310–321.

Marcuse, H. (1964) *One Dimensional Man*, London: Routledge & Kegan Paul.

Martin, G. (1981a) 'Introduction to block 4', *Form and Meaning: Block 1, Volume 4*, Milton Keynes: Open University Press, 3–10.

—— (1981b) 'Unit 13: Readers, viewers and texts', *Popular Culture: Block 4, Volume 4*, Milton Keynes: Open University Press, 14–36.

Marx, K. and Engels, F. (1965), *Selected Correspondence*, Moscow: Progress.

—— (1970) *The German Ideology Volume 1*, London: Lawrence & Wishart.

Mick, D.G. (1986) 'Consumer research and semiotics: exploring the morphology of signs, symbols and significance', *Journal of Consumer Research*, 13, September: 196–213.

—— and Buhl, K. (1992) 'A meaning based model of advertising', *Journal of Consumer Research*, 19, December: 317–338.

—— and Politi, L.G. (1989) 'Consumer's interpretations of advertising imagery', in E.C. Hirschman (ed.) *Interpretive Consumer Research*, Provo, UT: Association for Consumer Research, 85–96.

Montefiore, S.S. (1996) 'Anarchists living high on the hogwash', *Sunday Times*, London, 7.

Moores, S. (1992) 'Texts, readers and contexts of reading', in P. Scannell, P. Schlesinger and C. Sparks (eds) *Culture and Power*, London: Sage, 137–157.

—— (1993) *Interpreting Audiences: The Ethnography of Media Consumption*, London: Sage.

Morley, D. (1980) *The 'Nationwide' Audience*, London: British Film Institute.

Morrow, R. (1994) *Critical Theory and Methodology*, London: Sage.

Muncie, J. (1981) 'Pop culture, pop music and post-war youth: subcultures', *Popular Culture*, Milton Keynes: Open University Press, 31–62.

Murdock, G. and McCron, R. (1975) 'Consciousness of class and consciousness of generation', in S. Hall and T. Jefferson (eds) (1991) *Resistance through Rituals*, London: Routledge, 192–208.

—— and —— (1976) 'Youth and class', in G. Mungham and G. Parsons (eds) *Working Class Youth Culture*, London: Routledge.

Myers, K. (1986) *Understains: The Sense and Seduction of Advertising*, London: Comedia.

Ozanne, J.L. and Murray, J.B. (1996) 'Using critical theory and public policy to create the reflexively defiant consumer', in R.P. Hill (ed.) *Marketing and Consumer Research in the Public Interest*, London: Sage, 3–16.

Parker, I. (1992) *Discourse Analysis: Critical Analysis for Social and Individual Psychology*, London: Routledge.

Pollay, R.W. (1986) 'The distorted mirror: reflections on the unintended consequences of advertising', *Journal of Marketing*, 50, April: 18–36.

Radway, J. (1984) *Reading the Romance*, Chapel Hill, NC: University of North Carolina.

—— (1995) 'Interpretive communities and variable literacies: the functions of romance reading', in J. Munns and G. Rajan (eds) *A Cultural Studies Reader*, London: Longman, 334–366.

Ritson, M. and Elliott, R. (1995) 'A model of advertising literacy: the praxiology and co-creation of advertising meaning', in M. Bergadaa (ed.) *Proceedings of Annual Conference of the European Marketing Academy*, 1, Paris: ESSEC, 1035–1068.

—— and —— (1996) 'Reframing IKEA: commodity signs, consumer creativity and the social-self dialectic', in K.P. Corfman and J.G. Lynch (eds) *Advances in Consumer Research*, 23, Provo, UT: Association for Consumer Research, 127–131.

Roosens, E. (1992) *Creating Ethnicity: The Process of Ethnogenesis*, London: Sage.

Scannell, P., Schlesinger, P. and Sparks, C. (1992) 'Introduction', in P. Scannell, P. Schlesinger and C. Sparks (eds), *Culture and Power*, London: Sage.

Schouten, J.W. and McAlexander, J.H. (1995) 'Subcultures of consumption: an ethnography of the new bikers', *Journal of Consumer Research*, 22, June: 43–61.

Schudson, M. (1984) *Advertising the Uneasy Persuasion: Its Dubious Impact on American Society*, London: Routledge.

Sinclair, J. (1987) *Images Incorporated*, London: Croom Helm.

Solomon, M. (1996) *Consumer Behaviour: Buying, Having and Being*, 3rd edn, London: Prentice Hall.

Stern, B.B. (1989) 'Literary criticism and consumer research: overview and illustrative analysis', *Journal of Consumer Research*, 16, December: 322–334.

—— (1994) 'A revised communication model for advertising: multiple dimensions of the source, the message, and the recipient', *Journal of Advertising*, 23, 2: 5–16.

Tetzlaff, D. (1992) 'Popular culture and social control in late capitalism', in P. Scannel, P. Schlesinger and C. Sparks (eds) *Culture and Power*, London: Sage, 48–73.

Tharp, M. and Scott, L.M. (1990) 'The role of marketing processes in creating cultural meaning', *Journal of Macromarketing*, Fall: 47–60.

Thompson, J.B. (1990) *Ideology and Modern Culture*, Cambridge: Polity.

Weber, M. (1979) *Economics and Society: An Outline of Interpretive Sociology*, vol. 1, Berkeley, CA: University of California Press.

Weeden, C. (1987) *Feminist Practice and Poststructuralist Theory*, Oxford: Blackwell.

Wernick, A. (1991) *Promotional Culture: Advertising, Ideology and Symbolic Expression*, London: Sage.

Williamson, J. (1978) *Decoding Advertisements*, London: Marion Boyars.

Willis, P. (1990) *Common Culture: Symbolic Work at Play in the Everyday Cultures of the Young*, Milton Keynes: Open University Press.

Zizek, S. (1989) *The Sublime Object of Ideology*, London: Verso.

7   Beyond the semiotic strait-jacket

Everyday experiences of advertising involvement

Stephanie O'Donohoe and Caroline Tynan

All changed, changed utterly,
A terrible beauty is born
    (W.B. Yeats, *Easter 1916*)

INTRODUCTION

The involvement concept may well be the 'terrible beauty' of consumer behaviour. Adopted by rather than born into this discipline, it seems to have delivered more confusion and consternation than insight. Considering its fate, Belk (1995a) suggests that on the evidence to date, this 'promising brain child' was either stillborn or expired sometime during its troubled childhood. Others see it as dying if not already dead, to the extent that 'reviewers and editors are already writing involvement's eulogy' (Muncy 1990: 144). Such pessimistic prognoses arise because after thirty years of research, involvement remains an intriguing, intuitively appealing and ultimately elusive concept. This is certainly the case in an advertising context, where it seems relevant in two senses. First, involvement with goods, services, tasks or situations may influence consumers' response to advertising. Second, ads themselves may be the object of consumers' involvement.

This chapter outlines theoretical and methodological issues surrounding involvement and advertising, and argues that empirical research has effectively placed consumers in a semiotic strait-jacket. Relying heavily on laboratory experiments, studies have constrained consumers' freedom to communicate how they experience, relate to and make sense of ads. This is regrettable, particularly in light of recent theoretical and empirical work emphasising the active, sophisticated and socially situated nature of advertising consumption. The chapter considers how we may 'put consumer experience back into consumer research' (Thompson *et al.* 1989) in this area by broadening our perspectives and methods. Drawing on a study which obtained young adults' own accounts of their everyday advertising encounters, it seeks to indicate the richness of consumers' experiences of advertising involvement.

THE TIES THAT BIND: INVOLVEMENT AND ADVERTISING RESEARCH

Involvement is often understood as a sense of personal relevance or state of arousal regarding some consumption-related object, which increases with the object's closeness to an individual's central value system. While it appears to have a significant role to play in influencing consumer behaviour, Lastovicka and Gardner's (1979) description of involvement as 'a bag of worms' is supported by many reviews of the literature in this area (Antil 1984; Costley 1988; Laaksonen 1994; O'Donohoe 1992). Twenty years after Rothschild and Houston (1977) complained about the 'theoretical lipservice' and 'shallow empirical treatment' which it has received, involvement remains a mutant concept plagued by a plethora of objects, definitions, operationalisations and measurements. An indication of this conceptual minefield is provided by Andrews *et al.* (1990), who list twenty-eight definitions and numerous experimental attempts to manipulate involvement. Indeed, Poiesz and de Bont (1995) wonder whether there exists a core meaning for involvement, or whether it is simply a conceptual and statistical artefact.

The two most popular involvement measures are those developed by Zaichkowsky (1985) and Laurent and Kapferer (1985). Zaichkowsky's Personal Involvement Inventory measured involvement as a unidimensional construct relating to personal relevance, while Laurent and Kapferer's Consumer Involvement Profile measured the 'facets' or antecedents of involvement in terms of a product's perceived importance, its symbolic or sign value, its hedonic, emotional or pleasure value, and the perceived risk associated with its purchase. These scales and their conceptual implications have been extensively discussed, debated and revised, and it remains to be seen if researchers are indeed 'inching ever closer to a generally accepted involvement measurement scale' (Schneider and Rodgers 1996: 253).

An alternative approach was taken by Laaksonen (1994), who used a laddering technique to measure involvement in terms of the links between perceived product attributes and consumer values. Although she refers to hedonic and symbolic issues, Belk (1995a: 147) detects in this work 'the unexamined assumption that consumers are information processors and that this is what consumer involvement is destined to enlighten'. He argues that research on this topic still cannot account for consumers' actual involvement with marketing phenomena in everyday life, such as that indicated by distress at a scratch on a car. Furthermore, while researchers such as Poiesz and de Bont (1995) bemoan the fragmentation of involvement research, Belk challenges the notion of 'one true type' of consumer involvement, and suggests that there might well be multiple types. Such a stance resonates with the postmodern distrust of universal laws and celebration of the 'ephemerality, contingency and diversity of the physical and human worlds as we experience them' (Brown 1993: 22).

In any case, given such complexity, it is surprising that so little involvement research has focused on exploration and understanding rather than measurement or prediction. In this context, Zaichkowsky (1986) has suggest that in-depth interviews might be an 'interesting approach' in this area. However, only Laurent and Kapferer (1985) appear to have made extensive use of such interviews with consumers and/or practitioners in developing their scale. Indeed, Laaksonen herself recognises the need to broaden our scope and methods to consider the cultural context of involvement, its relationship with consumption issues beyond purchase decisions, and 'how consumers tend to perceive and think about the domain of involvement' (Laaksonen 1994: 135).

When we consider involvement in an advertising context, similar themes and tensions are evident. Even here, involvement has been associated with different objects and defined in different ways. As Mulbacher (1986) notes,

> The advertised product category, the brand, the purchase decision and consumption usage process, the executional framework of the advertisement, the media vehicle as well as parts of the situative context may evoke a person's arousal.

> (Mulbacher 1986: 464)

In many cases, the range of interpretations has confused attempts to measure involvement's persuasive effects (Andrews *et al.* 1990; Zaichkowsky 1986). Furthermore, various treatments have been guilty of 'circular misusage' (Laurent and Kapferer 1985) by defining the concept in terms of its consequences. For example, Greenwald and Leavitt's (1984) four levels of 'audience involvement in advertising' – preattention, focal attention, comprehension and elaboration – are defined in terms of how consumers process advertising messages.

Nonetheless, many studies have examined how involvement with products, brands or brand choice decisions may influence the way in which consumers respond to ads. Thus, the impact of involvement has been examined on the sequence of persuasion (e.g. C.W. Park and Mittal 1985; Ray 1973). Much attention has also been paid to the Elaboration Likelihood Model, or ELM (Petty *et al.* 1983, 1991), whereby involvement influences consumers' selection of 'central' or 'peripheral' ad processing strategies. While variations on the ELM theme are still popular (see e.g. J. Park and Hastak 1996), others have moved away from its much criticised dichotomies (Cole *et al.* 1990) and addressed instead the depth of information-processing arising from involvement. Thus, MacInnis and Jaworski (1989) discuss six levels of processing resulting from consumers' ability, opportunity and motivation. Although they explicitly avoid the term 'involvement', their view of motivation as based on product needs may be considered in terms of product involvement. These authors offer the most detailed and nuanced treatment of processing levels, but there is some common ground with earlier analyses by Greenwald and Leavitt

(1984) and Baker and Lutz (1987). Thus, the three models see ad elements as increasingly related to prior knowledge and experiences as the level of involvement increases. They also agree that higher levels of processing may be independent of the ad's actual content. Finally, all three models may be related to Mick's (1992) four levels of subjective comprehension, in that they propose a shift from message-based, superficial comprehension to receiver-based and deeper comprehension levels. Comparing his framework with that of MacInnis and Jaworski, however, Mick disputes their contention that at higher processing levels, consumers' attention turns inwards rather than externally towards the ad.

Several authors have focused on ads or advertising as the object of involvement. Indeed, it was in this context that involvement was introduced to the field of consumer research. Krugman (1965: 355) defined involvement with an ad in terms of 'the number of conscious "bridging experiences", connections, or personal references per minute that the viewer makes between his own life and the stimulus'. This appears to offer scope for research on the rich and idiosyncratic nature of advertising consumption. Unfortunately, however, Krugman defines the concept in terms of its consequences, emphasises the quantity rather than the quality or strength of connections, and ignores their dimensionality. Furthermore, he is interested only in connections made during exposure to the ad, denying the possibility that involvement could be more than instantaneous or ephemeral (O'Donohoe 1992). Many other treatments of 'advertising involvement' actually address the consequences of *product* involvement for the processing of an ad's overt brand information. Thus, Shimp (1981) argues that for consumers to be highly involved with an ad, they must be attentive to the ad 'message' and employ a brand evaluation strategy. Similarly, Muehling *et al.* (1990) measure advertising involvement in terms of attention, perceived relevance, or elaboration with respect to ad claims or message points. This restrictive view of advertising involvement, with all the associated problems of classifying ad elements as 'central' or 'peripheral', is highlighted by the manipulation checks offered by Andrews and Durvasula (1991), which address the attention and effort directed towards an ad's overtly brand-related content. As Boller and Olson (1991) observe, such classifications of content assume that ads are structured as 'lectures' rather than 'dramas' (Wells 1989).

According to Tyebjee (1979) and Batra and Ray (1983), involvement with ads may be multidimensional and directed towards any aspect of an ad. However, when others have addressed different kinds of advertising involvement, they tend to privilege those relating directly to brand choice. Thus, Baker and Lutz (1987) define *message* involvement as the effort devoted to processing an ad's 'contents' and *execution* involvement as the processing of an ad's executional properties, 'without regard to their brand relatedness'. These authors argue that execution involvement detracts from message involvement, as it directs attention and effort away from the message and inhibits the accessibility of brand information from memory. Muhlbacher (1986) also refers to 'advertisement involvement' in executional terms. He assigns this a residual role entailing less, more passive and visually dominated information-processing, in ways which may impede the processing of brand information.

Overall, the experimental research tradition has dominated empirical work on involvement and advertising. In this context, a review of thirty-five studies raised several questions about their ecological validity (O'Donohoe 1994a). Of the thiry-five studies, twenty-four were based entirely on full-time student samples. Indeed, the use of such convenience samples continues unabated (see e.g. Johar 1995; Tavassoli *et al.* 1995). Only ten of the studies reviewed by O'Donohoe embedded the test ads in editorial material; sixteen presented test ads in isolation, and the rest embedded them only in other ads. Simulated ads for fictitious brands were used in twenty-five studies, giving cause to reflect on Thorson's (1990) comment that

> A crucial but sadly unexamined question must precede any talk of theory, concepts and methodology: What constitutes an ad? ... is a line drawing of a ballpoint pen with eight product attributes typed below it an ad? Are three long paragraphs extolling the attributes of an automobile an ad?
>
> (Thorson 1990: 200–201)

Turning to the treatment of involvement itself, O'Donohoe (1994a) found this was manipulated rather than measured in twenty-three of the studies. While this allows for greater control, many manipulations confused the immediacy with the importance of brand choice. For example, 'Subjects in the high-involvement group were told that they would be able to select from a variety of disposable razor products, rendering our bogus razor ad highly involving' (Petty *et al.* 1983: 18).

As Scott (1994) remarks, equating involvement with the promise of product samples removes the concept from any individual sense of relevance or naturally occurring reading context. Indeed, it would be hard to find contexts any further removed from natural reception than those employed in this research stream. Thus, Petty *et al.* (1983) conducted their experiment among small groups in a very large classroom. Subjects were isolated from each other, and told to raise their hands when they had worked through the experimental booklet. Similar practices are still in use, although subjects may now find themselves isolated in computer booths (J. Park and Hastak 1996). At the more extreme end of the scale,

> subjects were seated in front of a screen, on which the slides were projected from the back, and were instructed to place their chin on a small chinrest. Eye movements were recorded by an infrared camera located at the subjects' left side, *such as not to interfere with the subjects' normal viewing behavior.*
>
> (Pieters *et al.* 1996: 244, emphasis added)

Clearly, these authors have a very restrictive notion of normal viewing behaviour. The argument here is not that involvement research has no place for rigorous and tightly focused laboratory experiments, but that positivistic, experimental and psychologically driven approaches have their limits. As Sahlins (1976, quoted in McCracken 1987: 123) observes, 'every theory makes a bargain with reality'. Here, it seems that reality comes off worse: much of our knowledge of involvement in an advertising context is based on surrogate consumers providing written responses to simulated ads for hypothetical products, in settings which are very different from the contexts in which they normally encounter advertising. The impression is of an academy preoccupied with derivative yet inconsistent studies, and perhaps more interested in tinkering with the twigs than tending to the tree of knowledge in this area. This is unfortunate, particularly in light of recent literature which indicates the active, sophisticated and socially situated nature of advertising consumption.

LOOSENING THEORETICAL TIES: RECENT INSIGHTS INTO ADVERTISING CONSUMPTION

Drawing on a wide range of disciplines and theories, two books have highlighted the central position of consumption in contemporary society and called for greater sensitivity to its dynamic and fragmented nature. Thus, Miller (1995: 51) laments the absence of 'the contradictory, inconsistent mess of ordinary mundane worlds' from literature addressing consumption. Similarly, Gabriel and Lang (1995) show how different traditions and discourses, working in isolation from each other, represent consumers variously as victims, choosers, hedonists, artists, identity-seekers, explorers, rebels, activists and citizens. The authors remind us that consumers are 'creative composites' of each of these facets, and that 'being a consumer dissolves neither class membership nor citizenship; it is not the case that one moment we act as consumers and the next as workers or as citizens, as women or men or as members of ethnic groups' (Gabriel and Lang 1995: 5).

Media consumption plays a particularly important part in contemporary social and cultural developments, and the media and cultural studies literature offers critical insights into issues which may bear on advertising consumption. Since the 1960s, there has been a shift away from seeing the media consumer as a passive dupe of the all-powerful Culture Industries (Morley 1995). Whereas the uses and gratifications perspective of the 1960s addressed active audiences within an individualistic psychological framework, later conceptualisations recognised readings of television texts as informed by membership of various social groups. In any event, there is now a well-trodden path from 'passive' to 'active' conceptualisations of audiences in communication and media studies (Roscoe *et al.* 1995); it is generally assumed that audiences are always active and media content is always polysemic (Evans 1990). This has led to some concern that active audience theorists, the 'revisionist celebrants of semiotic democracy' (Curran 1990, quoted in Seaman 1992: 310) exaggerate the power of the media consumer to resist dominant ideologies. Our ability to interpret what we see and hear does not mean that we shall reject the dominant reading of a text, nor does it equate with political power (Roscoe *et al.* 1995). Overplaying the active audience card may obscure the power of the media to present 'preferred meanings', set agendas or provide parameters for interpretation. Thus, Morley (1995) calls for models which reconcile a concern about media power and a view of audiences as more than dupes or victims.

The notion of the active audience has also been applied to advertising in recent years. Indeed, O'Donohoe (1994b) traces this line of reasoning among British advertising practitioners since the late 1960s. In an academic context, McCracken (1987) and Buttle (1991) have argued that ads constitute raw material which consumers use to make sense of themselves and their worlds. The integration of advertising meanings into everyday life is inevitable, because consumers are not 'unconnected to a social world, detached from culture, removed from history and biography' (Buttle 1991: 97). Indeed, Grafton-Small and Linstead (1989) demonstrate this clearly in their reading of an ad for a chauffeur-driven car service. These themes are developed in Mick and Buhl's (1992) meaning-based model of advertising experiences. Their model views consumers as embedded in a socio-cultural context, accumulating particular life histories, developing life themes and projects, and negotiating the meaning of ads in that context. Applying this model, Mick and Buhl conducted two semi-structured interviews with each of three Danish brothers. In the first interview, they were asked to talk about their 'experience' of five 'image' ads. Detailed miniature life histories were obtained later. Analysis of the interview data supported the model, in that what might appear as 'idiosyncratic meanings' could be understood as patterned readings, intertwined with the brother's life histories and current life world. Further support for such a view comes from Elliott and Ritson (1995), who discuss the meanings and rituals which a group of flatmates constructed from the overtly sexual ads for Häagen-Dazs ice-cream.

A related area of inquiry has involved treating ads as texts and drawing on theories from language, literary and literacy studies to consider how they might be read. Early indications of the insights to be gained from this approach are provided by the enduring work of Barthes (1977a) and Williamson (1978). More recently, Scott (1994) draws on reader-response theory (which also informs the Mick and Buhl model) to show how advertising texts imply active, selective, imaginative, sceptical and playful readers. By contrast, academic accounts of advertising response typically characterise consumers as rational, passive and lazy. As Scott (1994: 475) comments, 'This is not a reader any of us care to be, nor one that any of us probably know. This reader is an artefact of research methods that ignore textuality and what text implies about the people we study.'

Discussing the nature of reading, Scholes (1989, quoted in Appleyard 1991: vi) argues that

> We read life as well as books, and the activity of reading is really a matter of working through signs and texts in order to comprehend more fully and powerfully not only whatever may be presented therein but also our own situations, both in their particularity and historicity and in their more durable and inevitable dimensions.

This may explain how readers become 'lost in a book', immersed or swept into an experience described in it, and filled 'with the wonder and flavour of alternative worlds' (Nell 1988, quoted in Appleyard 1991: 101). In the case of adolescent readers, Appleyard notes that immersion was often accompanied by a strong emotional reaction. It tended to happen when readers identified with a book's characters and the situations in which they find themselves, and when readers used these to rehearse aspects of other identities for themselves.

Without wishing to inflate out of all proportion the significance of advertising in people's lives, there seem to be some tantalising glimpses here of what advertising involvement might mean for consumers. Scott (1994) speculates that 'being the reader' may entail experiencing a particular mood or attitude, sharing certain problems, or answering to particular social roles called forth in the ad. Indeed, ads often deal in issues of personal and social identity (Leiss *et al.* 1990; Williamson 1978) and take the form of dramas which invite consumers to project themselves into situations or emotions (Boller and Olson 1991). Similarly, Kover (1995: 603) notes that 'If resistance is overcome and advertising breaks through, people converse with advertising; that is they begin a dialogue with it. It may be positive or rejecting, but conversation is always a relatively high-involvement process.'

Barthes' (1977b) ideas concerning the pleasure of the text also seem pertinent here. He saw the text as 'a space where language circulates', inviting readers to engage in a 'practical collaboration . . . producing text, opening it out, *setting it going*' (1977b: 163, original emphasis). Elaborating on the forms of pleasure to be had with texts, Barthes (1975) referred to *plaisir* as a pleasure which is essentially cultural in origin, and related to issues of identity. He used the term *jouissance* to describe a more intense, physical and often sexual kind of pleasure. As Fiske (1994: 249) notes, in either case 'Pleasure may be *provoked* by the text, but it can only be *experienced* by the reader in the reading. It can thus differ from reader to reader, and even from reading to reading' (original emphasis).

While Fiske and others have been primarily concerned with issues of ideology and empowerment arising from this view of pleasure (Story 1993), Barthes' notion of *plaisir* in particular suggests ways of breathing life into the concept of advertising involvement. In this context, Cook's (1992: 226) notion of advertising's 'code-play' is useful; he suggests that joining in allows consumers to fulfil a need for language play. Indeed, the flatmates in the Elliott and Ritson (1995) study may have something to tell us about the possibilities for advertising *jouissance*!

Finally, Ritson and Elliott's (1995a) synthesis of literacy and advertising literature offers a powerful account of active audiences in terms of advertising literacy. They emphasise that literacy does not simply refer to a set of reading or decoding skills, but also the uses to which such skills are put. Their model incorporates 'practice' and 'event' accounts of advertising literacy. Practices refer to individual consumers' co-creation of advertising meanings for their own purposes, while events refer to consumers' social uses of such meanings to construct self and group identities. The two processes are interdependent, and together account for the creative negotiations of advertising meaning constantly undertaken by consumers. Indeed, the range and richness of such practices and events are suggested by advertising uses and gratifications theory, which considers how consumers use ads for purposes other than those the marketer may have had in mind (O'Guinn and Faber 1991). In this context, O'Donohoe (1994b) found ads to be used for a wide range of purposes such as structuring time, reinforcing attitudes and values, enhancing egos, and facilitating interactions with friends, family and strangers.

LOOSENING METHODOLOGICAL TIES: SOME ALTERNATIVE APPROACHES

The literature discussed above suggests that our understanding of advertising involvement could benefit by freeing consumers from the semiotic strait-jackets of positivistic and experimental research, and by inviting them to express their advertising experiences in less constrained ways. 'Naturalistic', 'interpretive' or 'post-positivistic' research has provided insights into consumer behaviour (see Sherry 1991 and Belk 1995b for reviews), and may do the same for our understanding of advertising involvement – 'opening it out, *setting it going*', as Barthes (1977b: 163) might describe it. This ventures into territory explored and contested by those interested in media consumption. As Schroder (1987, quoted in Morley 1995: 311) notes, qualitative researchers in this area have until recently suffered a 'spiral of silence' because they were interested in 'what mainstream sociology regarded as unresearchable, i.e. cultural meanings and interpretations'.

It is, however, precisely such cultural meanings and interpretations which have been illuminated by existential-phenomenological and hermeneutic studies of female consumers' 'lived experiences' (Thompson *et al.* 1989, 1990, 1994). As these approaches are discussed elsewhere in this book, the emphasis here is on their relevance to advertising research.

Although Thompson *et al.* foreground the meanings of shopping for and consuming products, there is certainly scope for extending these approaches to advertising consumption. Indeed, Mick and Buhl (1992) used phenomenological interviews to explore three Danish brothers' experiences of five 'image' ads. The richness of advertising meanings which emerged in these interviews suggests the potential of such an approach. Of course, if we are to examine real-life experiences of advertising involvement, it would not be possible to preselect particular ads to use in interviews. We may, however, expect that consumers would be able to discuss instances when they felt involved with ads in some way, just as Thompson found his informants capable of recounting and reflecting upon specific instances of product purchase or use.

Ethnographic research also appears to have potential for enhancing our understanding of advertising involvement. Ethnography is concerned with providing 'thick description' (Geertz 1973) of 'the entire tapestry of social life' (Radway 1988), within a particular culture. As Buttle (1991) sees it, this approach involves descriptive, cultural, focused, comparative and theoretical investigation. Typically, ethnographers take part in people's everyday lives for extended periods, watching, listening, asking questions, and collecting whatever data might illuminate the issue being studied. It is a practical process, requiring the exercise of judgement in context, and while it does not lend itself to a predetermined research design, it should nonetheless be systematic. It should also be a reflexive process, as ethnographers are effectively constructing interpretations of how others construct their social world (Hammersley and Atkinson 1995).

Since the mid-1980s there has been an explosion in the use of ethnographic research methods in studies of television viewing practices (Seaman 1992). According to Lull (1987: 319) researchers interested in the 'routine, taken-for-granted, assumptive world' of everyday life face three tasks: to observe and note the routine behaviour of those being studied, to do so in natural settings where that behaviour occurs, and to draw inferences carefully, mindful of different aspects of the context. Many studies of television audiences meet these criteria (e.g. Jenkins 1992; Lindlof 1987), but others have eschewed participant observation and relied on methods such as group discussions (e.g. Buckingham 1987; Roscoe *et al.* 1995). Doubts have been expressed about the extent to which such methods are ethnographic; indeed Seaman (1992: 304) charges many audience researchers with the 'pretence of conducting anthropological fieldwork'. Applying the full range of ethnographic methods to advertising consumption experiences would certainly be a challenging exercise. Ang (1991: 13) refers to the 'infinite, contradictory, dispersed and dynamic practices' of actual television audiences. This seems all the more true of advertising audiences: ads are encountered in many media, on many occasions, and in many contexts, and they may not be experienced simply at the point of exposure. As Buttle (1991: 107) observes, even focusing on families' advertising-related conversations would require the researcher to be present wherever that might occur, 'whether that is at the breakfast table or in front of the television watching the Saturday morning cartoons'. However, these obstacles are not insurmountable. Ritson and Elliott (1995b), for example, examined advertising literacy by observing and talking to teenagers during their free periods at school. Furthermore, research which does not involve participant observation may still benefit from what Ang (1991) calls an 'ethnographic attitude'. Hammersley and Atkinson (1995) have argued that the boundaries around ethnography are necessarily unclear, particularly as all social researchers are in some sense participant observers. Similarly, Moores (1993: 4) defends 'audience ethnography' studies which may not use the full range of ethnographic methods, but 'share some of the same general intentions as anthropological research. There may be a similar concern ... with questions of meaning and social contexts and with charting the "situational embeddedness of cultural practices".'

YOUNG ADULT EXPERIENCES OF ADVERTISING INVOLVEMENT

The next section seeks to indicate the potential for research exploring advertising involvement in this spirit. The findings discussed below are derived from a broader study examining the relationship between young adults and advertising. This relationship was expected to be particularly interesting, given both parties' preoccupation with issues of self and social identity, and young adults' reputation as sophisticated and cynical consumers of ads (Leiss *et al.* 1990; Ritchie 1995; Willis 1990). The study used both small group discussions and individual interviews. This was not intended to contrast social and psychological frameworks of interpretation, but to recognise that discourse occurs in different social contexts (Lunt and Livingstone 1996). Small groups (usually with four participants) were used for social interaction and idea stimulation, without losing the potential to explore individual comments and interpretations in some detail. Personal interviews were used to pursue individual experiences, interpretations and idiosyncrasies in more depth (Robson and Foster 1989). In order to address a range of experiences, age, gender and broad occupational status quotas were used. A pilot study involved four small group discussions and two individual interviews. The main research, conducted in Edinburgh in 1991, involved fourteen groups and fourteen individual interviews; informants located by a professional recruiter. In total, eighty-two young adults participated, and the tape-recorded part of the discussion generally lasted between one and a half to two hours.

Participants were encouraged to describe their experiences of advertising in their own words, in their own way, and with their own examples. Following some general media discussion, the young adults described ads which they liked, disliked or remembered for any reason, and from any time or medium. Subsequent discussion emerged from, and was grounded in, these experiences and descriptions of ads encountered in everyday life. Following Glaser and Strauss (1967), an attempt was made to develop grounded theory, emerging from and illustrated by the data collected. This calls for the joint collection, coding and analysis of data in so far as is possible, and a constant comparative method of analysis. Tentative categories and their properties were identified, explored in subsequent interviews, and compared with other transcripts; negative instances were also sought to challenge emergent theory. Interpretations were discussed with colleagues from a variety of social science backgrounds. In keeping with the ethnographic tradition, the young adults are referred to below as 'informants' rather than 'respondents', reflecting the attempt to ground the study in their language and culture, rather than those of the researcher (Spradley 1979).

The nature of advertising involvement

One indication of informants' involvement with ads was the strength of the vocabulary used at times. Some ads were described as 'absolutely brilliant', 'really effective', 'compulsive' or 'powerful', and reactions were described in terms such as 'addicted', 'intrigued' or 'engrossed'. For example,

> Every time that comes on I just sit and watch it and everybody says 'Are you around the bend or something?' . . . I'm just transfixed every time that's on the telly, I don't know why.
>
> (female worker 21–24)

Such expressions may simply suggest that informants had very favourable attitudes towards some ads, so that describing them as 'involved' adds little to our understanding. However, many comments could be related to traditional views of involvement. Thus, informants often described how they would notice particular ads as they flicked through a magazine or sat through a commercial break on television. A sense of alertness and anticipation was evident in many comments:

> You just saw it and thought, 'Hang on, what's this?' It's actually worth watching again.
>
> (male student 18–20)

> I might miss the first bit because I wouldn't be concentrating, and then I'd look out for it again.
>
> (female student 18–20)

Such comments indicate a degree of arousal in relation to particular ads. A sense of arousal, however, appeared to accompany rather than characterise instances of involvement, which could be understood as a relationship or connection between informants and ads. Individual ads, ad elements, campaigns and even advertising in a more general sense appeared to serve as objects of involvement: as one informant put it,

> I think folk are much more adjusted to thinking about adverts and getting into them, you know, than folk our age twenty years ago.
>
> (male graduate worker 21–24)

Expressions of involvement occurred most commonly in relation to particular ad elements, however. The range of elements discussed in this context emphasises the rich and idiosyncratic nature of the young adults' advertising experiences: even the smallest and most obscure details sometimes resonated with them. In some cases, Baker and Lutz's (1987) advertising 'message' appeared to be the object of involvement. More commonly, informants tended to express involvement with an ad's characters or plot, the situation portrayed in it, or the music, humour or imagery employed. The 'ideas' behind ads, the 'puzzles' they offered, and the technical skill with which they were executed, also appeared to serve as objects of advertising involvement. The relationship with ads or ad elements appeared to be a 'creative composite' (Gabriel and Lang 1995) of five dimensions. In some cases, it was characterised by a sense of ads being relevant to informants' own experiences or connecting with their personal values. In other cases, cognitive, emotional or hedonic dimensions seemed paramount.

The first dimension is consistent with Krugman's (1965) 'personal connections' and also bears some similarity with the notion of 'resonance' discussed by Gerbner *et al.* (1980). Highlighting the notion of advertising audiences as socially situated individuals, informants sometimes talked about how particular ads echoed their own experiences. Thus, an unemployed male who had visited New York described how an ad for Murphy's Stout set in a New York bar had 'brought it all back to me'. For other informants, an ad for Tennent's Lager (featuring a Scot giving up his London job to return home) related to their experiences. Many informants talked about homesick friends who were working in London. For someone else,

> It reminds me of the time I was in London. Like it's too big, ken. It's a big place, you just want to get back to Edinburgh to the wee pubs you know and everybody that you know in it, you know. I liked that advert. It was good. True to life I thought.
>
> (female worker 21–24)

In other cases, involvement with ads seemed to be based on a sense of shared values. In this context, someone offered a lengthy description of the same ad:

> It's sort of he's down in London and you see him walking through the busy streets, tube station and all that and you can see he's really pissed off with it all. And then he gets through in his office building, stands

in the lift, looks about him and says 'To hell with this!' Sort of walks away and the next minute you see him standing in Princes Street. And the music's quite good in the background, like a sort of song about Scotland and things like that. He comes into the bar, has his pint with his mates and then the next second you see is the bird, obviously his bird, on the tube in London opening up the letter with his photo. And she dinnae look too pleased about it.

(male worker 18–20)

This long and detailed account of the ad certainly indicates a great deal of involvement. The informant identified with the ad's main character, to the extent of putting words into his mouth. Several values implicit in the ad, such as the idea of a Scot rejecting life in London, also resonated with him. He seemed to relate to the idea that work might not be satisfying (hence the gusto accompanying the 'to hell with this' in the lift): what really counted in life was being with your mates and having a pint with them. Girlfriends ('birds') were not so important, and it did no harm to put them in their place. Such identification is consistent with the notion of parasocial interactions (Horton and Wohl 1956) between audiences and mass media characters, and indeed with Appleyard's (1991) discussion of involvement with a book's characters and their situations.

Cognitive aspects of involvement were suggested by various references to 'concentrating' to get a joke, catch a set of lyrics, or work out a puzzling visual image. For example, an unemployed woman mentioned that she did not understand a particular ad. Someone else in the group told her it was for Silk Cut cigarettes, but she knew that already: she just could not make sense of the picture which she knew was supposed to communicate the idea of silk being cut. Such incidents suggest that Cook's (1992) 'code-play' may well have contributed to the pleasure of the text for informants. Turning to hedonic aspects of involvement, informants often described ads as providing enjoyable experiences. This was sometimes the case with ads for products having a sensory appeal. Thus, a student described an ad for Galaxy Ripple as 'chocolate put on film' and proceeded to give the rest of the group a vicarious and quite sensual eating experience. In other cases, people talked about the fun they had in consuming ads. For example, a female worker remembered 'just crying with laughter' at the Hamlet *World Cup* ad which showed a footballer struck in a sensitive part of the male anatomy. Others thoroughly enjoyed ads with cartoon or puppet characters, such as the Heat Electric ad starring puppet parrots:

The two parrots, they just sit there on their perch and one of them really doesn't do much. The other one just sort of sits there and it goes 'Well yes, you know, I come home, I like to have controllable heating, I like it to be nice and warm', and its wings are moving about. You've just got to see it, it cracks me up.

(male student 18–20)

Expressions of emotional involvement tended to be less common, perhaps reflecting Holbrook and Batra's (1987) view that ads tend to engender mild rather than strong emotions. Sometimes, informants simply identified with warm or peaceful moods in ads. For example,

> That's like a really beautiful advert. It's a very painless advert. You know how Nurofen is a pain killer, it's a painless kind of an advert. It's like a really soft and gentle advert. That's a really good advert.
>
> (unemployed female 18–20)

This comment indicates the way in which different aspects of involvement were intertwined. Although the informant engages with the ad's emotional imagery, she has also made a cognitive connection between the imagery and the product's function. Many informants were attracted to the actor Rutger Hauer's character in ads for Guinness. While some simply described him as 'cool' or 'mysterious', others related to him on a deeper level.

> He's very different. He's very good-looking I think and he's got striking sort of grey hair. His eyes are really sort of piercing. Very fine, quite a sculptured face I see. Also he's old which is even better. Slightly haggard. Been places, you know . . . He's really, really cool. He just knows where it's at. He's calm . . . you couldn't imagine him getting stressed out and making a fool of himself.
>
> (unemployed female 21–24)

Most instances of strong emotional involvement, however, occurred in relation to 'public information' ads, associated with 'hard-hitting' approaches. For example, an ad appealing for blood donors showed the comedian Rowan Atkinson dressed as a doctor and literally trying to get blood from a stone:

> [It] sounds amusing, but it's not the way it's done. It actually strikes a chord . . . He's walking round it trying to talk this rock into giving blood and you see the pressure rising within him. He's actually getting quite aggravated . . . Then he goes down to it and says 'please' or something like that. And then he gets so angry he hits it with the end of the stethoscope and he walks away . . . then he just turns round and there's this blood coming out of the stone, and 'Oh, thank you'. You know, he's really grateful that this rock is giving blood. It's brilliant. It's really good. I think that's probably the best advert I've seen really.
>
> (male worker 18–20)

There are certainly similarities between these five dimensions and those identified in research on product involvement. For example, the perceived importance factor in Laurent and Kapferer's (1985) Consumer Involvement Profile may be related to the personal experience dimension discussed here. The absence of perceived risk dimensions may be understood as reflecting their association with brand choices rather than ads themselves. As symbolic values are essentially the currency of ads, it should not surprise us that they circulate around advertising involvement rather than forming a distinct dimension. Laurent and Kapferer's emotional and hedonic dimensions also emerged here, as did a cognitive dimension which presumably reflects advertising's explicit communicative or informative function. This explicit communicative function may also explain the emergence of a personal values dimension here. While the Consumer Involvement Profile may 'capture' some of the dimensions of advertising involvement, this study indicates that their meanings are more complex and intertwined.

Uninvolvement and negative involvement

On some occasions, informants seemed uninvolved or even negatively involved with ads. On the whole, there was relatively little discussion of ads which they found uninvolving. This is hardly surprising, as they would be less likely to remember or discuss such ads. Where comments indicated a lack of involvement with an ad or style of ad, these were often offered by way of comparison with ads which were liked or even disliked strongly. Instances of uninvolvement were described in terms indicating a lack of arousal, and a sense of indifference: as someone put it, 'it doesn't really strike a chord to you'. In some cases, this indifference seemed to be hedonically based, as when informants did not engage with the humour in an ad. In other cases, the relevance of an ad or ad element to informants' own lives was denied. Thus, someone compared the Andrex puppy ads with those for Kitekat cat food:

> I've got dogs at home so I'd watch those adverts more than Kitekat saying 'eight out of ten preferred it' ... I can't be bothered with any of that. Sort of, I'm happy for them.
>
> (male graduate worker 21–24)

While uninvolvement seemed related to a lack of arousal, negatively involved informants certainly appeared to be aroused, but related to ads in an antagonistic way. Extreme expressions of hostility were rare, but someone was moved to profanity at the thought of the Gold Blend ads featuring the 'yuppie couple':

> That bloody Gold Blend one, with the guy and the wifey. The minute that comes on I think 'oh for f–'s sake'. If that comes on I turn it off to get away from it.
>
> (male worker 18–20)

Informants who found ads contradicted their personal experience sometimes seemed to become negatively involved. For example, a student talked about a Nationwide Anglia Building Society ad which begins with a father writing a letter to his son, who is seen travelling in exotic parts of the world. The letter, read as a voice-over, says that the father knows his son will learn and grow from his experiences, and then return home. The Nationwide logo then appears, and a voice-over states that Nationwide helps someone buy a home every four seconds. Although the student claimed that the ad 'just didn't catch my attention', he talked about it at some length, criticising its 'terrible voice-over' and saying he 'didn't like the advert as a whole'. His main objection, however, was to the son

> travelling around the world with this Indiana Jones type hat! It just didn't seem to have anything to do with how I would be and I know. I've recently been abroad, in Sri Lanka studying, and it was quite a wild place in certain places. I still wouldn't be dressing up like Indiana Jones. It just didn't seem to strike a note with how I would act in those situations.
>
> (male student 21–24)

In other cases, negative involvement appeared to be related to a conflict between the values implicit in an ad and those held dear by informants. Thus, a group of male graduate workers lambasted the Nationwide Anglia ad, describing it as 'pretentious' and 'patronising'. Above all, they resented the assumed inevitability of the son's return home and settling down, and the implication that they might make a break for individuality and self-fulfilment, but were ultimately expected to conform. The ad was seen as 'ideologically just battering you':

> Nationwide is saying, you know. 'You will live your life in this direction ... You can go out and do all these wonderful things around the world and you can help the Third World. And you can come back and buy your Barratt house in Barnton' [laughter]. The messages that tells you, the whole package that it's saying.
>
> (male graduate worker 21–24)

> I hate having it rammed down my throat and it's just like saying, 'When you're young do what you want, but when you're ready to settle down, buy with us.' It's really ridiculous.
>
> (male graduate worker 21–24)

Informants also appeared to experience negative involvement along cognitive or emotional dimensions. For example, a student found a drink-driving ad upsetting, and she imagined it bringing back terrible memories to those who had suffered. Someone else explained how a 'silly' lingerie ad really annoyed her:

> it's just totally stupid. Honestly, I've thought about it and I've thought about it and I just can't get it at all.
>
> (female worker 18–20)

Again, this comment indicates arousal and a level of cognitive involvement. However, when she could not make sense of the ad to herself, her frustration appears to have manifested itself in a hostile relationship with the ad.

Consequences of involvement

In this study, the consequences of involvement with ads and advertising ranged from the visible and verbalised to the invisible and internal. Some were quite mundane, while others were dramatic or even downright embarrassing. Some occurred during exposure to the ad, and others took place quite a while afterwards. Three general groups of consequences emerged. Each of these reinforces a view of active and sophisticated audiences, integrating the raw material of ads into their daily lives through the literacy practices and events discussed by Ritson and Elliott (1995a).

Internal acts

Although this study did not set out to examine the young adults' advertising experiences in terms of information processing, there were certainly similarities between the internal consequences of involvement indicated here and the levels of processing mentioned earlier. There were also clear parallels with Mick's (1992) comprehension levels, in that the subjective meanings for ads ranged from surface to deep, with more intense involvement associated with receiver-based meanings. In contrast to the MacInnis and Jaworski (1989) framework, however, higher levels were not necessarily integrated with brand information or attitudes. The 'hang on, what's this?' reaction which so many informants described may be understood in terms of 'focal attention' or 'basic categorisation' levels. Such labels, however, hardly do justice to the attention devoted to some ad elements. For example, a male worker was not convinced by the trajectory of a ball:

> he bounces the ball, it goes out the window and the dog jumps out the window. The thing that gets me is, he's throwing the ball towards the window, it bounces off the unit. Therefore it should come back but it doesn't, it goes out the window.
>
> (male worker 18–20)

MacInnis and Jaworski describe brand inferences based on source credibility as heuristic and relatively superficial processing. Again, this does not begin to reflect the degree of elaboration which informants employed for example in associating the Rutger Hauer character with Guinness. Such processes seem closer to the higher processing levels, whereby message-relevant cues are integrated with other information to form inferential brand beliefs. There were many examples of MacInnis and Jaworski's role-taking, where informants projected themselves into situations, although they did not necessarily integrate these with the brand. For example, the male worker who put words in the mouth of the Scot in the Tennent's ad never referred to the advertised brand. In terms of MacInnis and Jaworski's highest level of processing, the student who described a Galaxy ad as 'chocolate put on film' seemed to undertake self-generated persuasion, although this process was not as independent of the ad content as those authors suggest. Informants who were negatively involved with ads also seemed to engage in self-generated persuasion on occasion. Certainly, the male graduate workers elaborated extensively on the Nationwide Anglia ad in ways which went well beyond its overt content. However, this was never going to bring them closer to the brand, as they associated it with distasteful values.

Finally, related to high levels of elaboration, the many detailed descriptions and interpretations of ads suggest that ads which informants found involving were retained in long-term memory. Indeed, informants sometimes referred to ads from 'years ago'. Even allowing for some distortion of the time periods involved, they frequently referred to ads which had long been superseded, such as the Levi's 'laundrette' ad from the mid-1980s. However, once again it should be noted that these were not necessarily related to brand information.

Individual acts

Advertising involvement sometimes seemed to draw the young adults into relationships with brands in the form of trial, repurchase or loyalty. Thus, a female worker attributed her brand loyalty to Maxell tapes to an ad which she had seen years before, and still considered her 'favourite'. Others had similar stories to tell about buying Guinness after seeing the Rutger Hauer ads. In many other cases, however, the young adults' involvement with ads and brands seemed completely independent. They frequently expressed involvement with ads for brands or products which they would never consider buying. Indeed, the brand was sometimes thought to intrude on or distract from the elements of an ad which informants found involving. In an ad for Flake chocolate bars, for example,

> A telephone's ringing constantly through it … I think that's quite annoying – 'Answer it!' You do get frustrated waiting for her to pick up the 'phone. You want to know who's on the other end, waiting for her, and she's eating the Flake!
>
> (female worker 18–20)

Thus, not surprisingly, informants commonly referred to acts which did not relate to the brand, such as reading articles or watching television programmes about advertising. There were also many references to 'watching out' for particular ads, and of physically stopping or sitting to look at them.

You've got to sit and watch until the end till you know what they're selling. You can't sort of leave halfway through and say 'Oh well'. You actually sit there glued to the screen.

(female worker 18–20)

Although marketers may be encouraged by such diligence, these instances seemed more to do with linking advertising codes and genres to product categories than with any interest in the particular brand being advertised. Among informants with access to video-recorders, there were various references to stopping the process of fast-forwarding to catch ads which they liked. A female worker had taped an ad for Togs nappies featuring humorous puppet characters, and she talked about how she would 'sit and watch the video of it'. Some students discussed how an automatic vending machine hit someone in an ad for Irn-Bru, a Scottish soft drink:

That bit at the end looks so sore when the guy goes to the machine [laughter].

The last time we seen it, it's classic, we just slow-motioned it down.

I've watched it on the video with the pause button.

(male students 18–20)

On some occasions, informants seemed to be involved with ads which they had not yet seen, but had heard about. This resulted in particular vigilance. For example, some had turned on the television at a particular (advertised!) time to see the next instalment of the Gold Blend campaign. In contrast, informants who were negatively involved talked about changing channels or even turning off the television to avoid ads which they hated:

That really nips my head. I've got to have the telly off when I see that.

(female worker 18–20)

Interpersonal acts

The consequences discussed above relate largely to individual thoughts and acts. Others were intrinsically interpersonal, relating quite clearly to the Ritson and Elliott category of literacy events. In some cases, involvement resulted in audience participation. For example, a student talked about how his flatmates would applaud when they saw a television ad featuring an attractive woman. An unemployed informant had been quite taken with the ads for Impulse body spray in which a man approaches an attractive female stranger in the street with some flowers, and is rewarded with a smile. Unfortunately, when he tried this approach with his hairdresser one day, 'it was dead embarrassing'. The female worker who had taped the television ad for Togs also referred to the bus shelter version:

with the baby standing on its head and the puppet, which has 'big news on the baby front'. I always laugh at that. I have that right on my roof above my bed because I think that it's really cool. My mum went 'Where did you get that from?' 'I found it'.

In fact, she later admitted that her sister's boyfriend misappropriated it from a bus-shelter for her. While this may seem to be taking advertising involvement to incredulous heights, this informant certainly knew the dimensions of the poster ('it's six foot by four foot'). Turning to more mundane consequences, talking to other people about ads emerged as the one of the most common consequences of advertising involvement. Such interactions were often characterised by playfulness and creativity on the part of the young adults, as they incorporated advertising jokes and catchphrases into their dealings with others. Other people's views and observations were frequently brought into the discussion, often indicating some involvement by these third parties:

> People at work have been talking about that a lot. They think that's great.
>
> (male worker 21–24)

> There's actually this woman appears in five different adverts. 'Cos my brother noticed her. She appears in the Galaxy adverts and adverts for Philips appliances and things like that.
>
> (female student 18–20)

While any aspect of any ad seemed a potential topic of conversation, informants generally thought they were most likely to talk about ads which were funny, new, 'different' or somehow controversial. Several people had discussed the Tennent's 'London' ad with friends, even telephoning people they knew who worked in London. Ads which were part of a big campaign or featured attractive models were also likely to be talked about, as were 'horrific', 'brilliant' or 'obscure' ads. Indeed, a male student had heard so much about the Levi's ads that he was thoroughly sick of them – before he had even seen them!

Antecedents of involvement

> You sit and take notice a bit more if you use the product or if it's of any relevance to you.
>
> (male worker 21–24)

Informants' advertising involvement sometimes suggested a level of prior brand or product involvement, as much of the literature would lead us to expect. As a corollary, dislike or disinterest regarding products sometimes seemed to carry through to ads. Thus, an informant talked about how she 'hated' the Oxo ads:

I hate the husband and I hate the woman. I just don't like the children. I hate Oxo, I think that's the problem. I don't like Oxo so I hate the advert.

(female student 21–24)

In many cases, it appeared that a lack of involvement with ads reflected the advertised product's lack of relevance to their own lives or experiences. Indeed, several people dismissed ads for furniture, carpets or electrical goods on that basis. While this may present product involvement as an antecedent of advertising involvement, that appeared to be a neither necessary nor sufficient condition. Furthermore, informants who expressed some form of product involvement did not restrict their comments about ads to overt brand arguments. In part, this reflects the focus on advertising dramas rather than lectures (Wells 1989) in the discussions. Such ads cannot be broken down easily into 'central' and 'peripheral' cues: brand attribute information was often inferred from advertising elements such as music or visual images. As several informants pointed out, goods and services aimed at them tended to use advertising images, music and styles which appealed to them. Similarly, ads not aimed at young adults often used approaches which did not appeal to them, leading to a lack of involvement. Thus, advertising tended to be consumed in a much more holistic manner than the involvement literature suggests.

In general, it seemed to be what informants brought to their encounters with ads, rather than the ads themselves, which led to their involvement. In some cases, this took the form of prior interest in the brand, but this was just one of many factors shaping involvement with ads. For example, one student seemed quite involved with advertising in general. She described how she had been asked to discuss a magazine ad during an English class at school:

And I never thought about adverts until then. Like I got really interested. Like it was a trifle in a fridge. But it went on about this celestial delight. I mean how a trifle in a fridge can be a celestial delight. And it had this sort of golden glow to it. I got really into it – golden glow, celestial, sort of heavenly thing ... and then after that ... I do think about adverts quite a lot.

(female student 18–20)

Thus, it was not the ad in itself which led to involvement, but the experience of being directed to examine it. This experience might reasonably be termed an antecedent of her involvement with advertising. As discussed earlier, however, involvement may be experienced cognitively, emotionally, hedonically and in relation to personal values or experiences. The antecedents of these dimensions seem to exist in people's own lives – their values and experiences, their personal, product and media relationships, and their general likes and dislikes. Thus, many of the informants who were involved with the Tennent's ad had friends in exile, and they brought this experience with them to their viewing of that ad. For the male graduates who were negatively involved with the Nationwide Anglia ad, the antecedents may be explained in terms of their own values, experiences and expectations. This offers further support for views of advertising audiences as socially and culturally situated, negotiating the meanings of ads through their own social actions, life histories, themes and projects. It also indicates that a socially situated examination of advertising uses and gratifications may help us to understand the factors motivating such negotiations (O'Donohoe 1994b).

CONCLUSIONS

Scott (1994: 478) calls for research linking 'the way we think about advertising in our work to the way we know it in our lives'. This chapter has attempted to do this for the concept of advertising involvement, considering how we may 'put consumer experience back into consumer research' (Thompson *et al.* 1989) in this area. Reviewing prior studies of involvement and advertising, it pointed to the conceptual confusion pervading the literature. It also argued that the psychological, positivistic and experimental orthodoxy has prevented consumers from expressing what involvement with ads and advertising might mean to them. The chapter located such concerns in the context of work in consumption, media, literary and literacy studies which highlights the active, meaningful and socially situated nature of consumption. Some research approaches which could accommodate such insights were discussed. Finally, a study conducted in the tradition of audience ethnography was discussed to indicate the richness of accounts which consumers could provide of advertising involvement.

The study demonstrates the active, sophisticated and socially situated relationships which constituted young adults' involvement with ads and advertising. Such relationships were seen as 'creative composites' of five dimensions: personal experiences, personal values, cognitions, emotions and hedonism. Such dimensions are not new to the consumer research literature on involvement, but this chapter has focused on 'showing' rather than 'telling', so that the depth and richness of consumer experiences which they imply may be understood. Various consequences of advertising involvement were also identified. Internal consequences related to the degree of message elaboration undertaken. High levels of elaboration, however, were not necessarily directed towards overt brand information, or even integrated with brand attitudes. Individual consequences of advertising involvement sometimes took the form of brand trial, purchase or even loyalty. More common, however, were activities such as offering ads undivided attention or actively seeking them out. Interpersonal consequences of involvement centred on talking about ads to others. The antecedents of advertising involvement sometimes appeared to be prior brand attitudes or product involvement. However, these were neither a necessary nor sufficient condition for advertising involvement. In general, its antecedents appear to reside in individual informants – in their personal life histories, life themes and life projects, as Mick and Buhl (1992) have argued. These factors certainly seemed to facilitate involvement with ads. Given the active and discriminating nature of the young adults' advertising encounters, however, an understanding of factors motivating advertising involvement is also required. Here, uses and gratifications theory offers a useful framework, and serves to emphasise the active and independent nature of the young adults' advertising consumption.

Presumably, practitioners would be gratified that young adults can be so involved with ads and advertising. Furthermore, informants reported many conversations with other people about ads, highlighting the potential contribution of word-of-mouth communications to advertising campaigns. Practitioners may wish to consider ways of further stimulating and managing such activity. Integrated communications campaigns which require novel forms of consumer participation may be one way forward here. For example, the 'beautiful people' campaign for Martini invited consumers to audition for roles in the television ads. Furthermore, consumers sending in photographs of themselves received T-shirts which reproduced their image with text to the effect that they were not quite beautiful enough to drink Martini! The extent of involvement with ad elements and characters, and the young adults' proficiency in decoding these, indicate the importance of creative approaches which do more than make overt brand claims; such so-called 'peripheral' elements may be central to a brand's positioning strategy, for example. However, as we have seen, the relationship between advertising involvement and brand involvement or choice was often complex and tenuous, if it existed at all.

These findings offer further support to those emphasising the holistic and socially situated nature of consumer behaviour. Conceptualisations of advertising involvement which restrict themselves to issues of brand choice miss a vital and vibrant part of everyday advertising consumption. Indeed, the independent consumption of ads and brands observed in this study suggests that advertising is a site with great potential for exploring consumption practices which are consummatory rather than instrumental (Millar and Tesser 1990). Holbrook (1985) for one has argued that if consumer behaviour is to be understood, theory and research should serve the discipline as well as managerial interests. Addressing consummatory aspects of advertising consumption seems a useful way of advancing this project. It is hoped that this chapter will encourage others to do so, and to broaden the range of methods used in researching advertising consumption and involvement. It is time for consumers to slip out of the semiotic strait-jacket of experimental studies, into something more comfortable and amenable to the study of advertising meanings.

ACKNOWLEDGEMENTS

The authors are grateful to Robert Grafton-Small for helpful comments on an earlier version of this chapter. The first author also thanks the Nuffield Foundation and the University of Edinburgh's Faculty of Social Sciences for funding of the fieldwork.

REFERENCES

Andrews, J.C. and Durvasula, S. (1991) 'Suggestions for manipulating involvement in an advertising message context', in R. Holman and M.R. Solomon (eds) *Advances in Consumer Research*, 18, Provo, UT: Association for Consumer Research, 194–201.

——,—— and Akhter, S.H. (1990) 'A framework for conceptualizing and measuring the involvement construct in advertising research', *Journal of Advertising*, 19, 4: 27–40.

Ang, I. (1991) *Desperately Seeking the Audience*, London: Routledge.

Antil, J.H. (1984) 'Conceptualisation and operationalization of involvement', in T.C. Kinnear (ed.) *Advances in Consumer Research*, 11, Provo, UT: Association for Consumer Research, 203–209.

Appleyard, J.A. (1991*) Becoming a Reader: The Experience of Fiction from Childhood to Adulthood*, Cambridge: Cambridge University Press.

Baker, W.E. and Lutz, R.J. (1987) 'The relevance-accessibility model of advertising effectiveness', in S. Hecker and D.W. Stewart (eds) *Nonverbal Communication in Advertising*, Lexington, MA: Lexington Books, 59–84.

Barthes, R. (1975) *The Pleasure of the Text*, New York: Hill & Wang.

—— (1977a [1964]) 'Rhetoric of the image', *Image, Music, Text*, London: Fontana, 32–51.

—— (1977b [1971]) 'From work to text', *Image, Music, Text*, London: Fontana, 155–164.

Batra, R. and Ray, M.L. (1983) 'Operationalizing involvement as depth and quality of cognitive response', in R. Bagozzi and A. Tybout (eds) *Advances in Consumer Research*, 10, Ann Arbor, MI: Association for Consumer Research, 309–313.

Belk, R. (1995a) 'An uninvolving look at consumer involvement', *Irish Marketing Review*, 8, 146–148.

—— (1995b) 'Studies in the new consumer behaviour', in D. Miller (ed.) *Acknowledging Consumption: A Review of New Studies*, London: Routledge, 58–95.

Boller, G.W. and Olson, J.C. (1991) 'Experiencing ad meanings: crucial aspects of narrative/drama processing', in R.H. Holman and M.R. Solomon (eds) *Advances in Consumer Research*, 18, Provo, UT: Association for Consumer Research, 172–175.

Brown, S. (1993) 'Postmodern marketing?', *European Journal of Marketing*, 27, 4: 19–34.

Buckingham, D. (1987) *Public Secrets: EastEnders and its Audience*, London: British Film Institute.

Buttle, F. (1991) 'What do people do with advertising?', *International Journal of Advertising*, 10, 2: 95–110.

Cole, C., Ettenson, R., Reinke, S. and Schrader, T. (1990) 'The elaboration likelihood model (ELM): replications, extensions and some conflicting findings', in R. Pollay and G.J. Gorn (eds) *Advances in Consumer Research*, 17, Provo, UT: Association for Consumer Research, 231–236.

Cook, G. (1992) *The Discourse of Advertising*, London: Routledge.

Costley, C. (1988) 'Meta analysis of involvement research', in M.J. Houston (ed.) *Advances in Consumer Research*, 15, Provo, UT: Association for Consumer Research, 554–562.

Curran, J. (1990) 'The new revisionism in mass communication research: a re-appraisal', *European Journal of Communication*, 5: 135–164.

Elliott, R. and Ritson, M. (1995) 'Practising existential consumption: the lived meaning of sexuality in advertising', in F. Kardes and M. Sujan (eds) *Advances in Consumer Research*, 22, Provo, UT: Association for Consumer Research.

Evans, W.A. (1990) 'The interpretive turn in media research: innovation, iteration, or illusion?', *Critical Studies in Mass Communication*, 7, 2: 147–168.

Fiske, J. (1994) 'Television pleasures', in D. Graddol and O. Boyd-Barrett (eds) *Media Texts, Authors and Readers*, Clevedon: Multilingual Matters and Open University, 239–255.

Gabriel, Y. and Lang, T. (1995) *The Unmanageable Consumer: Contemporary Consumption and its Fragmentations*, London: Sage.

Geertz, C. (1973) *The Interpretation of Cultures*, New York: Basic Books.

Gerbner, G., Gross, L., Morgan, M. and Signorelli, N. (1980) 'The mainstreaming of America', *Journal of Communication*, 30: 10–29.

Glaser, B. and Strauss, A. (1967) *The Discovery of Grounded Theory*, Chicago: Aldine.

Grafton-Small, R. and Linstead, S. (1989) 'Advertisements as artefacts: everyday understanding and the creative consumer', *International Journal of Advertising*, 8, 3: 205–218.

Greenwald, A.G. and Leavitt, C. (1984) 'Audience involvement in advertising: four levels', *Journal of Consumer Research*, 11, June: 581–582.

Hammersley, M. and Atkinson, P. (1995) *Ethnography: Principles and Practice*, London: Routledge.

Holbrook, M. (1985) 'Why business is bad for consumer research', in E.C. Hirschman and M. Holbrook (eds) *Advances in Consumer Research*, 12, Ann Arbor, MI: Association for Consumer Research, 145–156.

—— and Batra, R. (1987) 'Assessing the role of emotions as mediators of consumer response to advertising', *Journal of Consumer Research*, 14, December: 444–456.

Horton, D. and Wohl, R. (1956) 'Mass communication and para-social interaction', *Psychiatry*, 19: 215–229.

Jenkins, H. (1992) *Textual Poachers: Television Fans and Participatory Culture*, London: Routledge.

Johar, G.V. (1995) 'Consumer involvement and deception from implied advertising claims', *Journal of Marketing Research*, 32, August: 267–279.

Kover, A.J. (1995) 'Copywriters' implicit theories of communication: an exploration', *Journal of Consumer Research*, 21, March: 596–611.

Krugman, H. (1965) 'The impact of television advertising: learning without involvement', *Public Opinion Quarterly*, 29, Fall: 349–356.

Laaksonen, P. (1994) *Consumer Involvement: Concepts and Research*, London: Routledge.

Lastovicka, J. and Gardner, D. (1979) 'Components of involvement', in J. Maloney and B. Silverman (eds) *Attitude Research Plays for High Stakes*, Chicago: American Marketing Association, 53–73.

Laurent, G. and Kapferer, J. (1985) 'Measuring consumer involvement profiles', *Journal of Marketing Research*, 22: 41–53.

Leiss, W., Kline, S. and Jhally, S. (1990) *Social Communication in Advertising*, London, Routledge.

Lindlof, T. (ed.) (1987) *Natural Audiences: Qualitative Research of Media Uses and Effects*, Norwood, NJ: Ablex.

Lull, J. (1987) 'Audience texts and contexts', *Critical Studies in Mass Communication*, 4, 1: 318–322.

Lunt, P. and Livingstone, S. (1996) 'Rethinking the focus group in media and communications research', *Journal of Communication*, 46, 2: 79–98.

McCracken, G. (1987) 'Advertising: meaning or information?', in M. Wallendorf and P. Anderson (eds) *Advances in Consumer Research*, 14, Provo, UT: Association for Consumer Research, 121–124.

MacInnis, D.J. and Jaworski, B.J. (1989) 'Information processing from advertisements: toward an integrative framework', *Journal of Marketing*, 53, October: 1–23.

Mick, D.G. (1992) 'Levels of subjective comprehension in advertising processing and their relations to ad perceptions, attitudes and memory', *Journal of Consumer Research*, 18, March: 411–424.

—— and Buhl, C. (1992) 'A meaning-based model of advertising experiences', *Journal of Consumer Research*, 19, December: 317–338.

Millar, M. and Tesser, A. (1990) 'Attitudes and behaviour: the cognitive-affective mismatch hypothesis', in M. Goldberg, G. Gorn and R. Pollay (eds) *Advances in Consumer Research*, 17, Provo, UT: Association for Consumer Research, 86–89.

Miller, D. (1995) 'Consumption as the vanguard of history', in D. Miller (ed.) *Acknowledging Consumption: A Review of New Studies*, London: Routledge.

Moores, S. (1993) *Interpreting Audiences: The Ethnography of Media Consumption*, London: Sage.

Morley, D. (1995) 'Theories of consumption in media studies', in D. Miller (ed.) *Acknowledging Consumption: A Review of New Studies*, London: Routledge, 296–328.

Muehling, D.D., Stoltman, J.J. and Mishra, S. (1990) 'An examination of the cognitive antecedents of attitude-toward-the-ad', in J.H. Leigh and C.R. Martin (eds) *Current Issues and Research in Advertising*, 12, Michigan: Michigan Business School, 95–117.

Muhlbacher, H. (1986) 'An involvement model of advertising information acquisition and processing motivation', in K. Moller and M. Paltschik (eds) *Contemporary Research in Marketing*, Proceedings of the 15th Annual Conference of the European Marketing Academy, Helsinki: European Marketing Academy, 461–480.

Muncy, J.A. (1990) 'Involvement and perceived brand similarities/differences: the need for process oriented models', in M. Goldberg, G. Gorn and R. Pollay (eds) *Advances in Consumer Research*, 17, Provo, UT: Association for Consumer Research, 144–148.

Nell, V. (1988) *Lost in a Book: The Psychology of Reading for Pleasure*, New Haven, CT: Yale University Press.

O'Donohoe, S. (1992) 'Towards an understanding of advertising involvement?', in K. Grunert and D. Fulgede (eds) *Marketing for Europe: Marketing for the Future*, Proceedings of the European Marketing Academy Conference, Aarhus: European Marketing Academy, 905–924.

—— (1994a) 'Postmodern poachers: young adult experiences of advertising', unpublished PhD thesis, University of Edinburgh.

—— (1994b) 'Advertising uses and gratifications', *European Journal of Marketing*, 28, 10: 52–75.

O'Guinn, T. and Faber, R.J. (1991) 'Mass communication and consumer behavior', in T.S. Robertson and H.H. Kassarjian (eds) *Handbook of Consumer Behavior*, Englewood Cliffs, NJ: Prentice Hall, 349–400.

Park, C.W. and Mittal, B. (1985) 'A theory of involvement in consumer behavior: problems and issues', in J.N. Sheth (ed.) *Research in Consumer Behavior*, 1, Greenwich, CT: JAI Press, 201–231.

Park, J. and Hastak, M. (1996) 'Effects of involvement on on-line brand evalua-tions: a stronger test of the ELM', in F.R. Kardes and M. Sujan (eds) *Advances in Consumer Research*, 22, Provo, UT: Association for Consumer Research, 435–439.

Petty, R.E., Cacioppo, J.T. and Schumann, D. (1983) 'Central and peripheral routes to advertising effectiveness: the moderating role of involvement', *Journal of Consumer Research*, 10, September: 135–146.

——, Unnava, R. and Strathman, A.J. (1991) 'Theories of attitude change', in T.S. Robertson and H.H. Kassarjian (eds) *Handbook of Consumer Behavior.* Englewood Cliffs, NJ: Prentice Hall, 241–280.

Pieters, R., Rosbergen, E. and Hartog, M. (1996) 'Visual attention to advertising: the impact of motivation and repetition', in K. Corfman and J.G. Lynch (eds) *Advances in Consumer Research*, 23, Provo, UT: Association for Consumer Research, 242–248.

Poiesz, T. and de Bont, C. (1995) 'Do we need involvement to understand consumer behavior?', in F. Kardes and M. Sujan (eds) *Advances in Consumer Research*, 22, Provo, UT: Association for Consumer Research, 448–452.

Radway, J. (1988) 'Reception study: ethnography and the problems of dispersed audiences and nomadic subjects', *Cultural Studies*, 2, 3: 359–376.

Ray, M. (1973) 'Marketing communication and the Hierarchy-of-Effects', in P. Clarke (ed.) *New Models for Mass Communication Research*, Beverly Hills, CA: Sage, 147–176.

Ritchie, K. (1995) *Marketing to Generation X*, New York: Lexington Books.

Ritson, M. and Elliott, R. (1995a) 'A model of advertising literacy: the praxiology and co-creation of advertising meaning', in M. Bergadaa (ed.) *Proceedings of the European Marketing Academy Conference*, Paris, 1035–1054.

—— and —— (1995b) 'Advertising literacy and the social signification of cultural meaning', in F. Hansen (ed.) *European Advances in Consumer Research*, 2, Provo, UT: Association for Consumer Research, 113–117.

Robson, S. and Foster, A. (eds) (1989) *Qualitative Research in Action*, London: Edward Arnold.

Roscoe, J., Marshall, H. and Gleeson, K. (1995) 'The television audience: a recon-sideration of the taken-for-granted terms "active", "social" and "critical"', *European Journal of Communication*, 10, 1: 87–108.

Rothschild, M. and Houston, M.J. (1977) 'The consumer involvement matrix: some preliminary findings', in B. Greenberg and D. Bellenger (eds) *Contemporary Marketing Thought*, Chicago: American Marketing Association, 95–98.

Sahlins, M. (1976) *Culture and Practical Reason*, Chicago: University of Chicago Press.

Schneider, K.C. and Rodgers, W.C. (1996) 'An "importance" subscale for the Consumer Involvement Profile', in K.P. Corfman and J.G. Lynch (eds) *Advances in Consumer Research*, 23, Provo, UT: Association for Consumer Research, 249–254.

Scholes, R. (1989) *Protocols of Reading*, New Haven, CT: Yale University Press.

Schroder, K. (1987) 'Convergence of antagonistic traditions?', *European Journal of Communications*, 2: 14.

Scott, L.M. (1994) 'The bridge from text to mind: adapting reader-response theory to consumer research', *Journal of Consumer Research*, 21, December: 461–480.

Seaman, W.R. (1992) 'Active audience theory: pointless populism', *Media, Culture and Society*, 14: 301–311.

Sherry, J.F. (1991) 'Postmodern alternatives: the interpretive turn in consumer research', in T.S. Robertson and H.H. Kassarjian (eds) *Handbook of Consumer Behavior*, Englewood Cliffs, NJ: Prentice Hall, 548–591.

Shimp, T.A. (1981) 'Attitude toward the ad as a mediator of consumer brand choice', *Journal of Advertising*, 10, 2: 9–15.

Spradley, J.P. (1979) *The Ethnographic Interview*, New York: Holt, Rinehart & Winston.

Storey, J. (1993) *An Introductory Guide to Cultural Theory and Popular Culture*, New York: Harvester Wheatsheaf.

Tavassoli, N.T., Schultz, C.J. and Fitzsimons, G.J. (1995) 'Program involvement: are moderate levels best for ad memory and attitude toward the ad?', *Journal of Advertising Research*, September–October: 61–72.

Thompson, C., Locander, W. and Pollio, H. (1989) 'Putting consumer experience back into consumer research: the philosophy and method of existential-phenomenology', *Journal of Consumer Research*, 16, September: 133–145.

——,—— and —— (1990) 'The lived meaning of free choice: an existential-phenomenological description of everyday consumer experiences of contemporary married women', *Journal of Consumer Research*, 17, December: 346–361.

——,—— and —— (1994) 'The spoken and unspoken: a hermeneutic approach to understanding the cultural viewpoints that underlie consumers' expressed meanings', *Journal of Consumer Research*, 21, December: 432–452.

Thorson, E. (1990) 'Consumer processing of advertising', in J.H. Leigh and C.R. Martin (eds) *Current Issues and Research in Advertising*, 12, Michigan: Michigan Business School, 197–230.

Tyebjee, T.T. (1979) 'Refinement of the involvement concept: an advertising planning point of view', in J. Maloney and B. Silverman (eds) *Attitude Research Plays for High Stakes*, Chicago: American Marketing Association, 94–111.

Wells, W.D. (1989) 'Lectures and dramas', in P. Cafferata and A.M. Tybout (eds) *Cognitive and Affective Responses to Advertising*, Lexington, MA: Lexington Books, 13–20.

Williamson, J. (1978) *Decoding Advertisements*, London: Marion Boyars.

Willis, P. (1990) *Common Culture*, Milton Keynes: Open University Press.

Zaichkowsky, J. (1985) 'Measuring the involvement construct', *Journal of Consumer Research*, 12, December: 341–352.

—— (1986) 'Conceptualizing involvement', *Journal of Advertising*, 15, 2: 4–14, 34.

8 Semiotics in marketing and consumer research

Balderdash, verity, pleas

David Glen Mick

INTRODUCTION

Semiotics is one of those distinctly arcane words that academics and consultants enjoy uttering. So effortlessly it conjures up a virtual *terre haute* of philosophical insights about human nature and society. Say it slowly and it spins off the tongue, glazes the eyes, and expands the mind. To where, one is often unsure.

My courtship with semiotics started in the early 1980s as I sought to explore her implications for marketing and consumer behaviour. At different times she has been profound, vacuous, intoxicating, solemn, demanding, common-sensical and baffling. As this chapter indicates, our love–hate affair lives on.

Since the mid-1980s, conference activities and publications on semiotics and marketing have swelled worldwide (e.g. Aoki 1988; Grandi 1994; Holbrook and Hirschman 1993; *International Journal of Research in Marketing* 1988, vol. 4, nos. 3 and 4; Larsen *et al.* 1991; Mick 1986, 1988; Umiker-Sebeok 1987a; Vihma 1990). Concomitantly, several fictions about semiotics have spread throughout the marketing field, some of which, *mea culpa*, I may be partially responsible for. For instance, consider the following terms, and ask yourself: which among them do you think semiotics should be equated with or, at least, strongly associated with?

- semiology
- structuralism
- post-structuralism
- semantics
- symbolism
- subconscious meaning(s)
- analytic (Freudian) psychology
- postmodernism
- post-positivism
- theory
- science

- method
- qualitative-interpretive analysis

Balderdash! As I outline in this chapter, there is convincing evidence that semiotics should not be interchanged with or strongly associated with any of these terms or concepts.

Since this chapter is not a tutorial, for conciseness I assume that the reader has already been exposed to the basics of semiotics (if not, see Deely 1990; Fiske 1982; Innis 1985; Mick 1986; Sebeok 1976, 1994). Also, during the ensuing discussion of misconceptions about semiotics, I have avoided referencing specific authors in marketing and consumer research because doing so would serve no effect but petty embarrassment (of myself included!). Nonetheless, in addressing the issues in general terms, my hope is to encourage marketing and consumer researchers toward a more refined and more accurate use of semiotics. I conclude this chapter with commentary on my beliefs about the core verity of semiotics and some simple pleas to those who may implement semiotics in future research.

FOUNDATIONS

Etymologically, the term 'semiotics' originates from the Greek words for sign and signal. Although a number of philosophers during the Middle Ages and the Renaissance remarked on semiotics to varying degrees (e.g. St Augustine, Poinsot, Vico, Locke), it is principally associated with scholarly developments at the turn of the twentieth century by two independent scholars. The prominent Swiss linguist F. de Saussure (1916) referred to it as semiologie (spelled in English as semiology), while the American philosopher C.S. Peirce (1935–66) tended to refer to it as semiotic (without the 's' on the end). Other competing but less commonly used terms have included semasiology, sematology and sensifics. How it has come today to be called semiotics by most leading authorities worldwide, but still resisted by others, is a fascinating topic unto itself, but outside the purview of this chapter (see Deely 1990; Nöth 1990).

Multiple definitions of semiotics exist (Pelc 1981). For consistency, I shall use the term semiotics broadly, to refer to any study of communication that uses the concept of the sign as its fundamental unit (see also Eco 1976; Sebeok 1976). Saussure, who was solely interested in language, maintained a bilateral model of the sign, consisting of the signifier (a spoken word) and the signified (the concept or thought which the spoken word refers to). A sign, according to Peirce's more comprehensive perspective, is anything that can stand for something else to an animate being (i.e. an interpreter) in some context. Since everything is capable of standing for something else, everything is capable of being a sign. Examples of signs in the consumer world are everywhere a person wishes to look, listen, smell, feel or taste: brand names and logos; lyrics, melodies and tempos in music; deodorants and perfumes; wool sweaters and silk pillows; pizza and whisky; and so on, ad infinitum. What do these signs stand for? Meanings of all kinds, some of which are widely shared, while others are more specific to given subcultures, households or individuals. For instance, the Marlboro cowboy partly stands for American culture, independence and self-reliance, but may also stand for rebellion, chauvinism, fatalism, ill-health or the genocide of Native American Indians, depending on the communication context and the particular interpreter. The communication of meaning(s) through signs is often referred to as semiosis. It is fruitfully understood, as implicated in the example of the Marlboro man, according to Peirce's (1935–66) model of semiosis which involves three indissoluble components: a sign, its object and its interpretant.

Pinpointing the introduction of semiotics to marketing and consumer research is difficult, occurring at least by the early 1970s in Europe and shortly afterwards in North America and Asia (see discussions by Mick 1986, 1988; Pinson 1988, 1993; Umiker-Sebeok 1987b). As suggested earlier, the application of semiotics in marketing and consumer research has since burgeoned across the world. Unfortunately, the wide-ranging and rapid growth of applications has also led to a number of continuing misconceptions about semiotics that threaten to turn this emerging spire of insights into another tower of Babel.

A LITANY OF BALDERDASH

The first, and perhaps most pernicious, balderdash is that semiotics is a consolidated field of ideas about signs and semiosis. In truth, one must be very cautious in using the term semiotics, as if to suggest that it is unified. Casual use of the term leads to the implication that most semioticians agree about such things as the nature of signs, their numbers and varieties, their operations, and so on. In fact, there is considerable divergence even about essential issues, including the definition of semiotic concepts such as sign, symbol and code. While these disagreements make semiotics appear chaotic, the situation is only exacerbated by the one-term-fits-all mentality when the word semiotics is used without qualification or further specification. (For those readers already feeling dubious about semiotics and for whom this first balderdash deserves ample snickering, you might wish to check your self-righteousness at the door before entering the central domains of marketing, psychology and anthropology, for example, where widely accepted definitions of foundational concepts are similarly elusive.)

In semiotics there exist several traditions, most of which trace their lineage either to Saussure (semiology) or Peirce (semiotic). Not only are these two forefathers and their philosophies vastly different, their progeny are quite varied as well (e.g. Barthes, Eco, Jakobson, Morris, Sebeok). In addition, it is quite misleading to assume that the Saussurean and Peircean distinction maps onto the Atlantic divide between North America and Europe. In fact, renowned American scholars have drawn heavily from Saussure (e.g. Jonathan Culler), while eminent European scholars have done the same with respect to Peirce (e.g. Umberto Eco).

Another common balderdash is that semiotics is equivalent to structuralism. Slightly less onerous is the belief that semiotics is mostly concerned with structural issues. It is certainly true that the organisation of marketing signs (e.g. words and pictures in an advertisement) is pre-governed by cultural conventions (rules) whose identification and elaboration are crucial to understanding semiosis. But semiotics is not strictly focused on structural issues in communication (see e.g. Sebeok's 1984 fiery emphasis of this same point). Indeed, semiotics is more expansive than structuralism (Deely 1990). For example, semiotics also addresses the different processes (e.g. induction, deduction, abduction) and reactions (e.g. types of interpretants) that consumers evoke when confronting marketing signs. If semiotics is not structuralism in disguise, then perhaps semiotics is similar to post-structuralism. This too, however, is a slippery connection. In the first place, many of the major post-structuralists such as Derrida and Foucault still concentrate so intensely on structural issues that one observer has referred to them as superstructuralists (Harland 1987). On the other hand, some post-structuralists deny any affinity or interest in semiotics. Hence, while structural relationships among signs in a given system, or within a given message, are tantamount to communication and meaning, structural issues are only one aspect of semiotics *per se.*

Another balderdash is that semiotics is synonymous with semantics. In fact, semantics is usually characterised as the study of the relation between signs and their objects. Since semiotics also considers the relations of signs to other signs (syntactics or structural issues) and the relations of signs to their interpretants (pragmatics), it is wrongly delimiting to associate semiotics narrowly with semantics.

A related balderdash and another gross simplification is that semiotics is chiefly concerned with symbolism or symbolic meaning. In fact, symbolism is only one of many possible sign–object relations within the study of semantics. Saussure, the linguist, emphasised that the relationship between words and their referents is arbitrary. For instance, the word 'dog', which English speakers use to refer to a four-legged carnivorous animal that is commonly kept as a pet or hunting aide, could just as well be replaced by the word 'zog' to refer to the same category of animate beings. This characteristic of arbitrariness is thought-provoking, particularly when one begins observing all the other things that serve as signifiers that have strictly arbitrary relationships with their signifieds. In fact, the meaning of nearly every socio-cultural artefact or event (material or otherwise) seems to be constructed from mere human agreement, including marketing and consumer phenomena such as jewellery, clothing, television programmes, books, beer, cigars, computers, discos and football. Since the early 1970s there have been numerous efforts to analyse the complex, subtle, and arbitrary meanings of marketing stimuli and consumption. These studies represent some of the most fertile and provocative insights produced from a semiotic perspective. One of the earliest and most widely known analysts in this genre of semiotic research is, of course, Roland Barthes. Dozens of others have followed closely in his footsteps.

Unfortunately, the rise and predominance of symbolism analysis under the rubric of semiotics has led many writers to use the terms interchangeably. This is doubly bothersome since, in addition, the word symbol is arguably the most abused semiotic term, having been subjected to 'unjustifiably excessive generalization and overly broad application' (Sebeok 1994: 34). Eco's (1986) historical and philosophical examination of the symbol concept underscores Sebeok's indictment. But as Peirce and other semioticians have argued, the relationship between sign and object (i.e. semantics) can take many forms. Only one of these is characterised in terms of arbitrariness, that being the relationship which should be properly called symbolic. In fact, Peirce maintained that there were sixty-six different types of sign–object relations and many of these apply to non-linguistic signs. Two of the other most commonly acknowledged sign–object relations are iconic (based on similarity or likeness) and indexical (based on causality or other existential connection). Thus, even though symbolism is a crucial and inescapable aspect of semiosis in marketing and consumer behaviour, it is inauspicious and misleading that 1/66 of sign–object relations has come to be equated by some researchers with the whole of the semiotic field.

Yet another occasional balderdash is that semiotics is chiefly concerned with hidden or subconscious meanings. This belief implies that semiotics and analytic (Freudian) psychology are similar or equivalent. In twentieth-century semiotics there certainly have been some significant psychoanalytic semioticians, chief among them being Jacques Lacan and Julia Kristeva. However, meanings as communicated by signs exist at multiple levels. While many researchers exhibit an inherent bias toward looking for 'deeper', less obvious meanings in every phenomenon, 'surface' meanings can be (and often are) more influential and determinant in everyday communicative acts. A realistic and comprehensive view of semiotics acknowledges multiple levels of meaning.

A recent and growing balderdash maintains that semiotics is elemental to postmodernism. Brown (1995) has done an admirable job in previously unveiling this misconception, though not necessarily for the same reasons I would. Among other things, postmodernism is associated with the idea that meanings are profuse, indeterminate and provisional in the interpretation of virtually anything. If one primarily associates semiotics with semiology or structuralism (as Brown tends to do), then one is drawn to the conclusion that semiotics is not postmodern because semiology and structuralism have together fostered the view that meaning is imminent in, and determined by, fixed codes that predicate the selection of signs and their combination in a given message. However, the Peircean approach to semiotics admits the possibility of an infinite regress of interpretations of signs, an idea that is actually substantial to postmodernism. As Partmentier (1994) writes,

> Peirce offers the possibility that meaning is more than an operation of mental decoding, since semiosis is an open-ended process in which each moment of interpretation alters the field for subsequent interpretations. In contrast, Saussure's theory focuses on the preestablished, fixed code shared equally by ideal speaker and ideal hearer.
>
> (Partmentier 1994: xiii)

Nonetheless, semiotics is not necessarily postmodern because it is just as readily applicable to messages in which meanings are not blatantly underdetermined or wildly multifarious. For example, consider simple marketing slogans such as 'Come Shop at Wagner's Supermarket' or 'Introducing the New Manna Portable Computer' to which semiotics could be applied to analyse the process and content of their meanings (see also Johansen's (1993: ch. 8) thorough semiotic analysis of the traffic light system). There is nothing inherent to semiotics that prevents it from addressing the four Ps of postmodernism (Brown 1995), namely paradox, profusion, plurivalence and polysemy. Equally, however, there is nothing incorrect about semiotics addressing simplicity, scarcity, monovalence and singularity in marketplace meanings. As such, semiotics is not necessarily postmodern.

Akin to the previous balderdash is the claim or implication that semiotics is conterminous with post-positivism. Generally speaking, postpositivists maintain that multiple realities exist which are social constructed; the goal of research is understanding; and the knowledge gained from research is time-bound and context-dependent. Alternatively, positivistic researchers tend to believe that reality is singular, objective and tangible; the goal of research is explanation; and the knowledge gained is time-free and context-independent. In terms of epistemological foundations, it actually appears that many semioticians are situated between the positivist and post-positivist poles (see Figure 8.1).

Positivists tend to be realists who assume that the human mind is independent of the physical world and that people have direct, unmediated

Positivist view:	individual ⟶ reality	= realism
Semiotic view:	individual ⟷ signs ⟷ reality	= representationalism
Post-positivist view:	individual ⟶ sense data	= phenomenalism

Figure 8.1   Three epistemologies

contact with reality. This hard-core realist position is, of course, thoroughly rejected by most semioticians (e.g. Deely 1990; Sebeok 1994). Instead, they adhere to idealism to varying degrees (Savan 1983). Radical idealism assumes that people have contact only with sense data, behind which no independent reality exists. Sometimes this epistemological stance is called phenomenalism. The moderate form of semiotic idealism maintains that our most immediate contact is with sense data (signs) that are inter-dependent with a definitive reality, though the linkages between signs and reality are poorly understood. This latter type of idealism is sometimes known as representationalism and it closely approximates the epistemo-logical position of many leading semioticians. Perhaps most noteworthy, Peirce was a representationalist in so far as he believed in the existence of an ultimate independent reality, but he also believed that human percep-tion was of signs only and that human beings use signs to construct their views of what that reality may be. Consequently, he concluded that 'the word or sign which humans use are the humans themselves' (Peirce 1868). As such, the semiotic-representationalist position actually accepts the real-ist supposition about a singular, objective reality, but it also emphasises that knowing reality is complicated by, perhaps prevented by, an inevitable reliance on sign perceptions, interpretations, and use.

Another repeated balderdash is that semiotics is a theory. The word theory, like semiotics itself, supplies an appearance of intellectualism wherever it turns up. When applied to a set of ideas, the word theory also suggests rigour, sophistication, generality and timelessness. But problems quickly begin when the user of the T-word does not define it. Not surpris-ingly (given the arbitrary nature of words), theory has been defined in many different ways. It is not uncommon, however, to find many philos-ophers of science characterising theory as Rudner (1966) does:

> A theory is a systematically related set of statements, including some lawlike generalizations, that is empirically testable. The purpose of theory is to increase scientific understanding through a systemized struc-ture capable of both explaining and predicting phenomena.
>
> (Rudner 1966: 10)

Thus, explanation and prediction are often considered crucial to estab-lishing a theory and empirically supporting it. Hempel (1965) suggests that the core of explanation is providing answers to 'why' questions. Answers to 'why' questions, according to many philosophers of science, should facilitate the ability to expect certain outcomes surrounding a given phenomenon, in view of specific antecedent conditions. In so far as expec-tation is similar to prediction, then explanation and prediction are highly related terms in the eyes of many philosophers of science.

If one accepts the preceding characterisations of theory, explanation and prediction, then it seems clear that semiotics is not a theory, despite Morris's (1938) and Eco's (1976) distinguished books with their arresting titles. For example, Eco (1976: 3) begins by asserting that 'a *general semiotic theory* [should be] able to explain every case of sign-function in terms of underlying systems of elements mutually correlated by one or more codes.' Note that Eco uses the notion of explanation in his definition of semiotics, though it is not clear that he equates explanation with prediction. Two pages later, however, Eco (1976: 5) asserts that 'A general semiotic theory will be considered powerful according to its capacity for offering an appropriate definition for every sort of sign function.' By using the notion of definition to further clarify what he means by theory, Eco seems to be adopting a view of theory in which explanation does not mean prediction, since defining something says nothing about its predictive association with something else. In fact, nowhere in Eco's work is there the unmistakable aim to use semiotic concepts and related premises to predict aspects of communication (e.g. comprehension, attitudes, specific meaning content). Overall, Morris's and Eco's works are definitional or descriptive of semiosis, and not at all explanatory in a predictive sense. According to many philosophers of science, definitions and descriptions alone are not sufficient to establish a theory. These comments should not be taken as criticism of Morris's or Eco's research, as their reputations for advancing semiotics are well earned and rightly guaranteed for scholastic history. However, semiotics has not achieved the status of theory as the word theory is often used in scientific or philosophical circles. Whether semiotics will one day be the kind of theory many philosophers of science have in mind remains to be seen. And let me be clear, I am not necessarily advocating that semiotics should strive to become a theory which is evaluated in terms of its predictive strength. I am simply saying that if one believes that explanation-as-prediction is essential to what constitutes a theory, then it is balderdash to call semiotics a theory.

Hence, marketing and consumer researchers who have tended to write the word theory in the neighbourhood of the word semiotics (e.g. 'semiotic theory') are creating false impressions. Searching such writings for the semblance of predictions about marketing or consumer behaviour that have followed solely from semiotics is generally fruitless. It is possible, nevertheless, to combine semiotics with theories and insights from the social sciences to derive predictions (for one of my attempts, see Mick 1991; Mick and DeMoss 1992). But combining semiotics with social science theories and findings is one thing, claiming or implying that semiotics is itself a theory is the B-word.

Another potential balderdash is that semiotics is a science, as in calling it 'the science of signs'. If the word science is used to mean 'the study of', then it is appropriate and correct to call semiotics a science. However, according to Buzzell (1963: 37), the word science is often used to indicate that a particular discipline has matured to the point where it is:

- a systematised corpus of knowledge
- organised according to central theories and principles

- typically characterised in quantitative terms
- able to make predictions and, under some circumstances, control future events.

Semiotics meets some of these criteria, but certainly not all. Some semioticians would say that these are criteria that semiotics should be neither concerned about nor aspiring to. Leaving that debate aside, there are some convincing indications that semiotics is not currently a science.

Yet another potential balderdash is the belief or implication that semiotics is a method. In the context of consumer research, the word method conjures up data collection techniques such as interviews, participant observations, surveys, simulations and experiments. Obviously, semiotics is not a method in the same sense as these techniques. Nonetheless, if one thinks of semiotics as a refined approach to understanding or interpreting the meaning(s) of some idea or phenomenon, then it might be properly said that semiotics includes special tools, techniques, or methods. For example, one of the most distinguished tools for analysing meaning is Greimas's Semiotic Square (see e.g. Floch 1988; Mick 1991; Verba and Camden 1987). It could also be said that Peirce's sixty-six distinctions among sign–object relations form a taxonomic technique for understanding meaning (semantics particularly). Nevertheless, marketing and consumer researchers must be cautious in writing phrases such as 'semiotic method' without specifying what is entailed by the combination of those words. In fact, there is no singular 'semiotic method' and, thereby, it is confusing to call semiotics a method.

Related to this latter balderdash is another that equates semiotics with qualitative data and interpretive analyses, juxtapositioned to quantitative data and statistical analyses. Here again, there is nothing inherent to Peirce, Saussure, Eco, Sebeok or most other major semioticians that necessitates qualitative-interpretive approaches to understanding semiosis. Granted, many applications of semiotics in marketing and consumer research have been based on qualitative data and interpretive analyses (see e.g. Bertrand 1988; Hirschman 1988; Holbrook and Grayson 1986; Mick and Buhl 1992). But there is nothing to prevent the use of quantitative-statistical analyses in semiotic research (see e.g. Kaiser *et al.* 1987) or the combination of qualitative and quantitative data in a semiotically-oriented project (see e.g. McQuarrie and Mick 1992). Not only is semiotics not a method generally, but also it is not implemented strictly through qualitative-interpretive approaches.

A MODICUM OF VERITY

With all this balderdash bantered about, what then is semiotics? Semiotics is a multi-traditioned, transdisciplinary doctrine. The notion that semiotics is a doctrine has been suggested by (Sebeok 1976) and supported by parallel assertions that semiotics is a point of view (Deely 1990) or framework (Deely *et al.* 1986). As a doctrine, semiotics incorporates a wide set of concepts, principles and tools for explicating communication and meaning.

First and foremost, semioticians believe in the primacy of signs and sign systems. Equally critical is their unwavering focus on the nature and variety of signs, sign systems, sign uses, sign interpretations and sign effects. Semioticians continue to ply their doctrine across numerous disciplines, from phytosemiotics, zoosemiotics and medical semiotics, to the semiotics of law and of marketing. Within and across the applications of semiotics in these disciplines, there exists a range of ontological, epistemological, theoretical and methodological positions.

The semiotic doctrine is not one that is fathomed quickly or characterised concisely. It is, therefore, not surprising that semiotics is often described or criticised in terms of spurious equivalences, associations or caricatures. A serious negative outcome is that those who read such claims and who know little about semiotics go on to adopt a narrow and fallacious understanding. Consumer researchers who have definitive interests in communication and meaning must recognise that the level of semiotic-oriented insights they produce is directly proportional to the dedication they give to learning about the fuller history and range of semiotic ideas and applications. Perhaps no one in recent years has done more to assist in this task than Winfried Nöth (1990) in his impressive *Handbook of Semiotics*.

PLEAS: LET US BE EXPLICIT, RIGOROUS, AUTHENTIC AND INCREMENTAL

Beyond the balderdash and verity of semiotics, I wish to offer some heartfelt pleas for future semiotic research in marketing and consumer behaviour. First, as intimated in the opening paragraphs, there is a troubling tendency on the part of marketing and consumer researchers to use terms such as semiotics or semiology in a flippant manner. Apparently many researchers believe that any time the topic of communication or meaning is being discussed, it is perfectly appropriate to drop in the word semiotics or semiology. Unfortunately, all too often these words are raised in marketing and consumer research without a reasonable discussion of which particular semiotic tradition or concepts the research is drawing on, and even sometimes without any accompanying references to major semioticians. In fact, there are published articles in marketing and consumer research in which the title or opening section includes the term semiotic or semiology, and the articles then proceed with no further visible connection to the doctrine. This would be the equivalent of writing an article on 'The Behaviourism of Consumer Behaviour' and never citing Skinner or Watson and never using any key behaviourism concepts (e.g. stimulus, response, conditioning or reinforcement). Unless consumer researchers are prepared to be more explicit in their use of semiotic principles and concepts – not just invoking the word for its mesmerising effect – then there is little hope that semiotics will achieve the value and respect it has earned in other disciplines and which it deserves in marketing and consumer behaviour.

Second, it is equally important that researchers strive for greater rigour in applying semiotics. All too often semiotic concepts and analytic approaches are not adequately clarified before their implementation. As a result, the value of using semiotics is ambiguous. Since many semiotic terms and tools have been characterised in different ways, it is incumbent upon researchers to apply them in a lucid and precise manner. Further rigour is achieved through stronger efforts to show that semiotic concepts and approaches are applicable across multiple persons, stimuli and/or conditions. That is, semiotic-related insights are strengthened to the extent that understanding of communication and meaning is facilitated across several exemplars within the focus of a given study (products, brands, ads, consumption events, etc.). In short, semiotic research is more rigorous when researchers attend intensely to both the internal and the external validity of their applications and contributions.

Third, much semiotic research has involved qualitative data and subjective text analysis. Certainly, there has been some strong semiotic research of this variety that relates to marketing and consumer behaviour, advertising particularly (see e.g. Bertrand 1988). However, most of this work does not involve actual data from consumers for the purposes of verifying, enhancing or modifying the conclusions reached through subjective text analyses. As a result, there is a gap of authenticity or relevance to pure text analysis findings (cf. Mick 1994; Schroder 1991). It would be quite valuable for marketing and consumer researchers who have interests in semiotics to make stronger efforts to combine their qualitative data and text analysis with managerial or consumer responses (e.g. through thought listings, verbal protocols, interviews, surveys or experiments). Currently, few semiotic projects have adopted this tactic (see e.g. McQuarrie and Mick 1992; Mick and Politi 1989).

A fourth plea is for semiotic consumer researchers to demonstrate more convincingly that the application of semiotics in their work has led to truly incremental insights. By incremental I do not mean small. By incremental I mean an unmistakable knowledge advance, something that adds to and/or changes prior beliefs about the focus in the given study (e.g. theory, methodology, substantive domain). In general, semiotic researchers across many disciplines have been too complacent about this issue. Reaching the end of their articles the reader is often hard pressed to know exactly what new knowledge has been learned through the exercise of semiotics' esoteric terminology or techniques. The knowledge base that marketing and consumer researchers must extend is most definitively established by reference to first-rate journals such as the *Journal of Consumer Research*, the *Journal of Marketing* or the *International Journal of Research in Marketing*. The application of semiotics must result in new theoretical, substantive or methodological insights in light of prior work in leading journals. If the research is about advertising, for example, then the reader must be clearly informed about the knowledge base the semiotic application is seeking to advance (e.g. insights about the structure of language or images; consumer processing of advertising language and images; the influence of surrounding editorial material on the meaning of advertisements). Without establishing the baseline of current knowledge, the promise and application of semiotics are not fulfilled.

CONCLUSION

Semiotics is one of the richest sources of principles, concepts and tools for studying communication and meaning. It is unfortunate and ironic that the doctrine which focuses on communication and meaning has been mired in miscomprehension and misrepresentation. My hope is that this chapter has made a small step toward rectifying these problems in marketing and consumer research.

REFERENCES

Aoki, S. (1988) 'Semiotics of significance in advertising text', *Studia Semiotica: Journal of the Japanese Association for Semiotic Studies*, 8: 249–264.

Bertrand, D. (1988) 'The creation of complicity: a semiotic analysis of an advertising campaign for Black and White whiskey', *International Journal of Research in Marketing*, 4, 4: 273–289.

Brown, S. (1995) *Postmodern Marketing*, London: Routledge.

Buzzell, R. D. (1963) 'Is marketing a science?', *Harvard Business Review* 41, January–February: 32–40, 166–170.

Deely, J. (1990) *Basics of Semiotics*, Bloomington, IN: Indiana University Press.

——, Williams, B. and Kruse, F.E. (eds) (1986) *Frontiers in Semiotics*, Bloomington, IN: Indiana University Press.

Eco, U. (1976) *A Theory of Semiotics*, Bloomington, IN: Indiana University Press.

—— (1986) 'On symbols', in J. Deely, B. Williams and F.E. Kruse (eds) *Frontiers in Semiotics*, Bloomington, IN: Indiana University Press.

Fiske, J.C. (1982) *Introduction to Communication Studies*, London: Methuen.

Floch, J.M. (1988) 'The contribution of structural semiotics to the design of a hypermarket', *International Journal of Research in Marketing*, 4, 4: 233–252.

Grandi, R. (1994) *Semiotica Al Marketing*, Milan: FrancoAngeli.

Harland, R. (1987) *Superstructuralism*, London: Methuen.

Hempel, C.G. (1965) 'Aspects of scientific explanation', in *Aspects of Scientific Explanation and Other Essays in the Philosophy of Science*, New York: Free Press.

Hirschman, E.C. (1988) 'The ideology of consumption: a structural-syntactic analysis of *Dallas* and *Dynasty*', *Journal of Consumer Research*, 15, December: 344–359.

Holbrook, M.B. and Grayson, M.W. (1986) 'The semiology of cinematic consumption: symbolic consumer behavior in *Out of Africa*', *Journal of Consumer Research*, 13, December: 374–381.

—— and Hirschman, E.C. (1993) *The Semiotics of Consumption: Interpreting Symbolic Consumer Behavior in Popular Culture and Works of Art*, New York: Mouton de Gruyter.

Innis, R.E. (1985) *Semiotics: An Introductory Anthropology*, Bloomington, IN: Indiana University Press.

Johansen, J.D. (1993) *Dialogic Semiosis: An Essay on Signs and Meaning*, Bloomington, IN: Indiana University Press.

Kaiser, S.B., Schutz, H.G. and Chandler, J.L. (1987) 'Cultural codes and sex role ideology: a study of shoes', *American Journal of Semiotics*, 5, 1: 13–33.

Larsen, H.H., Mick, D.G. and Alsted, C. (1991) *Marketing and Semiotics: Selected Papers from the Copenhagen Symposium*, Copenhagen: Handelshojskolens Forlag.

McQuarrie, E. and Mick, D.G. (1992) 'On resonance: a critical pluralistic inquiry into advertising rhetoric', *Journal of Consumer Research*, 19, September: 180–197.

Mick, D.G. (1986) 'Consumer research and semiotics: exploring the morphology of signs, symbols, and significance', *Journal of Consumer Research*, 13, September: 196–213.

—— (1988) 'Contributions to the semiotics of marketing and consumer behavior (1985–1988)', in T.A. Sebeok and J. Umiker-Sebeok (eds) *The Semiotic Web*, Berlin: Mouton de Gruyer.

—— (1991) 'Giving gifts to ourselves: a Greimassian analysis leading to testable propositions', in H.H. Larsen, D.G. Mick, and C. Alsted (eds) *Marketing and Semiotics: Selected Papers from the Copenhagen Symposium*, Copenhagen: Handelshojskolens Forlag, 142–159.

—— (1994) 'Per un' integrazione delle analisi semiotiche della pubblicita con i dati delle reazioni dei consumatori', in R. Grandi (ed.) *Semiotica al Marketing: Le Tendenze della Ricera nel Marketing, nel Consumo, nella Pubblicita*, Milan: FrancoAngeli.

—— and Buhl C. (1992) 'A meaning-based model of advertising experiences', *Journal of Consumer Research*, 19, December: 317–338.

—— and DeMoss M. (1992) 'Further findings on self-gifts: products, qualities, and sociodemographic correlates', in J.F. Sherry, Jr and B. Sternthal (eds) *Advances in Consumer Research*, 19, Provo, UT: Association for Consumer Research.

—— and Politi, L. (1989) 'Consumers' interpretations of advertising imagery: a visit to the hell of connotation', in E.C. Hirschman (ed.) *Interpretive Consumer Research*, Provo, UT: Association for Consumer Research, 85–96.

Morris, C. (1938) *Foundations of the Theory of Signs*, Chicago: University of Chicago Press.

Nöth, W. (1990) *Handbook of Semiotics*, Bloomington, IN: Indiana University Press.

Partmentier, R.J. (1994) *Signs in Society: Studies in Semiotic Anthropology*, Bloomington, IN: Indiana University Press.

Peirce, C.S. (1868) 'Some consequences of four incapabilities', *Journal of Speculative Philosophy*, 2: 140–151.

—— (1935–66) *Collected Papers*, C. Hartshorne, P. Weiss, and A.W. Burks (eds) Cambridge, MA: Harvard University Press.

Pelc, J. (1981) 'Theoretical foundations of semiotics', *American Journal of Semiotics*, 1: 15–45.

Pinson, C. (1988) 'Editorial', *International Journal of Research in Marketing*, 4, 3: 167–172.

—— (1993) 'Marketing: semiotics', in R.E. Asher (ed.) *The Encyclopedia of Language and Linguistics*, Oxford: Pergamon.

Rudner, R.S. (1966) *Philosophy of Social Science*, Englewood Cliffs, NJ: Prentice Hall.

Saussure, F. de (1916) *Cours de Linguistique Generale*, Wiesbaden: Otto Harrassowitz.

Savan, D. (1983) 'Toward a refutation of semiotic idealism', *Semiotic Inquiry* 3: 1–8.

Schroder, K. (1991) 'Marketing and semiotics as a challenge to critical semiotics', in H.H. Larsen, D.G. Mick, and C. Alsted (eds) *Marketing and Semiotics: Selected Papers from the Copenhagen Symposium*, Copenhagen: Handelshojskolens Forlag, 177–195.

Sebeok, T. (1976) *Contributions to the Doctrine of Signs*, Bloomington, IN: Indiana University Press.

—— (1984) 'Signs of life', *International Semiotic Spectrum*, 2, June: 1–2.

—— (1994) *Signs*, Toronto: University of Toronto Press.

Umiker-Sebeok, J. (ed.) (1987a) *Marketing and Semiotics: New Directions in the Study of Signs for Sale*, New York: Mouton de Gruyter.

—— (1987b) 'Preface', in J. Umiker-Sebeok (ed.) *Marketing and Semiotics: New Directions in the Study of Signs for Sale*, New York: Mouton de Gruyter, x–xii.

Verba, S. and Camden, C. (1987) 'Writing with flesh: a semiotic interpretation of research findings on body image attitudes and behaviors in the U.S.', in J. Umiker-Sebeok (ed.) *Marketing and Semiotics: New Directions in the Study of Signs for Sale*, New York: Mouton de Gruyter, 165–186.

Vihma, S. (ed.) (1990) *Semantic Visions in Design: Proceedings from the Symposium on Design Research and Semiotics*, Helsinki: Publications of the University of Industrial Arts.

9 Consumer rules

Gordon R. Foxall

PROEM

Dozens of consumer behaviour textbooks – every one bearing the stunningly original title, *Consumer Behaviour* (though not always correctly spelt) – scarcely mention consumers' *behaviour* at all. This is not, perhaps, because their authors think consumers' behaviour irrelevant. It is simply that the prevailing paradigm for consumer research emphasises the alleged pre-behavioural determinants of choice – the procedures theoretically implicated in human information processing which culminate in brand beliefs, brand attitudes and brand purchase intentions – almost to the exclusion of the observable activities of those who purchase and use, give and receive, accumulate and dispose of social and economic products and services.

Some redress of this proclivity is apparent in the work of interpretive consumer researchers who have taken the bold step of going out to see what consumers *do* (e.g. Belk 1991). But too little of this has trickled down as yet to textbook writers. As one myself, I have to say *mea culpa* to this, even though people will think I've got religion.

But far be it for me to suggest that the cloning of these texts has become such an artform that they have barely changed since the mid-1960s. A penchant of comparatively recent origin which now impinges on the writing of consumer behaviour texts is the inclusion of a short section on classical and instrumental conditioning as these might apply to consumer choice in the grocery store. Sadly, the practice has been to blend these uncritically into cognitive consumer research, as though the ontological and epistemological gulfs that separate them did not exist. We await a textbook of consumer psychology which informs students (as well as many practising consumer researchers) of these matters. Judging by the impact of the research programme dedicated for some sixteen years to the Behavioural Perspective Model, we apparently await an author capable of elucidating the implications of a radical behaviourist interpretation of consumer choice. *Hey ho.*

In the mean time, to use the adjective 'behavioural' in reference to *behaviour* rather than the organocentric, psychological processes held to determine choice will be to invite misunderstanding, as a reviewer of my *Consumer Psychology in Behavioural Perspective* eloquently demonstrated. (Ralph Waldo Emerson had something to say about being misunderstood but I am not going to quote him here: people will think I'm egocentric.) On the other hand, critics who complain that I use big words and long sentences are entirely correct. *Professors*, some of them! But of *Marketing*, most of them.

INTRODUCTION

In spite of the widespread belief that behaviourism has been superseded in 'the cognitive revolution' (e.g. Baars 1986; Keehn 1996; Kimble 1996; Mandler 1985), some schools of behaviourist thought currently exhibit a considerable intellectual dynamic, especially in the analysis of thinking, reasoning and decision making – areas of human endeavour widely considered to fall exclusively within the province of cognitivism (e.g. Blackman and Lejeune 1990; Chase and Parrott 1986; Guerin 1994a; L.J. Hayes and Chase 1991; S.C. Hayes and L.J. Hayes 1992a; S.C. Hayes *et al.* 1993; S.C. Hayes *et al.* 1994; Lowe *et al.* 1985; Modgil and Modgil 1987; Reese and Parrott 1986; Richelle 1993). Far from being a supplanted paradigm, *radical* behaviourism is a flourishing area of intellectual activity in both its neo-Skinnerian and post-Skinnerian accentuations (e.g. Alessi 1992; Fallon 1992; S.C. Hayes *et al.* 1993; Kimble 1994; Lee 1988, 1992; Morris 1993a, 1993b; Rachlin 1992, 1995; Staddon 1993; Thompson 1994). In particular, theoretical and empirical work on verbal behaviour has transformed radical behaviourism since the fundamentals of operant conditioning were tentatively applied to marketing and promotions in the 1970s and 1980s (Berry and Kunkel 1970; Nord and Peter 1980; Peter and Nord 1982; Rothschild and Gaidis 1981). Much of this work has implications for consumer research.

First, it facilitates a comprehensive radical behaviourist interpretation of consumer behaviour, which incorporates the verbal antecedents of observed consumer choice. Prior use of this paradigm in marketing/ consumer research has generally assumed that its explanatory system can be extrapolated from the non-human animal laboratory, where supporting evidence has accumulated, to complex human behaviour such as purchase and consumption. However, an operant analysis of complex human behaviour need not rely upon principles of contingency-shaped behaviour gained from laboratory research with non-humans: it is now possible to incorporate the distinctively human capacity for language and rule governed behaviour. Consequently, operant analysis need not be restricted to simpler, routine consumer behaviours while a cognitive account is necessary for more complex behaviours based on decision making and problem solving. A behaviourist analysis may prove capable of handling both.

Second, study of the relationship between behaviour and its controlling environment promises to supply a much needed systematic understanding of the situational influences on consumer choice. Because of the emphasis in consumer research on the social-cognitive determinants of consumption, the field currently lacks an integrated model of consumer behaviour in the context of its social, physical, temporal and regulatory surroundings. Radical behaviourism, a discipline concerned almost entirely with the explanation of behaviour as an environmentally determined phenomenon, can be expected to contribute importantly to the required understanding. The advent of research on consumers' verbal behaviour means that this comprehension can incorporate the social influence of rule provision.

Third, consideration of radical behaviourist explanation of consumer behaviour permits discussion of a number of epistemological issues that are germane to contemporary debates about the nature of 'scientific' and 'interpretive' approaches to consumer research. By showing how an interpretation of consumer choice would proceed within a highly developed behavioural science paradigm, such analysis reveals the strengths and weaknesses of a specific ontology and methodology for consumer research and facilitates comparison with other modes of inquiry and explication. For example, the divergent ways in which social-cognitive and operant approaches interpret the role of prior behaviour in the shaping of current responding provide insight into the varied perspectives available for comparative consumer research.

The remainder of the chapter is structured as follows. The social-cognition approach to consumer research is briefly reviewed and contrasted with operant behaviourism. By way of contrast, recent developments in behaviourist theory and research are reviewed with special reference to verbal behaviour and the proximal causative role of private events. The differences between social-cognitive and operant interpretations of thinking and reasoning, and their relationships to overt consumer behaviour, are drawn out by reference to recent work on attitude-intention-behaviour consistency in the former and the role of instructed behaviour in behaviour analysis. Third, the components of the consumer situation – learning history, sources of reinforcement and behaviour setting scope – are elucidated and incorporated in an operant model of consumer choice. This is applied briefly to the analysis of purchase and consumption, saving, the diffusion of innovations, marketing management and social marketing. Finally, epistemological implications of the analysis are discussed with reference to the nature of behaviourist interpretation (illustrated by the treatment of prior behaviour in social-cognitive and operant frameworks), and the empirical correspondence of the model of the consumer situation previously derived.

OPERANT BEHAVIOURISM AND CONSUMER RESEARCH

The social-cognitive basis of consumer research

Models of consumer behaviour which since the mid-1960s have summarised the dominant paradigm for academic consumer research contain a distinctive amalgam of cognitive and social psychologies (Andreasen 1965; Bettman 1979, 1986; Bettman *et al.* 1991; Engel *et al.* 1968; Howard and Sheth 1969; Nicosia 1966). Fundamental to this paradigm are the goal-oriented reception, encoding, representation and processing of information; but equally definitive is the way in which this cognitive procedure is related to behaviour through a sequence of belief-, attitude- and intention-formation. The consumer theory of the 1960s thus anticipated the social-cognitive psychology of the 1980s and 1990s (Fiske 1993; Ostrom *et al.* 1981; Wyer and Srull 1986, 1989, 1994a, 1994b). Social cognition and consumer research are symbiotically related: while social-cognition provides the dominant paradigm for consumer research, consumer researchers have made theoretical and methodological advances, notably in the area of attitudinal-intentional-behavioural consistency, which are equally contributions to social psychology (e.g. Bagozzi 1992; Folkes and Kiesler 1991; Kardes 1994; Petty *et al.* 1991; 1994).

Nonetheless, the legacy of this relationship is that consumer research lacks a systematic framework of conceptualisation and analysis for the explanation of situational influences on consumer choice. Consumer research contains no paradigm which allows the situational influences on consumer choice to be identified and investigated in an organised way, or which promotes theoretical understanding of how the environment shapes consumer behaviour over time. Advances in ecological psychology since the late 1960s have drawn attention to the ways in which behaviour in specific settings retains a remarkable consistency irrespective of who is performing it, their attitudes, intentions, dispositional traits and motives (Barker 1968, 1987; Wicker 1979, 1987). The implication is that these behaviour settings deserve serious analysis based on the finding that the objective environment is responsible for the shape and content of our ultimate explanandum, behaviour itself. But, apart from a few ad hoc studies of consumers' subjective reactions to hypothetical situations described by researchers, there has been no such investigation of situational influences on consumer choice, no appreciation of how the meaning of consumer behaviour is systematically related to the circumstances in which it takes place. We do not know – that is we can neither understand nor explain – where consumer behaviour is: we are unable to trace its occurrence, form and persistence in familiar locations. At the same time, consumer researchers are failing to come to terms with the most complete explanatory and interpretive framework in behavioural science, one which is thoroughly, indeed exclusively, concerned with the influence of context on behaviour – radical behaviourism (Hillner 1984; Leahey 1987; Marx and Hillix 1979; Valentine 1992).

Radical behaviourism as science and interpretation

Radical behaviourism explains behaviour in terms of the contingent relationships of a response and the consequences it produces in the presence of an antecedent (discriminative) stimulus (Malott 1986; Skinner 1953, 1969). This 'three-term contingency', which can be summarised as

$$S^D \rightarrow R \rightarrow S^{R/A}$$

where S^D is a discriminative (setting) stimulus,

R is a response, and

$S^{R/A}$ is a positive or aversive (consequent) stimulus,

is the distinctive explanatory device of the paradigm (Hineline 1990, 1992; Iversen 1992; Morris and Midgley 1990; Morris *et al.* 1990). Since behaviour is understood in radical behaviourism as a function of the consequences of similar behaviour in the past, any causal reference to attitudes, intentions and other pre-behavioural mental, neural or hypothetical entities is redundant (Skinner 1971: 18). Such theoretical entities which exist in some realm other than that in which the behaviour in question is observed are mere 'explanatory fictions', inferred from the behaviour they purport to explain and thus leading only to a circular account. Nor is the antecedent discriminative stimulus an initiating cause of behaviour (Skinner 1988a): it simply signals the availability of reinforcement contingent upon the emission of the appropriate response. Its significance as a setting variable derives from its role in the individual's learning history. When learning has occurred, behaviour may come under the proximal control of the antecedent (discriminative) stimulus in the temporary absence of the reinforcing consequence. The variables of which behaviour is ultimately a function are the consequences such behaviour has produced in the course of that learning history (Delprato and Midgley 1992; Morris 1991).

Radical behaviourism is often criticised for its apparent extrapolation of the results of laboratory experiments conducted with non-human subjects to the human sphere, leading to prescriptions for social control and cultural engineering unsupported by either direct empirical evidence or a coherent theory of human behaviour (see, for instance, the review of Skinner's (1971) *Beyond Freedom and Dignity* by Chomsky (1972), plus the critical analyses, and Skinner's response to them, contained in Wheeler (1973)). This view overlooks, first, the large proportion of operant research which nowadays involves human participants, especially in the context of verbal behaviour, and, second, the role of interpretation in operant accounts of complex human behaviour. A review of research on verbal behaviour is presented on pp. 269–275; but radical behaviourist interpretation requires elaboration at this point, especially in view of the fact that while radical behaviourists have long recognised its inevitability, little has been done by them to establish methods or procedures of interpretation and canons of judgement by which it might be evaluated.

Interpretation becomes inevitable when the elements of the three-term contingency are not amenable to public confirmation. This does not indicate that they are unobservable, for radical behaviourism differs from metaphysical and methodological behaviourisms in its insistence that phenomena observable by only one person – for example, the private events of consciousness – properly form part of the subject matter of behavioural science, even though the private events attributed to others are no more than inferences (Moore 1985; Skinner 1953: 282; see also Mackenzie 1988; Skinner 1988b). However, both private events, which are observable by the individual who has them, and complex contingencies which, although publicly observable, are ambiguous when it comes to identifying the elements of the three-term contingency, cannot occasion the degree of prediction and or control that can be secured in the laboratory. Verbal reports of private events must not be confused with the private events themselves, though the reports may provide valuable information about those events (Skinner 1953: 282). Interpretation is, therefore, indispensable when the precise consequent and antecedent stimuli that control complex behaviour are not consensually obvious; for example, what attributes of the product class are sufficient for reinforcement of purchasing to take place? What are the exact discriminative stimuli under the control of which eating chocolate occurs (cf. Chomsky 1959; Schwartz and Lacey 1982)? In portraying consumer choice as influenced by environmental considerations, behaviour analysis can contribute to consumer research by providing a coherent framework of conceptualisation and analysis for understanding how situational factors influence consumer choice. Previous mention of this paradigm in the marketing and consumer research context (e.g. Berry and Kunkel 1970; Nord and Peter 1980; Rothschild and Gaidis 1981) has failed to accomplish this because of its apparent assumption that radical behaviourist explanation can be extrapolated unadorned from experimental research with non-humans to complex human interactions such as purchase and consumption. There appears to have been no recognition of the need for such an account to encompass either recent findings in the experimental analysis of human behaviour or the ramifications of radical behaviourist interpretation (Foxall 1995a). Both require that attention be accorded the verbal control of behaviour in humans and that Skinner's (1969) distinction between contingency-shaped and rule-governed behaviour be recognised. We turn to several recent developments in the analysis of verbal behaviour which are relevant to the operant interpretation of consumer choice.

OPERANT ANALYSIS OF VERBAL BEHAVIOUR

Verbal behaviour and schedule performance

The operant behaviour of non-humans is shaped entirely by direct contact with the contingencies (Lowe 1989); human behaviour is also frequently contingency-shaped but it is also uniquely subject to verbal control. That is, human behaviour may be controlled as a result of instructions irrespective of the individual's direct experience of the contingencies to which the instructions refer. Young consumers do not require an extended period of trial and error learning before they effectively operate an automatic teller machine: instructions given by a parent or other experienced person can lead to similar consequences. Both the provision and the following of verbal rules are aspects of verbal behaviour which has a long history in behaviour analysis (Skinner 1945, 1957, 1969).

Verbal behaviour is behaviour that is reinforced through the mediation of the social, rather than the physical environment, that is, through the mediation of other people (Skinner 1957). Verbal behaviour is treated by radical behaviourists as any other behavioural phenomenon: it is defined functionally, not logically, and the style of its analysis does not differ from that of operant behaviour in general (Moore 1994: 289; Skinner 1957). Consonant with the metatheoretical stance of radical behaviourism (Skinner 1945), functional analysis of this type diverges fundamentally from the formalism preferred by linguists such as Chomsky (1959, 1971; cf. MacCorquodale 1969, 1970; Richelle 1993). Skinner's (1957) work of interpretation, *Verbal Behaviour,* concentrated upon the verbal behaviour of the speaker and, by comparison, largely disregarded that of the listener (Hayes and Hayes 1989; cf. Skinner 1989). Hence, some authors have drawn attention to the 'unwarranted dominance' of Skinner's book in its having found acceptance as the sole behaviour theoretic approach to verbal responding and its consequent overshadowing of other theoretical approaches including relational frame analysis (L.J. Hayes 1991, 1994; S.C. Hayes 1994; Hayes and Hayes 1992a; Parrott 1986). The radical behaviourist analysis of verbal control is still inescapably influenced by, but by no means restricted to, Skinner's interpretive stance (e.g. Chase and Parrott 1986; Guerin 1994a; L.J. Hayes and Chase 1991; Hayes and Hayes 1992; S.C. Hayes *et al.* 1993, 1994).

Rule-governed behaviour

The contingency-shaping of human behaviour occurs when the consequences of responding are immediate, that is, sizeable, quick-acting and probable (Malott 1989). However, when behavioural consequences are remote, that is, small, delayed and improbable, behaviour is likely to be rule-governed (Malott 1989). For example, the immediate consequences of dieting, quitting smoking and dental flossing are unlikely to exert control of these behaviours; however, verbal rules may act as discriminative stimuli, delineating the outcomes of behaving in the specified ways, and thereby providing motivation to act appropriately. In the case of instructed or rule-governed behaviour, the rule provided by the speaker acts as a verbal discriminative stimulus which substitutes for the contingencies themselves.

Human vs. non-human schedule performances

Evidence for the role of verbal stimuli in human responding derives from the notable observed differences between non-human and human experimental schedule performances, which appear to stem from the human capacity for language. Human behaviour in experimental settings not only diverges from that of animals on prespecified schedules of reinforcement, but also is usually insensitive to changes in the schedule parameters in operation. Thus humans' patterns of responding on both fixed interval (FI) and fixed ratio (FR) schedules markedly depart from the scalloped pattern found in animal experiments in which, after a post-reinforcement pause, rate of responding gently increases over time (Horne and Lowe 1993). By contrast with the pattern typically found for non-human behaviour subject to these contingencies, human responding shows either a continuous high response rate between reinforcements, or an exceptionally low rate of responding in which one or two responses are emitted immediately prior to the presentation of the reinforcement. Non-humans' sensitivity to changes in schedule parameters renders their behaviour highly 'economical': they promptly accommodate their rates of responding to new contingencies. Yet human behaviour in similar experimental circumstances reveals a rigidity which impedes economic rationality (Lowe 1979, 1983; Lowe and Horne 1985; cf. Catania *et al.* 1982; Matthews *et al.* 1985).

The matching law

Non-human choices on concurrent variable interval (VI) schedules are described by the matching law, which states that subjects emit alternative responses with frequencies in direct proportion to the frequency of reinforcement available for each response (Herrnstein 1970, 1974); that is

$$\mathbf{R_A} = \frac{\mathbf{Kr_A}}{\mathbf{r_A} + \mathbf{r_B} + \mathbf{r_0}} \tag{1}$$

and

$$\mathbf{R_B} = \frac{\mathbf{Kr_B}}{\mathbf{r_A} + \mathbf{r_B} + \mathbf{r_0}} \tag{2}$$

where R_A and R_B are the number of responses accorded respectively to **A** and **B**, r_A and r_B are the respective frequencies of reinforcement for these alternatives, and **K** and r_0 are empirically derived parameters, **K** the response rate at asymptote; r_0 the reinforcement rate at half-maximal response rate which is theoretically equivalent to all of the implicit sources of reinforcement available in the experimental setting (Herrnstein 1970; Horne and Lowe 1993). The matching law may be derived by combining equations 1 and 2 as long as **K** and r_0 are invariant. Hence the matching law which states that the relative rates of responding on the alternatives **A** and **B** are roughly equal to the relative reinforcement frequencies of the two alternatives:

$$\frac{R_A}{R_A + R_B} = \frac{r_A}{r_A + r_B} \tag{3}$$

Expressed as a power function (Baum 1974), this becomes

$$\frac{R_A}{R_B} = k\left(\frac{r_A}{r_B}\right)^a \tag{4}$$

where k and a are empirically derived free parameters.

Human responding has been described in several studies as conforming to these equations (e.g. Bradshaw *et al.* 1976, 1977, 1979a, 1979b, 1981; Ruddle *et al.* 1979). Moreover, the potential of the matching law to describe non-human behaviour accurately and consistently has been indicatively extended to human behaviour in several applied settings (Epling and Pierce 1983; Hamblin 1979; McDowell 1982; Pierce and Epling 1980, 1983; Rachlin 1980; Schwartz 1984; Winkler 1980). However, some researchers (notably Lowe 1983) have argued that human responding frequently deviates substantially from the matching relationships found for other animals. Horne and Lowe (1993: 53) summarise six experiments involving human performances on concurrent VI schedules by noting that

> In our studies, unlike those conducted by Bradshaw and colleagues with humans, less than half the subjects' performances resembled those typically found in animal choice studies. For many of the remaining subjects, there were not mere 'deviations' from the matching typically observed in nonhumans; rather their performance was qualitatively different and could not be described by the matching equations.
>
> (Horne and Lowe 1993: 53)

Departures from the matching law have been reported by several other researchers (e.g. Oscar-Berman *et al.* 1980; Pierce *et al.* 1981; Schmitt 1974; Schroeder 1975; Schroeder and Holland 1969; Silberberg *et al.* 1991; Takahashi and Iwamoto 1986; Wurster and Griffiths 1979). Horne and Lowe (1993: 54) comment that 'Together with the data from our six experiments, these findings clearly demonstrate that human subjects showing ideal matching, or even a close approximation to it, are the exception rather than the rule in the literature.'

Departures such as these are apparently explained by the human capacity for verbalising the contingencies of reinforcement which they believe to be in operation. Information, accurate or otherwise, about the contingencies operating in experimental settings is provided in the instructions given by the experimenter: use of such information may account for the digressions shown in human behaviour from patterns found in experiments with non-humans (Catania *et al.* 1982; Hayes *et al.* 1986; Horne and Lowe 1993; Lowe 1979, 1983; Lowe and Horne 1985; Matthews *et al.* 1985). Verbal behaviour may thus be invoked in the search for the causes of both the relatively simple behaviours emitted in experimental settings and the more complex patterns of response found in the situations of purchase and consumption. The interpretations of such complex behaviour can and should be submitted to further experimental analysis (Horne and Lowe 1993).

Instructional Control

There is, moreover, extensive experimental evidence to suggest that language plays a definitive part in determining behaviour. Whereas pre-verbal infants' behaviour on FI and FR schedules resembles that of other animals, the behaviour of children of 5 or 6 who have acquired verbal skills is akin to that of adult humans, exhibiting comparable rates of response and the same insensitivity to schedule parameter changes. This is presumably because the acquisition of language permits children to characterise the contingencies that control their responding (Horne and Lowe 1993; Lowe 1983; Lowe and Horne 1985; Lowe *et al.* 1983). These behavioural changes in children are accelerated by the provision of appropriate verbal instructions (Horne and Lowe 1993; Lowe and Horne 1985). The behaviour of adults is also frequently under verbal control: behaviour modification programmes based on token economies and contingency management (Ayllon and Azrin 1968) indicate that changes in participants' behaviour are sensitive to the instructions provided them, including feedback on performance and descriptions of the prevailing contingencies (Lowe *et al.* 1987).

Instructed behaviour and contingency-shaped responding differ in view of the insensitivity of the former to changes in behavioural consequences (Catania *et al.* 1989, 1990). The distinction is further complicated in that instructed (or rule-governed) behaviour is governed by two classes of contingencies: the social consequences which maintain rule following itself, and the natural contingencies which come to exert control independently of the rule (Baum 1994). A parent might, for instance, advise a child to save a portion of his or her allowance each week in an account. The child's saving behaviour is maintained by the social contingencies of rule conformity (suppose that the parent has usually scolded the child for not following advice in the past); gradually, it comes under the influence of the 'natural' contingencies of saving: accrual of interest, planning of purchases, and so on. Instructed behaviour is usually effectively learned only if the consequences of rule-compliance are more powerful than the natural consequences that would otherwise follow trial-and-success behaviour (e.g. spending all of one's allowance, trying to save in the absence of advice on how to do it, etc.) Such natural contingencies are usually remote, delayed and weak so that learning from them alone (i.e. in the absence of instructions) would be tardy, dangerous, or possibly infeasible.

Functional analysis of rule-following

Skinner's (1957) *Verbal Behaviour* presents a functional analysis of verbal behaviour – which consists of certain gestures, and covert behaviour such as thinking and reasoning, as well as vocal behaviour (see also Skinner 1974). A functional analysis proceeds in terms of the consequences of the verbal response rather than its structure, form or topography. Skinner evolved several functional units of verbal behaviour, of which the most important in the current context are the mend and the tact. A *mend* is an element of verbal behaviour which indicates the consequences contingent upon following the instructions of the speaker or of imitating his or her example. Much advertising consists of mends – 'Buy three and get one free!' 'Don't forget the fruit gums, mum' – which indicate contingencies that are under the control of the speaker. *Tacts* present the listener with a part of the environment which he or she thus contacts and, depending on learning history, behaves toward. A trade mark or logo may be followed by making a purchase or entering a store.

Zettle and Hayes (1982) propose several functional units for analysis of the behaviour of the listener which has promoted several empirical and theoretical investigations (Chase and Danforth 1991; S.C. Hayes 1989; Hayes and Hayes 1989; Malott 1989; Poppen 1989). *Pliance* is rule-governed behaviour controlled by consequences that the speaker (or his/her agent) regulates (or claims to regulate). The rule, or ply, alludes to the social consequences of compliance or non-compliance: 'Keeping my breath fresh will get me more dates.' The ply corresponds to the *mend*. Zettle and Hayes (1982) propose a second functional unit of listener behaviour, *tracking*, instructed behaviour which the rule designates as under the control of the non-social environment. A *track* is, therefore, a rule that specifies the arrangement of contingencies within that physical or temporal context: 'If I turn left at the next intersection, I'll come to Sainsbury's.' 'If I arrive by five, the shop will still be open.' Tracking corresponds to tacting on the part of the speaker. A third functional unit of listener behaviour, which apparently has no corresponding unit for the speaker, is the *augmental* (Zettle and Hayes 1982), a highly motivating rule that states emphatically how a particular behaviour will be reinforced or avoid punishment. 'Just one more packet top and I can claim my watch!' The reason for the difficulty of defining plying and tracking exclusively is that a single rule often embodies elements of both (Poppen 1989): sometimes both elements of such a rule require the same behaviour to be performed (in which case the rule is a *congruent*); sometimes there is conflict (when the rule is known as a *content!*).

Private events

An operant account of a person's behaviour which employs his or her own rule generation as proximally causative requires an understanding of the private (though not mental or cognitive) events, that is, covert behaviours which are performed in rule formulation. These verbal events entail thinking, reasoning, deliberating and other *behaviours*. The subject of private events is central to the theme of radical behaviourist interpretation generally; the analysis of such verbal activity relies on the assumption of private causes that are inferred rather than observable in objective scientific investigation (Reese 1986; Skinner 1953, 1988b). The radical behaviourism of Skinner (1938, 1945, 1963) differs from methodological behaviourism by accepting private events as a part of its legitimate subject matter (Baum 1994; Moore 1994). Such events are not construed as unobservables, though they are observed by only one person. Radical behaviourism *infers* however that other people have private events which act as verbal discriminative stimuli for their behaviour (Mackenzie 1988). This inferential process differs nonetheless from the treatment of unobservables such as attitudes, personality traits and intentions by social cognitivists: radical behaviourism portrays those 'mental way stations' (Skinner 1963) as explanatory fictions that bring inquiry to a premature end by diverting attention from the ultimate causes of behaviour in an attempt to shift the environment 'into the head' (Skinner 1969). Some behaviour analysts view private events as proximal causes of behaviour (e.g. Malott and Garcia 1991); others have argued that, on the contrary and in keeping with the methodology of the experimental analysis of behaviour, only things whose role in prediction and control can be demonstrated in the laboratory deserve a place in an operant analysis (e.g. S. C. Hayes *et al.* 1986; Perone *et al.* 1988). The assumption that private events are proximal causes of behaviour certainly blurs the distinction between behaviourist and cognitive modes of explanation (Overskeid 1995).

Stimulus Equivalence

Non-humans have proved capable of learning complex relationships if they are appropriately reinforced but generally do not innovate by initiating relationships they have not been explicitly taught (Lowe 1989). By contrast, even young humans display the emergent behaviour of relating A to C having been taught that A is related to B and that B is related to C. This capacity for transivity is one of three criteria used to establish *stimulus equivalence,* a phenomenon which appears peculiar to human animals (Dugdale and Lowe 1990). The other criteria are symmetry (i.e. matching A to A) and reflexivity (i.e. matching B to A having learned that A relates to B) (Catania 1992a, 1992b; Sidman 1990, 1992). The implication is that these stimuli (A, B and C) belong to the same *stimulus class* since they evoke the identical response: for instance, a picture of a car (A), the written word 'car' (B) and the written word 'auto' (C) are all likely to evoke the oral response 'car'; but learning stimuli that belong to the same stimulus class is not sufficient for equivalence.

Stimulus equivalence is relevant to rule-governed behaviour in that a rule and the contingencies it describes presumably belong to the same equivalence class since they are functionally identical (Dugdale and Lowe 1990; cf. Sidman 1990, 1992).

BEHAVIOUR ANALYSIS OF CONSUMER DECISION MAKING

Consistency of verbal and non-verbal behaviours

Words and events are linked by a web of contingencies arranged by the verbal community (Catania 1992a: 250). The relationship between what a person says and what he or she does is central to the establishment and maintenance of social consistency. This is the heart of the attitude-behaviour problem in social cognitivism, though in a behavioural analysis the problem is reformulated as that of how and when verbal rules come to guide behaviour. These rules may originate in one of two ways. Either the behaviour may be instructed by others or it may be self-instructed as the individual describes the apparent contingencies to him or herself. An individual's behaviour may be changed, therefore, either by instruction or by shaping what he or she says about it; in the latter case, 'one's own verbal behaviour may thus become effective as an instructional stimulus' (Catania 1992a: 251). Of the two, shaped verbal behaviour has a greater effect on the individual's propensity to act than either direct shaping through modification of the contingencies or instruction (Catania *et al.* 1990: 217). In other words, encouraging people to formulate their own rules by altering the contingencies that govern their verbal behaviour is the most effective persuasive strategy (though the danger of false rules, leading to superstitious behaviour, is ever-present: Ono 1994). The resulting behaviour is then sensitive to the natural contingencies only to the extent that changes in those contingencies result in changes in the corresponding verbal behaviour (Catania *et al.* 1990: 217) The corollary is that only changes in the contingencies that are mediated by verbal behaviour, self-instructing, will change behaviour. None of this implies that behaviour formed through instruction does not come into contact with the contingencies. The natural contingencies remain the ultimate causes of behaviour and, therefore, rule-governed behaviour will at some point become contingency-shaped. Perhaps it is from the contingencies that we can ultimately predict behaviour most successfully, as well as explain it. Hence the contingency category analysis of consumer behaviour must include reference to both rules that are the proximal causes of behaviour and the natural contingencies in which their distal causes reside.

Attitudes and intentions as verbal behaviour

Guerin (1994a, 1994b) argues that attitudes and intentions can be behaviouristically interpreted. Hence attitudes constitute 'a generalised affective response to stimuli and contexts': the things that individuals report they like, favour or prefer are those which have relatively strong reinforcing effects (1994a: 236). Beliefs, consisting predominantly of intraverbals and facts, do not control overt behaviour, any more than attitudes control behaviour. Attitudes are simply a commentary on one's behaviour which one makes to oneself (ibid.), though we should wish to add that they are an *evaluative* commentary (Lalljee *et al.* 1984). But attitudes are not comments on elusive beliefs or latent behavioural processes: rather, the elements on which they provide a commentary are the individual's overt (public) and covert (private) behaviours. This goes beyond the simpler behaviouristic stratagem of using the term attitude to describe the consistency of behaviour: while this is sometimes a useful approach (Foxall 1983, 1996), it fails to acknowledge the evaluative nature of verbal behaviour and its capacity to direct other verbal and non-verbal behaviours, that is, to provide a truly behaviouristic counterpart to the attitude concept of social cognition. The distinction is that between attitudes as verbal behaviour that is contingency-shaped (under the direct control of the environment) as in saying that 'This book is enjoyable' because I have been reading it and have found it so – and attitudes under social control – as in saying the same thing about a book I have not read but about which my mentor has expressed a favourable view. The result of an operant analysis of such verbal behaviour is a functional view of attitudes. Functioning as facts, attitudes may be simply reports on the environment, replies to questions, social rituals or self-regulating verbal behaviours that involve self reinforcement (Guerin 1994a: 237–238). Expressed to others, attitudes may also function as mends.

The so-called 'problem' of attitudinal-behavioural consistency disappears on this view: both attitudinal and non-attitudinal acts are operant behaviours in their own right, each maintained by its own context of contingencies. Consistency cannot, therefore, be expected unless the contingencies happen to be functionally equivalent, perhaps as a result of a verbal community arranging the contingencies so as to produce consistency.

Guerin (1994a) identifies the interesting question for behaviourists
of isolating the effect of attitudes on the person who hears them ͻ
since, as the previous section showed, the verbal control of behavio
far short of perfection, the surprising thing is that any degree of consi
at all is observable, especially in view of the large repertoires of behɑʋiour
that people have and the reinforcement available for inconsistency (lying,
for instance: Sato and Sugiyama 1994). The compatibility required for the
predictive success of the Theory of Reasoned Action (TRA) and other
models that stress deliberative processing thus demands the verbal detail-
ing of specific contingencies rather than the provision of generalised
statements about possible outcomes. Such statements of attitude and intention act as verbal instructions to guide behaviour. Actual responding is
predictable from them in circumstances where the individual has control
over the contingencies of the situation, where he or she is familiar with
behaving in that context and the consequences that have previously
followed it. The evaluative beliefs elicited by questionnaires based on such
theories actually record what the respondent takes to be the contingencies
entailed in acting in a particular way (belief strength) and the likelihood
of reinforcement/punishment resulting from the performance of the
behaviour in question (evaluation). The summation of these evaluative
beliefs entails the combination of the positive and negative aspects of the
contingencies, which Guerin (1994a: 244) likens to 'a multiple contingency
Matching Law for verbally governed behaviour'. Both the beliefs and their
evaluations have their origins in the individual respondent's learning
history. Subjective norm similarly records the contingencies laid down by
the respondent's verbal community, reflecting social pressure (Guerin
1992). But learning history is significant here and is overlooked by cognitivists only because it is not immediately obvious, leading to the ontological inference that the causes of behaviour must lie within the individual.
Guerin (1994a: 245) sums up: 'The TRA brings together the major variables also dealt with by behaviour analysis: verbally governed behaviour,
verbal facts about contingencies and reports of their value, combining
the multiple contingencies involved to get an overall prediction, and the
verbal community contingencies.'

The behavioural perspective model

In order to construct a general theory of consumer behaviour in the
terms of the three-term contingency, it is necessary to define them more
closely in three respects (Foxall 1990). First, the nature of the setting
variables and the influence they exert must be clarified in view of the
complexity of the environments in which human economic behaviour takes
place. Second, the nature of reinforcement must be refined in the context
of human behaviour which, even in the operant laboratory, is multiply
motivated. Third, the nature and influence of verbal behaviour, which

regulates behaviour only in humans, must be considered. The behavioural perspective model (BPM) proposes that consumer behaviour is situated at the intersection of the behaviour setting in which it occurs (the spatial perspective) and the learning history of the consumer (the temporal perspective) (Foxall 1990). The resulting synomorphic construct of the *consumer situation* has been used to interpret observed patterns of consumer behaviour including purchase and consumption, saving and domestic asset management, the adoption and diffusion of innovations and 'green' consumption (Foxall 1993a, 1994a, 1994b, 1994c, 1995c). The interpretation proceeds essentially in terms of the three-term contingency, albeit critically appraised and re-presented in line with the provisions outlined above (Figure 9.1). The consumer behaviour setting consists of the current discriminative stimuli that signal reinforcement and punishment contingent upon the emission of a purchase or consumption response. The discriminative stimuli that compose the setting may be physical (e.g. point-of-sale advertising, the product array, a store logo), social (principally the physical presence of co-shoppers, other diners in a restaurant, the waiter, the salesperson), temporal (the hours of opening of a store, the duration of a special offer, Christmas) or regulatory (self- and other-rules that specify contingencies). Rule-governed behaviour is actually a social phenomenon but deserves separate treatment (Guerin 1994a; Hyten and Burns 1986). The consequences of responding in the setting which have played a role in shaping the individual's *learning* history and which are now signalled as behaviourally contingent by these setting elements, have three functions. Aversive consequences that are suffered punish the behaviour that produced them, that is, make it less probable in future. Any behaviour that avoids or escapes aversive consequences is (negatively) reinforced, that is, made more probable in similar circumstances in the future. Positive consequences of a behaviour also strengthen or reinforce it, that is, increase its probability of recurrence (Foxall 1992a). Such positive reinforcement may occur in two ways.

Hedonic reinforcement refers to the acceptance of positive benefits of purchasing, owning or consuming economic products and services (goods); these benefits are utilitarian, conferring material satisfactions, the utility of orthodox microeconomic theory. Hedonic reinforcers are frequently referred to as incentives both in general discourse and in applied behaviour analysis. *Informational* reinforcement is performance feedback, an indication of how well the consumer is doing. It may confer social status and/or self-satisfaction, or it may simply constitute a reference point denoting progress to date. Informational reinforcement is associated with verbal behaviour because the meaning of the behaviour is always mediated by a person, usually someone other than the actor but perhaps by him/herself. There is empirical evidence that hedonic and informational reinforcement have separate influences on behaviour in both human operant experiments conducted under laboratory conditions (Wearden

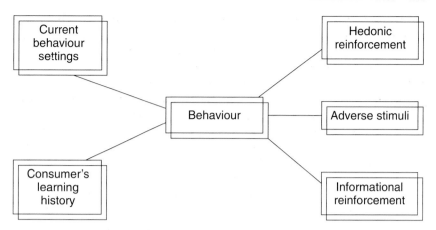

Figure 9.1 Summary of the Behavioural Perspective Model

1988), in token economy studies, and in the field experiments of applied behaviour analysis directed toward the reduction of environmentally-deleterious consumption (Foxall 1995a, 1995b, 1995c, 1996).

The extent to which consumer behaviour can be attributed to control by environmental contingencies varies with the closedness of the setting in which it takes place. The animal laboratory, from which principles of operant behaviourism were derived, presents a particularly closed setting, one in which the elements of the three-term contingency can be objectively identified and behaviour therefore traced unambiguously to its environmental effects. The further behaviour settings stray from this degree of closedness, the harder it is for the operant psychologist to ascribe activities within them unreservedly to operant conditioning. Even in the animal laboratory, there exists scope for alternative interpretations: in terms, for instance, of classical conditioning or cognitive decision making. The human operant laboratory, for example, presents a less closed context, one from which escape is relatively easy; while non-humans face no option but being in the setting, human participants on occasion remove themselves from the experimental situation. The settings in which human consumer behaviour takes place are more open still: though a continuum of such settings is evident, from the relatively closed confines of a large group awareness training session to the relatively open variety store. Closed and open settings may also be distinguished in terms of the verbal behaviour that characterises each. In closed settings, the other instructions and contingencies are precise: in order to get a passport, a consumer must obey the rules to the letter. In open settings, the consumer has more control over his or her behaviour through self-instructions, and specific other rules are less likely to be determinative. There may be several other-rule configurations to 'choose' from; further, there is the possibility of behaviour being directly controlled by the contingencies: as one spots new products, devises new ways of finding presents, and so on. Even if the view is taken that most consumer behaviour is rule-governed, open settings allow self-rules to a far greater extent than closed. Moreover, human behaviour that is entirely contingency-shaped is rare. Self-rules, devised and followed by the same individual, are particularly effective instructions, which may be more isolated from the contingencies than other-rules (Catania *et al.* 1990: 227). Employing dichotomous variables to represent the causative elements of the model, actual consumer situations can be categorised among eight contingency configurations, depending on whether the consumer behaviour setting is relatively closed or relatively open, whether hedonic reinforcement is relatively high or low, and whether informational reinforcement is relatively high or low. Moreover, depending on the strength of the sources of reinforcement, four operant classes of consumer behaviour can be defined: accomplishment (where both are high), pleasure (where hedonic reinforcement is high but informational is low), accumulation (where informational reinforcement is high but hedonic is low), and maintenance (where both are low) (Foxall 1993b). The consumer situations and behaviours assigned to each of these eight contingency categories are defined functionally rather than morphologically and topographically identical behaviours may be assigned at different times to different operant classes and contingency categories depending on the interpretation of the combination of contingencies maintaining them. The labels employed in Figure 9.2 are, therefore, ultimately arbitrary, though they have proved useful in the interpretation of consumer behaviour (Foxall 1994a).

Learning history

The importance of learning history is amply demonstrated by the repeated finding that prior behaviour is an important determinant of current responding. It is not sufficient to attribute the influence of prior behaviour simply to 'habit', which is to redescribe it rather than explain it. The continuance of behaviour is accounted for by the consequences it produces; whether or not a stream of behaviour is continued into the near future depends on the stimulus control which influences it and the maintenance of the pattern of reinforcement that is its distal cause. The deliberative processing models such as the TRA are centrally concerned with the self-reported consequences of behaving in a given way, which constitutes a personal summary of the respondent's learning history. The elicitation of subjective norm beliefs and evaluations is also indicative of a history of rule-compliance. The spontaneous processing models emphasise direct experience with the attitude object, which both constitutes a learning history in itself and serves to establish the attitude object as a

Behaviour setting

	closed	Scope	open
Accomplishment	Fulfilment		Status consumption
		2	1
Pleasure	Inescapable entertainment		Personal entertainment
		4	3
Accumulation	Token-buying		Saving and collecting
		6	5
Maintenance	Mandatory consumption		Routine purchasing
		8	7

Figure 9.2   Contingency categories

discriminative stimulus for further responding. The rehearsal of attitude statements, especially if they have their origin in other-instructions, constitutes prior *verbal* behaviour which also exerts an environmental influence on the probability of current responding. The potency of a learning history is manifested within a particular behaviour setting: prior learning establishes what will act as a discriminative stimulus in that setting by embodying the consequences, reinforcing and punishing, of earlier behaviour in the presence of the relevant setting elements. The functional approach to attitude theory and research taken by Shavitt (1989) corroborates the BPM by indicating several functions of behavioural consequence in controlling verbal and non-verbal current responding (usually via preceding verbal behaviour/instructional control). The bases of the attitude functions she proposes appear closely related to the nature of the reinforcement associated with these products – hedonic (utilitarian) and informational (social identity). The distinction between hedonic and informational reinforcement is consonant with that between the utilitarian and social identity functions of attitudes (Shavitt 1989). Shavitt argues that the function of a person's attitude toward an air conditioner is principally utilitarian because one's attitude toward it should be based largely on rewards (e.g. comfort) and punishments (e.g. high energy bills) intrinsically associated with it . . . one's attitude toward an air conditioner should guide behaviours that maintain the rewards and avoid the punishments associated with this object (e.g. using the air conditioner on a hot day, turning it off at times to conserve energy).

(Shavitt 1989: 324)

However, an individual's attitude toward a wedding ring performs contrasting functions:

one's attitude toward it should be based largely on what it symbolises. Furthermore, wedding rings are worn (in public) primarily to communicate information to others about the wearer, and one's attitude toward wedding rings and what they symbolise should guide this behaviour.

(Shavitt 1989: 324)

The components of Eagly and Chaiken's (1993) composite model of attitude-behaviour relationships are also supportive of the BPM: all of the determinants of attitude toward behaviour – habit, attitudes toward the target, utilitarian, normative and self-identity outcomes – are indicative of learning history. Habits form only if the behaviour of which they are composed is sequentially reinforced; attitudes toward target develop only through experience; and, although conceptualised as expectations of what will result from behaving in a specified way, the outcomes can result only from environmental history, either in the form of contingency-shaping or through instruction. Moreover, utilitarian outcomes closely resemble the hedonic reinforcement of the BPM, while normative (including self-identity) outcomes are akin to informational reinforcement. The BPM links past behaviour, behaviour setting elements and outcomes by arguing that learning history primes elements of the setting to act as discriminative stimuli for hedonic and informational reinforcement/punishment contingent upon the performance of specific responses. Like Eagly and Chaiken's model, the BPM is untested but it provides an alternative, noncognitive synthesis of empirical results gained in both attitude research and operant investigations of instructed behaviour.

Consumer decision making as behaviour

Work in the social cognition of decision processes has led to several theoretical frameworks which attempt to explain the nature of the information processing utilised by consumers in varying circumstances. In the MODE model (motivation and opportunity as determinants), Fazio (1990) points to two ways in which attitudes guide behaviour – spontaneously and through deliberation – and argues that one or other of these processing modes will be activated according to the circumstances of motivation and opportunity present. Deliberative processing is probable when the expected costliness of the prospective behaviour induces rational evaluation of the merits and demerits of assuming a given course of action. At this time, motivation to avoid the expense of making and acting upon a poor judgement overrides the spontaneous mechanism whereby attitudes might be activated from memory without cognitive effort. Assuming that an opportunity to deliberate is available, the individual can be expected to engage in extensive prebehavioural mental deliberation. Where the motivation to avoid heavy costs misjudgement is low and/or an opportunity to deliberate is not forthcoming, attitudinal influences on behaviour will occur via spontaneous processing. The extent to which attitude influences behaviour in these circumstances reflects the strength of evaluative association that has been built with respect to the attitude object through direct experience or by means of verbal rehearsal of the attitude. Provided that this association is sufficiently strong, the individual's definition of the event will be wholly or predominantly attitude-determined. When the attitude association is weak, however, this definition of the event will be based mainly on non-attitudinal factors: behaviour toward the attitude object will then depend predominantly on the salient features of the attitude object itself and the situation (Fazio 1990: 93–94).

A broadly similar spectrum underlies Chaiken's (1980) heuristic-systematic model (HSM) which arrays processing strategies on the basis of the amount of cognitive effort they involve. The extremes of the processing continuum she proposes are *systematic* processing which is potentially effortful, requiring the evaluation of multiple interpretations of the situation before a definitive impression is formulated, and *heuristic* processing which requires minimal information handling, relying on established rules to make sense of the current situation. On the understanding that individuals minimise effortful activity, systematic processing is likely only when the person is highly motivated and has the cognitive capacity and resources to engage in it. Nevertheless, individuals are also assumed to balance effort minimisation with the confidence they feel in their social perceptions. When heuristics based on experience can be substituted for systematic processing, they will be activated by elements of the current situation that signify their relevance (Bohner *et al.* 1995). Decision making may, however, result from the simultaneous activation of both processes, reflecting both 'content-related thinking' (systematic) and 'cue-related evaluations' (heuristic) (van Knippenberg *et al.* 1994). Reviews of the empirical work prompted by the HSM can be found in Eagly and Chaiken (1993); in addition, Bohner *et al.* (1995) present the most recent version of the model and review research which has applied the model in the spheres of mood, persuasion and minority influence.

Finally, Eagly and Chaiken (1993) present an integrative model of the attitude–behaviour relationship which incorporates both the attitudes toward objects ('targets') implicated in spontaneous processing and the attitudes toward behaviours implicated in deliberative processing. Each kind of attitude is operational at a different stage in a dynamic sequence leading to behaviour. Attitude toward a behaviour is determined by *habit* (successive instances of an action that occur automatically or at least in the absence of self-instruction); *attitude toward the target*; and three sets of outcomes: *utilitarian*, rewards and penalties expected to follow from the performance of the behaviour; *normative*, the endorsement or denunciation expected of significant others toward the action, plus the self-administered rewards like pride and punishments like guilt resulting from internal moral rules; and, when these self-administered consequences relate to the self-concept, *self-identity*. Attitude toward behaviour impacts in turn upon intention which impacts upon behaviour. Intention is also partly determined by normative and self-identity outcomes; and behaviour, by habit and attitude toward behaviour (Eagly and Chaiken 1993: 209–211). This is corroborated by the functional approach to attitude theory and research taken by Shavitt (1989) who proposes that an object may evoke one or more of three functions: *utilitarian* (coffee, for instance) which arises from the reinforcing and punishing outcomes of using the item; *social identity* (e.g. a wedding ring) that communicates social status, identity and prestige; and *ego defensive/self-esteem* (e.g. one's appearance). Shavitt has shown that many objects evoke a single attitude function and that promotional appeals based on the appropriate function for each product are more persuasive than appeals based on different criteria.

How do the mechanisms for decision making and persuasion proposed by Fazio's (1990) MODE model, the Elaboration Likelihood Model (Petty and Cacioppo 1984a) and the Heuristic Systematic Model (Chaiken 1980) relate to consumer decision making in behavioural perspective? In the BPM interpretation 'motivation' is supplied by the individual's learning history or lack thereof. It is this which determines the likelihood that the outcome of a particular action will be relatively costly or rewarding and which leads to more or less prebehavioural reviewing of the contingencies, that is, the probability of particular positive and aversive outcomes emerging from each of the behaviours available. This review is not mental processing: it is behaviour, verbal behaviour which is often private. Where deliberation takes place it consists of a review of rules, self-rules generated on the basis of direct learning experience of the contingencies, and other-rules provided by those whose instructions have proved accurate and reinforcing if followed in the past and/or who themselves have relevant experience of the consequences which can be publicly ascertained. Self-rules correspond to the attitude toward the act of the Fishbein/Ajzen formula (Fishbein and Ajzen 1975): how else would one identify learning history through self-report than by asking an individual what he or she believed would be the outcome of acting in a given way in specific circumstances and weighting this by his or her appraisal of those consequences? Questions that elicit attitude toward the act may be equally understood as indicating a history of reinforcement. The rules revealed in this manner ('Eating fresh greens every day will result in a clear complexion') are akin to the tracks identified by Zettle and Hayes (1982): they specify how to get to a particular goal point. By this time, behaviour is 'scripted' (Langer 1989a, 1989b), following not from conscious intentions or plans but under the control of self-rules and/or immediate stimuli. Other-rules correspond to the subjective norm of the Fishbein/Ajzen model: acting as plys, they specify the social consequences of compliance or non-compliance with a specified course of action. Evidence for the progression from other-rules, via deliberation, experience and self-observation, to action based on self-rules is provided by research on the Theory of Planned Behaviour (TPB) by East (1992, 1997) which was reviewed above. (A comparative review of the cognitive and behaviourist approaches to problem solving is found in Reese 1994; cf. Chase and Bjamadottir 1992; Ito 1994; Reese 1992a, 1992b.)

The probability of a particular response depends also upon the non-regulatory components of the consumer behaviour setting, the physical, social and temporal discriminative stimuli given meaning in any particular setting by the individual's learning history. Where they have figured in the past as controlling antecedents, they will now act to signal the kinds of consequences that are contingent on each possible response. They will thus play an integral role in pre-behavioural deliberation, each setting the occasion for behaviour with predictable results in the form of positive and aversive consequences. When the learning history of the individual is such that known consequences have followed regularly and unimpeded from specific acts, the discriminative stimuli in the current setting will provide signals that quickly result in the performance of the requisite behaviour, when the individual has little appropriate learning history, or the history is ambiguous with respect to the kinds of reinforcer or punisher likely to result from behaviour, the magnitude of these consequences and their probability, greater deliberation including the formulation, weighing and use of rules will be normal.

The self- and other-instructions activated to a greater or lessser extent in either deliberative or spontaneous processing, plus the power of current discriminative stimuli – conferred in a history of reinforcement and punishment – determine the probability of a specific response. The immediate pre-behavioural verbal self-instruction or prediction the individual is capable of making (on the question of introspection entering into rule-formulation, see Moore 1994; on that of self-editing in rule formulation, see Hyten and Chase 1991; cf. Vaughan 1991) – equivalent to what deliberation theorists call his or her behavioural intention – is another kind of rule, an augmental, the proximal motivating factor leading to the consummation of a particular act.

Behaviour formed through direct experience is contingency-shaped: its persistence is due to continued reinforcement and its emission is likely to come under the stimulus control of the physical, social and temporal elements of the behaviour setting. Such behaviour may be described as 'spontaneous' or 'automatic' – finger tapping, for instance – when it is entirely under the control of these historical and current contingencies (Catania 1992a). However, it is unlikely that a great deal of human behaviour is formed and maintained entirely through the direct action of the environmental contingencies. Humans are rule-formulating animals and routine/habitual behaviour is likely to be guided by self-rules, formed through experience and observation, and taking the form largely of tracks. Private tracking probably controls a great deal of repetitive consumer behaviour such as weekly or monthly supermarket shopping. Although such behaviour as brand choice shows 100 per cent loyalty in only a small minority of the users of a product class, most consumers' multi-brand purchasing is confined to a small repertoire of tried and tested brands in each class (Ehrenberg and Uncles 1995). Brand choice within this repertoire may look haphazard but it is far from random. It differs from finger tapping in that it is highly functional and economically/consumption rational, and most consumers have no difficulty in describing the rules employed in finding and selecting brands of fast-moving consumer goods, as protocol analysis readily shows (O'Shaughnessy 1987). Self-rules in the form of tracks are undoubtedly analogous to global attitudes toward the object – in this case a known subset of substitutable brands within a product class – which are easily/automatically elicited by the discriminative stimuli in the purchase setting. Formed through repeated purchasing, observation and imitation, including a long period of consumer socialisation, they are readily available to guide immediate, familiar purchasing in the presence of such antecedent controlling stimuli as the label on a can, a familiar brand name or a logo. This resembles the spontaneous processing in the presence of a known attitude object identified by Fazio (1990) as prerequisite to unpremeditated, automatic, routine processing.

Behaviour instructed by the rules provided by others is formed through indirect experience: TV advertisements, neighbours' recommendations, parents' approbation and so on. Such rules are most likely to be effective when the listener's relevant learning history is minimal or non-existent and/or when the behaviour setting in which he or she is acting is closed (the latter is a function of how much control the speaker has over the setting). Other-instructions are far more likely to be productive in situations unfamiliar to the listener, when a novel course of action is commended – perhaps buying a radically innovative product or moving house or just trying a new make of computer disc. Such behaviours usually require some degree of deliberation since no self-rules exist to 'spontaneously' guide action. Depending on the consumer's history of rule-compliance, he or she will be more or less disposed to follow the other-instructions without demur: a friend whose advice has proved worthwhile may be able to offer recommendations that are immediately taken up and acted upon, providing the new sphere of consumption is not too far removed from that previously instructed. But a stranger appearing in a TV commercial may not be able to rely on audience members' having so motivating a reinforcement history with respect to following other-rules. Other-rules of these kinds take the form of plys: in the absence of direct experience on the part of the listener, and especially if the rules come from a remote/unfamiliar/impersonal source, they are more likely to lead to deliberation than immediate action. The consequent review of the contingencies is not mental but behavioural (Skinner 1974), a series of private events in which the ultimate causes of behaviour are scrutinised. Verbal rules toward specific courses of action (like attitudes toward target behaviours in the cognitive theories) may result from this process. The consumer who initially had no self-rules for the proposed course of action (because he or she had little or no direct experience thereof, little or no relevant learning history) eventually may form such rules, translating the plys provided by others into the private tracks necessary to guide particular behaviour in a clearly defined situation (corresponding to that defined in terms of target, action, timing and context by the multiattribute modellers).

To reach a decision, determining to adopt one action among several, is to form a behavioural intention in the deliberative models; in the BPM, it appears to involve a third kind of rule, an augmental, which motivates the individual to behave in a specific manner. Augmentals of this kind result from deliberation and are succeeded by positive motivation, perhaps the outcome of a cost-benefit analysis that indicates that the reinforcing consequences of the proposed act are likely to exceed the aversive, a review of the contingencies that suggests one action will generate greater net benefits than any other. If the action is performed and reinforced, the plys provided as other-rules gradually become track-based self-rules and, ultimately, the contingencies themselves exert a greater share of control than instructions: the behaviour becomes routinised and apparently habitual. Much behaviour is of course a mixture of contingency-shaped and rule-governed, subject to adjustment as new contingencies arise and as new instructions from others and oneself emerge to be evaluated and otherwise deliberated upon. Guerin (1994a: 192) distinguishes two kinds of decision making which have the capacity to bring together the findings of social cognitive research and those of behaviour analysis. 'Intuitive decision making', he writes, 'refers to behaving in accordance with the multiple environmental contingencies acting at that time [while] nonintuitive means that decision behaviour has become verbally governed in some way and verbal rules are controlling the decision behaviour through pliance or tracking.' The preceding analysis goes beyond this, however, eschewing the simple dichotomy it implies. The theory expounded above casts behaviour where there is little direct learning history as guided by other-rules (plys), and that where there is a well-established learning history as guided by prior contingency shaping and the discriminative stimuli of the current behaviour setting including self-rules (tracks). Between the two is a period of contingency shaping through which the self-rules that come to guide behaviour apparently spontaneously are formulated. At this stage, the non-verbal contingencies that guide current behaviour are notoriously difficult to distinguish from the self-rules that may do so (Hackenberg and Joker 1994; S.C. Hayes *et al.* 1986). The choice of explanation is methodologically based: some behaviour analysts refuse to admit variables represented by private events that are not amenable to an experimental analysis of their subject matter (e.g. S.C. Hayes 1986); others are willing to interpret observed behaviour in terms of non-publicly available entities of this kind (e.g. Catania 1992a; Horne and Lowe 1993).

Hence, the debate about the direction of causation between attitudes and behaviour is redundant: a consumer who has simply seen an advertisement for a brand will have an attitude in the sense of being able to express some verbal evaluations, perhaps only in the form of echoics (Skinner 1957) though he or she may be capable of some minimal verbal evaluation of the brand. But such an attitude is less likely to act as a self-instruction to guide behaviour than that which is formed through experience with the brand.

SUMMARY AND CONCLUSION

According to the social cognition interpretation, consumer behaviour is the result of information processing in a social context. It is attitude-consistent either because prior experience of the object is sufficient to allow evaluations to control behaviour spontaneously or because, in the absence of such experience, the individual must deliberate, examining the likely consequences of each course of action apparently available and consciously selecting one which he or she intends to perform if circumstances permit. Most consumer behaviour contains elements of both spontaneous and deliberative processing. The tendency of adherents to this paradigm is to interpret evidence for the environmental control of behaviour in terms of additional cognitive processing.

Behaviour analytic consumer research portrays consumer behaviour as the outcome of environmental consequences, acting either directly or through verbal descriptions (rules). Behaviour is contingency-shaped when the person has much experience of the outcomes of this or similar behaviour. When this is not the case, behaviour is usually preceded by a review of the contingencies described by other-rules (instructions provided by other people). In this process, and through direct behavioural experience, the individual forms his or her own self-rules about how the contingencies operate. As behaviour comes under the control of self-rules, it appears spontaneous and routine, though it has a long history in which it was shaped by successive approximations to what it has become. Most human behaviour is rule-governed to some extent but ultimately the contingencies themselves determine what people actually do. Adherents of this viewpoint interpret prebehavioural deliberation not as mental processing but as a behaviour in its own right in which the consequences of acting are reviewed and evaluated.

The behavioural perspective model (BPM) proposes that consumer behaviour is a function of the interaction of the scope of the current consumer behaviour setting and the individual's learning history. This interaction motivates a specific behaviour by prefiguring the hedonic and informational consequences it is likely to produce. A relatively closed behaviour setting involves mainly other-rules which describe not only the contingencies but the social reinforcements and punishments of compliance or non-compliance. Compliant behaviour in these settings is negatively reinforced while non-compliance is punished. Relatively open settings involve mainly self-rules. The individual's learning history encapsulates his or her disposition toward complying with the instructions of others (which is activated by the discriminative stimuli that compose a closed setting) and his or her derivation of self-rules (which are activated by the elements of an open setting). Hedonic reinforcement consists in the utilitarian benefits of purchase and consumption: the behaviour that produces it is contingency-shaped. Informational reinforcement consists in social standing and the achievement of personal norms: the behaviour that produces it is rule-governed. Self-rules appear to refer to the attitudes formed through deliberation; other-rules, to subjective norms; when self-rules have been employed frequently, the behaviour appears to come under the automatic stimulus control of the behaviour setting.

ACKNOWLEDGEMENTS

The author thanks Professors R.P. Bagozzi, University of Michigan, A.L. Minkes, University of Oxford, and J. O'Shaughnessy, Columbia University, for their valuable comments on earlier drafts.

REFERENCES

Alessi, G. (1992) 'Models of proximate and ultimate causation in psychology', *American Psychologist*, 47: 1359–1370.

Andreasen, A.A. (1965) 'Attitudes and customer behaviour: a decision model', in L.E. Preston (ed.) *New Research in Marketing*, Berkeley, CA: University of California Press.

Ayllon, T. and Azrin, N.H. (1968) *The Token Economy: A Motivational System for Theory and Rehabilitation*, New York: Appleton.

Baars, B. (1986) *The Cognitive Revolution in Psychology*, New York: Guilford.

Bagozzi, R.P. (1992) 'The self-regulation of attitudes, intentions, and behaviour', *Social Psychology Quarterly*, 55: 178–204.

Barker, R.G. (1968) *Ecological Psychology*, Stanford, CA: Stanford University Press.

—— (1987) 'Prospecting in environmental psychology: Oskaloosa revisited', in D. Stokols and I. Altmann (eds) *Handbook of Environmental Psychology*, New York: Wiley, 1413–1432.

Baum, W.M. (1974) 'On two types of deviation from the matching law: bias and undermatching', *Journal of the Experimental Analysis of Behaviour*, 22: 231–242.

—— (1994) *Understanding Behaviourism: Science, Behaviour and Culture*, New York: HarperCollins.

Belk, R.W. (ed.) (1991) *Highways and Buyways: Naturalistic Research from the Consumer Behaviour Odyssey*, Provo, UT: Association for Consumer Research.

Berry, L.L. and Kunkel, J.H. (1970) 'In pursuit of consumer theory', *Decision Sciences*, 1: 25–39.

Bettman, J.R. (1979) *An Information Processing Theory of Consumer Choice*, Reading, MA: Addison Wesley.

—— (1986) 'Consumer psychology', *Annual Review of Psychology*, 37: 257–289.

——, Johnson, E.J. and Payne, J.W. (1991) 'Consumer decision making', in T.S. Robertson and H.H. Kassarjian (eds) *Handbook of Consumer Behaviour*, Englewood Cliffs, NJ: Prentice Hall, 50–84.

Blackman, D.E. and Lejeune, H. (eds) (1990) *Behaviour Analysis in Theory and Practice: Contributions and Controversies*, London: Erlbaum.

Bohner, G., Moskowitz, G.B. and Chaiken, S. (1995) 'The interplay of heuristic and systematic processing of social information', in W. Stroebe and M. Hewstone (eds) *European Review of Social Psychology*, vol. 6, Chichester: Wiley, 33–68.

Bradshaw, C.M., Ruddle, H.V. and Szabadi, E. (1981) 'Studies of concurrent performances in humans', in C.M. Bradshaw, E. Szabadi and C.F. Lowe (eds) *Quantification of Steady State Operant Behaviour*, Amsterdam: North Holland, 225–259.

——, Szabadi, E. and Bevan, P. (1976) 'Behaviour of humans in variable-interval schedules of reinforcement', *Journal of the Experimental Analysis of Behaviour*, 26: 135–141.

——,—— and —— (1977) 'Effect of punishment on human variable interval performance', *Journal of the Experimental Analysis of Behaviour*, 27: 275–279.

——,—— and —— (1979) 'Effect of punishment on free operant choice behaviour in humans', *Journal of the Experimental Analysis of Behaviour*, 31: 71–81.

——,——,—— and Ruddle, H.V. (1979) 'The effect of signalled reinforcement availability on concurrent performance in humans', *Journal of the Experimental Analysis of Behaviour*, 32: 65–74.

Catania, A.C. (1992a) *Learning*, Englewood Cliffs, NJ: Prentice Hall.

—— (1992b) 'B.F. Skinner, organism', *American Psychologist*, 47: 1521–1530.

——, Matthews, B.A. and Shimoff, E. (1982) 'Instructed versus shaped human verbal behaviour: interactions with non-verbal responding', *Journal of the Experimental Analysis of Behaviour*, 38: 233–248.

——, —— and —— (1990) 'Properties of rule-governed behaviour and their implications', in D.E. Blackman and H. Lejeune (eds) *Behaviour Analysis in Theory and Practice: Contributions and Controversies*, London: Erlbaum, 215–230.

—— , Shimoff, E.H. and Matthews, B.A. (1989) 'An experimental analysis of rule-governed behaviour', in S.C. Hayes (ed.) *Rule-Governed Behaviour: Cognition, Contingencies, and Instructional Control*, New York: Plenum, 119–150.

Chaiken, S. (1980) 'Heuristic versus systematic information processing and the use of source versus message cues in persuasion', *Journal of Personality and Social Psychology*, 39: 752–766.

Chase, P.N. and Bjamadottir, G.S. (1992) 'Instructing variability: some features of a problem-solving repertoire', in S.C. Hayes and L.J. Hayes (eds) *Understanding Verbal Relations*, Reno, NV: Context Press, 181–196.

—— and Danforth, J.S. (1991) 'The role of rules in concept formation', in L.J. Hayes and P.N. Chase (eds) *Dialogues on Verbal Behaviour*, Reno, NV: Context Press, 205–225.

—— and Parrott, L.J. (eds) (1986) *Psychological Aspects of Language: The West Virginia Lectures*, Springfield, IL: Charles C. Thomas.

Chomsky, N. (1959) 'Review of B.F. Skinner's *Verbal Behaviour*', *Language*, 35: 26–58.

—— (1971) 'Review of B.F. Skinner's *Beyond Freedom and Dignity*', *New York Review of Books*.

Cohen, J.B. and Chakravarti, D. (1990) 'Consumer psychology', *Annual Review of Psychology*, 41: 243–288.

Davey, G. C. L. and Cullen, C. (eds) (1988) *Human Operant Conditioning and Behaviour Modification*, Chichester: Wiley.

Delprato, D.J. and Midgley, B.D. (1992) 'Some fundamentals of B.F. Skinner's behaviourism', *American Psychologist*, 47: 1507–1520.

Dugdale, N. and Lowe, C.F. (1990) 'Naming and stimulus equivalence', in D.E. Blackman and H.H. Lejeune (eds) *Behaviour Analysis in Theory and Practice*, London: Erlbaum, 115–138.

Eagly, A.H. and Chaiken, S. (1993) *The Psychology of Attitudes*, Fort Worth, TX: Harcourt Brace Jovanovich.

East, R. (1992) 'The effect of experience on the decision making of expert and novice buyers', *Journal of Marketing Management*, 8: 167–176.

—— (1997) *Consumer Behaviour: Advances and Applications in Marketing*, London: Prentice Hall.

Ehrenberg, A.S.C. (1972) *Repeat Buying*, Amsterdam: North Holland, 2nd edn 1988, London: Griffin.

—— and Uncles, M.D. (1995) 'Dirichlet-type markets: a review', unpublished manuscript, South Bank Business School, London.

Engel, J.F., Blackwell, R.D. and Miniard, P.W. (1995) *Consumer Behaviour*, 8th edn, Fort Worth, TX: Dryden.

——, Kollat, D.T. and Blackwell, R.D. (1968) *Consumer Behaviour*, New York: Holt, Rinehart & Winston.

Epling, W.F. and Pierce, W.D. (1983) 'Applied behaviour analysis: new directions from the laboratory', *Behaviour Analyst*, 6: 27–37.

Fallon, D. (1992) 'An existential look at B.F. Skinner', *American Psychologist*, 47: 1441–1453.

Fazio, R.H. (1990) 'Multiple processes by which attitudes guide behaviour: the MODE model as an integrative framework', in M.P. Zanna (ed.) *Advances in Experimental Social Psychology*, 23, San Diego, CA: Academic Press, 75–109.

Feyerabend, P. (1970) 'Consolations for the specialist', in I. Lakatos and A. Musgrave (eds) *Criticism and the Growth of Knowledge*, Cambridge: Cambridge University Press.

—— (1975) *Against Method*, London: New Left Books.

Fishbein, M. and Ajzen, I. (1975) *Belief, Attitude, Intention and Behavior*, Reading, MA: Addison-Wesley.

Fiske, S.T. (1993) 'Social cognition and social perception', *Annual Review of Psychology*, 44: 155–194.

Folkes, V.S. and Kiesler, T. (1991) 'Social cognition: consumers' inferences about the self and others', in T.S. Robertson and H.H. Kasarjian (eds) *Handbook of Consumer Behaviour*, Englewood Cliffs, NJ: Prentice Hall, 281–315.

Foxall, G.R. (1983) *Consumer Choice*, London: Macmillan.

—— (1984) 'Consumers' intentions and behaviour', *Journal of the Market Research Society*, 26: 231–241.

—— (1987) 'Radical behaviourism and consumer research: theoretical promise and empirical problems', *International Journal of Research in Marketing*, 4: 111–129.

—— (1990) 'The consumer situation: an integrative model for research in marketing', *Journal of Marketing Management*, 8: 392–404.

—— (1992) 'The behavioural perspective model of purchase and consumption: from consumer theory to marketing management', *Journal of the Academy of Marketing Science*, 20: 189–198.

—— (1993a) 'Consumer behaviour as an evolutionary process', *European Journal of Marketing*, 27, 8: 46–57.

—— (1993b) 'Situated consumer behaviour: a behavioural interpretation of purchase and consumption', in J.A. Costa and R.W. Belk (eds) *Research in Consumer Behaviour*, 6, Greenwich, CT: JAI Press, 113–152.

—— (1993c) 'Variety seeking and cognitive style', *British Food Journal*, 95, 7: 32–36.

—— (1994a) 'Behaviour analysis and consumer psychology', *Journal of Economic Psychology*, 15: 5–91.

—— (1994b) 'Consumer choice as an evolutional process: an operant interpretation of adopter behaviour', *Advances in Consumer Research*, 21: 312–317.

—— (1994c) 'Environment-impacting consumer behaviour: a framework for social marketing and demarketing', in M.J. Baker (ed.) *Perspectives on Marketing Management*, 4, Chichester: Wiley, 27–53.

—— (1994d) 'Consumer initiators: adaptors and innovators', *British Journal of Management*, 5: S3–S12.

—— (1994e) 'Consumer decision-making', in M.J. Baker (ed.) *The Marketing Book*, London: Butterworth-Heinemann, 193–215.

—— (1995a) 'Science and interpretation in consumer research: a radical behaviourist perspective', *European Journal of Marketing*, 29, 9: 3–99.

—— (1995b) 'The psychological basis of marketing', in M.J. Baker (ed.) *The Companion Encyclopedia of Marketing*, London: Routledge.

—— (1995c) 'Environment-impacting consumer behaviour: an operant analysis', *Advances in Consumer Research*, 22: 262–268.

—— (1996) *Consumers in Context: The BPM Research Program*, London: Routledge.

du Gay, P. (1995) *Consumption and Identity at Work*, London: Sage.

Guerin, B. (1992) 'Behaviour analysis and the social construction of knowledge', *American Psychologist*, 47: 1423–1432.

—— (1994a) *Analyzing Social Behaviour: Behaviour Analysis and the Social Sciences*, Reno NV: Context Press.

—— (1994b) 'Attitudes and beliefs as verbal behaviour', *The Behaviour Analyst*, 17:

Hackenberg, T.D. and Joker, V.R. (1994) 'Instructional versus schedule control of humans' choices in situations of diminishing returns', *Journal of the Experimental Analysis of Behaviour*, 62: 367–383.

Hamblin, R.L. (1979) 'Behavioural choice and social reinforcement', *Social Forces*, 57: 1141–1156.

Hayes, L.J. (1991) 'Substitution and reference', in L.J. Hayes and P.N. Chase (eds) *Dialogues on Verbal Behaviour*, Reno, NV: Context Press, 3–18.

—— (1992) 'Equivalence as process', in S.C. Hayes and L.J. Hayes (eds) *Understanding Verbal Relations*, Reno, NV: Context Press, 97–108.

—— (1994) 'Thinking', in S.C. Hayes, L.J. Hayes, M. Sato and K. Ono (eds) *Behaviour Analysis of Language and Cognition*, Reno, NV: Context Press, 149–164.

—— and Chase, P.N. (eds) (1991) *Dialogues on Verbal Behaviour*, Reno, NV: Context Press.

Hayes, S.C. (1986) 'The case of the silent dog: verbal reports and the analysis of rules', *Journal of the Experimental Analysis of Behaviour*, 45: 351–363.

—— (ed.) (1989) *Rule-Governed Behaviour: Cognition, Contingencies and Instructional Control*, New York: Plenum.

—— (1994) 'Relational frame theory: a functional approach to verbal events', in S.C. Hayes, L.J. Hayes, M. Sato and K. Ono (eds) *Behaviour Analysis of Language and Cognition*, Reno NV: Context Press, 9–30.

—— and Hayes, L.J. (1989) 'The verbal action of the listener as a basis for rule-governance', in S.C. Hayes (ed.) *Rule-Governed Behaviour: Cognition, Contingencies and Instructional Control*, New York: Plenum, 153–190.

—— and —— (1992a) 'Verbal relations and the evolution of behaviour analysis', *American Psychologist*, 47: 1383–1395.

—— and —— (eds) (1992b) *Understanding Verbal Relations*, Reno, NV: Context Press.

——, Brownstein, A.J., Haas, J.R. and Greenway, D.E. (1986) 'Instructions, multiple schedules and extinction: distinguishing rule-governed from schedule-controlled behaviour', *Journal of the Experimental Analysis of Behaviour*, 46: 137–147.

——., Hayes, L.J. Reese, H.W. and Sarbin, T.R. (eds) (1993) *Varieties of Scientific Contextualism*, Reno, NV: Context Press.

——, ——, Sato, M. and Ono, K. (eds) (1994) *Behavior Analysis of Language and Cognition*, Reno, NV: Context Press.

Herrnstein, R.J. (1970) 'On the law of effect', *Journal of the Experimental Analysis of Behavior*, 13: 243–266.

—— (1974) 'Formal properties of the matching law', *Journal of the Experimental Analysis of Behaviour*, 21: 159–164.

Hillner, K.P. (1984) *History and Systems of Modern Psychology: A Conceptual Approach*, New York: Gardner.

Hineline, P. (1990) 'The origins of environment-based psychological theory', *Journal of the Experimental Analysis of Behavior*, 53: 305–320.

—— (1992) 'A self-interpretive behaviour analysis', *American Psychologist*, 47: 1274–1286.

Horne, P.J. and Lowe, C.F. (1993) 'Determinants of human performance on concurrent schedules', *Journal of the Experimental Analysis of Behavior*, 59: 29–60.

Howard, J.A. and Sheth, J.N. (1969) *The Theory of Buyer Behaviour*, New York: Wiley.

Hyten, C.M. and Burns, R. (1986) 'Social relations and social behaviour', in H.W. Reese and L.J. Parrott (eds) *Behaviour Science: Philosophical, Methodological, and Empirical Advances*, Hillsdale, NJ: Erlbaum, 163–183.

—— and Chase, P.N. (1991) 'An analysis of self-editing: method and preliminary findings', in L.J. Hayes and P.N. Chase (eds) *Dialogues on Verbal Behaviour*, Reno, NV: Context Press, 67–81.

Ito, Y. (1994) 'Models and problem solving: effects and use of the "views of probability"' in S.C. Hayes, L.J. Hayes, M. Sato and K. Ono (eds) *Behaviour Analysis of Language and Cognition*, Reno, NV: Context Press, 259–280.

Iversen, I.H. (1992) 'Skinner's early research: from reflexology to operant conditioning', *American Psychologist*, 47: 1318–1328.

Kardes, F.R. (1988) 'Spontaneous inference processes in advertising: the effects of conclusion omission and involvement on persuasion', *Journal of Consumer Research*, 15: 225–233.

—— (1994) 'Consumer judgment and decision processes', in R.S. Wyer and T.K. Srull (eds) *Handbook of Social Cognition, Volume 2, Application*, 2nd edn, Hillsdale, NJ: Erlbaum.

Kassarjian, H.H. (1982) 'Consumer psychology', *Annual Review of Psychology*, 33: 619–649.

Keehn, J.D. (1996) *Master Builders of Modern Psychology: From Freud to Skinner*, London: Duckworth.

Kimble, G.A. (1994) 'A new formula for behaviourism', *Psychological Review*, 101: 254–258.

—— (1996) *Psychology: The Hope of a Science*, Cambridge, MA: MIT Press.

Kohlenberg, B.S., Hayes, S.C. and Hayes, L.J. (1991) 'The transfer of contextual control over equivalence classes through equivalence classes: a possible model of social stereotyping', *Journal of the Experimental Analysis of Behaviour*, 56: 505–518.

Kuhn, T.S. (1962) *The Structure of Scientific Revolutions*, 2nd edn 1970, Chicago IL: Chicago University Press.

—— (1963) 'The function of dogma in scientific research', in A.C. Crombie (ed.) *Scientific Change*, London: Heinemann, 347–369.

Lalljee, M., Brown, L.B. and Ginsburg, G.P. (1984) 'Attitudes: disposition, behaviour or evaluation?', *British Journal of Social Psychology*, 23: 233–244.

Langer, E.J. (1989a) *Mindfulness*, Reading, MA: Addison-Wesley.

—— (1989b) 'Minding matters: the consequences of mindlessness–mindfulness', in L. Berkowitz (ed.) *Advances in Experimental Social Psychology*, 22, San Diego, CA: Academic Press, 137–173.

Laudan, L. (1984) *Science and Values: The Aims of Science and their Role in Scientific Debate*, Berkeley, CA: University of California Press.

Leahey, T.H. (1987) *A History of Psychology: Main Currents in Psychological Thought*, Englewood Cliffs, NJ: Prentice Hall.

Lee, V.L. (1988) *Beyond Behaviourism*, London: Erlbaum.

—— (1992) 'Transdermal interpretation of the subject matter of behaviour analysis', *American Psychologist*, 47: 1337–1343.

Lowe, C.F. (1979) 'Determinants of human operant behavior', in D.M. Zeiler and P. Harzem (eds) *Advances in Analysis of Behavior, Volume 1, Reinforcement and the Organization of Behavior*, Chichester: Wiley, 159–192.

—— (1983) 'Radical behaviorism and human psychology', in G.C.L. Davey (ed.) *Animal Models of Human Behavior: Conceptual, Evolutionary, and Neurobiological Perspectives*, Chichester: Wiley, 71–93.

—— (1989) *From Conditioning to Consciousness: The Cultural Origins of Mind*, Bangor: University of North Wales.

—— (1993) 'Determinants of human performance on concurrent schedules', *Journal of the Experimental Analysis of Behavior*, 59: 29–60.

—— and Horne, P.J. (1985) 'On the generality of behavioural principles: human choice and the matching law', in C.F. Lowe, M. Richelle, D.E. Blackman and C.M. Bradshaw (eds) *Behaviour Analysis and Contemporary Psychology*, London: Erlbaum, 97–116.

——, Beasty, A. and Bentall, R.P. (1983) 'The role of verbal behavior in human learning', *Journal of the Experimental Analysis of Behavior*, 39: 1 57–164.

——, Horne, P.J. and Higson, P.J. (1987) 'Operant conditioning: the hiatus between theory and practice in clinical psychology', in *Theoretical Foundations of Behaviour Therapy*, London: Plenum.

——, Richelle, M., Blackman, D.E. and Bradshaw, C.M. (eds) (1985) *Behaviour Analysis and Contemporary Psychology*, London: Erlbaum.

MacCorquodale, K. (1969) 'B.F. Skinner's *Verbal Behaviour*: a retrospective appreciation', *Journal of the Experimental Analysis of Behaviour*, 12: 831–841.

—— (1970) 'On Chomsky's review of Skinner's *Verbal Behaviour*', *Journal of the Experimental Analysis of Behaviour*, 13: 85–99.

McDowell, J.J. (1982) 'The importance of Herrnstein's mathematical statement of the law of effect for behaviour therapy', *American Psychologist*, 37: 771–779.

Mackenzie, B. (1988) 'The challenge to Skinner's theory of behaviour', in A.C. Catania and S. Harnad (eds) *The Selection of Behaviour: The Operant Behaviourism of B.F. Skinner – Comments and Consequences*, New York: Cambridge University Press, 111–113.

Malott, R.W. (1986) 'Self-management, rule-governed behaviour and everyday life', in H.W. Reese and L.J. Parrott (eds) *Behaviour Science: Philosophical, Methodological, and Empirical Advances*, Hillsdale, NJ: Erlbaum, 207–228.

—— (1989) 'The achievement of evasive goals: control by rules of describing contingencies that are not direct acting', in S.C. Hayes (ed.) *Rule-Governed Behaviour: Cognition, Contingencies and Instructional Control*, New York: Plenum, 269–324.

—— and Garcia, M.E. (1991) 'Role of private events in rule-governed behaviour', in L.J. Hayes and P.N. Chase (eds) *Dialogues on Verbal Behaviour*, Reno, NV: Context Press, 237–254.

Mandler, G. (1985) *Cognitive Psychology: An Essay in Cognitive Science*, Hillsdale, NJ: Erlbaum.

Marr, J. (1983) 'Memory, models and metaphors', *The Psychological Record*, 33: 12–19.

Marx, M.H. and Hillix, W.A. (1979) *Systems and Theories in Psychology*, 3rd edn, New York: McGraw-Hill.

Matthews, B.A., Catania, C.A. and Shimoff, E. (1985) 'Effects of uninstructed verbal behavior on nonverbal responding: contingency descriptions versus performance descriptions', *Journal of the Experimental Analysis of Behaviour*, 43: 155–164.

Modgil, S. and Modgil, C. (eds) (1987) *B.F. Skinner: Consensus and Controversy*, Brighton: Falmer.

Moore, J. (1980) 'On behaviourism and private events', *The Psychological Record*, 30: 459–475.

—— (1984) 'On privacy, causes and contingencies', *The Behaviour Analyst*, 7: 3–16.

—— (1985) 'Some historical and conceptual relations among logical positivism, operationism and behaviourism', *The Behaviour Analyst*, 8: 53–63.

—— (1994) 'On introspection and verbal reports', in S.C. Hayes, L.J. Hayes, M. Sato and K. Ono (eds) *Behaviour Analysis of Language and Cognition*, Reno NV: Context Press, 281–299.

Morris, E.K. (1991) 'The contextualism that is behaviour analysis: an alternative to cognitive psychology', in A. Still and A. Costall (eds) *Against Cognitivism: Alternative Foundations for Cognitive Psychology*, Hemel Hempstead: Harvester Wheatsheaf, 123–149.

—— (1993a) 'Behaviour analysis and mechanism: one is not the other', *The Behaviour Analyst*, 16: 25–43.

—— (1993b) 'Mechanism and contextualism in behaviour analysis: just some observations', *The Behaviour Analyst*, 16: 255–268.

—— and Midgley, B.D. (1990) 'Some historical and conceptual foundations of ecobehavioral analysis', in S.R. Schroeder (ed.) *Ecobehavioral Analysis and Developmental Disabilities*, New York: Springer-Verlag, 1–32.

——, Todd, J.T., Midgley, B.D., Schneider, S.M. and Johnson, L.M. (1990) 'The history of behaviour analysis: some historiography and a bibliography', *The Behaviour Analyst*, 13: 131–158.

Navarick D. I. and Chellsen, J. (1983) 'Matching versus under-matching in the choice behavior of humans', *Behavior Analysis Letters*, 3: 325–332.

——, Bernstein, D.J. and Fantino, E. (1990) 'The experimental analysis of human behaviour', *Journal of the Experimental Analysis of Behaviour*, 54: 159–162.

Nicosia, F.M. (1966) *Consumer Decision Processes*, Englewood Cliffs, NJ: Prentice Hall.

Nord, W. and Peter, J.P. (1980) 'A behaviour modification perspective on marketing', *Journal of Marketing*, 44: 36–47.

Ono, K. (1994) 'Verbal control of superstitious behaviour: superstitions as false rules', in S.C. Hayes, L.J. Hayes, M. Sato and K. Ono (eds) *Behaviour Analysis of Language and Cognition*, Reno, NV: Context Press, 181–196.

Oscar-Berman, M., Heyman, G.M., Bonner, R.T. and Ryder, J. (1980) 'Human neuropsychology: some differences between Korsakoff and normal operant performance', *Psychological Research*, 41: 235–247.

O'Shaughnessy, J. (1987) *Why People Buy*, New York: Oxford University Press.

—— (1992) *Explaining Buyer Behaviour*, New York: Oxford University Press.

Ostrom, T.M. (1994) 'Foreword', in R.S. Wyer and T.K. Srull (eds) *Handbook of Social Cognition, Volume 1: Basic Processes*, Hillsdale, NJ: Erlbaum, vii–xii.

——, Prior, J.B. and Simpson, D.D. (1981) 'The organization of social information', in E.T. Higgins, C.P. Herman and M.P. Zanna (eds) *Social Cognition: The Ontario Symposium*, Hillsdale, NJ: Erlbaum, 3–38.

Overskeid, G. (1995) 'Cognitive or behaviourist – who can tell the difference? The case of implicit and explicit knowledge', *British Journal of Psychology*, 46: 312–319.

Parrott, L.J. (1986) 'The role of postulation in the analysis of inapparent events', in H.W. Reese and L.J. Parrott (eds) *Behaviour Science: Philosophical, Methodological, and Empirical Advances*, Hillsdale, NJ: Erlbaum, 35–60.

Perone, M., Galizio, M. and Baron, A. (1988) 'The relevance of animal-based principles in the laboratory study of human operant conditioning', in G.C.L. Davey and C. Cullen (eds) *Human Operant Conditioning and Behaviour Modification*, Chichester: Wiley, 59–86.

Peter, J.P. and Nord, W.R. (1982) 'A clarification and extension of operant conditioning principles in marketing', *Journal of Marketing*, 46: 102–107.

—— and Olson, J.C. (1993) *Consumer Behaviour and Marketing Strategy*, Homewood, IL: Irwin.

Petty, R.E. and Cacioppo, J.T. (1984a) 'The effects of involvement on responses to argument quantity and quality: central and peripheral routes to persuasion', *Journal of Personality and Social Psychology*, 46: 69–81.

—— and —— (1984b) 'Source factors and the elaboration likelihood model of persuasion', *Advances in Consumer Research*, 11: 668–672.

—— and —— (1986a) *Communication and Persuasion: Central and Peripheral Routes to Attitude Change*, New York: Springer-Verlag.

—— and —— (1986b) 'The elaboration likelihood model of persuasion', in L. Berkowitz (ed.) *Advances in Experimental Social Psychology*, 19: 123–205.

——, Priester, J.R. and Wegener D.T. (1994) 'Cognitive processes in attitude change', in R.S. Wyer and T.K. Srull (eds) *Handbook of Social Cognition, Volume 2: Application*, 2nd edn, Hillsdale, NJ: Erlbaum.

——, Unnava, R. and Strathman, A.J. (1991) 'Theories of attitude change', in T.S. Robertson and H.H. Kassarjian (eds) *Handbook of Consumer Behaviour*,

Englewood Cliffs, NJ: Prentice Hall, 241–280.

Phillips, D.C. (1992) *The Social Scientist's Bestiary: A Guide to Fabled Threats to, and Defences of, Naturalistic Social Science*, Oxford: Pergamon.

Pierce, W.D. and Epling, W.F. (1980) 'What happened to analysis in applied behaviour analysis?', *Behaviour Analyst*, 3: 1–9.

—— and —— (1983) 'Choice, matching, and human behaviour', *Behaviour Analyst*, 6: 57–76.

——, —— and Greer, S.M. (1981) 'Human communication and the matching law', in C.M. Bradshaw, E. Szabadi and C.F. Lowe (eds) *Quantification of Steady State Operant Behaviour*, Amsterdam: North Holland, 345–348.

Poppen, R.L. (1989) 'Some clinical implications of rule-governed behaviour', in S.C. Hayes (ed.) *Rule-Governed Behaviour: Cognition, Contingencies and Instructional Control*, New York: Plenum, 325–357.

Rachlin, H. (1980) 'Economics and behavioural psychology', in J.E.R. Staddon (ed.) *Limits to Action: The Allocation of Individual Behaviour*, New York: Academic Press, 205–236.

—— (1992) 'Technological behaviourism', *American Psychologist*, 47: 1371–1382.

—— (1995) *Behaviour and Mind: The Roots of Modern Psychology*, New York: Oxford University Press.

Reese, H.W. (1986) 'On the theory and practice of behaviour analysis', in H.W. Reese and L.J. Parrott (eds) *Behaviour Science: Philosophical, Methodological, and Empirical Advances*, Hillsdale, NJ: Erlbaum, 1–33.

—— (1992a) 'Rules as non-verbal entities', in S.C. Hayes and L.J. Hayes (eds) *Understanding Verbal Relations*, Reno, NV: Context Press, 121–134.

—— (1992b) 'Problem solving by algorithms and heuristics', in S.C. Hayes and L.J. Hayes (eds) *Understanding Verbal Relations*, Reno, NV: Context Press, 153–180.

—— (1994) 'Cognitive and behavioural approaches to problem solving', in S.C. Hayes, L.J. Hayes, M. Sato and K. Ono (eds) *Behaviour Analysis of Language and Cognition*, Reno, NV: Context Press, 197–258.

—— and Parrott, L.J. (eds) (1986) *Behaviour Science: Philosophical, Methodological, and Empirical Advances*, Hillsdale, NJ: Erlbaum.

Ribes, E. (1991) 'Language as contingency-substitution behaviour', in L.J. Hayes and P. Chase (eds) *Dialogues on Verbal Behaviour*, Reno, NV: Context Press, 47–58.

—— (1992) 'An analysis of thinking', in S.C. Hayes and L.J. Hayes (eds) *Understanding Verbal Relations*, Reno, NV: Context Press, 209–224.

Richelle, M.N. (1993) *B.F. Skinner: A Reappraisal*, London: Erlbaum.

Ronis, D.L., Yates, J.F. and Kirscht, J.P. (1989) 'Attitudes, decision and habits as determinants of repeated behaviour', in A.R. Pratkanis, S.J. Beckler and A.G. Greenwald (eds) *Attitude Structure and Function*, Hillsdale, NJ: 213–240.

Rothschild, M.L. and Gaidis, W.C. (1981) 'Behavioural learning theory: its relevance to marketing and promotions', *Journal of Marketing*, 45: 70–78.

Ruddle, H., Bradshaw, C.M., Szabadi, E. and Bevan, P. (1979) 'Behaviour of humans in concurrent schedules programmed on spatially separated operanda', *Quarterly Journal of Experimental Psychology*, 31: 509–517.

Sato, M. and Sugiyama, N. (1994) 'Lying', in S.C. Hayes, L.J. Hayes, M. Sato and K. Ono (eds) *Behaviour Analysis of Language and Cognition*, Reno, NV: Context Press, 165–180.

Schmitt, D.R. (1974) 'Effects of reinforcement rate and reinforcer magnitude on choice behaviour of humans', *Journal of the Experimental Analysis of Behaviour*, 21: 409–419.

Schnaitter, R. (1978) 'Private causes', *Behaviourism*, 6: 1–12.

Schroeder, S.R. (1975) 'Perseveration in concurrent performances by the developmentally retarded', *Psychological Record*, 25: 51–64.

—— and Holland, J.G. (1969) 'Reinforcement of the eye movement with concurrent schedules', *Journal of the Experimental Analysis of Behaviour*, 12: 897–903.

Schwartz, B. (1984) *Psychology of Learning and Behaviour*, 2nd edn, New York: Norton.

—— and Lacey, H. (1982) *Behaviorism, Science, and Human Nature*, New York: Norton.

—— and Reisberg, D. (1991) *Learning and Memory*, New York: Norton.

Shavitt, S. (1989) 'Operationalizing functional theories of attitude', in A.R. Pratkanis, S.J. Breckler and A.G. Greenwald (eds) *Attitude Structure and Function*, Hillsdale, NJ: Erlbaum, 311–337.

Sidman, M. (1990) 'Equivalence relations: where do they come from?', in D.E. Blackman and H.H. Lejeune (eds) *Behaviour Analysis in Theory and Practice*, London: Erlbaum, 93–114.

—— (1992) 'Equivalence relations: some basic considerations', in S.C. Hayes and L.J. Hayes (eds) *Understanding Verbal Relations*, Reno, NV: Context Press, 15–28.

Silberberg, A., Thomas, J.R. and Berendzen, N. (1991) 'Human choice on concurrent variable-interval variable ratio schedules', *Journal of the Experimental Analysis of Behaviour*, 56: 575–584.

Skinner, B.F. (1938) *The Behaviour of Organisms*, New York: Century.

—— (1945) 'The operational analysis of psychological terms', *Psychological Review*, 52: 270–277, 291–294.

—— (1950) 'Are theories of learning necessary?', *Psychological Review*, 57: 193–216.

—— (1953) *Science and Human Behaviour*, New York: Macmillan.

—— (1957) *Verbal Behaviour*, New York: Century.

—— (1963) 'Behaviourism at fifty', *Science*, 140: 951–958.

—— (1967) 'B.F. Skinner', in E.G. Boring and G. Lindzey (eds) *A History of Psychology in Autobiography*, vol. V, New York: Appleton, Century, Crofts.

—— (1969) *Contingencies of Reinforcement: A Theoretical Analysis*, Englewood Cliffs, NJ: Prentice Hall.

—— (1971) *Beyond Freedom and Dignity*, New York: Knopf.

—— (1974) *About Behaviourism*, New York: Knopf.

—— (1988a) 'Reply to Schnaitter', in A.C. Catania and S. Harnad (eds) *The Selection of Behaviour: The Operant Behaviourism of B.F. Skinner – Comments and Consequences*, New York: Cambridge University Press, 354.

—— (1988b) 'Reply to Mackenzie', in A.C. Catania and S. Harnad (eds) *The Selection of Behaviour: The Operant Behaviourism of B.F. Skinner – Comments and Consequences*, New York: Cambridge University Press, 113–114.

—— (1989) 'The behaviour of the listener', in S.C. Hayes (ed.) *Rule-Governed Behaviour: Cognition, Contingencies and Instructional Control*, New York: Plenum, 85–96.

—— (1990) 'Can psychology be a science of mind?', *American Psychologist*, 45: 1206–1210.

Staddon, J.E.R. (1993) *Behaviourism*, London: Duckworth.

Steele, D. and Hayes, S.C. (1991) 'Stimulus equivalence and arbitrarily applicable relational responding', *Journal of the Experimental Analysis of Behaviour*, 56: 519–555.

Takahashi, M. and Iwamoto, T. (1986) 'Human concurrent performances: the effects of experience, instructions, and schedule-correlated stimuli', *Journal of the Experimental Analysis of Behaviour*, 45: 257–267.

Thompson, R.F. (1994) 'Behaviourism and neuroscience', *Psychological Review*,

101: 259–265.

Todd, J.T. and Morris, E.K. (1992) 'Case histories in the great power of steady misrepresentation', *American Psychologist*, 47: 1441–1453.

Troye, S.V. (1985) 'Situationist theory and consumer behaviour', in J.N. Sheth (ed.) *Research in Consumer Behaviour* 1, Greenwich, CT: JAI Press, 285–321.

Tversky, A. and Kahneman, D. (1974) 'Judgment under uncertainty: heuristics and biases', *Science*, 185: 1124–1131.

Valentine, E.R. (1992) *Conceptual Issues in Psychology*, 2nd edn, London: Routledge

Van Knippenberg, D., Lossie, N. and Wilke, H. (1994) 'In-group prototypicality and persuasion: determinants of heuristic and systematic message processing', *British Journal of Social Psychology*, 33; 289–300.

Van Raaij, W.F. (1988) 'Information processing and decision making: cognitive aspects of economic behaviour', in W.F. Van Raaij, G.M. Van Veldhoven and K.-E. Warneryd (eds) *Handbook of Economic Psychology*, Dordrecht: Kluwer, 74–106.

—— (1991) 'The formation and use of expectations in consumer decision making', in T.S. Robertson and H.H. Kassarjian (eds) *Handbook of Consumer Behaviour*, Englewood Cliffs, NJ: Prentice Hall, 401–418.

——, Van Veldhoven, G.M. and Warneryd, K.-E. (eds) (1988) *Handbook of Economic Psychology*, Dordrecht: Kluwer.

Vaughan, M.E. (1991) 'Toward a methodology for studying verbal behaviour', in L.J. Hayes and P.N. Chase (eds) *Dialogue on Verbal Behaviour*, Reno, NV: Context Press, 82–84.

Wearden, J. (1988) 'Some neglected problems in the analysis of human operant behaviour', in G.C.L. Davey and C. Cullen (eds) *Human Operant Conditioning and Behaviour Modification*, Chichester: Wiley.

Wheeler, H. (ed.) (1973) *Beyond the Punitive Society*, London: Wildwood House.

Wicker, A.W. (1979) *An Introduction to Ecological Psychology*, Cambridge: Cambridge University Press.

—— (1987) 'Behavior settings reconsidered: temporal stages, resources, internal dynamics, context', in D. Stokols and I. Altmann (eds) *Handbook of Environmental Psychology*, New York: John Wiley, 613–653.

Winkler, R.C. (1980) 'Behavioural economics, token economies and applied behaviour analysis', in J.E.R. Staddon (ed.) *Limits to Action: The Allocation of Individual Behaviour*, New York: Academic Press, 269–297.

Wurster, R.M. and Griffiths, R.R. (1979) 'Human concurrent performances: variation of reinforcer magnitude and rate of reinforcement', *Psychological Record*, 29: 341–354.

Wyer, R.S. and Srull, T.K. (1986) 'Human cognition in its social context', *Psychological Review*, 93: 322–359.

—— and —— (1989) *Memory and Cognition in its Social Context*, Hillsdale, NJ: Erlbaum.

—— and —— (eds) (1994a) *Handbook of Social Cognition, Volume 1: Basic Processes*, 2nd edn, Hillsdale, NJ: Erlbaum.

—— and —— (eds) (1994b) *Handbook of Social Cognition, Volume 2: Application*, 2nd edn, Hillsdale, NJ: Erlbaum.

Zettle, R.D. and Hayes, S.C. (1982) 'Rule-governed behaviour: a potential theoretical framework for cognitive-behavioural therapy', in P.C. Kendall (ed.) *Advances in Cognitive-Behavioural Research and Therapy*, 1, New York: Academic Press, 73–118.

Zuriff, G.E. (1979) 'Ten inner causes', *Behaviourism*, 7: 1–8.

10 Cyberspace as the next marketing frontier(?)

Questions and issues

Alladi Venkatesh, Laurie Meamber and A. Fuat Firat

In the late twentieth century, with modernity having lost its innocence, and its transparency having yielded to an unsettling opaqueness, a search for alternative categories of life has begun. The defining moments are no longer the dichotomies of time and space, past and future, near and far, but only the present and here. As Foucault (1979) noted, we are busy constructing the history of the present, freezing time into a new set of practices and discourses, and unburdening ourselves from the weight of history and the uneasy anticipation of the future. What we are creating is a world where we can lose ourselves and escape into the world of the hyperreal (or hype and real) manipulated by the ideologies and the technologies of the digital. In this phantasmagoric world, in trying to relinquish the vestiges of modernism, we are preparing to enter a futuristic world replete, however, with the symbolism of the distant past. Paradoxically, we seem to be seeking a reassurance that our physicality is still intact (if not real), and that we can touch, feel, see and smell the various (artificial?) life forms that spin around us. It is as if we are moving in a gigantic circulating machine where both fission and fusion, fact and fiction are caught in a vertiginous web. No doubt, all of this seems to have inspired the sci-fi writer, Gibson (1984), to characterise what was previously thought of as mere fiction but today experienced as the reality of our living space as *cyberspace*. To quote Gibson from his serious yet frolicsome classic, *Neuromancer*:

> Cyberspace. A consensual hallucination experienced daily by billions of legitimate operators ... A graphic representation of data abstracted from the banks of every computer in the human system. Unthinkable complexity. Lines of light ranged in the nonspace of the mind, clusters and constellations of data. Like city lights, receding.
>
> (Gibson 1984: 51)

Cyberspace and cyberculture are terms that are now in vogue (Escobar 1994). They represent the new electronic world of social activity, language, commerce, discursive practices that seem to have suddenly overtaken our lives, but, in reality, have been years in the making. The new manifestation of cyberspace is a dimensionless web-like space (WWW) and what we are witnessing today is the continuation of a long process which Daniel Bell (1973) identified in the mid-1960s as the beginnings of the post-industrial society that was becoming more knowledge based. He called the emerging industries the knowledge industries, the workers the knowledge workers, and the machines responsible for this transformation the knowledge-based machines, or more popularly the computers. Over the years, the prefix, knowledge, has given way to terms such as 'intelligence', 'information', and more recently to 'cyber'.

In this chapter, we shall provide an analysis of how cyberspace is beginning to impact on consumers, and what theoretical and practical implications emerge from this. Writing this chapter at this juncture is akin to studying the raging waters of a river while standing right in the middle of it and hoping to make sense of the mysteries of the river current. By the time one is able to grasp the phenomena one intends to study, the very ground on which one stands has moved leaving no anchor from which an observation can be made. Detached observation is more difficult when the observer is also moving along with the observed.

That the new technologies of information and communication are all around us needs no special mention. They seem to be per(in?)vading our universe with sovereign vengeance. The information revolution which was heralded almost a quarter century ago is taking place as we are writing these lines. A good measure of the revolution is motivated by commercial opportunities that now involve markets and consumers as part of everyday life. This chapter is about the nature of cyberspace as it pertains to consumers and their identities, and to the co-optation of this space by eager marketers. For some people, the term 'cyberspace' seems to be pretentious because it is evocative of hype and exaggeration. Perhaps, there is some truth to it. However, if history teaches us any lesson, an important one is that today's hypes could become tomorrow's realities. It is in this spirit that we want to examine several key issues. Our chapter will address the following questions/issues.

1 What is cyberspace? How is it related to physical space? Are they (cyberspace and physical space) parallel spaces, or each a mirror of the other, or oppositional to each other?
2 What are the limits of cyberspace (as constructed and experienced)? How does it challenge modernist categories such as artificial and natural, culture and nature, real and virtual, mechanistic and organismic?
3 How are consumer identities established in cyberspace?
4 What technological possibilities exist in cyberspace that are relevant to consumer behaviour and marketing? (Why is cyberspace a site of marketing control?)

WHAT IS CYBERSPACE?

Is cyberspace (the allegorical space?) the same as physical space?

Where in the world is Cyberspace? . . . How is cyberspace also a space? First, in mathematics, logic and computer science, it is common to speak of a space as a subset of a world . . . For any initial configuration of elements and a set of rules, there is a space of possibilities defined. The system can assume many states, and the total of all states constitutes a space . . . There is a sense in which cyberspace is such a space.

(Coyne 1995: 155)

In many respects, cyberspace is similar to physical space. Objects can occupy cyberspace . . . There is the sense of [cyber]space as coordinate and measurable space . . . Cyberspace constrains and enables human interaction in ways similar to physical space . . . Behavioral patterns are intimately connected as in physical space . . . Cyberspace is thought to reproduce or represent Cartesian space. If physical space can be represented with three-dimensional coordinates, then this information can be stored, manipulated, and transformed by computer and displayed, using monitors, plotters, digital devices, flight simulators, and stereo-scopic virtual-reality head sets. Furthermore, any information can be transformed into visual, audile, and now tactile form. In this sense, cyber-space reproduces and even transcends physical space.

(Coyne 1995: 155–156)

Cyberspace is thought to be a space in these four senses. It defines spaces of possibilities, it is measurable and numerically specifiable, it enables and constrains social activity, and it reproduces physical space.

(Coyne 1995: 157)

Cyberspaces are basically computer mediated environments. They give rise to various kinds of simulacra, such as virtual environments, MUDs (Multi-User Dungeons), digital images and sounds, and to new under-standing of the relationship between the natural and the artificial, real versus imaginary, or as Massumi (1987) would call it, 'realer than real' (see also Baudrillard 1983). Cyberspace is the furthest we have travelled into the world of reality if we do not count the magical and the supernatural. It is also far removed from the mechanical conception of modernity. Several developments in the cyberspatial culture are crucial for us here.

1   Cyberspace as parallel to the physical space.
2   Cyberspaces as the site of fragmented virtuality, as highly individu-alised, decentralised spaces of human subjectivity.
3   Cyberspaces as providing a different order of navigation.
4   Cyberspaces as subversive and transgressive of many of our established norms and expectations of behaviour.

5 Cyberspaces as organismic while seeming to mimic the mechanistic view of physical space which is linear and one of sequential ordering.
6 Cyberspace as giving rise to clans and anonymous communities.

Abandon realism: cyberspace is a new conception of space and is oppositional to physical space

> in patently unreal and artificial realities such as cyberspace, the principles of ordinary space and time, can in principle(!), be violated with impunity . . . After all, the ancient worlds of magic, myth, and legend to which cyberspace is heir, as well as the modern world of fantasy, fiction, movies, and cartoons, are replete with violations of the logic of everyday space and time: disappearances, underworlds, phantoms, warp speed travel, mirrors and doors to alternate worlds, zero gravity, flattenings and reconstitutions, wormholes, scale inversions, and so on. And after all, why have cyberspace if we cannot (apparently) bend nature's rules there?
>
> (Benedikt 1991: 128)

Cyberspaces are both imaginary and constructed spaces, products of digital frontierism and science fiction, and follow no predetermined principles of order and structure. They exist as much in human imagination as they do in everyday reality and there is no particular theoretical framework within which the spaces can be configured. There are no walls to bound these spaces, no physical terrain on which they can be cartographed, but they are nevertheless spaces where people move around (roam about?) without having to face each other. What characterises the cyberspaces is the *physical location* of the subject independent of the *body,* embedded in a system of symbolic forms and information nodes. Cyberspaces are full of paradoxes, they are spaces where human beings can be in contact with one another on an instantaneous basis and still remain anonymous, where identities are hidden and camouflaged, and people can enter and withdraw, meet and discuss, see and not be seen. All of this is possible while sitting at home and gazing at the electronic screen (Turkle 1995). In spite of this seeming ethereality, the actual rhetoric of this new spatial adventure is cast in terms of established vocabulary, awash with the ideas of community, social interaction, the meeting of minds, and the exchange of ideas.

Of course, the object is to render the cyberspace familiar and ensure that it approximates the real world. But then there are some features of cyberspace not found in the real space. Virtual environments are both marginal (in the sense that they are not accorded equal status with real life) environments and simulated environments. They do not need physical referents and individuals can experience virtual conditions not encountered in the real world. People can construct virtual objects in cyberspace and interact with them as both real and imaginary objects.

Cyberspace is a communication and an information space

> Cyberspace is a vast media matrix of the actual and the potential that incorporates the activities of telephone conversations, data transfer, electronic mail, computerized transactions, ATM transactions, on-line information services, video-conferencing, the new mass media, virtual reality ... Cyberspace promises a bright and exciting technological future of unfettered communication and a reinvigoration of liberal and democratic community.
>
> (Coyne 1995: 150)

> Cyberspace is a globally networked, computer-sustained, computer-accessed, multidimensional, artificial, or 'virtual reality.' In this reality, to which every computer is a window, seen or heard objects are neither physical nor, necessarily, representations of physical objects but are, rather, in form, character and action, made up of data, of pure information.
>
> (Benedikt 1991: 122)

Cyberspace is a repository of information. It is not a conventional 'air space' in the sense of a broadcasting channel. It is limitless. The information can be accessed by anybody with very limited investment. Unlike the broadcast space it need not be regulated for there is no space to distribute in the sense of allocating a limited resource among competing demands. Since the cyberspace is practically limitless, it presents its own problems. First, for any single individual, the need is finite but perhaps focused. The needs are not limitless. The challenge facing the individual is how to choose from the limitless world of information. In other words, the individual needs to have information about information. This is a new twist to information access. It is similar to another information space, the traditional library. In a typical library, the size of the library is not that critical for locating a book. Once there is a cataloguing system any library material can be accessed if the user knows the author or the title. The difficulty arises when the user knows neither. However, it is still possible to do something about it via key words or doing subject search. In a similar fashion we can think of cyberspace information as a digital library. In any event, search engines are available to meet these needs and are constantly being updated.

CYBERSPACE IS POSTMODERN

(Descartes! Move over and make room for Heidegger)

> I used to date a woman who lived in a different city. We spent a lot of time together on e-mail. And we figured out a way we could sort of go to the movies together. We'd find a film that was playing at about

the same time in both our cities. We'd drive to our respective theaters, chatting on our telephones. We'd watch the movie, and on the way home we'd use our cellular telephones again to discuss the show. In the future this sort of 'virtual dating' will be better because the movie watching could be combined with a videoconference.

(Gates 1995: 206)

Today the computer is an actor in a struggle between modern and post-modern understandings ... Prefigured by Neuromancer's matrix of informational space, postmodernism's objects now exist outside science fiction. They exist in the information and connections of the Internet and the World Wide Web, and in the windows, icons, and layers of personal computing. They exist in the creatures on a SimLife computer game, and in the simulations of the quantum world ... All of these are life on the screen. And with these objects, the abstract ideas in Jameson's account of postmodernism become newly accessible and even consumable.

(Turkle 1995: 43, 45)

In a deep (ontological sense) we are in *the* world.

(Coyne 1995: 167)

As has been noted before (Brown 1995; Firat and Venaktesh 1993), postmodernism is sceptical of fundamentals and foundations. In the context of information technology, Coyne (1995) observes that, as opposed to systems theory which has for decades provided the basic principles of the structure of computerised environments, cyberspatial culture is viewed as postmodern in nature. It is postmodern because the conventional thinking about what is reality, how representational systems work and significatory systems perform is different from the modernist understanding. Postmodernism is a cultural position that introduces non-linearities in time and space, in virtual environments, in chains of signifiers, in decentred self, in the breaking down of the mind–body dualism, in the creation of expressive forms, in resurrecting language as a critical narrative, in decentring the gendered relationship and in general, in the breaking down of modernist dichotomies. Postmodernist discourse renounces hierarchical reasoning and closed systems approach to the study of computerised environments. It acknowledges that human systems are open systems and cautions against universalising the principles of behaviour in living organisms and human organisations which are characterised by complex transactions within their environments and which are poorly understood. Heidegger (1964) distinguishes between the ontic and the being in human discourse. Conventional sciences are ontic in nature looking for regular patterns of behaviour and neat classification schemes. These approaches, useful as they are, are also limited in their appeal. To quote Coyne:

Much postmodern writing follows Heideggerian line. Studies in information technology or design that accord primacy to information systems theory are categorized by postmoderns as ontic ... [The] indifference on the part of postmodernism to systems theory means that postmodernism focuses on ... power, how texts operate, questions about the constitution of the subject, how we are constituted by our technologies, and the dismantling of metaphysics.

(Coyne 1995: 206)

Therefore, in the discourse on cyberspace our concerns are more with

- simulation or the construction of simulacra
- signification and identity formation
- objects without referent – mechanistic versus organismic forms
- virtual communities
- virtual spaces and interactivity.

Cyberspaces are not only cognitive spaces but also behavioural spaces and experiential spaces. They are there to explore, and to create new possibilities. There is no need for prior knowledge as to what the space is, nor how to navigate it. One can enter cyberspace as the new born turtle reaches the deep waters within an instant of its birth. It is a place where one can experience new behaviours, repeat past behaviours, and hide behind the conscious. People can simulate the spaces they roam, manipulate the texture of the spaces and find new ways to settle or colonise them. Because there are no physical boundaries in cyberspace, there are no limits to behaviour or standardised responses. Euclidean parameters do not apply to cyberspaces. Cyberspaces permit considerable exploration of the kind unattainable in the real world. In other words, it is a world of simulation as well as exploration.

Cyberspace as simulacrum

In this section we shall examine four different dichotomies of modernity and how they have become problematic in the discourse on cyberspace. We identify the dichotomies as artificial and natural, culture and nature, real and virtual, and mechanistic and organismic.

One point of departure for this discussion is 'the sciences of the artificial' as enunciated by Herbert Simon (1982). Another point of departure is related to Simon's notion of artificiality but has origins in a different paradigm, 'the social construction of reality' by Berger and Luckmann (1966). Berger and Luckmann focus on the social/cultural world while Simon's focus is on a cognitive and mechanistic world. Simon (1982) makes three arguments which must be taken seriously whether we agree with him or not.

- *Argument 1*: 'The world we live in today is much more a man-made, or artificial than it is a natural world. Almost every element in our environment shows evidence of artifice.'

- *Argument 2*: '[We] must be careful about equating "biological" with "natural." A forest may be a phenomenon of nature; a farm is certainly not. The very species on which man depends for his food – his corn and cattle – are artifacts of ingenuity. A plowed field is no more part of nature than an asphalted street, no less.'
- *Argument 3*: However, in this artificiality of the world 'man must obey the law of gravity as surely as does stone.'

The first argument sets the record straight that the modern person lives in the world of artifice more than in the world of nature. The second argument points to a distinction between biological and natural by stating that biological does not necessarily imply that the object is also natural. Thus biological life can be constructed by the human being in the same way as an inanimate object (e.g. automobile) can. The third argument points to an inevitable irony in all of this. Whether we live in a world of nature or in a state of artifice, we still follow the laws of nature. The airplane which flies at high altitudes does not defy the law of gravity but does in fact obey it to the last detail. Whatever tricks we play with nature are subject to what nature imposes on us. We shall return to this natural–artificial issue later on. Let us turn to the nature–culture issue.

The nature–culture issue is more complex, and historically has been more central to the practice of the social sciences. We do not look for the laws of nature – and, if at all, only marginally – to guide us in developing appropriate norms of social or cultural behaviours. Without meaning to be tautological, all social behaviour is socially constructed. For example, certain types of behaviour are permitted and certain others are not, based on social expediency. Many ritualistic practices are socially determined and regulated. To the extent social is not natural, we may even say that it is artificial – artificial as understood to be opposite to natural. Enter cyberspace which is an amalgam of artifice and a socially constructed, technologically mediated world of (un)reality. Cyberspace is where perhaps Simon on the one hand and Berger and Luckmann on the other can find a common ground.

The real and the virtual

The relationship between virtual/simulated environments and real environments can be conceptualised in several ways. Let us begin with a simple case of how simulation works and proceed progressively to more complex relationships between simulation and reality.

In the conventional discourse, the 'real' environment is where the 'real' action is, and the simulated environment becomes an exploratory, or preparatory environment. So, for example, a pilot using a flight simulator is trained in a simulated environment. This is an 'as if' environment. The relationship between the simulated flight and real flying is as follows.

The objective here is to use the flight simulator as an artificial training ground that approximates real/natural flying conditions. There is no pretence here that the simulated environment is imbued with the characteristics of the real environment, but it nevertheless serves an important purpose. The risks are lower both to the flyer and the machine, the costs of mistake negligible, and the dangers of flying absent. The simulator provides necessary learning opportunities, that is, as a preparatory device to real life experience. If we were to use a semiotic framework, the simulator can be considered the signifier and the real environment the signified. In this representational scheme, the signifier is not a perfect substitute and therefore occupies a less privileged position when compared to the signified. That is, even if individuals master the simulator, merely on that basis they cannot qualify as pilots unless they test their prowess in real conditions.

A critical aspect of the relationship between the simulation and the real that we just discussed is that no technology exists to make the simulation a perfect substitute for the real. This is the basic structural limitation and is the starting point of the problematic of representation in cyberspace.

Let us now look at a marketing example which in most respects is similar to the flight simulator example. When an advertisement for ice-cream appears in a magazine, there is no misconception that the ice-cream in the ad is capable of satisfying one's appetite, for, obviously, the physiological condition of the body requires the real ice-cream. One cannot eat ice-cream that appears on the advertisement page however appetising it might appear. As in the previous example, the virtual cannot compete with the real in its essential aspects and therefore we may say with some confidence that the real is superior to the virtual in a phenomenological sense. It is obvious in this example that no amount of virtuality can come close to a real scoop of ice-cream if the objective is to satisfy one's physiological need of hunger. There is, however, a key difference between the flight simulator example and the ice-cream example. The real flying conditions are not only real but also natural (even allowing for Herbert Simon's extreme examples from above) while the real ice-cream is not a natural product but human-made.

Be that as it may, both the examples cited above provide a unidimensional perspective of the relationship between the virtual and the real in that the virtual falls short of the real in some 'essential aspects' and therefore is considered inferior. But this is not the only relationship that we encounter in our everyday lives. For instance, in a different context, we might ask the question, is the movie better than the book? Here the virtual is the movie, but can we say that the book is the real in the ice-cream sense? In this example, the notion of the real breaks down. The movie is based on the book but the book has no greater reality than the movie but perhaps only a different reality. The only thing we can say about the book is that it has a temporal priority, and therefore we can call it the original (and not the real). The virtual represents the original but not in the sense of the ice-cream ad representing the real scoop of ice-cream. We have now come to an interesting theoretical position. In the flight simulator example, the flight simulator is a simulation and the flying conditions are not only real but also *natural*; in the ice-cream example, the ice-cream ad is virtual but the scoop of ice-cream is real and *constructed*, and in the movie example, both the movie and the book are equally real and constructed.

In spite of these distinctions, were we to use a semiotic framework, these distinctions would disappear because all the three of them, the flight simulator, the ice-cream ad and the movie can be called the signifier and what they represent as the signified.   .

Let us now stretch the book example a little bit further. Supposing the book is a mediocre or an obscure book, and would have never risen to any prominence without the movie which is both an artistic and commercial success. Although the book is the temporal prior and therefore the original, the movie is certainly the more privileged if we accept a different set of criteria to judge their relative phenomenologies based on aesthetic and commercial considerations. The movie begins to exist in its own reality, independent of the book whose reality is not the same. To say that the movie simulates the book does not have much meaning, at least not in the ice-cream sense where the real ice-cream is also the 'edible' product, a characteristic denied to the ad.

Now, let us give one last twist to the relationship between the simulation and the real to make one more important point. In the ice-cream example, the real refers not so much to the ice-cream but to its fundamental property that it satisfies a biological need that the simulation does not. There is no other privileged element in this relationship other than the biological-need-satisfying-ability. Let us now imagine a food situation where a food designer designs a new ice-cream product that does not exist in reality. That is, the designer concocts a recipe purely out of his or her imagination from some sort of deductive scheme and the edible product does not yet exist. Supposing somebody comes up with the actual ice-cream based on the designed model. If we use a temporal priority argument we may be obliged to say that the 'real' ice-cream is the simulation and the non-real ice-cream is the original. And if we use a semiotic framework, we can similarly argue that the edible ice-cream is the signifier and the design of it is the signified. In this example, the original and the signified are different from the real. The real becomes the signifier in a sort of semiotic role reversal.

The above examples and discussion lead to a fundamental theoretical issue concerning the relationship between the simulation and the real. Normally, when we use the term, 'simulation', we assume that there is something 'real' that is being represented. We are now ready to ask the question, is it possible to have simulation without the real? What does this mean? Here the problematic word is not simulation but the word 'real'. The previous discussion was designed to show that in common discourse we tend to use the words the 'real', the 'simulation' and the 'original' in a rather uncritical fashion whereas in actual fact, these terms take on meanings based on the context. The reality of these terms is much more complex for what is 'real' is as much a construction as the simulation is. That is, as Baudrillard (1983) never tires of reminding us, the simulation can become more real than the real and sometimes simulation is its own reality, and there is nothing but signifiers.

When we move to the technological realm, the problem is compounded. Let us briefly examine the various technologies of everyday (real?) life. What is an automobile? It does not simulate anything. It is a reality in itself as is any technology in the home, the telephone, the refrigerator, the vacuum cleaner, the video-recorder, TV, camera, stereo-recorder and so on. Each of them was a new reality when it was invented and continues to be one in its own right. These are constructions with no resemblance to anything prior to that. These examples suggest that they are neither simulations nor are they the simulated. They are their own reality not in the sense of a natural real or organic real, but something that exists outside these two frames of reference. They constitute a 'cultural real'. The cultural real privileges neither the simulation nor the simulated.

Cyberspace is a combination of the new and the old. It is new in the sense that new technological possibilities create new social spaces but it is also old in the sense that the social/cultural imperatives have remained unaltered. But as Poster (1995) reminds us, cyberspace is not a Greek agora, but a new territorial concept completely (if not, over-) determined by the late twentieth-century technology.

From the virtual/real to the mechanistic/organismic: mechanistic ideas of representation

Beginning with Descartes our understanding of the world has followed a mechanistic route. Essentially, the mechanistic approach formalises the ideas or symbols we use to represent the world in a rationalistic fashion. In addition, it also attempts to formalise the process of thinking itself. Thinking in this perspective means instrumental reasoning, calculation, using formal rules of evidence and monitoring standardised/predictable performance. Rational thinking is a conscious, competent administration of an idea, aided by procedural methods.

The mechanistic and formalistic idea of representation was also at the heart of computing in its beginning stages and continues even today to some extent. Data are representations of facts and computer technology is essentially directed toward storing and manipulating of data.

The mechanistic paradigm underlies the design of various domestic technologies that exhibit a purpose, are singular, and well ordered. To the extent that mind is presumed to control matter, we view these machines as controllable devices whose functions are dictated by human needs and dictates, and whose operations and purposes appear to be very transparent. Any interaction with the machine implies this relationship.

But in parallel to this mechanistic view of the world, there always existed a romantic view. Human emotions and unconscious desires always resisted these mechanistic and formalistic norms of behaviour and looked for forms of liberatory moments. Poetry always existed side by side with logic. However, in all of these cases, the romantic elements played a secondary role to the rationalistic framework because of social norms and institutional structures.

While the mechanistic view lent itself to collective order and rationality, the romantic view was a privileged, individualistic, artistic expression, which allowed for physical and bodily articulations.

We elaborate this idea further in Figure 10.1. The rectangular formulation is a modified Greimasian square which pits mechanism against organism. Familiar domestic technologies (kitchen appliances and automobiles) are classified as mechanistic devices characterised by singularity of purpose and well-defined systems. Together they constitute the mechanistic space. At the opposite end are computers and the new cyberspace technologies (World Wide Web) that occupy the organismic space. They are both ill-defined relative to the mechanistic technologies. The relationship of the technologies to the human agency varies. The mechanistic technologies serve the human being in the performance of various mechanical chores.

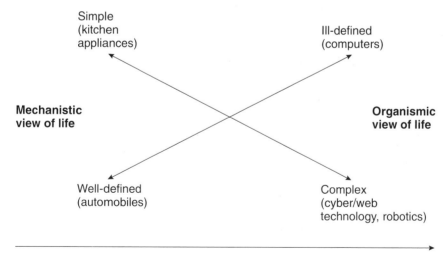

Figure 10.1 Greimasian square of the configuration of mechanistic and organismic views of life

The organismic technologies mimic human intelligence and also serve human needs at a higher level. The extreme form of this relationship is where the computer can act as a simulated human being. Writing in 1984, Turkle (1984) compared the computer to the mirror in which the human being could see himself or herself. This imagery was further modified in her book, *Life on the Screen* (Turkle 1995). Using a postmodern interpretation, she characterised the computer screen as the door behind which other humans reside and can be contacted. We have moved a long way from the kitchen appliances to the Web technology.

Computers are no longer viewed as merely computational devices working with mass amounts of data. The cyberspace has become a site of romantic vision and experience, and all the suppressed emotional areas of life are blossoming in cyberspace. One can see this in various technological manifestations of cyberspace – interactive media, virtual technologies, simulated art and a host of similar developments.

Mechanical to computational to bio-technical

We are moving from a mechanical concept of the world to a computational concept and further into a bio-technical concept of the world. For centuries, a key argument centred around culture and nature dichotomy, questioning which of the two was superior in explaining or guiding human behaviour. The debate continues and keeps some of us occupied. A few thinkers have suggested that the dispute between nature and culture is itself socially constructed, for according to some of them what is natural is cultural and what is cultural is natural. While the debate regarding nature–culture goes on, a parallel debate has surfaced in recent years, natural vs. artificial. Whatever progress we have recorded in the past three hundred years is in the world of the artificial. For more than three decades our focus has been on not just artificial but artificial intelligence (AI). This has more recently expanded into artificial life (AL) suggesting that we are moving away from AI to AL. The aesthetic of the body has also accordingly shifted to artificial formulations of the body.

Mechanism versus organism: a final note

The basis of computerisation is the effacement of the distinction between mechanism and organism. We are now picturing machines as organisms or self-replicating artifices. Organisms do not have a purpose, at least one that we can theorise about. For example, we cannot easily ask a question why cats, dogs or humans inhabit the planet. What we can say, if we are not atheists, is that God willed it. Of course, we can also say that because dogs have a keen sense of smell, they are good in finding criminals. But this is not why the dog was created in the first place. We invented the purpose once we knew what dogs could do. On the other hand, mechanisms have purpose (granted 'purpose' is culturally determined and signified); we build a machine so the machine can do something. We can talk about the automobile having a purpose, that is, as a means of transportation. The main purpose of an organism seems to be self-replication and this is as close as we can get in uncovering its purpose. The site for the effacement of the distinction between mechanism and organism is cyberspace.

Computerised aesthetic

If the basis of cyberspace is the effacement of the distinction between mechanism and organism, we may be looking at machine-organisms as self-replicating artifices. The main purpose of an organism is to self-replicate but, as we stated earlier, this is true of a machine. However, this traditional distinction between mechanism and organism is being eroded with the entry of new technologies of information. Of particular interest for our discussion is how the blurring of this distinction has an impact on individual identity. We discuss individual identity by first exploring the notion of body in cyberspace.

Aestheticisation of the body

We would like to find a position for the body in cyberspace. Since cyberspaces are virtual, or more real than real, our conceptualisations of the body also follow these virtualities.

The field of marketing has historically and quite aggressively appropriated the human body as the site of its discourse (Joy and Venkatesh 1994). Hundreds of products are manufactured and sold with human anatomy and clothing as the prime targets of marketing. One can argue that a major part of consumer culture is devoted to the aestheticisation of the body culture. Marketing has been simultaneously exploitative and seductive, and has universalised this aesthetic temporally and spatially. Because of the modernist hang-up with mind–body dichotomy, with mind being given a preferred status, marketing had to contend with a defensive posture in promoting the body culture.

With the emergence of the sciences of the artificial, and the new technologies of computerised aesthetic, the very notion of the body is undergoing serious and active debate. These new disciplines of the artificial are high status scientific disciplines and their approaches to the cultivation of the physical via the artificial have received much intellectual support. These new disciplinary ideas are penetrating into our notions of subjectivities not simply metaphorically or phenomenologically but by creating a social problematic of the contemporary world. The question then is what is the nature of subjectivity in cyberspace.

In the Cartesian framework, the mind-centredness dominates our view of the world. In the postmodern world, we are moving more and more into a body-centred framework. Two important manifestations permit this conclusion. First of all, the architecture of cyberspace lends itself to the permutations of bodily expressions and displays through the use of colour, three-dimensional graphics and other visual imagery. Cyberspatial manipulations are subject to interactivity, which means that the user is more a bricoleur in Lévi-Strauss's sense. Second, the manipulation of cyberspace needs no special skills. Many of them are available for mere asking at the touch of a button and the manipulation of objects in cyberspace is as easy as lifting a pen.

Cyberspace is not only the realm of the artificial but also the realm of artificial life. In a Cartesian world, artificial intelligence (AI) provides the dominant model for thinking. The best example is the computer in the famous movie, *2001 A Space Odyssey* with a mind but no movable body. In a non-Cartesian world, artificial intelligence slowly gives way to artificial life (AL). The earliest manifestation of artificial life is the computer virus. Computer virus is a self-replicating organism with minimum intelligence and maximum destructive power. The principle of self-replication can be easily extended to other cyber forms.

Social body versus ontological body

Stone (1995) uses virtuality in terms of the relationship between the sense of self and the body. As she says, this is 'virtual because the accustomed grounding of social interaction in the physical facticity of human bodies is changing' (Stone 1995: 17). For example, what she has in mind is a socially constructed body instead of an ontologically present body. In a move similar to Turkle's (1995), Stone considers her approaches as a shift from modernity to postmodernity, as shown in the following.

Modernity	Self and body	Located in the same physical space
Transition	Self and body	Both socially constructed, both socially mediated
Cyber technology	Spatial location of the subject independently of the physical body	

Stone (1995: 17) also raises some interesting questions. How are bodies represented through technology? How is desire constructed through representation? What is the relationship between the body and self-awareness? What is the role of play in the emergent paradigm of human–computer interaction? And overall, what is happening to sociality and desire at the end of the mechanical age?

According to Stone (1995) there are many historical developments leading to the issue of current virtuality. These include suburban living and the use of automobiles (virtual geography), shopping malls and spectacularisations. The technologies of cyberspace, the electronic media, computers, large-scale information networks, automated teller machines, arcade games, etc., are nothing but manifestations of these postmodern fragmented life patterns.

Consumer subjectivity in cyberspace

The models of virtuality in cyberspace provide new forms of subjectivity. For example, many of the contingent essentialisms of cyberspace come from science fiction – *Neuromancer, Bladerunner*. Hollywood presents the realms of possibility and advertising takes its cue from what happens in Hollywood – where hi-tech determines the protocols of contemporary consumer culture.

BODIES AND SPACES

Global identities

A world in which the global traffic of knowledge, secrets, measurements, indicators, entertainments, and alter-human agency takes on form . . . entered equally from a basement in Vancouver, a boat in Port-au-Prince, a cab in New York, a garage in Texas City, an apartment in Rome, an office in Hong Kong, a bar in Kyoto, a cafe in Kinshasa, a laboratory in the moon.

(Benedikt 1991: 1)

As an acknowledgment of this paradoxical, postmodern space, Appadurai (1993) identifies five different scapes: ethnoscapes, technoscapes, financescapes, mediascapes and ideoscapes. The first refers to the movement of populations around the world – tourists, immigrants, exiles, refugees, guestworkers – all of which is happening at unprecedented levels. The movement of these groups is closely linked to the movement of international economic and cultural capital. The second refers to the generation and movement of new technologies creating new global grids and the shifting of know-how. The third refers to the shifting of financial capital through a labyrinth of institutional arrangements and application of information technologies in an instantaneous fashion. The fourth refers both to the distribution of electronic capabilities to produce and disseminate information (newspapers, magazines, television stations, film production studios, etc.) and to the images of the world created by these media. Mediascapes have a postmodernist character, because they are image-based, and they fragment cultural realities and complicate the imagined lives of passive consumers. They are, in a sense, the apostles of a new world (religious?) order where techno-fantasies are allowed to clash with immediate life experiences. Finally, ideoscapes refer to a concatenation of images guided by political and ideological considerations. The global flows occur in and through the growing disjunctures between the five landscapes as they collide in cyberspace.

These cultural flows, notes Appadurai, create two kinds of fetishism – the fetishism of production and the fetishism of consumption. By production fetishism, he means

> an illusion created by contemporary transnational production which masks translocal capital, transnational earning flows, global management and often faraway workers in the idiom or spectacle of local control, national productivity and territorial sovereignty.
>
> (Appadurai 1990: 6)

In this formulation, the locale becomes the fetish which disguises the globally dispersed forces that actually drive the production process. Consumer fetishism represents the idea that the consumer is transformed, through commodity flows (and the mediascapes) into a sign, with global electronic communications assuming the role of key technology in the worldwide dissemination of cultural ideas. Although these messages are globally standardised, globalisation is not synonymous with homogenisation, it is just that globalisation uses the instruments of homogenisation – clothing and fashion, music and entertainment, food and aesthetic experience – to create heterogenised markets, that is, to serve and service the locals with global universal signs, transmitted through cyberspace.

Identity and virtual communities

> The idea of a community accessible only via my computer screen sounded cold to me at first, but I learned quickly that people can feel passionately about e-mail and computer conferences. I've become one of them. I care about people I meet through my computer, and I care deeply about the future of the medium that enables us to assemble ... People in virtual communities use words on screens to exchange pleasantries and argue, engage in intellectual discourse, conduct commerce, exchange knowledge, share emotional support, make plans, brainstorm, gossip, feud, fall in love, find friends and lose them, play games, flirt, create a little high art and a lot of idle talk. People in virtual communities do just about everything people do in real life, but we leave our bodies behind.
>
> (Rheingold 1993: 1, 3)

New members meet every evening at 9.00p.m. in the NEW MEMBERS LOUNGE. On-line conversations are often punctuated with textual 'smileys' and on-line shorthand.

Below is a list of some of the common ones you might come across,

:) Smile
:D Laughing
;) Wink
:* Kiss

:X My lips are sealed
:(Frown
:P Stick out Tongue. . .
{ } Hug
brb be right back

. . . Ask a Guide. Go into the People Connection Lobby (Command L) and find someone with the word 'Guide' in their name. Parents can limit their child's on-line activities – use KEYWORD PARENTAL CONTROL.

(From a membership promotional blurb – America On Line)

Very few terms in contemporary linguistics evoke such images as community. Contemporary societies, or the so-called developed, industrial societies, seem to yearn for lost symbols and institutional orders that are difficult to retrieve in these ever-changing times. Western societies, and, in particular, the American society, are nostalgic about the notion of community which, over the years, has taken a back seat in the face of rampant individualism and modernistic logic. In the emerging postmodern cyberculture, two aspects remain critical to our understanding of human behaviour in cyberspace – the constitution of identity and the formation of community. Durkheim (1964) was one of the first social theorists to raise the issue of balancing individual autonomy and social solidarity as the basis of community formation. In the past hundred years much has been written in this area and the popular work by Bellah *et al.* (1985) further confirms that this issue is very much alive even today. The notion that the sense of community has been eroded significantly in industrial societies is a frequently discussed issue in the academic circles as well as in political discourse (Etzioni 1993). Habermas (1987) has pushed this idea still further by stating that the 'system' has replaced the 'life world' as the organising principle of human existence and has therefore given rise to an interesting paradox that in industrial democracies both individual freedom and communal spirit are becoming the ultimate casualties. The loss of individual freedom means a loss of individual identity. The loss of individual identity means the loss of community. Well, enter cyberspace.

Some authors believe that perhaps in cyberculture both individual identity and the sense of community can be restored. However, within the cyberculture, these terms may not mean the same. In contradistinction to the 'real cultural space' which has marked human life over the course of history, cyberculture is not a face-to-face culture. While we can still use the terms 'freedom', 'identity' and 'community' the question needs to be asked, do they really mean the same thing in the context of cyberculture? This issue has never been more urgent.

In terms of identity formation in cyberspace, some psychoanalytical and dramaturgical approaches have been proffered (Stone 1995; Turkle 1995). The primary emphasis in these approaches is to explore how individuals project themselves on the screen and what personalities they assume in such projections. The underlying idea is that the cyber medium lends itself to certain changes in this projection process, so individuals can assume any persona of their choice which may be different from the persona in the real space. There is a distinction between the more familiar 'role' playing in 'real' life and changing one's persona on the cyberscreen. In role playing, the individual identity is not altered and everybody knows that it is the same individual who is assuming a different role because the social circumstances warrant it. Thus an individual can play the role of a parent or a manager or a teacher depending on the social situation. The role that the individual plays in real life is public knowledge. But life on the screen allows people to assume different identities so they can play the same role in multiple ways and this is not known to anybody except the individual. Cyberspace permits this because the individual is able to hide behind the screen under an identity of his or her choice. What is the motivation for identity change or identity concealment? It ranges from the simple thrill of novelty seeking to seeking a new set of experiences not possible in the real space. In either case, individuals are able to protect their real identity and revert to it without having to surrender their entire persona to strangers. Thus cyberspace is a space for strangers who can behave as if they are intimate friends. This certainly is a new dimension to human experience bordering on the magical or schizophrenic depending on one's point of view.

In a paradoxical fashion to this simultaneous identity construction and identity concealment, or because of it, the cyberspace is also viewed as a community space. In this virtual land, people can become part of a community and share their experiences with others as if they are in a real community. Nobody has promoted the idea of community in cyberspace as 'Well' as Howard Rheingold (1993). In a narrative that almost borders on fiction, Rheingold waxes eloquent on the pristine notion of virtual community. We know from the writings of sociologists that communities are social groupings in perpetuity, sharing a common language, a common physical/experiential setting that gives rise to face-to-face contact, a common set of practices, and a common set of expectations. Communities provide mechanisms for socialisation, a sense of individual identity and a site where individuals prepare themselves for the life of adulthood and family/work life. Communities provide continuity in terms of generational structure, provide psychological spaces and zones of comfort. Because community members develop a sense of solidarity, there is a lot of mutual help and understanding. People *give* without necessarily expecting immediate returns. Besides, communities provide social memory and continuity of the species. Evidently, not all of these are possible within the context of cyberculture, at least not in the precise fashion. By the same token, what is possible in cyberculture is not possible in real culture. Virtual communities do offer their members a shared space, a shared language, and an intimate communication space. Advice is sought and given, friendships are developed and lasting intimacies are attempted.

Virtual community spaces also offer a culture of freedom, freedom of accessing information, freedom of travel. The mobilities that are characteristic of cybertravel provide distinct experiences for 'cybertravellers' for whom these experiences may include seeing different worlds and seeing themselves in these worlds. The cybertraveller can say, 'that's me there, I can freely roam about in that world'. This form of cybertravelling relies on the construction of identity both by identifying oneself with, and differentiating oneself from, other cybertravellers. The cybertraveller can enter the world of others without intruding on them and without being intruded upon by others. This is the essence of cybercommunity or the virtual community. Since such a community is supportive and non-threatening, individuals can build empathetic identities. Empathetic identities can be relationally autonomous. They exist separately and yet inform and draw on each other, shape each other through cybercontact. In other words, going back to the issues we raised earlier, looming behind this identity construction is the construction of a virtual community. Thus the Durkheimian balancing act, between individual autonomy and social solidarity, is supposedly resolved in cyberspace for individuals do not lose their individuality but only gain by being part of the community.

SOME FINAL THOUGHTS: CYBERSPACE AS THE SITE OF (MARKETING) CONTROL

Given the liberatory potential of cyberspace, where does it leave the individual ultimately? In the name of consumer freedom, we are seeing many dark forces of control. Parallel to the possibility of creating new freedoms in cyberspace one also sees spheres of control – the control of consumer space by marketers. Various statistics show that 80 per cent of the Internet is now completely occupied by merchants of commerce. The rhetoric of cyberspace is full of choice, freedom, dispersed identities for the consumer. But marketers are gradually moving into this social space and redefining the notions of consumer choice and freedom. If indeed the cyberspace were to really become a world of consumer freedom, this might mean that marketers might lose grip over their consumers. But this ought not to happen. So the marketing question is, not how to preserve the true intent of the rhetoric, but only its apparent meaning. In an article in the *Harvard Business Review* (*HBR*), this issue was raised with great concern and anxiety (Hagel and Rayport 1997). As everybody knows, *HBR* is primarily a management-orientated journal and is an unabashed handmaiden of commerce. There are usually no surprises in the journal's orientation. The concerns expressed by the authors are real. They acknowledge that with the new technologies of cyberspace, it is now possible to collect more information about individual customers. In other words, there is very little that one could not know about a consumer for everything resides in the cyber database for every one to see – that is, every one who can afford to see. Consumer identities are being totally appropriated by marketers via the information data base in the name of providing better services and products. The control of the consumer is through a web of information whose net is cast wide and far. The more information one has about the consumer the more control one has over the consumer. This obvious principle is being fully tested in the world of virtuality and in the name of consumer freedom. As consumers strive to build new identities on the internet, they are also being quickly transformed into data points in databases. Getting back to the *HBR* article, instead of raising the issue that consumers might become the ultimate losers in the information war, the authors' concern is not the consumer but the marketer. One can rephrase their concern as a new title of their article, 'How to protect marketing while collecting information about the consumer.' As marketing unleashes its beguiling power over the cyberspace, the question we must ask is, whither the life of consumer freedom in cyberspace?

REFERENCES

Appadurai, A. (1990) 'Disjuncture and difference in the global cultural economy', *Public Culture*, 2, Spring: 1–24.

Baudrillard, J. (1983) *Simulations*, trans. P. Foss, P. Patton and P. Beitchman, New York: Semiotext(e).

Bell, D. (1973) *The Coming of Post-Industrial Society: A Venture in Social Forecasting*, New York: Basic Books.

Bellah, R.N. *et al.* (1985) *Habits of the Heart: Individualism and Commitment in American Life*, Berkeley, CA: University of California Press.

Benedikt, M. (ed.) (1991) *Cyberspace: First Steps*, Cambridge, MA: MIT Press.

Berger, P.L. and Luckmann, T. (1966) *The Social Construction of Reality: A Treatise in the Sociology of Knowledge*, Garden City, NY: Doubleday.

Brown, S. (1995) *Postmodern Marketing*, London: Routledge.

Coyne, R. (1995) *Designing Information Technology in the Postmodern Age: From Method to Metaphor*, Cambridge, MA: MIT Press.

Durkheim, E. (1964) *The Rules of Sociological Method*, trans. S.A. Solovay and J.H. Mueller, Glencoe, IL: Free Press.

Escobar, A. (1994) 'Welcome to Cyberia: notes on the anthropology of cyberculture', *Current Anthropology*, 35, June: 211–231.

Etzioni, A. (1993) *The Spirit of Community: Rights, Responsibilities, and the Communitarian Agenda*, New York: Crown.

Firat, A.F. and Venkatesh, A. (1993) 'Postmodernity: the age of marketing', *International Journal of Research in Marketing*, 10, 3: 227–250.

Foucault, M. (1979) *Discipline and Punish: The Birth of the Prison*, trans. A. Sheridan, New York: Viking.

Gates, B. (1995) *Looking Ahead*, New York: Viking.

Gibson, W. (1984) *Neuromancer*, New York: Ace.

Habermas, J. (1987) *The Theory of Communicative Action*, trans. T. McCarthy, Boston, MA: Beacon, vol. II, ch. VI, 113–198.

Hagel, J. and Rayport, J.F. (1997) 'The coming battle for customer information', *Harvard Business Review*, 75, January–February: 53–57.

Heidegger, M. (1964 [1927]) *Being and Time*, trans. J. Macquarrie
Robinson, New York: Harper & Row.

Joy, A. and Venkatesh, A. (1994) 'Postmodernism, feminism and the body: the
visible and the invisible in consumer research', *International Journal of Research
in Marketing*, 11, September: 333–358.

Massumi, B. (1987) 'Realer than real: the simulacrum according to Deleuze and
Guattari', *Copyright*, 1, Fall: 90–96.

Poster, M. (1995) *The Second Media Age*, Cambridge: Polity.

Rheingold, H. (1993) *The Virtual Community: Homesteading on the Electronic
Frontier*, Reading, MA: Addison Wesley.

Simon, H. (1982) *The Sciences of the Artificial*, Cambridge, MA: MIT Press.

Stone, A.R. (1995) *The War of Desire and Technology at the Close of the
Mechanical Age*, Cambridge, MA: MIT Press.

Turkle, S. (1984) *The Second Self: Computers and the Human Spirit*, NewYork:
Simon & Schuster.

—— (1995) *Life on the Screen: Identity in the Age of the Internet*, New York:
Simon & Schuster.

...ng out of the box

...yle a construct or a construction?

...ael R. Solomon and Basil G. Englis

Lifestyle is a widely used and very familiar construct to marketing researchers and laypeople alike. Indeed, the application of lifestyle analyses by managers to identify, understand and reach distinct consumer groups arguably is the most visible 'contribution' of consumer behaviour research to business practice. A *lifestyle marketing perspective* is predicated on the recognition that people sort themselves into groups on the basis of the things they like to do, how they like to spend their leisure time, and how they choose to spend their disposable income (Solomon 1996; Zablocki and Kanter 1976).

The identification and targeting of these categories has become 'The Holy Grail' for many practitioners. Psychographically orientated managers believe that consumers' lifestyle choices create opportunities for market segmentation strategies; they are instrumental in determining both the types of products purchased and the specific brands likely to appeal to a designated segment. This fine-tuning of consumer profiles allows the firm to go beyond mere demographics, as it seeks to truly understand what motivates the consumers it seeks to reach. Thus, the race is on to devise the most efficient way to divide the mass market into 'boxes' that will distil a complex morass of choices into actionable and distinct segments.

Despite the pervasiveness of this perspective, shifting views on the philosophy of science toward a post-positivist stance impel us to question the veridicality of these empirically derived 'categories' of meaning. The evolving perspective instead emphasises the subjectivity and fluidity of epistemology. It calls into question many of our most cherished assumptions about the stability of events assumed to be objectively 'out there' as opposed to being constructed in the minds of observers.

If we truly consider pledging our allegiance to this new research paradigm, then we are obligated to round up the usual suspects and call in our tried-and-true constructs for interrogation. The lifestyle construct would have to be among the first to be subjected to scrutiny. So, how valid is the lifestyle construct as it has been 'interpreted' by most researchers and marketing managers?

In this chapter we argue that the popular application of the lifestyle construct has in fact managed to leave out one important part of the phenomenon – the person whose life is being scrutinised. The *modus operandi* of those who trained and who work in the positivist tradition (as two experimental social psychologists, we plead *mea culpa*) is to distil idiosyncratic observations into broad, generalisable categories (ideally in the form of a 2×2 matrix!) and to reify these phenomena in sterile laboratory settings, the better to generate causal suppositions.

Lifestyle analyses as typically conducted follow this pattern precisely: a set of immutable categories is generated statistically and consumers are clustered in terms of their goodness of fit with each. These categories are duly named (e.g. Shotguns and Pickups, Slatherers, Oceanic Drinkers), and in their incarnation as market segments then go on to take on a life of their own – to the point that even religious congregants (or potential ones) are described in terms of such labels as 'seekers', 'true believers', etc. (Lewis 1996).

Ironically, though, this rational quest to reduce the complexities of existence to a set of finite categories has strayed from the original intent of lifestyle research. Furthermore, even from a managerial perspective this strategy may do us a disservice, in so far as it blinds us to the potential richness of adopting the consumer's point of view when studying consumer behaviour (truly a heretical concept!). Our modest goal here is to apply a corrective to the positivist approach to lifestyle analysis. We support this effort by noting the conceptual parallels with two other major perspectives in our field – models of fashion diffusion and of communication – both have to some extent returned to the fold of subjectivism from which they originated. We shall emphasise that for conceptual *and* methodological reasons it behoves us to regard lifestyle not as a 'virtual' *construct* computed in the rational but barren confines of a statistical package, but rather as a *construction* interpreted and enacted in the rough-and-tumble, chaotic world we know as daily life.

We argue that lifestyles can be understood not only in terms of the *actual* patterns of behaviour that marketers measure and use to cluster consumers, but also in terms of the *social categories*, or idealised patterns of consumption, that lifestyles represent for consumers and marketers alike (Englis and Solomon 1995b). The use of a lifestyle-orientated approach to market segmentation is based on the assumption that a 'lifestyle campaign' will provide a more effective means of contextualising a product in the daily life of the target consumer. But ultimately the notion of lifestyle has meaning only if it is meaningful to consumers themselves. It is precisely the issue of what lifestyles *mean* to consumers that in our estimation has been underemphasised by lifestyle marketers.

LIFESTYLE: AN ABBREVIATED HISTORY

In an economic sense, a lifestyle is a sort of shorthand that denotes the way members of a market have allocated their income, both in terms of relative allocations to different products and services and to specific alternatives within these categories (Zablocki and Kanter 1976). Other somewhat similar distinctions have been invented to describe consumers in terms of their broad patterns of consumption as, for example, differentiating social class categories in terms of those who devote a high proportion of total expenditures to food, advanced technology, or to such information-intensive goods as entertainment and education (Douglas and Isherwood 1979).

As defined by sociologists, the idea takes on a bit more texture and richness. Lifestyle refers to a pattern of consumption reflecting a person's choices of how he or she spends time and money. In his seminal development of the concept, Simmel (1921) used the term 'styles of life' to discuss how consumption was altered by the money economy. Weber elaborated on this perspective by observing that social classes were stratified according to consumption of goods. Many factors, such as a person's self-concept, ethnicity and social class, are 'raw ingredients' that contribute to the recipe for a lifestyle.

This general sociological approach that views consumption as a medium through which pre-existing group differences are manifested later made its way into the marketing literature, largely due to Sidney Levy's influential early writings on brand symbolism (e.g. Levy 1959, 1963). These developments were contiguous with the brief heyday of motivational research in the late 1950s and early 1960s as Ernest Dichter (1964) and others championed the value of examining deep-seated, subjective motivations for purchases.

Enter the social psychologists. Controlled, reductionist laboratory studies of attitudes and group dynamics gained ascendancy in the mid-1960s (and sophisticated computers came on the scene to analyse large data sets like a large hammer in search of a nail). Marketing researchers eagerly bought into the potential of personality inventories and other aggregated instruments to sort quirky consumers into a set of finite, predictable and, ultimately, controllable 'types' that could then empirically be related to market behaviours.

This methodology was dubbed *psychographics*, which one practitioner defined as the

> use of psychological, sociological, and anthropological factors ... to determine how the market is segmented by the propensity of groups within the market and their reasons to make a particular decision about a product, person, ideology, or otherwise hold an attitude or use a medium.

> (Demby 1989: 21; see also Alpert and Gatty 1969; Wells 1968)

Psychographic research was developed to address the perceived short-comings of both qualitative motivational research and quantitative survey research. It was felt that motivational research, which involves intensive one-on-one interviews and projective tests, yields a lot of information about a few people. The information, however, is often idiosyncratic and hence not very useful or reliable.

At the other extreme, quantitative survey research, or large-scale demographic surveys, yields only a little information about a lot of people. As Bill Wells and Doug Tigert observed in the early 1970s:

> The marketing manager who wanted to know why people ate the competitor's cornflakes was told '32 percent of the respondents said taste, 21 percent said flavor, 15 percent said texture, 10 percent said price, and 22 percent said don't know or no answer'.
>
> (Wells and Tigert 1971: 27)

Psychographics was touted as the panacea that would rectify this empirical sterility.

In many applications, the term psychographics is used interchangeably with lifestyle to denote the separation of consumers into categories based on differences in choices of consumption activities and product usage. While there are many psychographic variables that can be used to segment consumers, they all share the underlying principle of going beyond surface characteristics (most notably, demographics) to understand consumers' motivations for purchasing and using products.

Despite the early promise of psychographics, however, the bloom was soon off the rose. Many studies 'borrowed' standard psychological scales (often used to measure pathology or personality disturbances) and tried to relate scores on these tests to product usage. As might be expected, such efforts were largely disappointing. These tests were never intended to be related to everyday consumption activities and yielded little in the way of explanation for purchase behaviours.

Later psychographic research attempts to group consumers according to some combination of three categories of variables – Activities, Interests, and Opinions (AIOs). Using data from large samples, marketers created profiles of customers who resemble each other in terms of their AIO profiles (Boote 1980; Wells 1975). To group consumers into common AIO categories, respondents are given a long list of statements and are asked to indicate how much they agree with each one. Lifestyle is thus 'boiled down' and aggregated over a large number of respondents, generating a profile that describes how the sample spends its time, what it finds interesting and important (or at least how this is reported on a pencil-and-paper instrument), and how members view themselves and the world around them.

Demographics allow us to describe *who* buys, but psychographics allow us to understand *why* they do (or so its adherents argue). To illustrate how this approach works, consider a very popular Canadian campaign for Molson Export beer that based its advertising strategy on psychographic research. The company found that Molson's target customers tended to be like boys who never grew up, who were uncertain about the future, and who were intimidated by women's new-found freedoms. Accordingly, the ads featured a group of men, 'Fred and the boys', whose get-togethers emphasise male companionship and protection against change – the beer 'keeps on tasting great' (Pearson 1985). Psychographics allowed the company to firmly anchor the beer in a way that was appealing to this group (even though members of this segment could not necessarily say *why* such commercials resonated with them).

As researchers expanded the net of measures used to cluster consumers into lifestyle groups, though, the models that were developed took on the form of an explanatory tautology. Instead of sampling measures from one domain (e.g. psychological variables, beliefs) and attempting to predict another (e.g. specific brand choices, product category usage), by including consumption-related variables as predictors, these models tended to predict overlapping (and, therefore, partially redundant) domains. Thus, although the incorporation of consumption-relevant measure improved the ability of researchers to tie AIO segments to actual purchase behaviours, most of the work did not live up to early expectations of predictive power (Kassarjian 1971; Wells 1975).

The disappointing results of this psychographic approach led later researchers to attempt to ground lifestyle more theoretically by relating overt consumption practices to underlying values – as quantitatively assessed on large samples of respondents (Beatty *et al.* 1985; Mitchell 1983; Vinson *et al.* 1977). This approach assumes that lifestyles can be identified by partitioning the relative importance of a set of universal values and that consumers can be 'ranked' and hence clustered into lifestyle categories in terms of their endorsement of these values. Commercial applications of lifestyle segmentation approaches – most notably VALS (Values and Lifestyles) and to a lesser extent VALS2 – are rooted in a values-based perspective.

TROUBLE IN PARADISE: SHORTCOMINGS OF THE POSITIVIST APPROACH TO LIFESTYLE

The positivist spin on the lifestyle construct ironically mutated from murkier qualitative origins. A dynamic perspective on lifestyle as initially articulated by sociologists is far removed from the familiar application of consumption data as input into 'lifestyle segmentation' strategies. The holistic orientation was obscured when operationalised via clusters of AIOs, which tend to take on a life of their own and consequently obligate us to view the dynamic nature of everyday existence through the static lens of the modernist.

Although later research did attempt to provide linkages between broad cultural values and specific consumption choices, this approach still assumes that such patterns are ahistorical, and that stable phenomena can be isolated without reference to the social context in which they occur (Holt 1996). The AIO approach, which focuses us on creating categories rather than viewing lifestyle choices as social constructions, has several shortcomings (cf. Holt 1996; Solomon 1996).

First, the richness of many lifestyle choices depends upon nuance rather than categorical choice. The more sophisticated values-based approach, for example, can perhaps help us to discriminate between the heavy versus light user of fragrance products, but not necessarily between the heavy user of Chanel No. 5 and the heavy user of White Linen. These subtle differences may be meaningful only to members of an in-group who are able to make fine-grained discriminations among brands that may not be apparent to the detached researcher.

Second, the treatment of lifestyle as a personality trait ignores the basic premise that lifestyles serve as symbolic boundaries that distinguish between social/cultural *groups*. Lifestyle is more than the allocation of discretionary income. It is a statement about who one is in society and who one is not. Group identities, whether of hobbyists, athletes, or drug users, gel around forms of expressive symbolism. The self-definitions of group members are derived from the common symbol system to which the group is dedicated. Such self-definitions have been described by a number of terms, including *lifestyle, taste public, consumer group, symbolic community* and *status culture* (Peterson 1979).

Third, the AIO approach assumes the meaning of each specific AIO-based category is singular, durable and self-evident. Thus, simple knowledge of a person's consumption choice and its frequency is sufficient to infer an underlying lifestyle. This does not permit a relational approach to lifestyle – viewing what each activity means in the context of the group. As Holt (1996) observes, for example, both poor people and counter-culture youth shop at thrift stores, but for very different reasons. The static approach also assumes a static self, yet consumers can and do shift lifestyle definitions periodically, whether out of whimsy or necessity. Furthermore, lifestyle patterns reflect a particular collectivity in relation to alternative ones, for example the 'skinhead' lifestyle is meaningful only when juxtaposed with those of middle-class and adult working-class populations (Hebdige 1979).

Fourth, the AIO structure is assumed to be constant across persons and time, yet lifestyles mutate over time and clearly are subject to the whims of fashion. Indeed, products that serve as emblems of a lifestyle at T_1 may become stigmatised as other groups adopt or co-opt them, to the extent that they may literally be 'anti-emblems' at T_2. For example, the Playboy bunny, once the totem of the 'sophisticated man', now appears to be declassé and its display is passionately avoided by its original target audience. Indeed, a bunny mirror ornament is more likely to be spotted hanging from a beat-up Chevrolet than from a sleek Lexus or even a shiny Cadillac – yet another deposed lifestyle emblem. Furthermore, one of the conditions of postmodernism is the fragmentation of lifestyles – as people become multiple role players, so too are they likely to claim membership in several lifestyle groups. This renders the implicit notion of 'one group to a consumer' especially problematic.

Fifth, the 'New Age' author Douglas Coupland protested in *Generation X*, 'I am not a target market' (Coupland 1991: 17). One implication of this rebellion is that while a pattern of consumption is often composed of many ingredients that are shared by others in similar social and economic circumstances, each person also provides a unique 'twist' to this pattern that allows him or her to inject some individuality into a chosen lifestyle. For example, a 'typical' college student (if there is such a thing) may dress much like his or her friends, hang out in the same places, and like the same foods, yet still indulge a passion for running marathons, stamp collecting, or community activism, that makes him or her a unique person.

Finally, and perhaps as importantly, the static AIO conception fails to recognise that consumption choices may be driven by an individual's motivation to attain membership in some (idealised) AIO category to which he or she does *not* belong – there is little room for aspiration and emulation in an AIO matrix. Furthermore, a lifestyle can be defined as much by what is *not chosen* as by what is. While the role of avoidance motivation has yet to be adequately addressed in this literature, any researcher who happens to have adolescents living at home surely would appreciate the extent to which a lifestyle is constructed in terms of acts of rebellion, symbolic or actual, against an imposed lifestyle (Englis and Solomon 1995a, 1995b; Solomon and Englis 1996).

GETTING BOXED IN: LESSONS LEARNED FROM FASHION AND COMMUNICATIONS THEORY

The perils inherent in the attempt to impose an overarching causal structure on what is at heart a fluid phenomenon in some ways markedly resemble the conceptual evolution of other important and related domains of aggregate social behaviour. Perhaps lessons can be learned by briefly tracing the development of two such areas: models of fashion diffusion and of communication. In both cases, attempts at explanation began with the imposition of a positivist linear process that lacked the recognition that these processes actually are the product of a complex series of social constructions. In each case, initial models ignored the crucial role of feedback and interactivity and the crucial role played by various cultural intermediaries during the creation and enactment of the phenomenon in question (Solomon 1988).

Consider first how social scientists have attempted to understand the workings of the fashion system. Trickle-down theory, first proposed in 1904 by Georg Simmel, has been one of the most influential approaches to understanding fashion. It essentially states that subordinate groups try to adopt the status symbols of the groups above them as they attempt to climb up the ladder of social mobility. Dominant styles thus originate with the upper classes and trickle-down to those below (Simmel 1904).

This worldview was quite useful for understanding the process of fashion changes when applied to a society with a stable class structure that permitted the easy identification of lower- versus upper-class consumers. This task is not so easy in modern times. In contemporary western society, then, this approach must be modified to account for new developments in mass culture (McCracken 1985). For example, a perspective based on class structure cannot account for the wide range of styles that are simultaneously made available in our society. Modern consumers have a much greater degree of individualised choice than in the past because of advances in technology and distribution.

Elite fashion has been largely replaced by *mass fashion,* since media exposure permits many groups to become aware of a style at the same time. In addition, current fashions often originate with the lower classes and are more likely to trickle-up. Grassroots innovators typically are people who lack prestige in the dominant culture (like urban youth). Since they are less concerned with maintaining the status quo, they are more free to innovate and take risks (Walle 1990).

Current treatments of fashion thus are more likely to recognise the dynamic nature of style creation, as well as focusing on how the meanings of certain styles can be understood only in light of the subcultural milieu to which they belong (Hebdige 1979). Rather than viewing the transmission of fashion as a one-sided attempt by authority figures to impart their received wisdom to the waiting masses (the 'conspiracy theory' of fashion change), current approaches are also likely to add a crucial feedback loop from consumers to producers. They also may emphasise such issues as the co-optation of style from marginalised groups and the effect of aspirational media images on consumers' ideal styles, body images, etc. (Solomon 1996). Some researchers have begun to develop phenomenological approaches to fashion choices that transcend the meanings supposedly 'embedded' in clothing by the fashion industry (Thompson and Hirschman 1995).

As a second parallel, consider the tremendously influential communications model. This worldview also has to some degree metamorphosed from a passive, linear perspective to an interactive one. It began as a rather simplistic notion of a message, encoded by a source, and then transmitted via some medium to a passive perceiver. Later, the influential moderating role of opinion leaders who filter the information received from mass media was acknowledged. The process was simple and neatly bundled, an ideally modernist invention.

Now, however, it is acknowledged that much communication is in fact a dynamic process; opinion leaders are as likely to be opinion receivers, and the meanings taken from messages by individuals often bear little resemblance to those intended by the source. Even this amended version, however, does not address criteria by which opinion leaders choose to transmit and filter information, nor does it typically consider the differential motivation of perceivers to receive and process this information – with the exception of the significant body of research on the ELM (Elaboration Likelihood Model, see Solomon 1996). Nonetheless, hope springs eternal: as the communications discipline also confronts its own paradigm shift, increasingly work is embracing emphases such as reader-response theory that acknowledge and indeed celebrate the active process of meaning construction by the receiver (Scott 1994).

THE MODEL TRAP: OR, IMPOSING A STRUCTURALIST VIEW ON A POST-STRUCTURALIST WORLD

This very brief historical overview brings us full circle back to a box. Conventional applications of the lifestyle construct by marketers mainly derive from a positivist model: people are assigned to lifestyle 'categories' based upon contemporary consumption choices and other overt behaviours; these classifications are implicitly assumed to attain the status of objective reality. And, this is a static process – consumers typically are placed in *one and only one* box. Multiple roles, developmental transitions and consumer aspirations are not taken into account in formulating 'so-called' predictive models.

However, lifestyle viewed through post-positivist lenses looks quite different (for an example, see Thompson 1996). If we adopt this perspective, we might ask such questions as:

- How accurate are the neat little lifestyle categories constructed (at great expense) by marketers and then incorporated into decisions ranging from package design to marketing communications?
- How do people themselves incorporate their lifestyle choices into self-concept(s)? And, how do marketer-created categories relate to self- and social-meaning?
- How fluid and fuzzy are lifestyle categories, and how do these correspond to the rigid meanings imposed upon them by marketing strategists? Do consumers passively accept their 'assignment' or can attempts at insurrection succeed in allowing individuals to break out of the box in which they have been placed?
- What role do idealised lifestyle images presented to us by the media play in influencing the structure of our own lifestyle 'dreams and nightmares'?

- What is the origin of these meanings and how are they diffused and acted upon?
- How do researchers go about uncovering these meanings?

Obviously we cannot hope to answer or even to address all of these questions here. However, we can take a stab at the last issue, in so far as we have attempted to develop a research programme that in a variety of applications focuses on the general issue of uncovering symbolic meanings (see Englis and Solomon 1996b for a review): to wit, how do consumers incorporate information about products, services and activities in the process of developing representations and meanings connected with different lifestyles?

In thinking about the importance (or lack thereof) of lifestyle clusters as discrete social categories, we shall discuss the stages involved in uncovering these meanings, beginning with some conjectures as to how these categories are created and ending with what they mean to the people who have often been left out of the lifestyle equation – consumers themselves. These four stages are (1) category creation, (2) consumer self-selection into social/lifestyle categories, (3) category associations and (4) category meanings.

We shall highlight two research projects that have employed methods designed to examine each of these four stages of meaning creation. In one study consumers were asked to generate social categories that represent important meaning categories for themselves and their peers; these do not necessarily reflect marketer-created lifestyle categories (Englis and Solomon 1995a). In a second study, we started with marketer-created categories and then examined the lived meanings associated with these categories by actual, breathing consumers (reported in detail in Englis and Solomon 1995b).

CATEGORY CREATION

Traditional approaches to lifestyle-based market segmentation employ empirical methods to cluster consumers based on commonalities among their market behaviour, their attitudes, interests and opinions, and among other pertinent demographic and psychographic characteristics. Notably lacking in these approaches is a touchstone of meaning: namely, how do these empirically derived patterns accord with consumers' perceptions of these occurrences?

Although the creation of artificial market categories may provide insights for marketers into the behaviour of potential markets for their products, they provide little insight into the social meaning of these distinctions for consumers. At the same time that marketers are trying to understand how consumers 'load' in terms of patterns of market behaviour, consumers themselves are busy trying to understand and categorise their own more chaotic social reality. This mutual drive to form recognisable and useful categories is most valuable to consumers and marketers alike when there is convergence in the categories formed and in the meanings ascribed to those categories. However, little attention is paid to consumer-formulated social categories and their meaning (for an exception, see Schouten and McAlexander 1995).

Thus, one point of departure from traditional AIO-based lifestyle research is to ask the general question of how consumers formulate meaningful social categories and then use these as guideposts for behaviour. Socially meaningful categories such as reference groups are of particular interest as they impact on consumers' desires to adopt or reject specific products, services and activities. The overlap between the social categorisation process of consumers and that of lifestyle marketers is of course an interesting and important question (one that we raise elsewhere: Englis and Solomon 1995b, 1996a, 1996b; Solomon and Englis 1994).

For our present purpose, however, we hark back to the perspective of early sociologists and argue that perceived differences in patterns of consumption are used as social category markers by consumers, and thus become intimately connected to the social meaning of different lifestyle groups.

From this perspective, we form clusters by asking *consumers themselves* to provide input into their own subjective experiences of group boundaries and of the markers that serve to delineate one group from another. In this manner, we begin by anchoring the categories to motivationally significant and subjectively meaningful groups for the consumers we wish to study and whose consumption behaviour we wish to understand.

Both studies that we touch upon here examined college-age consumers. Owing to the importance of social acceptance and peer approval this is an ideal group in which to study symbolic consumption. Group boundaries and consumption-related markers that communicate group affiliation should be particularly salient to these consumers. In addition, the college student market is a group facing several important life/role transitions. As graduation approaches, much of the consumption behaviour of college students may be best understood in relation to their anticipated transition to a new role upon graduation. Since our conceptual framework emphasises the role of consumer aspirations (and anticipatory consumption), this is a particularly suitable age group for study.

Using just this approach we conducted a study that examined the 'universe' of social types on the campus of a major university in the northeastern region of the United States (Englis and Solomon 1995a). We began by having students act as participant observers who visited several social venues and photographed other students. Photographs were taken over a two-month period at sites including campus student centres and dining commons as well as concert venues and local bars frequented by students. Their task was to collect photographs of people who would exemplify the meaningful social distinctions and groups (or cliques) on campus. Our participant-observers then sorted the full set of photographs (over 100) into categories that were meaningful as representing distinct 'social types' within the current social landscape at the university. The confederates then provided narrative descriptions of these types as well as labels that represent (to them) the 'natural' language used to describe these social categories. Participant-observers combined their individual 'clustering schemes' into a single set of eleven categories: exemplars of each category were selected from the full set of photographs on the basis of their perceived prototypicality by the judges. In examining these narratives, emphasis was placed on identifying distinctive features of each category given the overall social typology created. The following examples of relevant 'types' within this one university are taken from the narratives provided by the participant-observers.

Hip-Hop: . . . baggy pants, oversized shirts and jackets, baseball caps, hooded shirts, starter jackets and tennis shoes. Cross Colours Clothing and other African-American owned [labels] . . . sold in mainstream retail outlets including Macy's and J.C. Penney's. Slogans like 'Stop the Violence' and 'peace N the Hood' are emblazoned on these fashions.

Preppie School Boy: . . . with oversized V-neck sweaters worn over white t-shirts, khaki trousers rolled-up to the ankles and chunky brogues. A prep always dresses in a crisp manner, clothes are pressed and [dry] cleaned. He . . . would shop at Abercrombie and Fitch and The Gap.

Alternative: . . . sport side burns, rock band t-shirts, loose fit faded jeans and bright colors worn down around their knees. Doc Martens and Combat boots are found on their feet . . . sure to be found attending Lollapalooza [a major alternative rock festival].

Athletics: They are the most comfortably dressed group . . . . They wear sneakers, sweats, t-shirts, shorts and sweat socks. Women sport scrunchies in their hair . . . men sport baseball caps of their favorite teams. Their clothes are untucked most of the time and without any defined shape. Shopping for their wardrobe is done at the Sports Authority and The Gap.

Rough Cycle: . . . includes leather motorcycle jackets (Harley Davidson is preferred) paired with faded jeans for both men and women. Dark sunglasses and cowboy boots often accompany this fashion statement. Stores in malls [carrying this style include] . . . the Merry Go Round and Contemp Casuals.

One interesting outcome of this approach is that it quickly becomes obvious that consumption behaviours (actual or inferred) play an important role in delineating category boundaries. Categories were typically described with rich, detailed reference to personal style ('sport side burns'), fashion ('khaki trousers rolled-up to the ankles and chunky brogues') and brand/retail usage information. A similar approach can be used to study category creation by marketing gatekeepers (e.g. art directors or fashion editors as attempted by Solomon *et al.* 1992). It would be particularly helpful to compare the category creation of gatekeepers with that of consumers – differences might highlight social terrain where communications strategies based on gatekeeper perceptions may not be particularly effective (Ashmore *et al.* 1996).

CONSUMER SELF-SELECTION INTO SOCIAL/LIFESTYLE CATEGORIES

The second layer of meaning focuses on consumers' own efforts at self-categorisation, or how they go about describing their own discretionary preferences in terms of broader lifestyle and social distinctions. We can delineate several bases upon which consumers self-select into different social categories. These include racial/ethnic group ties, membership in a particular social class, occupation, subcultural identity that may be linked to a certain lifestyle choice (hunters, die-hard Elvis fans, and so on) or aesthetic preferences (fans of 'gangsta rap' versus alternative music; for a look at how these identities are linked to MTV videos in two cultures, see Englis *et al.* 1993).

Relevant categories include most prominently those groupings that consumers admire and aspire to as compared with those categories that represent their current status. In addition, we feel it is important to compare these desired groups with those that are meaningful to consumers in a different way – namely, that they are motivated to avoid being placed in these groups and may partly define themselves in terms of how successful they have been in doing so.

Consumers are active agents in the process of adopting products and in innovating their usage and meaning. Categories that are either emergent (derived from consumers' own active process of typing their social world) or imposed (by the communication and merchandising systems that perpetuate and reinforce marketer-created lifestyle categories) are useful as social landmarks to consumers. In the process of decision making, consumers are placing themselves, consciously or not, into one or another category that has meaning for them, and for their significant others and reference groups.

We argue, therefore, that as consumers decide whether or not to purchase a particular item, they are in effect judging 'goodness-of-fit' with their idealised category membership. In the process of trying to understand how consumers formulate and utilise social typologies we should ask consumers how they type themselves. This approach can be used with marketer- as well as consumer-created categories. For example, a consumer may as readily develop a desire for a particular hairstyle (or form of nose-jewellery) by observing a member of an aspirational reference group on campus, as by emulating idealised college students depicted in a magazine ad.

Self-generated categories

As a follow-up to our category-creation study described earlier, in-depth interviews were conducted with a sample of sixty business school students drawn from the same campus. We deliberately limited our interviews to a homogeneous sample in order to ensure greater consistency of meaning across respondents. As part of the interview process, consumers were asked to sort the photographs into three piles that represented their aspirational group (others with whom they would desire to affiliate, whom they admire and would like to emulate), their avoidance group (others with whom they would choose to avoid affiliation, whom they would probably dislike and would not wish to emulate), and a third pile to represent 'neutral' others.

Respondents were randomly assigned to the aspirational or avoidance condition and were asked to look back through the relevant group of photographs and to pick the one photograph most representative of the category. Overall, there was high consensus in the selection of aspirational and avoidance categories – especially for the avoidance category. In the following, the descriptive passages used to identify avoidance and aspirational categories were taken from the narratives provided by the participant-observers during the category formation part of the study. Of the sample 58 per cent selected Grunge as the avoidance group:

> Sloppily dressed in black baggy outfits, cut-off jean shorts that extend past their knees, overalls with absolutely no shape and birkenstocks [sandals] ... They are depressed and aloof ... They walk the streets ... alone, giving the impression that they do not want to be bothered with the nonsense of the world around them ... They purchase their attire at flea markets and Army/Navy surplus stores.

Respondents asked to select an aspirational type showed greater variability in their choices. In this case, three categories comprised 74 per cent of the sample: Trendy JAP ('Jewish-American Princess' but apparently used more generically to describe highly materialistic and/or pampered students; 28 per cent), Preppie (22 per cent), Conservative (19.4 per cent). Descriptive passages for these three categories included the following:

Trendy JAP/Preppie/Conservative

> JAP – Her wardrobe centers around body suits, tight shirts, short skirts, blue jeans, vests ... short flowery baby dolls, and opaque stockings ... chokers, earth costume jewelry, and ... clunky shoes and espadrille

sandals ... She purchases her clothing at retail department stores and mainstream mall stores, as well as privately owned boutiques ... She epitomizes the trends of the time that is seen on the hottest new television shows on Fox.

Preppie – with oversized V-neck sweaters worn over white t-shirts, khaki trousers rolled-up to the ankles and chunky brogues. A prep always dresses in a crisp manner, clothes are pressed and [dry] cleaned. He ... would shop at Abercrombie and Fitch and The Gap.

Conservative – frequent J. Crew and The Gap ... Bucks, braided belts, and penny loafers are common accessories ... neatly put together people who shy away from flashy, bright colors and stick to the more earthy tones in their polos, flannels, and collared shirts from Britches.

Marketer-generated categories

We used a similar approach in identifying how consumers self-select into marketer-created categories using the geodemographically derived PRIZM clusters created by Claritas, Inc. (Englis and Solomon 1995b). In this case, respondents sorted the PRIZM clusters into four categories, comprised of 'people very similar to how I would like to be' (aspirational group); 'people very similar to how I currently see myself' (occupied group); 'people very similar to how I would *not* like to be' (avoidance group).

About 61 per cent of the sample selected 'Money & Brains' as the aspirational lifestyle cluster. In his narrative descriptions of the PRIZM clusters Weiss (1988) notes that among members of this cluster

it's easier to find a tin of caviar in local shops than a box of nails. Houses ... come with pedigrees to go with their price tags ... Residents buy investment property, sailboats, classical records and designer telephones at many times the national average ... They're big purchasers of salted nuts, snack cheeses and specialty wines – all the ingredients for a cocktail party except stimulating conversation.

(Weiss 1988: 272–275)

About 82 per cent of the sample selected 'Smalltown Downtown' as the avoidance lifestyle category. This group is comprised of consumers who tend

to travel less by plane or train than average Americans, and they buy few cars at above-average rates. Their idea of a vacation is to go camping, fishing, and hiking, and their home-based leisure pursuits would make a preppie blanch: they like to watch wrestling and Roller Derby, go out for a cafeteria dinner or a Tupperware party and listen to gospel and country music.

(Weiss 1988: 364)

Both aspirational and avoidance categories contrast with consumers' self-placement into their current or 'occupied' lifestyle: 76 per cent of the sample identified 'Young Suburbia' as their current lifestyle category:

> Young Suburbia has the kind of lifestyle amenities trumpeted in real-estate ads: new homes, modern schools, gleaming shopping centers and a reasonable commute downtown – the nesting ground for the nation's nuclear families of Mom, Dad and the kids. So what if the freshly built subdivisions are often a maze of uniformity, with brick veneer split-levels pressed together like sausages? [Young Suburbanites] buy ... cheese spread, baked beans, pretzels, dry soups ... lawn mowers and hedge clippers, automatic garage-door openers and sheet vinyl flooring. They put down payments on flashy Nissan 300ZXs, Chevrolet Corvettes, and Porsche 924s ... In this neighborhood type, success is measured by the width of your garage.
>
> (Weiss 1988: 291)

It is important to recognise that these self-categorisations of consumers do not necessarily accord with a so-called 'objective' approach based on demographic, psychographic or geodemographic characteristics (as in the case of PRIZM). That is to say, consumers who might fall into the 'Pools and Patios' PRIZM cluster based on their current behaviour, demographics, and so on, might subjectively place themselves into the 'Young Suburbia' cluster and, more importantly, might aspire to the 'Money & Brains' category. The critical issue is which of these methods of consumer categorisation is most related to the behaviour of consumers in the market-place as they create a pattern of purchases intended to aid them in realising long-term lifestyle goals that mesh with an ideal self-concept. Self-categorisations may be as, or more, important as determinants of consumer behaviour as the objective classification schemes commonly used by marketers.

CATEGORY ASSOCIATIONS

The primary thrust of the PRIZM study described earlier was to examine the groupings of consumption activities associated by consumers with marketer-created lifestyle categories. Our intention was to relate these associations to the meaning of the category for a particular group of consumers (i.e. whether the PRIZM cluster represented an aspirational or avoidance lifestyle). Overall, there was great diversity in the products mentioned, which included over two hundred different products across four product categories. The following descriptions of the products associated with aspirational and avoidance lifestyles include only those products mentioned by more than 15 per cent of the sample. It is important to note that none of these products was 'cross-listed'; avoidance and aspirational group products were never mentioned in association with the other group.

Aspirational group consumers ('Money & Brains') were perceived as likely drivers of BMWs (53.6 per cent), Mercedes (50.7 per cent), Cadillacs (30.4 per cent), Volvos (23.2 per cent), Porsches (21.7 per cent), Acuras (17.4 per cent) and Jaguars (15.9 per cent). This group of products compares well with the top cars actually purchased by this group according to the PRIZM database – BMWs, Jaguars, Mercedes, Rolls Royces and Ferraris. The aspirational group was perceived as reading travel magazines (21.7 per cent), *Vogue* (21.7 per cent), *Business Week* (20.3 per cent), *Fortune* (17.9 per cent) and *GQ* (15.9 per cent). The actual top magazines/newspapers are *Forbes, Barron's, The New Yorker* and *Gourmet*. The alcoholic beverages most closely associated with this group are Heineken beer (33.3 per cent), expensive wines (26.1 per cent), Scotch (18.8 per cent), champagne (17.4 per cent) and Beck's beer (15 per cent). Finally, they are perceived as likely users of Polo (27.5 per cent), Obsession (15.9 per cent) and Drakkar (15.9 per cent).

The avoidance lifestyle ('Smalltown Downtown') presents a sharp contrast to this aspired-to lifestyle. Although there were high levels of agreement concerning the products this group consumes, fewer products were mentioned. The cars most closely associated with this lifestyle group were pick-up trucks (34.8 per cent), Chevys (23.2 per cent) and Fords (18.8 per cent). According to PRIZM data Chevrolets (Chevettes and Spectrums), Isuzus and Plymouths (Gran Furys) are among those cars most likely to be purchased by this lifestyle cluster. The magazines associated with this group included *People* (30.4 per cent), *Sports Illustrated* (26.1 per cent), *TV Guide* (24.6 per cent), *Wrestling* (21.7 per cent), fishing magazines (20.3 per cent) and the *National Enquirer* (18.8 per cent). According to PRIZM data *Sporting News, Colonial Homes, True Story* and *Southern Living* are the magazines most widely read by this group.

One of the most distinctive product sets was alcoholic beverages, with Budweiser seen as the most preferred beer for this group (59.4 per cent); this product group also contained Miller (24.6 per cent), Coors (18.8 per cent) and Jack Daniels (15 per cent). Of note is the absence of any wine for this group. Finally, personal care products included Brut (15.9 per cent), Old Spice (15 per cent) and Mennen Speed Stick deodorant (15.1 per cent).

In the case of the PRIZM study, we were able to explore the issue of congruence between consumer perceptions and lifestyle cluster behaviour. In the 'fashion images' study our contrasts are more 'relativistic' and involve comparisons of the consumption patterns *perceived* to be associated with each social category without regard to 'accuracy'.

In this study we asked respondents to make product and lifestyle associations across eighteen categories of consumption behaviour. These included likely future careers, wardrobe and clothing store selections, automobiles, alcoholic beverages, hobby and leisure activities, and sports activities.

Estimates of the likely career paths for these groups were distinctive. Perceptions of the aspirational group career paths were quite homogeneous, with 82 per cent of responses falling into one of three categories: business profession (36 per cent), teacher (32 per cent) or doctor (18 per cent). For the avoidance group, there were only two career categories with frequencies higher than ten per cent: artist (29 per cent) and teacher (13 per cent). (Teacher for the aspirational lifestyle was more likely to be described as high-school or college, while it was more likely to be described as grade-school for the avoidance group.)

Respondents were also asked to give their impressions of the wardrobe of the person whose photograph they had selected and to name that person's favourite clothing store. Very few brands or clothing stores were named for the avoidance group; these associations appear to be concentrated more on an abstract, stylistic level. The styles and types of clothes for this group were described as baggy/loose (50 per cent), black or dark coloured (46 per cent) and second-hand (25 per cent). In addition, 29 per cent of respondents specified no-brand or brand avoidance for this group. In contrast, there was a high level of brand specificity for the aspirational group, including The Gap (68 per cent), Limited (23 per cent) and Levi's (18 per cent). Other than these three leading brands there were ten other brands/retailers mentioned with an aggregate frequency of 73 per cent of responses. Other than the style label 'preppie' (14 per cent), statements concerning style were also highly variable and idiosyncratic.

The avoidance category was associated with older cars (38 per cent), primarily Volkswagens (29 per cent) in grey, yellow or brown (33 per cent). In sharp contrast, the cars associated with the aspirational lifestyle were never described as old. Dominant brands were Honda (32 per cent) and Toyota (18 per cent) in either red (23 per cent) or blue (23 per cent). This group was associated with a wider range of alcoholic beverages, with beer (32 per cent), mixed drinks (32 per cent) and wine (23 per cent) the leading categories. About 18 per cent of respondents explicitly mentioned beer as an avoidance product for this group; in contrast, 75 per cent of respondents mentioned beer as the most preferred drink and a cheap beer at that (25 per cent qualified the type of beer as cheap), with Budweiser as the leading brand (25 per cent).

Aspirational and avoidance categories were also distinctive as concerns sports activities and hobby and leisure pursuits. The avoidance group was perceived as non-athletic, with 46 per cent of respondents responding 'none' to the question 'What sorts of sporting activities do you think this person enjoys participating in?' Aside from this response, basketball (21 per cent) was the only sporting activity to appear with a frequency higher than one or two mentions. In contrast, no respondent mentioned 'none' in response to this question for the aspirational group. Tennis (46 per cent) was the leading sporting activity (there was only one mention of tennis for the avoidance group), with other responses spread out over in-line skating, softball, soccer, swimming, basketball and volley-ball (68 per cent).

For the avoidance lifestyle leisure activities and hobbies included listening to music (42 per cent), arts-related activities (25 per cent), reading (25 per cent) and going to bars (17 per cent). Two respondents mentioned recreational drug use as a favoured hobby for this group! For the aspirational group, favoured leisure/hobby activities included 'hanging out' with friends (32 per cent), listening to music (23 per cent), reading (18 per cent), going to bars (18 per cent) and the arts (18 per cent). There was again more variety of response for the aspirational group.

Several conclusions may be drawn from these forms of category associations. First, it is clear that consumers' associations are not necessarily an accurate reflection of the consumption patterns that were used by marketers to form lifestyle clusters, and may instead reflect their own in-group, shared understanding of group boundary markers.

Second, it is important to recognise the relativistic nature of these associations: the content of these associative structures will vary for different groups of consumers as a function of the meaning and valuation of the category being described. For example, in our fashion images study, beer as a product category had different perceived likelihood of being consumed and brand/product symbolism in connection with avoidance as compared with aspirational groups. Finally, perceived category associations may provide a road map of opportunities for identifying new meaning niches for products. To the extent that consumer perceptions are the primary determinant of their market behaviour, then examination of their product associations may better inform positioning strategies than an examination of current markets for those products.

CATEGORY MEANINGS

In our more recent work, we have begun to explore deeper layers of meaning associated with lifestyle and social categories. Our methodological approach involves the use of visual or descriptive representation of diverse categories. Consumers are asked to generate narrative stories (much like a Thematic Apperception Test protocol); instructions contextualise the story (e.g. imagine the person on a Saturday night out), and prompt for categories of response (describe who is present, what is being said, and so on), but are otherwise non-directive. Thus far, we have explored this approach with homeowners who describe the imagined lifestyle of people as a function of their decorating style, of the experiences of guests at weddings of different ethnic/religious orientations, and in our fashion images study, which we shall briefly describe here.

In the fashion images study, each respondent selected a photograph that represented the most prototypic aspirational *or* avoidance type, and then was asked to tell a story about the person depicted in the photograph.

Thematic analysis was performed on these projective stories. It is of interest to note that all respondents were able to tell a 'story' about an aspirational other, but nearly 17 per cent of those who tried to tell a story about an avoidance other could not do so even upon repeated prompting by the interviewer.

There were several notable thematic features of these stories, which involved descriptions of the internal state of the person portrayed (i.e. their emotions, desires, attitudes, and so on), the social world of the person shown (whether they are 'loners' or surrounded by friends) and the kinds of activities (or lack thereof) that the person is likely to engage in. For all three thematic categories, sharp distinctions were noted between stories told about aspirational as compared with avoidance others.

Internal states

When the internal state of the person in the photograph was referred to there were very sharp differences in the themes for aspirational as compared with avoidance others. The internal states of avoidance others were described as generally negative and tended to involve feelings of loneliness, frustration, and anger:

> This guy went to a wild party, with headbanging music, got drunk, threw up and went home. Was angry he got sick.

> Getting dressed to go out, can't find anything to wear, yelling at people, goes out.

> She's kind of bummed out like something really bad happened to her ... something happened with one of her friends or she got into a fight with her boyfriend.

> He seems very alone like he has a problem and his friends know he doesn't deserve them. He's very confused ... and he doesn't work out his problem.

In contrast, if the internal mood or emotional state of an aspirational other was mentioned at all, the valence was positive.

> She is happy ... independent, getting things done. Always on the go ... laid back, relaxed.

> Walking along College Avenue, running for election, comes over to me, very friendly and nice, I voted for her because she was outgoing and nice.

She is going back from a Chinese take-out place, nice person, casual
... happy to hang out with friends.

Looks like she's got a little smile on her face, she's hanging out, she's
not too worried about how she is dressed ... she looks like she's fun
to hang out with. This girl just came back from going out one night
and she's all happy because she was so drunk ... She's happy because
she had a good time.

He likes to take easy classes, is easygoing, not that he doesn't care a
whole lot, but he shows up to class, takes the exams, hangs loose, parties
on the weekends, hits all the bars, likes to have a good time over Spring
Break.

She looks very naturry, like she has the zen on her shoulder. See here,
if a person wants to pretend something to you, the nature is standing
up. Here, the shoulders are both down.

Social worlds

The social world of the avoidance group images was described as more
lonely and isolated. Social relationships are fraught with peril and difficulties:

Looks like a loner, not with anyone, walks with his head down, avoids
contact – don't bother me.

This guy spends a lot of time by himself. Receives some strange looks
because he is solemn looking. Goes to class, speaks to one or two
people in the class. Nothing beyond Hi. Leaves class, takes a very long
walk by himself.

She probably doesn't have many friends. If she [has any], they are all
like her, a little different. She probably has a weird boyfriend. She's
very shy.

He doesn't look very sociable. He's just doing this [having his picture
taken] so this person will leave him alone. That's probably because he
looks like he's a loner. He looks like he's going to lunch or dinner by
himself.

In contrast, aspirational figures were described as more socially active and successful in their social relationships. Their social world is benign, full of friends, and is described with themes of connectedness rather than alienation.

Me and another friend and this girl, talking about professors, laughing.

Down to Earth, cool to hang out with. With lots of people.

Lives with other people, but is alone right now.

Happy to hang out with friends, do a little studying. Will share her food back at dorm room.

Looks like she's got a lot of friends and she seems easy to talk to because she has a big smile on her face. You can easily approach her.

Before taking the picture, we were studying, and we decided to take a break so we stopped at the camera. After taking the picture, we went back to studying. She's with a group of people.

There is a group of friends around her and they are making her take a picture in front of some kind of building ... She's going to graduate soon with her friends so they are all taking pictures to remember each other by and they are all very happy that they are going to graduate.

She seems like someone hanging out, talking to people. She seems like a friendly person. She like to tune in when people walk by her ... She seems like someone who would take care of her friends. This weekend [at a fraternity party] ... a couple of her friends got a little too drunk so she helped them home, got them away from those guys that were trying to take advantage of them.

Activities

In general, most of the stories told in response to a photograph of an aspirational other focused on mundane, normal activities.

Going to a party with other girls looking for guys at a club. Has a good time and meets some guy.

[He] likes to have a good time over Spring Break. He went down to Cancun, hitting the beaches, checking out the girls, dresses real casual ... throw it on and go.

To the extent that the activities associated with the aspirational group were at all unusual, they tended to emphasise positive, success- or career-orientated themes.

Walking along College Ave., running for election.

She's a student and she's probably studying to be someone who makes a lot of money like her parents did. She probably wants to follow in their footsteps.

A particularly striking feature of the stories told about aspirational images was the presence of numerous examples in which the respondent placed himself or herself in the story told about the person in the photograph.

In New York city, coming out of a bar late at night, she trips and falls and rips her jeans. We all laugh about it because we were wasted.

this girl, talking about professors, laughing and we get to class. Talking about school, work, what we are going to do tonight. Criticizing profs.

She had just picked up dinner from a local restaurant and was taking it back to her dorm and she was telling me about how her art was displayed at the student center and she invited me to take a look at it ... we make some informal plans to get together at some of the clubs.

In contrast, the activities associated with the avoidance category often suggest a lack of control (staying out too late, getting too drunk, and so on).

This guy went to a wild party, with headbanging music, got drunk, threw up and went home.

he wakes up in the morning, goes to the student center to get some breakfast, alone ... goes to a club with alternative music. Goes home very late and doesn't wake up until very late the next day.

In other cases activities contain elements of inappropriateness:

he gets his buddies to go with him in the car with loud music and they drive to the club and they're calling [out to] some women. They go into the club and they're dancing and they get kind of drunk.

She is definitely not going to get her hair done. Going to class. A Dead Head, a feminist.

Walking down the street, goofy with that walk, coming back from class waving to girls with that look.

She's trying to be different in dressing the way she does ... She's a good student, probably very smart.

He always wanted to be different and experience new and different things. He got a band together with a couple of people and tries to get on a label. They are going to go back in two years [*sic*] and he becomes a corporate executive.

The use of such projective storytelling has great potential to shed light on the psychic, social and cultural connotations elicited by consumer- as well as marketer-created categorisation schemes. The cultural meaning of a wide range of consumption activities may be best uncovered through this kind of approach and, in particular, may be best revealed by beginning with consumer-created categories. As noted earlier, future work needs to provide direct comparison between the meanings associated with marketer-created as compared with consumer-created categories. It is this last stage in uncovering the meaning that lifestyles have for consumers that, in our opinion, has the greatest potential of revitalising the lifestyle concept by re-anchoring to the social worlds of consumers themselves.

CONCLUSIONS: BOXES OR MÖBIUS STRIPS?

There is ample reason to conclude that the perspectives of marketers who create empirically driven lifestyle categories and consumers who actually experience consumption as part of their day-to-day realities may not necessarily coincide very well. Indeed, empirical data even indicate that marketing managers often harbour highly inaccurate images of the very target markets to which they are directing their efforts (cf. Hoch 1988). From the advertiser/marketer perspective, market data are filtered into the creative process, and then lifestyle-orientated communications are channelled through discrete media to separate audiences. In contrast, audiences/consumers integrate messages from a variety of sources, many of which are mass-media vehicles of popular culture.

Yet there must be a domain of shared reality between those marketing gatekeepers who instantiate empirically derived lifestyle groups and consumers who incorporate (rather than reject) these images into their own 'versions of reality'. It is in this intersection of meaning that marketers and consumers collude in the social construction of lifestyle meaning. As we have noted elsewhere, direct contact with the actual market behaviour of diverse social groups plays an increasingly peripheral role in shaping consumer perceptions as compared with media imagery (Englis and Solomon 1996b; Solomon and Englis 1994).

The pervasive images of popular culture become as, or more, important in shaping consumer understanding of lifestyle groups as the direct observation of these groups. Direct observation takes a back seat because consumer behaviour is often motivated *not* by a desire to emulate the lifestyle group to which the consumer *currently* belongs, but rather by the desire to emulate one that he or she *aspires* to join. Thus, either in their actual or anticipatory (e.g. fantasy) consumption behaviour, consumers are orientated toward lifestyle information that in some manner represents an aspirational social group – a desirable ideal.

In the process consumer perceptions may reflect selected or stereotypical perspectives on what a prototypic member of a particular lifestyle category 'ought' to look like. Such stereotypical images may originate in the subjective experiences and perceptions of media and marketing gatekeepers themselves and, thus, may represent yet another step away from 'reality'.

Paradoxically, the underlying accuracy of these simplifications of social reality may not matter – perception is paramount. As one critic noted,

> Everywhere the fabricated, the inauthentic [*sic*] and the theatrical have gradually driven out the natural, the genuine and the spontaneous until there is no distinction between real life and stagecraft. In fact, one could argue that the theatricalization of American life is the major cultural transformation of the century.
>
> (Gabler 1991)

Indeed, from a postmodern perspective we would argue that to ask the questions concerning the 'accuracy' of these social constructs is to miss the point altogether. What may be more important is to recognise this process of social construction as the 'factory' where meaning systems are created and then to recognise that the resulting behaviour of consumers will recursively create new market 'realities' for marketers to analyse. In this sense, the true paradox was duly noted by Boorstin over three decades ago:

> Humanist historians had aimed at individualized portrait. The new social science historians produced a group caricature. Oversimplified sociological concepts – 'status,' 'other-direction,' etc. – appealed because they

were so helpful in building images. These wide-appealing 'modes,' expressed in our dominating notions of norms and averages, led us unwittingly to try to imitate ourselves. We have tried to discover what it is really like to be a junior executive or a junior executive's wife, *so we can really be the way we are supposed to be, that is, the way we are.*

(Boorstin 1961: 202, emphasis added).

Can it be that in our zeal to 'classify' every imaginable consumer phenomenon we have lost sight of the very events we set out to study? Perhaps we need to replace our love of constructs with a renewed passion for constructions. If the post-positivist 'revolution' accomplishes nothing else, perhaps a sufficient contribution will be that it reminds us to put the consumer back in consumer behaviour.

REFERENCES

Alpert, L. and Gatty, R. (1969) 'Product positioning by behavioral life styles', *Journal of Marketing*, 33: 65–69.

Ashmore, R.D., Solomon, M.R. and Longo, L. (1996) 'Thinking about female fashion models' looks: a multidimensional approach to the structure of perceived physical attractiveness', *Personality and Psychology Bulletin*, 22, 11: 1083–1104.

Beatty, S.E., Kahle, L.R., Homer, P. and Misra, S. (1985) 'Alternative measurement approaches to consumer values: the list of values and the Rokeach Value Survey', *Psychology and Marketing*, 2: 181–200.

Boorstin, D.J. (1961) *The Image: A Guide to Pseudo-Events in America*, New York: Vintage.

Boote, A.A. (1980) 'Psychographics: mind over matter', *American Demographics*, April: 26–29.

Coupland, D. (1991) *Generation X: Tales for an Accelerated Culture*, New York: St Martin's Press.

Demby, E.H. (1989) 'Psychographics revisited: the birth of a technique', *Marketing News*, 2 January: 21.

Douglas, M.T. and Isherwood, B.C. (1979) *The World of Goods*, New York: Basic Books.

Englis, B.G. and Solomon, M.R. (1995a) 'Social typologies and their relationship to consumers' aspirations', unpublished manuscript, Rutgers University, NJ.

—— and —— (1995b) 'To be *and* not to be?: Lifestyle imagery, reference groups, and *The Clustering of America*', *Journal of Advertising*, 24, Spring: 13–28.

—— and ——(1996a) 'Using consumption constellations to develop integrated marketing communications', *Journal of Business Research*, 37, 3: 183–191.

—— and —— (1996b) 'Where perception meets reality: the social construction of lifestyles', in L. Kahle and L. Chiagurus (eds) *Values, Lifestyles, and Psychographics*, Hillsdale, NJ: Erlbaum.

——,—— and Olofsson, A. (1993) 'Consumption imagery in Music Television: a bi-cultural perspective', *Journal of Advertising*, 22: 21–34.

Gabler, N. (1991) *The New York Times*, 20 October, quoted in M. Dery (1993) 'Hacking, jamming and slashing in the empire of signs', *Adbusters Quarterly*, Summer: 55–61.

Hebdige, D. (1979) *Subcultures: The Meaning of Style*, London: Methuen.

Hoch, S.J. (1988) 'Who do we know?: predicting the interests and opinions of the American consumer', *Journal of Consumer Research*, 15: 315–324.

Holt, D.B. (1996) 'Post-structuralist lifestyle analysis: conceptualizing the social patterning of consumption in postmodernity', unpublished manuscript, Pennsylvania State University.

Kassarjian, H. (1971) 'Personality and consumer behavior: a review', *Journal of Marketing Research*, 8, November: 409–418.

Levy, S. (1959) 'Symbols for sale', *Harvard Business Review*, 37, July–August: 117–124.

—— (1963) 'Symbolism and lifestyle', in S. Greyser (ed.) *Toward Scientific Marketing*, Chicago: American Marketing Association, 140–150.

Lewis, M. (1996) 'God is in the packaging', *The New York Times Magazine*, 21 July: 14, 16.

McCracken, G.D. (1985) 'The trickle-down theory rehabilitated', in M.R. Solomon (ed.) *The Psychology of Fashion*, Lexington, MA: Lexington Books, 39–54.

Mitchell, A. (1983) *The Nine American Lifestyles: Who We Are and Where We're Going*, New York: Macmillan.

Pearson, I. (1985) 'Social studies: psychographics in advertising', *Canadian Business*, December: 67.

Peterson, R.A. (1979) 'Revitalizing the culture concept', *Annual Review of Sociology*, 5: 137–166.

Schouten, J.W. and McAlexander, J.H. (1995) 'Subcultures of consumption: an ethnography of the new bikers', *Journal of Consumer Research*, 22: 43–61.

Scott, L.M. (1994) 'The bridge from text to mind: adapting reader-response theory to consumer behavior', *Journal of Consumer Research*, 21: 461–480.

Simmel, G. (1904) 'Fashion', *International Quarterly*, 10, 4: 130–155.

—— (1921) 'Money and freedom', in *Introduction to the Science of Sociology*, trans. R.E. Park and E.W. Burgess, Chicago: University of Chicago Press, 552–553.

Solomon, M.R. (1988) 'Building up and breaking down: the impact of cultural sorting on symbolic consumption', in J. Sheth and E.C. Hirschman (eds) *Research in Consumer Behavior*, 3, Greenwich, CT: JAI Press, 325–351.

—— (1996) *Consumer Behavior: Buying, Having, and Being,* 3rd edn, Englewood Cliffs, NJ: Prentice Hall

—— and Englis, B.G. (1994) 'Reality engineering: blurring the boundaries between commercial signification and popular culture', *Journal of Current Issues and Research in Advertising*, 16, 2: 1–17.

—— and —— (1996) 'I am not, therefore I am: the role of anti-consumption in the process of self-definition', special session, Association for Consumer Research, Tucson, AZ, October.

——, Ashmore, R.D. and Longo, L. (1992) 'The beauty match-up hypothesis: congruence between types of beauty and product images in advertising', *Journal of Advertising*, 21: 23–34.

Thompson, C.J. (1996) 'Caring consumers: gendered consumption meanings and the juggling lifestyle', *Journal of Consumer Research*, 22: 388–407.

—— and Hirschman, E.C. (1995) 'Understanding the socialized body: a post-structuralist analysis of consumers' self-conceptions, body images, and self-care practices', *Journal of Consumer Research*, 22: 139–153.

Vinson, D.E., Scott, J.E. and Lamont, L.R. (1977) 'The role of personal values in marketing and consumer behavior', *Journal of Marketing*, 4, April: 44–50.

Walle, A.H. (1990) 'Grassroots innovation', *Marketing Insights*, Summer: 44–51.

Weiss, M. (1988) *The Clustering of America*, New York: Harper & Row.

Wells, W.D. (1968) 'Backward segmentation', in J. Arndt (ed.) *Insights into Consumer Behavior*, Boston, MA: Allyn & Bacon, 85–100.

—— (1975) 'Psychographics: a critical review', *Journal of Marketing Research*, 12, May: 196–213.

—— and Tigert, D.J. (1971) 'Activities, interests, and opinions', *Journal of Advertising Research*, 11, August: 27.

Zablocki, B.D. and Kanter, R.M. (1976) 'The differentiation of life-styles', *Annual Review of Sociology*: 269–297.

12 A postcard from the very edge
Mortality and marketing

Darach Turley

Dennis passed through and opening the door marked 'Inquiries' found himself in a raftered banqueting-hall. 'The Hindu Love-song' was here also, gently discoursed from the dark-oak panelling. A young lady rose from a group of her fellows to welcome him, one of that new race of exquisite, amiable, efficient young ladies whom he had met everywhere in the United Sates. She wore a white smock and over her sharply supported left breast was embroidered the words, *Mortuary Hostess* . . . She led him through the hall into a soft passage. The *décor* here was Georgian. The 'Hindu Love-song' came to its end and was succeeded by the voice of a nightingale. In a little chintzy parlour he and his hostess sat down to make their arrangements . . .

'Now Mr. Barlow, what had you in mind? Embalmment of course, and after that incineration or not, according to taste. Our crematory is on scientific principles, the heat is so intense that all inessentials are volatilized. Some people did not like the thought that ashes of the casket and clothing were mixed with the Loved One's. Normal disposal is by inhumement, entombment, inurnment, or immurement, but many people just lately prefer insarcophagusment. That is *very* individual. The casket is placed inside a sealed sarcophagus, marble or bronze, and rests permanently above ground in a niche in the mausoleum, with or without a personal stained-glass window above. That, of course, is for those with whom price is not a primary consideration.' . . .

'Then let me explain the Dream. The Park is zoned. Each zone has its own name and appropriate Work of Art. Zones of course vary in price and within the zones the prices vary according to their proximity to the Work of Art. We have single sites as low as fifty dollars. That is in Pilgrim's Rest, a zone we are just developing behind the Crematory fuel dump.'

(Waugh 1948: 37–38)

INTRODUCTION

Waugh's mordant spoof of the encounter between marketing and mortality at the Whispering Glades Parkland crystallises what continues to be a prickly and uneasy relationship. At one level, this failure to connect is understandable. Death marks the omega point for consumption, a guillotine on the procurement and use of artefacts, and a fate that seemingly can be neither bartered nor bartered with. There is also a qualitative dimension: 'There is obloquy for merchandising' (Douglas and Isherwood 1979: 3), a sense of the quintessentially profane marketing function being inappropriate, scabrous and ultimately at odds with the aura of sacredness and otherworldliness that, even in post-religious societies, prevails when a consumer dies. Wittgenstein's injunction – whereof one cannot speak thereof one must be silent – seems singularly apposite for the juxtaposition of death and marketing. The latter has nothing to say to the former. Death heralds an imperceptible and complete shift in marketing focus from the departed to the distraught survivors – funerary paraphernalia are purchased primarily by and for the left ones rather than the loved ones.

Marketing as an academic discipline seems equally uncomfortable and unforthcoming in the face of death. References to the subject in textual indices are rare, literature searches matching mortality and marketing yield little. Consumer researchers too, with the exception of a small and growing cadre, have eschewed death and dying either through omission or aversion. After all, marketing is young. Thankfully, many of the early settlers of consumer behaviour remain resolutely aboard this mortal coil. Through academic osmosis, the same message has been absorbed by students of the discipline. To cite a case in point, cohorts of consumer behaviour undergraduates have been presented with traditional family life-cycle segmentation as a composite variable, however, the role of dead/alive as one of its constitutive elements has been conveniently omitted; what was it anyway that turned a survivor into a *solitary* survivor? The reluctance to accord death and dying their rightful place on the consumer behaviour/research agenda is puzzling for more prosaic reasons as well. Marketing activity comprises an array of products and services that impinge in some fashion on human mortality. The mnemonic and intimatory possibilities of such a plethora of death-related offerings, financial services, life assurances, lump-sums and legal services have lain untapped, or have been deftly sidestepped.

Despite the prevailing antipathy, a number of considerations suggest themselves as possible justifications for incorporating more death-related research into the canon of consumer behaviour. First, Ariès (1981) states that there is a fundamental relationship between one's attitude towards death and awareness of self. While the centrality of the self-concept in consumer behaviour has been consistently confirmed (Belk 1988; Solomon

1983) the role of attitude towards death as constituent of that self-concept has lain fallow as a potential area of research. Second, marketing as an academic discipline is unquestionably a child of the twentieth century. Its birth and development have been contemporaneous with an unparalleled quantum leap in social attitudes towards death in the western world.

> During the long period ... from the Early Middle Ages until the mid-nineteenth century, the attitude toward death changed, but so slowly that contemporaries did not even notice. In our day, in approximately a third of a century, we have witnessed a brutal revolution in traditional ideas and feelings, a revolution so brutal that social observers have not failed to be struck by it. It is really an absolutely unheard-of phenomenon. Death, so omnipresent in the past that it was familiar, would be effaced, would disappear. It would become shameful and forbidden.
>
> (Ariès 1974: 85)

It would seem implausible to suppose that alterations in perception of the human condition of this magnitude would not impinge on consumption attitudes and behaviour in the contemporary marketplace. Third, while alternatives to the modern conception of marketing have come of age, academically speaking, the critique of the modernist conception of death has as yet failed to feature in the consumer behaviour literature. This modernist view emphasises personal death as a *terminus ad quem*, a distant end point, best forgotten or sublimated and certainly not to be talked about. The post-positivistic theorists to be discussed later reject this thesis and propose instead that death be reinstated on an equal footing with living, that it be woven into the fabric of life as opposed to being relegated to its termination. In a curious fashion this echoes Tucker's (1974) much quoted metaphorical injunction not to focus on the end point of the consumer decision process – as fish are viewed by fishermen – but rather to examine the life context from which such decisions emerge – as fish are studied by marine biologists. The second and third considerations above require some elaboration. To this end, the next section examines the genesis of current views of death and dying from a historical/anthropological perspective.

CHANGING ATTITUDES TOWARDS DEATH

Ariès (1974, 1981) discerns four broad stages in the emergence of contemporary attitudes towards death since the early Middle Ages. Arguably, one of the leading thanatologists of the twentieth century, he is not, however, without critics. In particular, the epochal shifts he proposes have been characterised as the product of overly generous theoretical and chronological brushstrokes; they also stand accused of succumbing to a purely linear conception of history (Walter 1992). His focus on the French experience of death in particular has been faulted for lacking sensitivity to influences from the Reformation (Walter 1994). However, for present purposes his classification merits interest for the light it throws on the array of possible cultural and historical antecedents of current perceptions of death and dying.

In the first phase, encompassing the early Middle Ages to the twelfth century, dying was essentially a public ritual presided over by the person in question. 'The dying man's bedchamber became a public place to be entered freely' (Ariès 1974: 12). The audience looked on passively, save when the ailing person either failed or was incapable of following the requisite protocol. This public dimension was borne of a conception of death as an element of collective destiny and common fate. Death was familiar and expected. It was precisely this notion of death being antici-pated that engendered an attitude of acceptance. Knowing that death was approaching meant that it could be met with a developed ritual of communal prayers, farewells and blessings. When this was accomplished, the person could wait peacefully for death. For this reason, sudden, aleatory and private death, precluding the possibility of requisite prep-aration, was to be avoided. 'Anyone other than a knight who died suddenly was cast to the outskirts of society and quickly and quietly forgotten' (Moller 1996: 5). They were forgotten precisely because there was no communal experience of their death and consequently no possibility of their sharing in the collective salvation they would otherwise have enjoyed. After death, the deceased was thought to persist in a prolonged sopor, typically in a bucolic and floral setting, awaiting bodily resurrection at the end of time. The contemporary practice of placing wreaths and floral tributes on caskets is thought to date from this period.

If contact between the dying and the living was a feature of this era so too was social commerce between dead and living. This was evidenced most clearly in contemporary burial practices. By the eighth century, corpses were interred within town or city boundaries usually adjacent to a church or abbey. Apart from social and ecclesiastical luminaries who qualified for burial under altars or flagstones within the church edifice, the norm was burial in common unmarked graves containing between 30 and 1,500 corpses. Grave space was at a premium and recyclable. So, once the flesh had decomposed, bones that came to the surface were dug up and deposited in dedicated storage rooms, or charnels, that cloistered the cemetery. In time this procedure was invested with aesthetic overtones. Exhumed bones were artistically arranged in ossuaries in the charnels for display and public perusal.

> By the turn of the twelfth century, the cemetery had become what the suburban shopping mall is to people of modern society. It was the centre of social life ... It became the central place of public interac-tion – of making speeches, of courting, of picnicking, of baking bread

in communal ovens, and so on ... An ironic relationship of indifference and intimacy between life and death was created. Living could proceed untroubled in the shadow of death itself, as its terrifying and frightful aspects had been stilled, that is to say, death was tamed.

(Moller 1996: 6–7)

Elias (1985) makes a number of cautionary observations on Ariès's analysis of death and dying in the Middle Ages. He censures him in general for looking 'mistrustfully on the bad present in the name of a better past' (Elias 1985: 12). While Elias concedes that dying was both spoken about and public during this era – it could hardly have been private given the prevailing domestic architecture – he strongly disputes Ariès's portrayal of death at this time as typically serene and peaceful. Elias would substitute terror for tranquillity as the characteristic emotional response to the prospect of death and dying. Towns were affording an unparalleled toe-hold for plagues and pestilence, fulminating preachers assured their hearers that, save for a sanctified select, limited or limitless suffering lay in store for the departed. Palliative interventions to assuage torment and agony were limited in number and effect. Finally, Elias cautions against the assumption that public death necessarily implied a benign death – conflict, taunting and mockery were not uncommon among onlookers.

Ariès traces the beginning of the second phase to the twelfth century. An inchoate sense of personal judgement paralleled and fuelled the emergent individualism of the era. A millennium of death as public and communal was replaced by death as inherently personal – *'mort de soi'*, my death, petrified for the first time in inscribed headstones. Death as collective destiny and death as individual event parted ways for good. The growth in courts and judicial process bolstered the notion of the individual as free agent, choosing between good and evil alternatives and, in the process, creating a personal biography that would be rounded in death. The powers of good and evil were thought to have monitored these mortal choices throughout the life course so that the moment of death was perceived as one of reckoning, a summation of sin and sanctity, leading to an overall judgement of the person as worthy of paradise or perdition. Towards the fifteenth century this inventory of actions became personified. Damnation or salvation depended now on the outcome of a struggle between the forces of good and evil for the soul of the dying person. The overtures of Satan had to be spurned at all costs; confession, deathbed reconciliation, and the last rites were requisite armour for this agonistic encounter between devil and deity. How one died assumed greater importance than how one lived. 'Books on the art of dying a good death became as popularised by the printing press of the fifteenth century as books on how to have good sex to-day' (Moller 1996: 7).

During the late Middle Ages this stark image of individual death – *mort de soi* – was paralleled by a growing fascination with grotesque images of death and decomposition. Art and drama of the period depict the living as vulnerable, separated out from the collective, pursued by prancing skeletons and ghoulish cadavers representing death. The ubiquity and capriciousness of such deadly visitations furnished the central theme for the European death play of the fifteenth century, Danse Macabre, where skeletal fingers tugged the coat-tails or tapped the shoulders of bewildered mortal folk going about their earthly chores.

The sixteenth and seventeenth centuries mark the third phase of Ariès's analysis of the evolution of European attitudes towards death – 'Death as remote and imminent'. In one sense, the prevailing view at this time represented a logical sequel to its predecessor. If death is as imminent as the Danse Macabre suggested, then a constant state of preparedness was the best course of action and this was taken to mean living one's lifespan to the full in a godly and upright fashion. Assured by such a lifestyle, the living could countenance the vagaries of sudden death with serenity and tranquillity. This importance of the quality and calibre of life served to render death, its final moment, less consequential, more remote, and to divest it of much of its earlier ineffable mystique. This remoteness of death was furthered by

> the arrival in the 1690's of the mathematical notion of probability ... Though no-one could predict exactly when the Grim Reaper would call your name, the new science of statistics made it possible to calculate the *chance* of your dying in any given year or living to a particular age.
>
> (Walter 1994: 9)

Paradoxically, this distancing of death went hand in hand with a preoccupation with its physical remains. At one level, the corpse was seen as a repository of worthy and useful knowledge.

> Anatomy was so popular in the seventeenth century that the anatomy lesson was often a social 'happening' that included good-natured joking, refreshments and people wearing gay, masquerade-like apparel. Dissection had become an ironically fashionable activity, an ancient version of the modern cocktail-theme party.
>
> (Moller 1996: 11)

However, there was an additional more salacious interest in the human corpse over this period. Necrophilic motifs were prevalent in both literature and drama adumbrating the queues for Dracula films three centuries later. Towards the end of this 'remote and imminent' phase, these erotic and seductive associations were extended to the process of dying itself.

> Like the sexual act, death was henceforth increasingly thought of as a transgression which tears man from his daily life, from rational society, from his monotonous work, in order to make him undergo a paroxysm,

plunging him into an irrational, violent, and beautiful world ... This idea of rupture is something completely new. Until this point the stress had been on the familiarity with death and with the dead ... from now on it would be thought of as a *break*.

(Ariès 1974: 57)

Ariès's fourth phase dates roughly from the beginning of the nineteenth century. Increasing urbanisation and its attendant sense of isolation had weakened communal solidarity and engendered greater reliance on the nuclear family. This development led to a similar contraction in the number of those surrounding the deathbed. The audience was likely to be limited to close relatives and friends and it was precisely this sense of intimacy between the dying and onlooker that infused death in the Victorian era with pathos and high drama. The impending rupture of a cherished friendship, the imminent loss of a loved one, redirected the observers' concern away from their own deaths towards the demise of the special other ailing before them. '*Mort de toi*', thy death, had supplanted '*mort de soi*'.[1] The ritual for dying epitomised by the protracted deathbed scene was unique among rituals. It permitted and encouraged 'hysterical mourning' born of a new intolerance of separation. Desolate and distraught survivors were accorded uncustomary latitude in their display of grief, however, in keeping with the Victorian crusade against hedonism and sex, the erotic overlay of the eighteenth century was replaced by a romantic sentimentalism.

Excessive grief called for commensurate mourning, mourning that would be lavish, regulated and couth. As with the deathbed scene, both funeral and mourning ritual were invested with climactic beauty and a dedicated aesthetic. Corpse, casket, costume and catafalque were all marshalled to this end; the first store specialising in black funeral attire in London had opened in 1780. 'Services to the bereaved and the deceased were the great standby of most Victorian drapers' (Adburgham 1989: 58). Outlets offered a plethora of paraphernalia to signal the various stages and degrees of ritualised mourning 'from a grief *prononcé* to the slightest *nuance* of regret' (p. 68).

The Victorian attitude to death also spawned a thriving market in consolation products – obituary cards, mourners' manuals, maudlin song sheets, souvenir rings and gloves, and a haemorrhage of twee consolation literature (Leming and Dickinson 1994). Burial arrangements too were not immune from aesthetic dictat. The receptacle for the remains underwent a change in name and design, from coffin containing and conveying the contour of the human corpse to rectangular casket housing a precious jewel. In Europe, with the departure of the loved one to an anthropomorphic beyond, those left behind sought to maintain the personal bond, to create a home away from home, preferably one that could be visited – the cult of the tomb was born (Ariès 1974: 70). In the United States, the rural cemetery on the edge of conurbations was to be a topographical lesson in beauty and decorum, its bucolic setting and rolling contours a counterpoint to the unbending streets of the heartless city. And orchestrating the entire process was the funeral *director*; the change in title from 'undertaker' in the 1880s was not inappropriate.

In keeping with the desire to have death's gruesome and discordant side-effects suppressed and to maintain a semblance of continuity in the severed relationship, the practice of embalming became a core specialism of the American funeral director's repertoire. Initially developed to facilitate the transport of Civil War dead to their homes for burial, it subsequently became a standard feature of the effort to maintain appearances and construe death as natural. Embalming received critical celebrity endorsement, albeit posthumously, for its success in preserving Abraham Lincoln's remains during his lengthy funeral procession by railroad (Moller 1996: 82).

Paradoxically, the effort expended in the Victorian era on solemnising death through ritual and exaggerated display of mourning ultimately produced a more secular approach to the event.

> At the death bed, the survivor's grief eclipsed any concern with the spiritual destination of the departing soul; the hope of an afterlife was not union with God but reunion with the beloved.
>
> (Walter 1994: 15)

This shift in attitude was bolstered by a number of apparently unrelated developments. The invention of ether in the 1840s lessened apprehension before death, the prospect of the painful death receded. The emergence of life assurance, by appropriating death actuarily, also meant a less worrisome leaving for the dying and enhanced security for the survivors (Leming and Dickinson 1994). The growing intervention of the funeral director marginalised the role of sacred ministers and softened the tenor of funeral sermons.[2]

DEATH TODAY

Adherence to Ariès's four chronological phases is perhaps less crucial than viewing them as thematic reservoirs for understanding the view of death shared by contemporary consumers. This view can be considered under a number of headings. First, personal death has assumed the status of taboo (Gorer 1965). The nineteenth-century endeavour to shield the dying from death has been extended beyond the bedroom to society at large (Ariès 1974). For those currently living in an age of death denial, 'Dying has become an unbearable and intolerable intrusion into the order of everyday life' (Moller 1996: 17). In the interests of the myth of modernity, that life should be happy, death has been expunged from the individual and social agenda:

the denial of death is openly acknowledged as a significant trait of our culture. The tears of the bereaved have become comparable to the excretion of the diseased ... Death has been banished.

(Ariès 1981: 580)

Second, death is essentially a private matter. Distaste of dying was bolstered by Victorian distaste of its unhygienic and unpleasant tumefactions and excretions. Modesty dictated greater privacy and, in the twentieth century, the move to the hospital. With this move, the home was saved the task of containing 'the promiscuity of terminal illness' and the gaze of prurient onlookers could be confined to visiting hours. In the twentieth century one dies essentially as one lives – alone. 'Never before in the history of humanity have the dying been removed so hygienically behind the scenes of social life' (Elias 1985: 23). This privatisation of death has been abetted by the fact that all those who currently handle the corpse, hospital personnel and funeral directors, do not *know* the deceased. This involvement of anonymous professionals has dispossessed family and the broader community (Leming and Dickinson 1994); the prospect of a twentieth-century *Pietà* would likely prove quite startling.

This growing concealment and sequestration of death and dying has been attributed by Giddens (1991) to the influence of the modernist agenda. The advent of the hospital as the proper place in which to die heralds the virtual concealment of human passing away. In pre-modern societies contact with death was immediate and prevalent. Disease and illness were familiar features of the everyday precisely because they had not been expropriated, professionalised and controlled.

The third feature of death in contemporary western society noted by thanatologists is the absence or paucity of mourning rituals. Overt demonstrations of grief are uncomfortable to witness and are viewed as dysfunctional, possibly pathological. 'House private' notices attest that this proscription has been duly internalised by the bereaved (Ariès 1981). Apart from the brief postmortem period, efforts are focused on distracting rather than facilitating grief.

At present death and mourning are treated with much the same prudery as sexual impulses were a century ago. As 'good' men and women harboured no sexual impulses, so sensible folks today keep a rein on mourning and, should they yield to the urge to mourn, do so furtively in private.

(Gorer 1965: 111)

This same discretion is reflected in the absence of sartorial signs of mourning and in the manner in which funerals are expected to cause minimal social disruption. Cremation, apart from disposing of the body totally, obviates the need for visitation rituals and constitutes an 'antidote to the cult of tombs'. In so far as ritual demands remain, they centre on an individual 'working through' of grief. There is no compulsion or desire on the part of society to know the contents of this process, it is private. The sole end of this 'emotional surveillance' is to ensure that the bereaved feel *something* (Walter 1994: 34). It is precisely the absence and mistrust of 'ready-made rituals and flowing phrases of earlier generations' (Elias 1985: 26) that places a greater onus on contemporary mourners and bereaved to extemporise in the presence of death and dying. A novel proposition advanced by Moller (1996) is that expenditure on lavish funerals has itself become an individualised bereavement ritual whose display represents a culturally approved means of registering estimation of the deceased.

Fourth, death has been bureaucratised. Drawing on Weber's portrayal of the emergence of bureaucracy, Moller (1996) claims that contemporary dying exhibits all the requisite hallmarks – specialisation, depersonalisation, elimination of personal and emotional considerations, and exercise of power through expert protected knowledge. The hegemony of the normalisers ensures that deaths that are abnormal necessitate the body being whisked away from the bereaved for autopsy; a cause must be found (Walter 1994: 10). Even grieving has been normalised into stages (Kübler-Ross 1970).

Medical service providers fare poorly from thanatologists espousing the critique of modernism particularly for their complicity in this bureaucratisation process. Disenfranchising the dying and their families, doctors have become 'masters of the moment as well as of the circumstances of death' (Ariès 1974: 89). The effort to eliminate any ambiguity or overlap between life and death is central. Curative and palliative possibilities are then predicated on whatever sensory, pulmonary or cerebral definition of the moment of death that prevails. Ariès (1981) traces this crusade to excise any ambiguity or overlap between life and death to late nineteenth-century medics. Their goal was to eliminate ghoulish tales of the living dead and superstitious accounts of premature burial from the medical lexicon and scientific discourse. Such a project underscored the need to appropriate the bar between life and death, to define the moment, and thereby lay claim to ultimate control over the process. It is worth noting that in the 'remote and imminent' phase delineated by Ariès the pendulum of the point of death had swung from one extreme to the other; from life encroaching on death as evidenced by growth of facial hair after death to death encroaching on life as evidenced by loss of consciousness, and coldness in the limbs.

Walter (1994) claims that prior to the eighteenth century the doctor's main function was to confirm and predict the time of death to allow for appropriate preparation. Medical intervention since then has led to the deconstruction of death. Instead of being pursued by the single skeleton of the Danse Macabre, humans are harried by hordes of germs, bacteria and diseases. A further offshoot of the medicalisation of dying has been that 'the prolongation of the dying process is a basic feature of death in modern society' (Moller 1996: 25). During this process the medieval bedside conflict between good and evil has been replaced by the struggle between doctor and dying, treatment and death have become mortal adversaries. To this end medical training has sought to innoculate physicians against personal involvement with the dying; most doctors tend to retire as death looms imminent leaving the patient to the ministrations of nurses and family (Moller 1996: 27). 'The dying patient is a deviant in the medical subculture because death poses a threat to the image of the physician as healer' (Leming and Dickinson 1994: 228).

While these four features constitute a rather bleak and sombre picture, Walter (1992) cautions against an extreme interpretation of the negativity currently attaching to death and dying, proposing instead a modified 'taboo plus coda thesis'. Accordingly, there is an endemic distrust of all formal rituals, not simply mourning rituals, in modern secular societies. Furthermore, lengthening of the lifespan means that the dying are likely to be older, more socially isolated. So, death is expected and the traumatic impact on the bereaved should thus be mitigated. Walter also detects a lack of appreciation in Ariès's work for the 'disparate frames' through which death is viewed in fragmented postmodern society. Finally a certain pre-modern nostalgia may have blurred the realisation that denial of death is not unique to the twentieth century and consequently simplistic designations of societies as 'taboo or not taboo' may be less than helpful (Elias 1985). It could also be argued that Ariès's rather stark analysis fails to do justice to the ethnic and religious diversity that still obtains in western society. Attitudes towards death in such groupings are likely to be quite nuanced and idiosyncratic (Firth 1993; Power 1993).

Whatever the levels of antipathy and denial of death, the twentieth century has given birth to its own characteristic array of death denying/defying projects. A seminal tenet of Bolshevik utopianism was the abolition of death, the conquest of finitude, and the defeat of time (Sypnowich 1995). The secretive production of the mysterious elixir to preserve Lenin's embalmed corpse and the comradely mutual exchange of blood transfusions to boost life expectancy were but two of its more vivid avatars. At the level of language, the current lexicon of the final things has managed to embalm death in a shroud of euphemisms, many with a provenance in the marketplace – 'cashed in', 'checked out', 'signed off', 'number's up'. Towards the end of the century financial and technical reservations have failed to quench a lively interest in cryonics. First carried out in 1967, consumers who refuse to stay dead are prepared to entrust their cadavers, frozen to minus 196 degrees centigrade, to a generation of as yet unborn scientists in the hope that they will develop the requisite technology and good faith to restore them to their former selves. Leming and Dickinson (1994) report that many have thawed out in the intervening years as their estates have failed to meet rising freezing costs.

Ethical and gerontological literature (Dworkin 1993; Kennedy 1990; O'Rourke 1980), together with popular media, increasingly debate the morality of the lethal ministrations of medics in euthanasia. At one level, the 'Right to Die' movement, by countenancing impending death, runs counter to the prevailing trend of defying death and the ageing process; however, others choose to interpret assisted death in a different light:

> is this philosophy a new, sophisticated confrontation of our mortality and control of our death? Or are the older persons in our society who kill themselves ... merely conforming to our society's implied 'final solution' to the 'problem' of age?
>
> (Friedan 1993: 16)

About 9 per cent of Americans have drawn up 'living wills', a form of passive euthanasia where people specify in advance their reluctance to accept medical intervention should it adversely affect their quality of life at some future juncture.

This overview of current perceptions of death suggests consumers are uncomfortable with its personal dimension, anxious not to speak of it, view it as a distant and private end-moment whose propinquity can be progressively postponed and, who knows, put on hold indefinitely. Medical and technological progress have paid a handsome dividend in terms of life expectancy increments over less than a century. Life can only get longer, death further away.

POST-POSITIVISTIC ALTERNATIVES

The prevailing scientific conception of death in modernity as observable terminus of life, an external event, has not gone unchallenged. In particular, post-positivistic approaches have emerged in the twentieth century from divergent intellectual traditions. The two alternatives chosen here are hermeneutics and postmodernism. While both of these traditions have given rise to identifiable groupings of consumer researchers (Arnold and Fischer 1994; Brown 1993, 1995; Firat and Venkatesh 1995; Ryan and Bristor 1987; Thompson *et al.* 1994), their respective views of death and mortality relative to those in the dominant rationalistic stream remain largely untapped. Heidegger is arguably the hermeneutic tradition's greatest exponent (Macquarrie 1973). Consumer behaviour authors have also begun to explore his thinking in this area (Young and Wallendorf 1989). The kernel of his approach to death is found in Division II of *Being and Time* (Heidigger 1962) where he elaborates a painstaking phenomenological description of 'dasein', human being-in-the-world, man as he actually lives.

This description reveals death as a fulcrum through which a variety of key lived themes intersect.[3] His scrutiny of what is nearest and most familiar in human existence discloses death as an immediate yawning chasm. Dasein *is* a 'being-towards-death'. This notion constitutes a stark counterpoint to the prevailing attitude to death discussed so far – death as external event, 'the stuff of obituaries', detached and distant. Such a perspective is inherently futile precisely because 'my death can never be an external, fact-in-the-world for me'. Construing death as a third person mishap masks the realisation that it is ineluctably mine. Humans cannot be replaced by someone else in death. Someone else could replace me as owner of my possessions, they could take my place on a holiday cruise, they could occupy my role at work, theoretically they could even substitute for me as spouse to my partner. However, death is the sole event precluding such substitutability. In this sense, death individuates and is primordially first person in character.

A further feature of dasein as 'being-towards-death' is the way in which death totalises or completes human being-there. To exist at all is 'to be ahead' of oneself, to be faced with choices, to be orientated towards the future, to be in the process of shaping one's identity. Product, service and career choices all possess this future trajectory; items bought today are to be worn at some future date, money lodged today may be spent tomorrow. In this sense, human being-there is inevitably incomplete and unfinished. Death extinguishes this identity-shaping process and totalises it.

> Dasein can only grasp its wholeness when it countenances its 'no-longer-being-there', the nearness of nothing.
>
> (Steiner 1978: 99)

Heidegger further characterises death as 'distinctively impending'. It can materialise at any moment and, by virtue of its not being tied to any specific configuration of events, is pure possibility. Death is an omnipresent vivifying threat, infusing being-there, engendering a healthy anxiety. Anxiety is human mortality and contingency resonating in consciousness. It is precisely this pervasive ever-present knowledge that life can be summarily terminated that makes people care about life, that generates involvement (comparisons with 'involvement' in consumer behaviour are not totally misplaced in this context!).

> my life matters to me, indeed must matter to me – only because I am aware that I don't have it 'forever' and 'once-for-all'; life matters only because I am aware that it can be snatched away from me by the power of death.
>
> (Hoffman 1993: 200)

This authentic appropriation of oneself as a being-towards-death, is contrasted by Heidegger with the inauthentic, banalised chatter of the collective that seeks to render death as external, third person event.

> In such a way of talking, death is understood as an indefinite something which, above all, must duly arrive from somewhere or other, but

which is proximally not yet *present-at-hand* for oneself, and is therefore no threat.

(Heidegger 1962: 296)

Heidegger's emphasis on death stems neither from a Germanic death obsession nor from a desire to round his system off with placatory addenda. His intent is to underscore the primordial proximity of death, a proximity predicated neither on chronological age nor on physical well-being, but on the power of death to self-define at any stage in the life course. In this sense his analysis represents both a counterpoint to the modern conception of death and a call to the human sciences to envision it as a positive and constitutive dimension of human existence rather than a distant *terminus ad quem* towards which we move reluctantly.

The second paradigm chosen is postmodernism with Baudrillard as its representative. Three considerations in particular guided this choice. First, while there is some doubt as to whether Baudrillard himself would warm to the designation 'postmodernist' (Genosko 1994), consumer behaviour commentators appear to find this appellation appropriate – Brown (1995) describes him as 'the high priest of postmodernism' – and, furthermore, judge his contribution to the study of contemporary consumption of considerable worth (Brown 1995; Firat 1991; Firat and Venkatesh 1995). Second, *Symbolic Exchange and Death* (Baudrillard 1993) arguably presents the most sustained critique of modern rational conceptions of death in the postmodern canon (cannon?). Third, this critique provides a stimulating counterpoint to and contrast with the views of Heidegger above.

Baudrillard's treatment of death draws much of its initial inspiration from Foucault's contention that scientific rationalism has abrogated to itself a power to control by naming, categorising and differentiating. Such rational disjunctions, achieved through the exercise of definitional 'power bars', result in classifications that are arbitrary, non-transcendental and historically conditioned. Typical postmodern disjunctions – mad/sane, deviant/normal – 'chains of discrimination' (Baudrillard 1993: 125) comport a hegemonic dynamic where one category is excluded, extradited albeit with the possibility of re-integration with the normal. Baudrillard's control thesis is that the dichotic disjunction between life and death marks the most fundamental of all such exclusive dichotomies, death is 'an incurable deviancy' (p. 126). In modern society, courtesy of a power bar, the dead are irretrievably separated from the living. They have been defined into 'social exile'. The project is to exclude the dead – Ariès makes the same point geographically: church close to suburban cemetery to crematorium – and to maintain control over dying. Baudrillard returns to this theme with fugal fervour throughout the text; typically he is at his most incisive and insightful when in ballistic mode.

At the very core of the 'rationality' of our culture ... is an exclusion that precedes every other, more radical than the exclusion of madmen, children, or inferior races, an exclusion preceding all these and serving as their model: the exclusion of the dead and of death.

(Baudrillard 1993: 126)

'Castes, priests, and the Church' (p. 144) promulgated and perpetuated the fissure between the living and the dead by investing the latter with immortality, the antibody of mortality, which served to render them totally other and unreachable. Contemporary society achieves the same end by stressing the objective, decisive and 'punctual' nature of biological death.

> The irreversibility of biological death ... is a modern fact of science. It is specific to our culture. Every other culture says that death begins before death, that life goes on after life, that it is impossible to distinguish life from death ... Our modern idea of death is controlled by a very different set of representations: that of the machine and the function. A machine either works or it does not. Thus the biological machine is either dead or alive.
>
> (Baudrillard 1993: 159)

The term 'every other culture' in this quotation is perhaps a little overstated. Baudrillard appears to hark back with a modicum of pre-modern nostalgia to primitive societies, archaic communities where reciprocal exchange between living and dead, 'an incessant cycle of giving and receiving', pre-dated the deadly disjunction of living and dead witnessed today. Protesting that he is not forwarding a 'utopian fusion' of living and dead, he posits a 'dual-mode' between them without necessitating social exile for the latter. He cites the case of the convent in Palermo where thousands of dead corpses stand propped up and dressed along corridors, visited for over three hundred years by cohorts of relatives who 'acknowledge them' and show them to their children. A society such as this, by recognising death as social, public and collective, by its symbolic exchange with the dead, by refusing to 'bar' them from the living, gives the lie to the 'dichotomania of structural systems'.

> If one's goal is to overcome the system which disbars the dead from the living by means of the 'power bar' between life/death, one is best on the side of the dead – Baudrillard's clever observation is well taken that in the West it is not normal to be dead.
>
> (Genosko 1994: xxi)

In this sense, Baudrillard's pre-occupation with pre-modern non-exclusive societies is more profitably seen as an attempt to subvert the prevailing biological power bar by looking at life from death's vantage point than an attempt to prescribe a social template to which modern societies should revert. In so doing he is essaying to undermine the control-inspired bifurcation between living and dead by adopting the position of the excluded; instinctively most consumers do the opposite: 'Does heaven have a McDonald's?'

For the present the hegemony of the 'natural, biological' conception of death prevails. As with nature, science endeavours to control this death, 'to push back the limits of life' (Baudrillard 1993: 162). However, this project has less to do with empowering and enfranchising people to take hold of their death and more to do with the administration and programming of death by State monopoly.

> We are all hostages in the sense that the system holds our death in the balance. My death is out of my hands – it will be minutely administered, officially announced . . . no matter how I die, my death will be found out.
>
> (Genosko 1994: 94).

Drawing on anthropological gift-giving metaphor, the form of biological death, given to us by the system – irreversible and final – precludes any return gift, any reciprocity by the dead. The system's power over death is thus confirmed.

> From birth control to death control, whether we execute people or compel their survival, the essential thing is that the decision is withdrawn from them, that their life and their death are never freely theirs, but that they live or die according to a social visa.
>
> (Baudrillard 1993: 174)

Social control over death has enlisted an array of agencies, 'security forces' to prevent the living from appropriating their own death. Aleatory death, suicide, hostage-taking are all fascinating precisely because they undermine and subvert this state control. There is also allusion to complicity on the part of product and service providers in this process. Car manufacturers ensure that all models are replete with an array of features that will render the driver secure from 'unnatural' death – seat belts, helmets, driver bags, safety frames. Similarly with the plethora of insurance offerings, MOT tests, speed limits, spot checks – all designed to protect the living from themselves. The fact that motorists resist this security regime by speeding, driving sub-standard vehicles, or not using a safety belt is vestigial evidence of the 'accursed fragment' of their lives they strive to retain free from the security apparatus. Funeral parlours (where no one speaks!), characterised as 'drug stores of smiling, sterilised death' (Baudrillard 1993: 181), also collude in this control and pushing back of death. They share the same impulse to 'sterilise death at all costs, to varnish it, cryogenically freeze it, air-condition it, put make-up on it' (p. 180) in order that the dead appear alive since death is unnatural. In sum, 'Our whole culture is just one huge effort to dissociate life and death' (p. 147).

In this overview of hermeneutic and postmodern views of death, a common theme of death being expunged and denied was in evidence.[4] In both exposés contemporary society was seen to relegate death to a remote and receding end-point, a development that, for Heidegger, militates against an appreciation of human existence as 'being-towards-death', for Baudrillard, precludes any possibility of reciprocal exchange between the living and their dead. This theme was also confirmed in Ariès's historical analysis of current attitudes towards death. Both writers also refute the hegemony of the rationalistic scientific view of death; for Heidegger a banal and collective understanding of biological extinction, for Baudrillard, a powerful and fetishistic disjunction. However, what is perhaps most remarkable of all in both of these writers, despite their obvious differences, is the prominence accorded the notions of death and dying in their thinking.

DEATH AND CONSUMER BEHAVIOUR

Given the foregoing discussion, the liminality of death in consumer behaviour research is not really surprising. Most references to the subject tend to be tangential. The small cadre of researchers who have broached the question of death and dying have in the main found post-positivistic, naturalistic forms of inquiry to be the most appropriate research orientation.

The relationship between objects and mortality has begun to attract the attention of a growing body of researchers. Belk (1988) notes how senescence can involve two parallel shifts; one's sense of mortality heightens and, due to a likely contraction of one's social orbit, the sense of self may diminish. Possessions can counter these developments by extending the self beyond death and facilitating their 'living on' through heirs or museums. If the item in question is an heirloom, particularly an heirloom that was handmade or worn close to the body, it can perpetuate family bonds beyond the grave thereby representing 'a gift to the living from the dead' (Belk *et al.* 1989). Researchers on the Odyssey further revealed that some bequests were willed to descendants with the express purpose of preserving their sacredness after the owner's death. Collections exemplified such bequests. However, here the emphasis was less on ensuring the bequester's immortality than on preserving the collection's sacred status. Despite this, recipients, even those without any interest in the collection, could choose to care for the collection as they would care for the donor's lover or mistress (Belk *et al.* 1989: 29). The endeavour to ensure immortality is even more pronounced when the collector is able to have the collection named after him or her (Belk 1995).

Hirschman (1990) has broadened this discussion by prescinding from specific possessions and focusing instead on the pursuit of secular immortality among US upper-middle-class and lower-upper-class consumers through the cultivation of affluence in general. This interpretive study revealed that when affluence is the product of independent entrepreneurial effort and manifests itself in certain forms of conspicuous consumption such as artistic collections and bequests, it can secure for its 'founder' and those who inherit this affluence an aura of immortality. This contagion of immortality appears to infect both possessors and possessions.

In its most manifest form this quest for immortality has as its primary intent the cultivation of the founder's name and achievements in the collective consciousness. To this extent, denial of human passing away *per se* is not at issue. However, Hirschman uncovered a further leitmotiv particularly evidenced in advertising copy directed at these two social classes that betokened a more radical agenda with regard to human finitude. Typically such copy lauded scientific and technological endeavours to control natural processes and singled out one such process in particular – human ageing and dying.

> nature is portrayed as flawed and destructive; one's material body – a natural entity – is depicted as inherently degenerate and imperfect. The superior powers of the mind, acting through technology and science are required to overcome undesirable natural processes such as ageing ... Those with money employ them to stave off the reality of ageing and death.
>
> (Hirschman 1990: 39)

While the import of Hirschman's research is confined to certain groupings in the US economic spectrum, it does break fresh ground by positing the quest for immortality as a central and salient motive underpinning the accumulation of possessions.

Moving to the more immediate postmortem period, a rich array of relationships between survivors and possessions has been uncovered. One such fundamental relationship arises from the capacity of some special objects to ground or 'anchor' a person either when current identity is threatened (Belk 1990) or in times of significant role transition (Solomon 1983). The loss of a close relative or friend is likely to result in either of these outcomes. It is the daunting, muddling and unfamiliar nature of the mourner's new situation that prompts reliance on familiar, special possessions. Parkes (1986) ascribes the 'alarm' experienced by the recently bereaved to this feeling of being in a completely altered environment. In such circumstances, there is need to simplify, to hold fast to possessions that self-define, and to maximise operative competencies. The family home is a possession commonly cited in this regard (Lopata 1996).

Gentry *et al.*'s (1995) phenomenological study of thirty-eight bereaved respondents has shed further light on the relationship between possessions and the grieving process. Drawing on the modes of sacralisation in Belk *et al.* (1989), they note that in the case of conjugal bereavement, the wedding ring of the deceased (and that of the survivor) assume a sacral status, redefining and perpetuating the relationship beyond the grave. A further use of possessions involved forging a link with the dead person through fondling, caressing or simply talking to some object worn by or associated with the deceased person. This use of objects as 'charms' was also recorded by Parkes (1986), however, he observed an additional olfactory dimension; garments were used to recall the body odour of the departed. The third use involved the creation of 'shrines' or memorials. Such objects, akin to formal religious shrines, were not physically manipulated in a direct sense, however this in no sense diminished their instrumental power. One particularly vivid example involved a widower leaving his late wife's purse on the bedroom dresser. Its power lay in acting as a *remedium concupiscentiae*, a check on future libidinal excess. A more common instance of possessions as shrine is the undisturbed bedroom of the deceased. While Gentry *et al.* (1995) ascribe a 'commemorative' impulse to such behaviour, Gorer (1965) likens it to mummification and claims that it is in fact an attempt to prolong grief and mourning. To this extent he views such shrines as dysfunctional and potentially pathological. The room is kept

> as though it were a shrine which would at any moment be reanimated. The most notorious exemplar of mummification in recent English history is Queen Victoria, who not only preserved every object as Prince Albert had arranged them, but continued the daily ritual of having his clothes laid out and having his shaving water brought.

Queen Victoria's behaviour bears remarkable similarity to the case of a contemporary widow interviewed by Czikszentmihalyi and Rochberg-Halton (1981: 103) who, twenty-five years after the demise of her spouse, continued to arrange his shaving implements each morning as she had done when he was alive.

Douglas and Isherwood (1979: 65) have shown how goods 'make sense of the inchoate flux of events'. One such sense-making process they instance involves the consensual use of clocks, calendars and certain foodstuffs to render time intelligible, to parcel it into meaningful categories. While they did not address the question of mourning, certain parallels do suggest themselves. For example, erection of a headstone (Gorer 1965), disposal of ashes, disposal of the deceased's possessions (Young 1991), return to normal attire (Adburgham 1989; Lopata 1973) and resumption of social activities (Lopata 1988), could all potentially serve as 'markers', differentiating stages in the mourning process.

One consumption topic relating to death that has attracted considerable attention from researchers is the dispossession of the dying or deceased person's belongings. It is one of the areas in consumer behaviour where the impact of death, imminent or actual, is most forcefully discernible. Death radically transforms the meanings of the goods involved – from bric-à-brac to treasured memento, from tawdry ornament to poignant souvenir. In Belk's (1988) terminology such dispossession is voluntary 'interpersonal contamination', the acquisition of intimate possessions of another. There are two distinct though related strands in the literature on this topic. The first focuses on the process of dispossession while the owner is still alive, the second on postmortem disposal of belongings usually by the deceased's family or friends.

Commenting on the first form of dispossession, Young and Wallendorf (1989) ask:

> Does our fear of the death of living beings, this thanatophobia, extend to the disposition of consumption objects? A resounding 'yes' is the position put forward here, if we are what we have, then, as our things die, so too do we.
>
> (Young and Wallendorf 1989: 33)

In this sense disposal of one's own possessions can be a significant 'message to oneself' (p. 37) comporting a considerable emotional and ritualistic dimension. For this reason, disposal of significant belongings is likely to have been preceded by a modicum of hesitation and deliberation (Young 1991). Disposition of self-defining goods is properly viewed as a process rather than a once-off discrete action. Young and Wallendorf's (1989) distinction between physical and emotional disposition stresses this point to considerable effect. A terminally ill woman may inform a son or daughter of her intention to leave them a valued item of furniture. The question of when precisely the parent takes her leave emotionally of the possession is a moot point. It is likely to have preceded the moment when the offspring was informed, but not necessarily so. Likewise, the mother's physical dispossession of the furniture piece could take place at a variety of junctures – when she ceases to use it, when she ceases to polish it, the day it is removed from her home. For this reason dispossession is best studied emically.

Protracted terminal illness provides an illuminating vantage point from which to research owner dispossession of belongings. Adelman (1992) and Pavia (1993) have both conducted depth interviews with respondents living with AIDS and HIV. The time interval between diagnosis and death for this illness is problematic and unpredictable; lengthy asymptomatic periods are not uncommon. As a result dispossession, when it does occur, tends to be idiosyncratic. Voluntary dispossession is made easier by the fact that respondents with life-threatening ailments are likely to have had a number of prior decumulations involuntarily foisted upon them, such as lowering of income, loss of occupation, mobility decrements, and disimproving appearance (Pavia 1993). The stigmatic nature of this particular illness delimits the number of potential recipients of dispossessions; 'contamination' is an issue although it can sometimes be remedied by giving the belonging to other people living with the illness.

Where the respondents reside in a communal care facility, belongings are characteristically employed to effect transitions in physical and social liminality. The move from an apartment to a room in this facility physically necessitates the discarding of several belongings. This distillation of personal inventory typically leaves a collection of small intimate possessions, a process that fosters acknowledgement of impending death and thereby facilitates social integration into the liminal residential community. By leaving such personal items to other residents after death, reintegration into the group collective memory is ensured (Adelman 1992).

In the case of the second class of dispossessions, postmortem dispossessions, the disposal of the dead person's belongings may be a group activity, conducted in an emotionally charged atmosphere (Gentry *et al.* 1995) and in the absence of clear directions from the departed owner. The mere physical presence of some items almost dictates that the dispossession process begins; the car in the driveway, the clothes in the wardrobe, the tennis racket in the hallway 'demand' some response (Gentry *et al.* 1994). When the process does begin it is likely to evince an attraction–repulsion dynamic, described vividly by one of Gentry *et al.*'s (1995) respondents.

> Getting rid of the possessions was very hard. When I found something associated with bad memories, I just threw it away. If she wore it when she got hurt, I just tossed it. If there were good memories, I kept the item for family and friends. The rest I just gave to the Salvation Army.
>
> (Gentry *et al.* 1995: 133)

There are also hierarchies operative in the way in which postmortem dispossessions take place. First, there is a hierarchy of sentiment. A belonging perceived to have been more closely associated with the deceased enjoys a higher emotional currency than one deemed less personal. This hierarchy is predicated more on perceived proximity to the deceased than on the cost of the item. The second hierarchy is one of kinship. Family members normally take a more prominent role in the actual disposition process than friends or acquaintances. Ritually speaking, mourning is primarily undertaken by immediate family in western industrial societies (Parkes 1986). This percolates through to the disposition process. Friends are more likely to receive dispossessions as deliberate tokens of appreciation from surviving family members than as direct bequests in the departed person's will (Gentry *et al.* 1995).

Authors drawing on the Symbolic Interactionist tradition commonly link dispossession to the first of van Gennep's (1960) three role transition phases (Schouten 1991). In this framework disposition is a stratagem the survivors engage in to facilitate transition to a new self-identity. According to this line of thinking, dispossession plays a crucial function by removing stimuli or 'props' that reinforce a previous but now defunct social status. The continued presence of the objects disposed of would inhibit the adoption of behaviour patterns consonant with the survivor's altered status (Young 1991).

Leming and Dickinson (1994) have outlined the proliferation of service offerings provided by US funeral directors to bereaved people. Seen from one perspective they comport many of the features of current service provision. Customer after-care has ensured 80 per cent repeat business. This after-care has a variety of incarnations – customised consultations for 'problematic grieving', grief support groups, bereavement workshops, sponsorship of seminars on financial management and car maintenance, and free limousine service for family weddings (Leming and Dickinson 1994: 482–483). However, seen from another perspective, death can be viewed not only as inaugurating a series of unusual service requirements but also as creating a context or environment in which regular consumer functioning becomes either altered or almost impossible.

Death of a close relative or friend is a stress-inducing change in life status that can disturb the inertia characterising much of consumer behaviour (Andreasen 1984). Research by Gentry *et al.* (1994, 1995) has sought to explore the attendant domestic atmosphere resulting from such a change in life status. In the first place, the prevalence of grief impairs normal cognitive activity; the bereaved feel distracted, unable to concentrate, removed from the flow of living, and pre-occupied with the lingering presence of the dead person (Parkes 1986). However, in the event that the bereaved person *could* muster the necessary psychological resources to address decisions relating to the funeral, the requisite information is generally not available. The prevailing denial of death and sequestration of mourning have drastically curtailed the extent of and access to information relating to funerals. Even those who have recently lost a close relative are typically unwilling or unable to engage in word of mouth communication on the subject with others. Gentry *et al.* (1994) advance this thesis further, arguing that at a time when ritual prescriptions for mourning are gradually disappearing, one proscription that continues to hold fast is the unacceptability of comporting oneself as a normal consumer in the early postmortem period. Put another way, a grieving consumer who was sufficiently minded, motivated and informed to make a funeral decision as other decisions are made, would likely incur a modicum of opprobrium.

Gentry *et al.* suggest that in practice many bereaved are content to abjure their everyday functioning as consumers and to relegate necessary decisions either to 'consumer surrogates' (1994: 134) such as non-immediate family members or close friends. Funeral directors too can fill this void. This need of the bereaved to have one person, one outlet to address their needs is well captured in an advertisement for the Argyll General Mourning and Mantle Warehouse in 1854:

> respectfully begging to intimate to ladies whose bereavements demand the immediate adoption of mourning attire, that every requisite for a complete outfit of mourning can be supplied at a moment's notice, and that many unpleasant occurrences arising from delay on melancholy occasions are thereby obviated.

(Adburgham 1989: 67)

Nonetheless, some decisions do necessitate the involvement of close family members and one promising line of investigation pursued by Gentry *et al.* (1995) concerns the impact of recent death on the manner in which such decisions are addressed. Their findings suggest that the nature of the recent death is a key determinant; the death of a child led to a more studied and explicit decision style, replacing the normal tacit or implicit way of deciding in families, whereas the death of a spouse resulted in difficulty in embracing unfamiliar consumer roles and responsibilities. In both cases it is clear that death has the ability to constitute a turbulent and traumatic environment in which significant changes in consumer functioning occur.

Apart from death's impact on the broad decision-making environment for families, it is also the harbinger of intense loss at the personal level.

> If I have relied on another person to predict and act in many ways as an extension to myself then the loss of that person can be expected to have the same effect upon my view of the world and my view of myself as if I had lost a part of myself.
>
> (Parkes 1986: 114)

This notion of coalescence of self-identities, especially between spouses, has been mooted by some consumer behaviour commentators; however, its ability to shed light on specific aspects of consumption remains unexplored. There are 'aggregate levels' of self-identity according to Belk (1990: 672) and possessions may in turn function as extensions of such a joint self (Solomon 1990). With conjugal bereavement the 'family self-conception carried out jointly by husband and wife' (Cavan 1962: 532) is irreparably sundered and the surviving spouse will typically describe a gap, a void, as though part of the self was taken away (Lopata 1996; Parkes 1986). Turley (1995) encountered older bereaved women being coaxed by well-meaning offspring and friends to resume a range of consumption activities to help fill this void and hasten their return to normalcy. These attentions overlooked the fact that the fusion of self-identities, usually over decades, had resulted in the couple engaging in many consumption activities as a unit. Using Fish's (1980) notion of 'interpretive community', these widows had lost someone with whom they shared interpretive strategies, strategies that shaped their joint watching of television programmes, shopping expeditions, vacation experiences and outings with grandchildren. Death had rendered this common 'world of already-in-place objects, purposes, goals, procedures, values' (Fish 1980: 304) obsolete. If they baulked at the prospect of resuming these activities it was often born of a reluctance to vacate this common world and an understandable aversion to unlearning, 'to experiment with new categories of meaning' (Schouten 1991: 49). Expressions of loneliness and desolation voiced by these widows were often explicated precisely in terms of a total inability to savour these once cherished consumer events; this may well represent death's most fundamental and tangible impact on consumer behaviour.

CONCLUSION

'Death is a problem for the living: the dead have no problems' (Elias 1985: 3). Implied in this dictum is an understanding that death is an ongoing problem, a persistent problem that successive generations have to countenance. Their typical response may take the form of sober acceptance, eschewal or outright denial, however the problem remains. Also implied in the saying is the fact that the 'death' that constitutes the problem is not an immutable and unitary event. The historical overview of the ancestry of western attitudes towards death, if nothing else, disclosed how emergent, variable and time specific its manifestations were over the centuries. In chronological terms, the dominant rationalistic view of death as distant and controllable end point into which we have been socialised is a relative newcomer to the thanatological scene. Death as natural and immutable has been one of modernity's more professionally packaged myths.

Scientific and technological conceptions of death have masked the fact that what is decisive in all this is not the termination of a biological process, the cessation of cerebral activity, the disappearance of the bleep on the monitor, but the 'image of death in the consciousness of the living' (Elias 1985: 3). More fundamentally it has failed to see that this pre-occupation with the moment of death is itself but one further emergent image. Death is always peculiar. The reactions it gives rise to, terror or tranquillity, will invariably stem from some stage and group-specific image. The prolegomenon to any concerted exploration of the role of death in consumer behaviour would profit considerably from first examining the features of its prevailing interpretive incarnation. Given the literature reviewed in this chapter, such an exploration would probably encounter the thematic pot-pourri intimated by the few consumer behaviour authors who have broached the topic. While the contemporary image of death features denial as one of its central motifs, this can and does comport an array of associated though distinct subsidiary themes. Clarification of these would help. For example, awareness of death, denial of death, quest for immortality – understood either as desire for posthumous remembrance or eternal youth – are each likely to inform consumer behaviour in a varied and idiosyncratic manner. Needless to say, these thematic substrata are also likely to prove antithetical to quantitative measurement (Belk 1989), a proviso that may explain the dearth of positivistic research contributions to date in this area.

The polysemous nature of death and dying was further instanced in the diverse and diffuse manner in which both were seen to impinge on consumers. They could invest what were formerly commonplace items with a fresh and valued poignancy, they could act as catalyst for traumatic dispossession, they could inaugurate an emotional domestic microclimate precluding or problematising customary consumer thinking and behaviour, they could necessitate a radical interpretive re-orientation precisely when the consumer's psychological resources were most depleted.

The more illuminating insights into the relationship between death and consumer behaviour so far have emanated from authors adopting a post-positivistic approach. Such an approach seems better equipped to capture the fluidity and overlap between life and death and the role that products and services may fulfil to this end. In Baudrillard's terms, this would represent subverting the power bar between life and death, going beyond death as discrete event. Gentry *et al.* (1995) probed the impact of recent death on decision making, however death can also be impending death; mourning can take place before the moment of departure (Gorer 1965: 63). This 'anticipatory grieving' is an accepted phenomenon in the literature on grief (Nussbaum *et al.* 1989; O'Bryant 1990) and it might be expected to give rise to a context embracing the dying person and significant others that functions analogous to but distinct from the context that ensues in the postmortem period.

A dominant theme in the writings of Paul de Man (1983) is the dialectic between blindness and insight specifically as it applies in the realm of literary criticism. In essence the deployment of any one method of literary criticism inevitably leads to the exclusion or disbarment of certain dimensions of the text in question. The resulting blindspots or endemic oversights can in turn serve as wellsprings of insight and illumination for others; there is a 'reward for peering into the dark' (Godzich 1983: xx). Paradoxically, such a blindspot is a prerequisite for and grounds the very possibility of further criticism, remaining 'itself radically blind to the light it emits' (de Man 1983: 16). Could it be that de Man's insight in literary criticism affords a metaphor for the virtual stand-off between marketing and human mortality? As with de Man's exculpation of individual critical methods, blame is not at issue here. No more than any other discipline, marketing is not immune from the prevailing thanatophobia, however, from here on it may serve it well to 'keep the eye trained on darkness knowing it to hold the secret the lightning will disclose' (Godzich 1983: xx).

NOTES

1 Walter (1994) questions the altruism underpinning this concern on the part of the audience speculating that the loss of the loved one may well have been feared less than the ability of the survivor to cope in the postmortem period. In other words, bereavement rather than death was the primary focus of fear.
2 For an insightful and comprehensive overview of service provision by US funeral directors in the first half of the twentieth century, see Mitford (1964).
3 Commentaries on the notion of death in Heidegger's philosophy may be found in Barret (1978), Hoffman (1993) and Steiner (1978).
4 Juxtaposition of Heidegger and Baudrillard in this chapter is not intended to downplay obvious and axiomatic differences between them. Baudrillard depicts death in Heidegger's writing as 'a tragic haunting of the subject, sealing its absurd liberty' (1993: 149).

REFERENCES

Adburgham, A. (1989) *Shops and Shopping: 1800–1914*, London: Barrie & Jenkins.

Adelman, M. (1992) 'Rituals of adversity and remembering: the role of posses-sions for persons and community living with Aids', in J.F. Sherry and B. Sternthal (eds) *Advances in Consumer Research*, 19, Provo, UT: Association for Consumer Research, 401–403.

Andreasen, A.R. (1984) 'Life status changes and changes in consumer preferences and satisfaction', *Journal of Consumer Research*, 11, December: 784–894.

Ariès, P. (1974) *Western Attitudes Towards Death: From the Middle Ages to the Present*, Baltimore, MD: Johns Hopkins University Press.

—— (1981) *The Hour of Our Death*, trans. H.Weaver, London: Allen Lane.

Arnold, S.J. and Fischer, E. (1994) 'Hermeneutics and consumer research', *Journal of Consumer Research*, 21, June: 55–70.

Barrett, W. (1978) 'Heidegger and modern existentialism', in B. Magee (ed.) *Men of Ideas*, London: BBC Publications, 74–95.

Baudrillard, J. (1993 [1976]) *Symbolic Exchange and Death*, trans. I.H. Grant, London: Sage.

Belk, R.W. (1988) 'Possessions and the extended self', *Journal of Consumer Research*, 15, September: 139–168.

—— (1990) 'The role of possessions in constructing and maintaining a sense of past', in M.E. Goldberg, G. Gorn and R.W. Pollay (eds) *Advances in Consumer Research*, 17, Provo, UT: Association for Consumer Research, 669–675.

—— (1995) 'Studies in the new consumer behaviour', in D. Miller (ed.) *Acknowledging Consumption*, London: Routledge, 58–95.

——, Wallendorf, M. and Sherry, J.F. Jr (1989) 'The sacred and profane in consumer behaviour: theodicy on the Odyssey', *Journal of Consumer Research*, 16, June: 1–38.

Brown, S. (1993) 'Postmodern marketing?', *European Journal of Marketing*, 27, 4: 19–34.

—— (1995) *Postmodern Marketing*, London: Routledge.

Cavan, R.S. (1962) 'Self and role in adjustment during old age', in A.M. Rose (ed.) *Human Behaviour and Social Processes*, London: Routledge & Kegan Paul, 526–536.

Czikszentmihalyi, M. and Rochberg-Halton, E. (1981) *The Meaning of Things: Domestic Symbols and the Self*, Cambridge: Cambridge University Press.

de Man, P. (1983) *Blindness and Insight: Essays in the Rhetoric of Contemporary Criticism*, 2nd edn, London: Routledge.

Douglas, M. and Isherwood, B. (1979) *The World of Goods*, New York: Basic Books.

Dworkin, R. (1993) *Life's Dominion: An Argument about Abortion and Euthanasia*, London: HarperCollins.

Elias, N. (1985 [1982]) *The Loneliness of the Dying*, trans. E. Jephcott, London: Basil Blackwell.

Firat, A.F. (1991) 'The consumer in postmodernity', in R.H. Holman and M.R. Solomon (eds) *Advances in Consumer Research*, 18, Provo, UT: Association for Consumer Research, 70–76.

—— and Venkatesh, A. (1995) 'Liberatory postmodernism and the reenchantment of consumption', *Journal of Consumer Research*, 22, 2: 239–267.

Firth, S. (1993) 'Approaches to death in Sikh and Hindu communities in Britain', in D. Dickenson and M. Johnson (eds) *Death, Dying and Bereavement*, London: Sage, 26–32.

Fish, S.E. (1980) *Is There a Text in this Class?*, Cambridge, MA: Harvard University Press.

Friedan, B. (1993) *The Fountain of Age*, London: Vintage.

Genosko, G. (1994) *Baudrillard and Signs: Signification Ablaze*, London: Routledge.

Gentry, J.W., Kennedy, P.F., Paul, C. and Hill, R.P. (1994) 'The vulnerability of those grieving the death of a loved one: implications for public policy', *Journal of Public Policy and Marketing*, 13, 2: 128–142.

——,——,—— and —— (1995) 'Family transitions during grief: discontinuities in household consumption patterns', *Journal of Business Research*, 34: 67–79.

Giddens, A. (1991) *Modernity and Self-Identity*, Cambridge: Polity.

Godzich, W. (1983) 'Introduction', in P. de Man, *Blindness and Insight: Essays in the Rhetoric of Contemporary Criticism*, 2nd edn, London: Routledge.

Gorer, G. (1965) *Death, Grief, Mourning in Contemporary Britain*, London: Cresset.

Heidegger, M. (1962 [1927]) *Being and Time*, trans. J. Macquarrie and E.S. Robinson, New York: Harper & Row.

Hirschman, E.C. (1990) 'Secular immortality and the American ideology of affluence', *Journal of Consumer Research*, 17, June: 31–42.

Hoffman, P. (1993) 'Death, time, history: division II of *Being and Time*', in C.B. Guignon (ed.) *The Cambridge Companion to Heidegger*, Cambridge: Cambridge University Press, 195–214.

Kennedy, L. (1990) *Euthanasia: The Good Death*, London: Chatto & Windus.

Kübler-Ross, E. (1970) *On Death and Dying*, London: Tavistock.

Leming, H.R. and Dickinson, G.E. (1994) *Understanding Dying, Death and Bereavement*, 3rd edn, Fort Worth, TX: Harcourt Brace.

Lopata, H.Z. (1973) *Widowhood in an American City*, Cambridge, MA: Schenkmann.

—— (1988) 'Support systems of American urban widowhood', *Journal of Social Issues*, 44, 3: 113–128.

—— (1996) *Current Widowhood: Myths and Realities*, Thousand Oaks, CA: Sage.

Macquarrie, J. (1973) *Existentialism*, Harmondsworth, Pelican.

Mitford, J. (1964) *The American Way of Death*, New York: Crest.

Moller, D.W. (1996) *Confronting Death: Values, Institutions and Human Mortality*, New York: Oxford University Press.

Nussbaum, J.F., Thompson, T. and Robinson, J.D. (1989) *Communication and Aging*, New York: Harper & Row.

O'Bryant, S.L. (1990) 'Forewarning of a husband's death: does it make a difference for older widows?', *Omega: Journal of Death and Dying*, 22, 3: 227–239.

O'Rourke, K.D. (1980) 'Christian affirmation of life', in D.J. Horan and D. Moll (eds) *Death, Dying, and Euthanasia*, Frederick, MD: Alethia, 362–368.

Parkes, C.M. (1986) *Bereavement: Studies of Grief in Adult Life*, 2nd edn, Harmondsworth: Penguin.

Pavia, T. (1993) 'Dispossession and perceptions of self in late stage HIV infection', in L. McAlister and M.L. Rotschild (eds), *Advances in Consumer Research*, 20, Provo, UT: Association for Consumer Research, 425–428.

Power, R. (1993) 'Death in Ireland: deaths, wakes and funerals in contemporary Irish Society', in D. Dickenson and M. Johanson (eds) *Death, Dying and Bereavement*, London: Sage, 21–25.

Ryan, M.J. and Bristor, J.M. (1987) 'The symbiotic nature of hermeneutical vs. classically generated knowledge', in R.W. Belk *et al.* (eds) *American Marketing Association Winter Educators' Conference*, Chicago: American Marketing Association, 191–194.

Schouten, J.W. (1991) 'Personal rites of passage and the reconstruction of self', in R. Holman and M.R. Solomon (eds) *Advances in Consumer Research*, 18, Provo, UT: Association for Consumer Research, 49–51.

Solomon, M. (1983) 'The role of products as social stimuli: a symbolic interactionism perspective', *Journal of Consumer Research*, 10, December: 319–329.

—— (1990) 'The imperial self', in M.E. Goldberg, G. Gorn and R.W. Pollay (eds) *Advances in Consumer Research*, 17, Provo, UT: Association for Consumer Research, 68–70.

Steiner, G. (1978) *Heidegger*, Glasgow: Collins.

Sypnowich, C. (1995) 'Death in Utopia: Marxism and the mortal self', in D. Bakhurst and C. Sypnowich (eds) *The Social Self*, London: Sage, 84–102.

Thompson, C.J., Pollio, H.R. and Locander, W.B. (1994) 'The spoken and the unspoken: a hermeneutic approach to understanding the cultural viewpoints that underlie consumers' expressed meanings', *Journal of Consumer Research*, 21, December: 432–452.

Tucker, W.T. (1974) 'Future directions in marketing theory', *Journal of Marketing*, 38, April: 30–35.

Turley, D. (1995) 'Dialogue with the departed', in F. Hansen (ed.) *European Advances in Consumer Research*, 2, Provo, UT: Association for Consumer Research, 10–13.

van Gennep, A. (1960 [1908]) *Rites of Passage*, trans. M.B. Vizedom and G.L. Caffee, London: Routledge & Kegan Paul.

Walter, T. (1992) 'Modern death: taboo or not taboo?', *Sociology*, 25, 2: 293–310.

—— (1994) *The Revival of Death*, London: Routledge.

Waugh, E. (1948) *The Loved One*, London: Chapman Hall.

Young, M.M. (1991) 'Disposition of possessions during role transitions', in R.H. Holman and M.R. Solomon (eds) *Advances in Consumer Research*, 18, Provo, UT: Association for Consumer Research, 33–39.

—— and Wallendorf, M. (1989) 'Ashes to ashes, dust to dust: conceptualising consumer disposition of possessions', in T.L. Childers *et al.* (eds) *American Marketing Association Winter Educators' Conference*, Chicago: American Marketing Association, 33–39.

Name index

Subject index

Learning Resources
Centre